The

American Vampire

AMERICAN

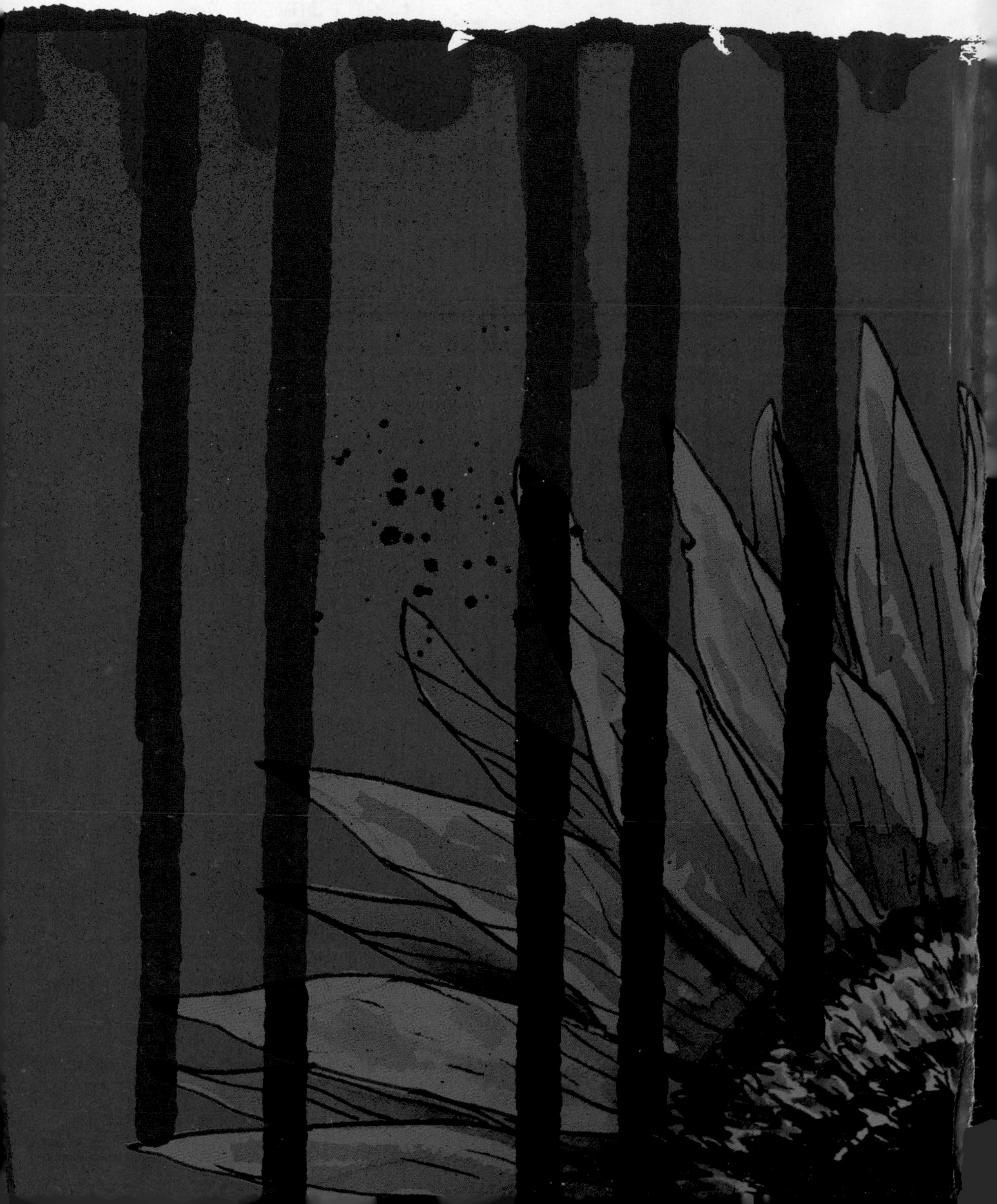

VAMPIRE

VOLUME FIVE

Scott Snyder Writer

Rafael Albuquerque Dustin Nguyen Artists

Dave McCaig John Kalisz Colorists

Jared K. Fletcher Steve Wands Letterers

Rafael Albuquerque Cover Artist

American Vampire created by Scott Snyder and Rafael Albuquerque

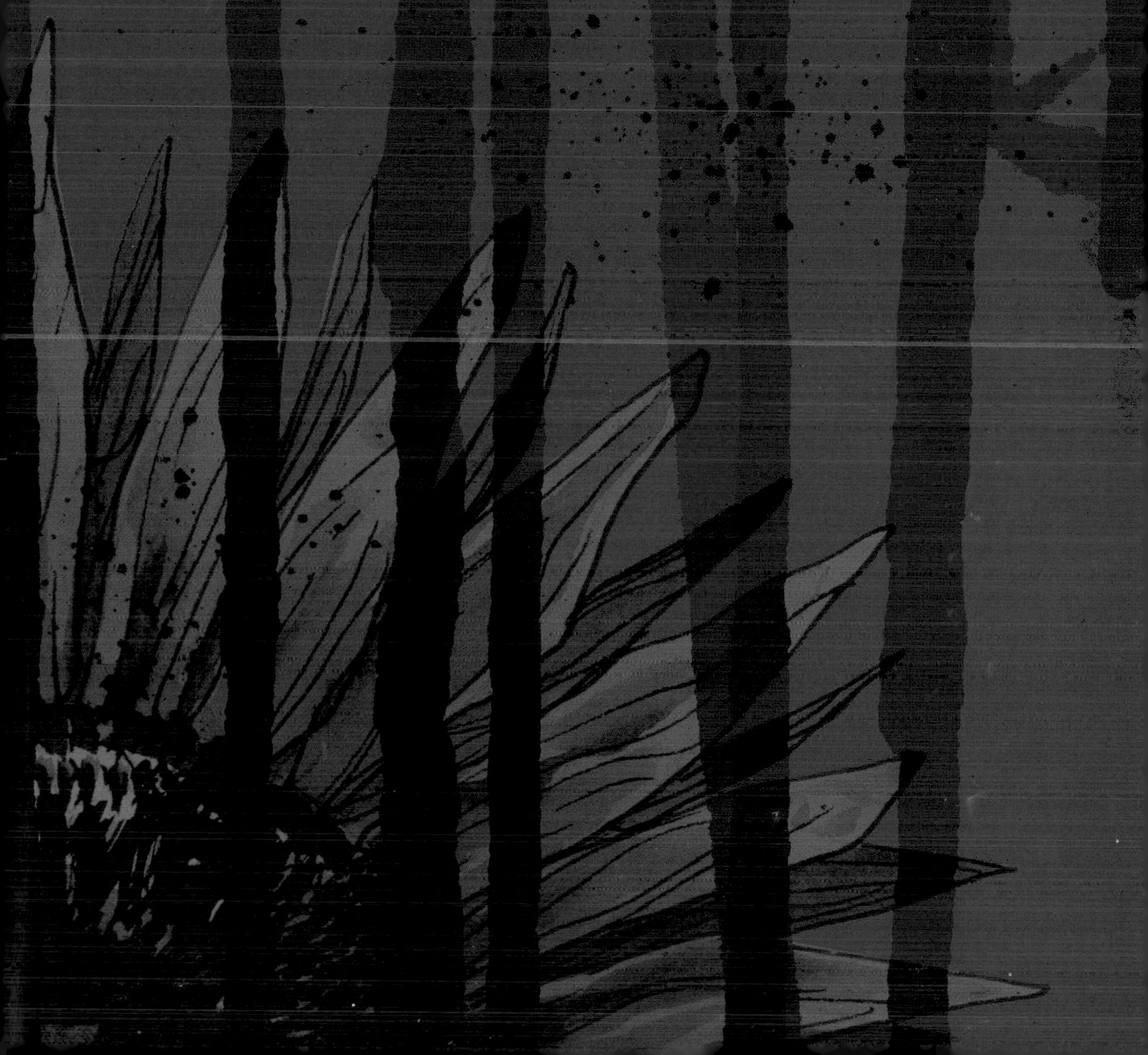

AMERICAN VAMPIRE Volume Five
Published by DC Comics. Cover and compilation Copyright © 2013 Scott
Snyder and DC Comics. All Rights Reserved.

Originally published in single magazine form in AMERICAN VAMPIRE
28-34, AMERICAN VAMPIRE: LORD OF NIGHTMARES 1-5 Copyright
© 2012, 2013 DC Comics. All Rights Reserved. VERTIGO and all characters,
their distinctive likenesses and related elements featured in this publication are
trademarks of DC Comics. The stories, characters and incidents featured in this
publication are entirely fictional. DC Comics does not read or accept unsolicited
ideas, stories or artwork.

DC Comics, 1700 Broadway, New York, NY 10019
A Warner Bros. Entertainment Company.
Printed in the USA. First Printing.
ISBN: 978-1-4012-3770-7

Library of Congress Cataloging-in-Publication Data

Snyder, Scott.
  American Vampire volume 5 / Scott Snyder, Rafael Albuquerque,
Dustin Nguyen.
      pages cm
  "Originally published in single magazine form in American
Vampire 28-34, American Vampire: Lord of Nightmares 1-5."
  ISBN 978-1-4012-3770-7
  1. Vampires–Comic books, strips, etc. 2. Graphic novels.
I. Albuquerque, Rafael, 1981- illustrator. II. Nguyen, Dustin,
illustrator. III. Title.
  PN6727.S555A47 2012
  741.5'973–dc23

2012047803

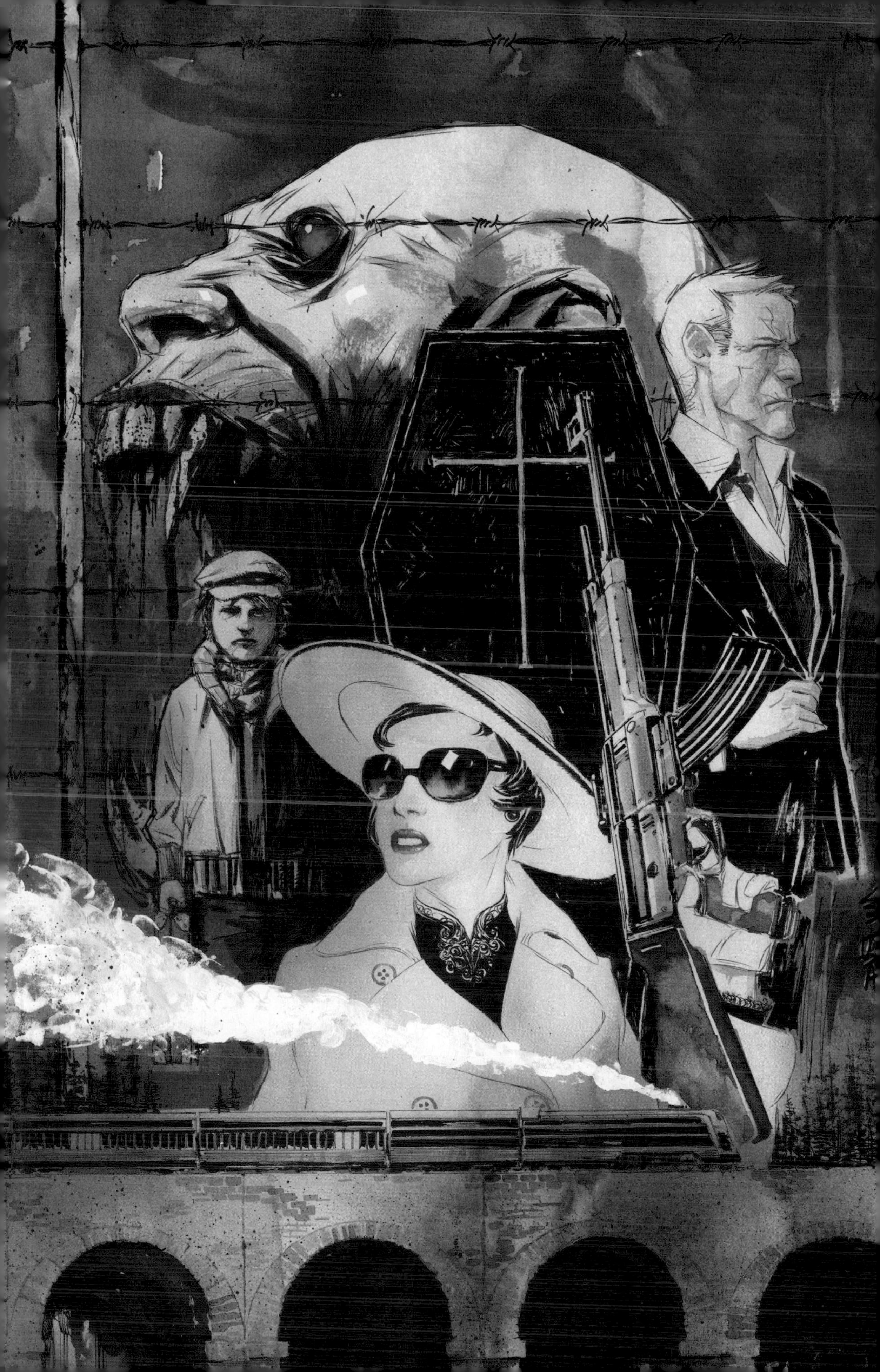

Lord of Nightmares

Scott Snyder
Writer

Dustin Nguyen
Artist and covers

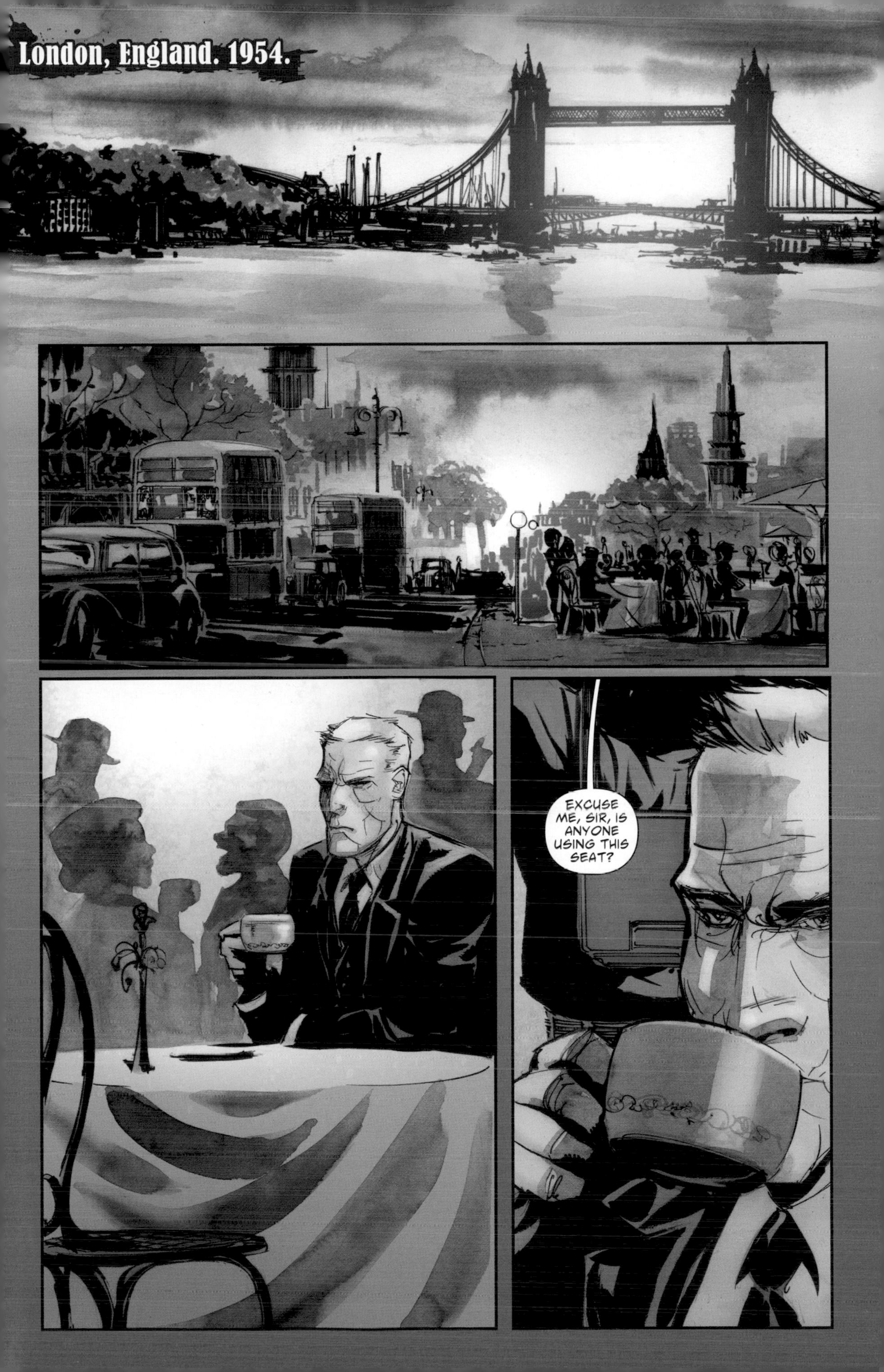
London, England. 1954.
EXCUSE ME, SIR, IS ANYONE USING THIS SEAT?

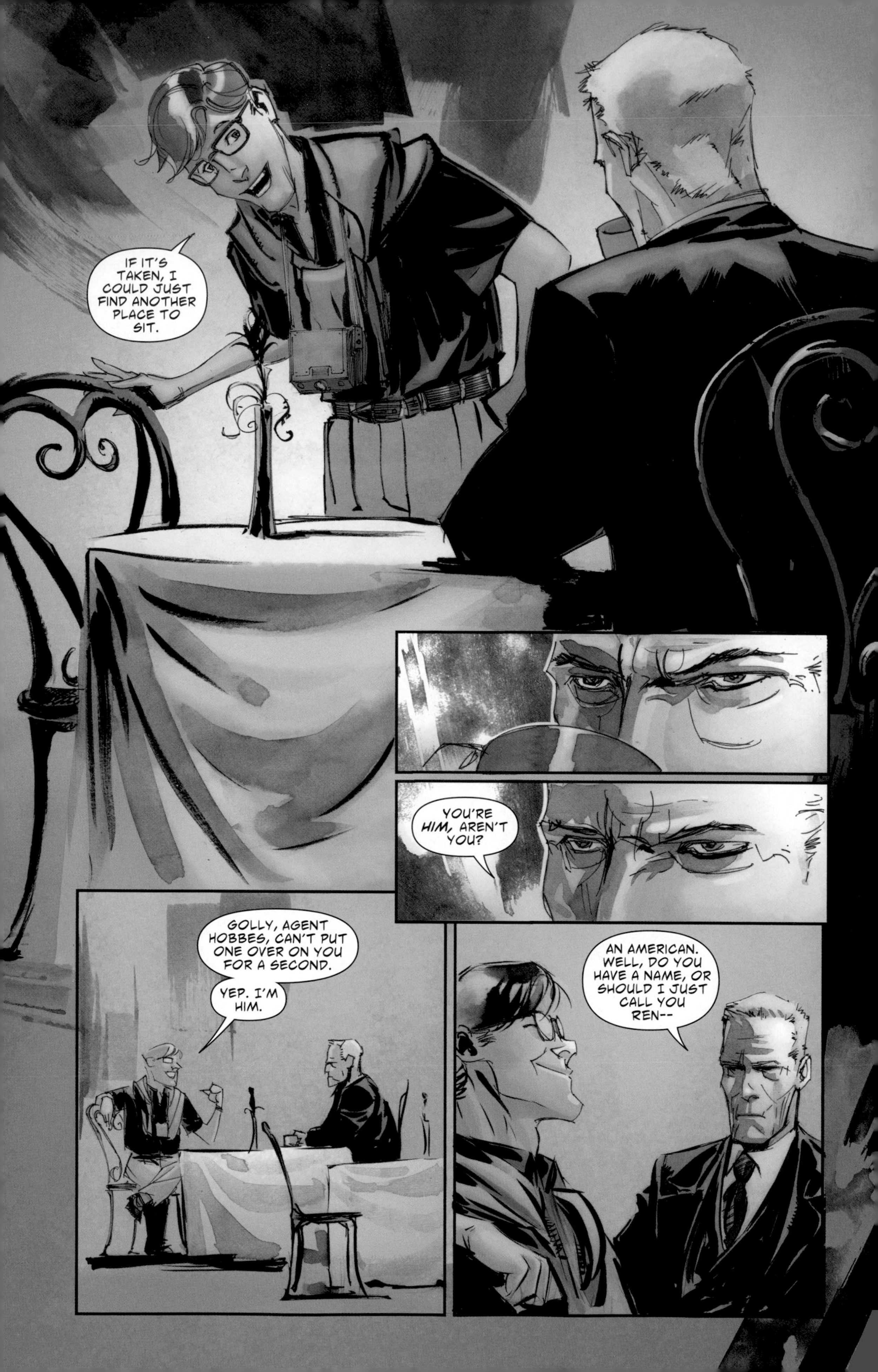
IF IT'S TAKEN, I COULD JUST FIND ANOTHER PLACE TO SIT.
YOU'RE *HIM*, AREN'T YOU?
GOLLY, AGENT HOBBES, CAN'T PUT ONE OVER ON YOU FOR A SECOND.
YEP. I'M HIM.
AN AMERICAN. WELL, DO YOU HAVE A NAME, OR SHOULD I JUST CALL YOU REN--

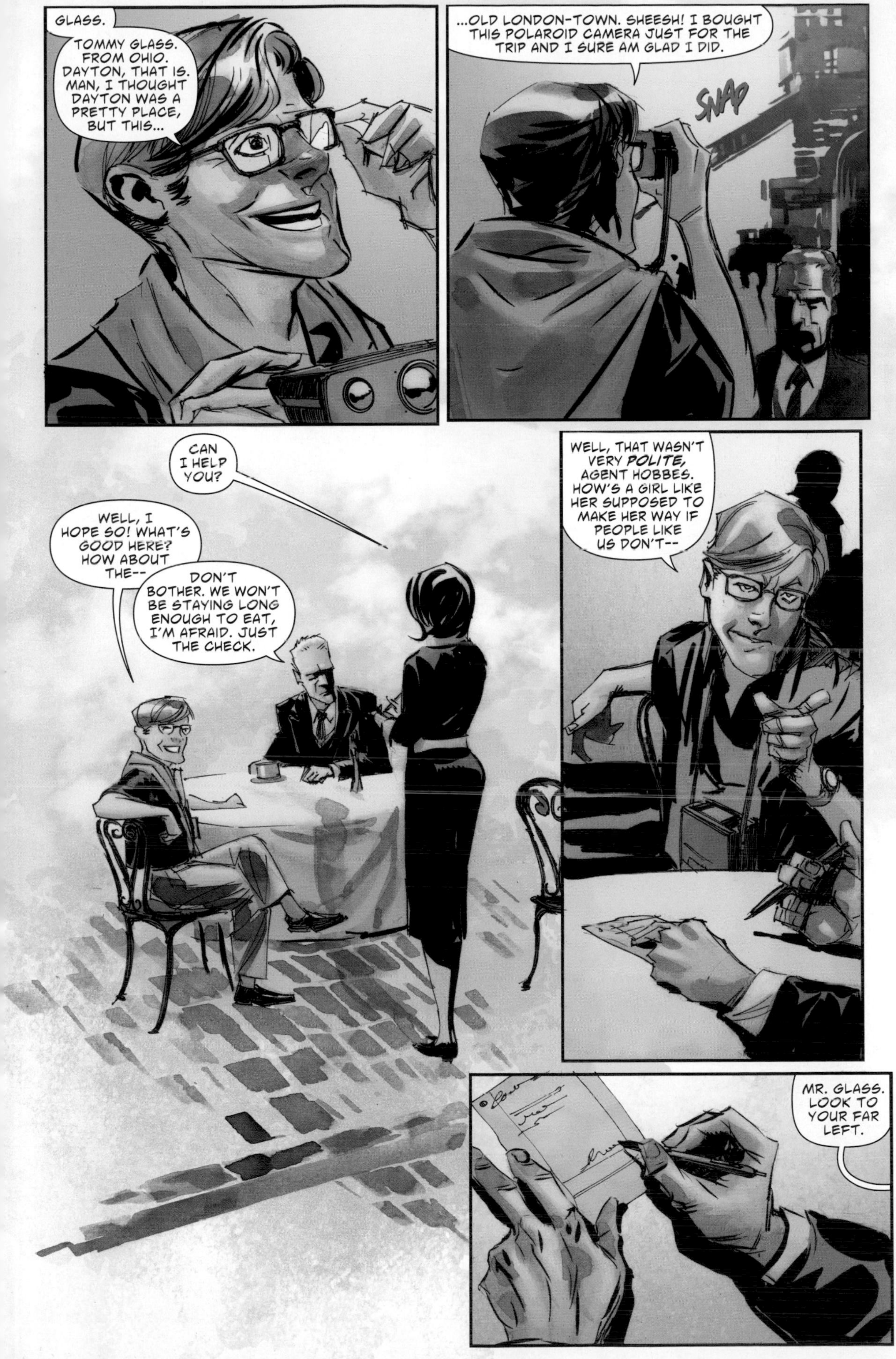
GLASS.
TOMMY GLASS. FROM OHIO. DAYTON, THAT IS. MAN, I THOUGHT DAYTON WAS A PRETTY PLACE, BUT THIS...
...OLD LONDON-TOWN. SHEESH! I BOUGHT THIS POLAROID CAMERA JUST FOR THE TRIP AND I SURE AM GLAD I DID.
SNAP
CAN I HELP YOU?
WELL, I HOPE SO! WHAT'S GOOD HERE? HOW ABOUT THE--
DON'T BOTHER. WE WON'T BE STAYING LONG ENOUGH TO EAT, I'M AFRAID. JUST THE CHECK.
WELL, THAT WASN'T VERY POLITE, AGENT HOBBES. HOW'S A GIRL LIKE HER SUPPOSED TO MAKE HER WAY IF PEOPLE LIKE US DON'T--
MR. GLASS. LOOK TO YOUR FAR LEFT.

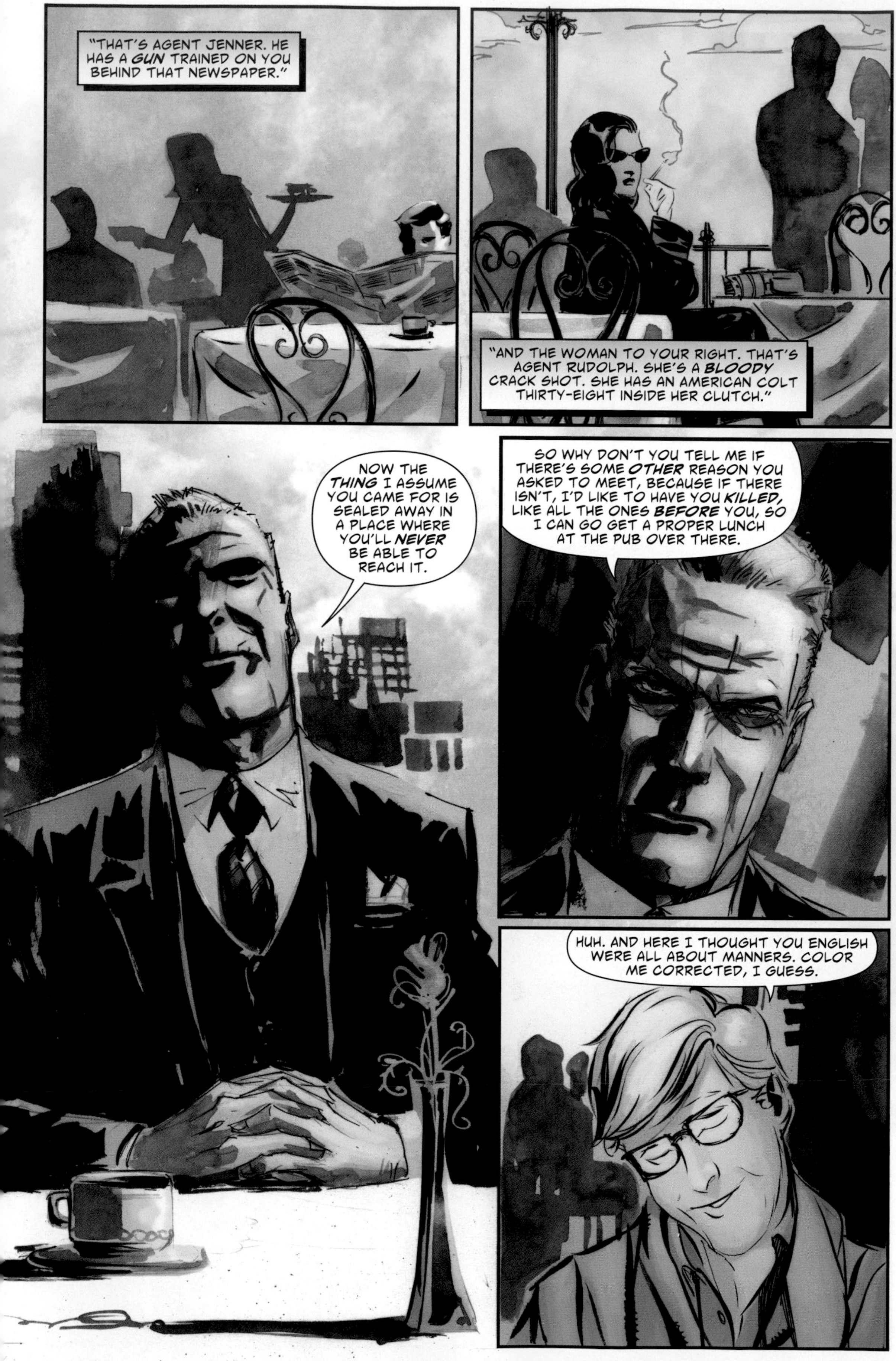
"THAT'S AGENT JENNER. HE HAS A GUN TRAINED ON YOU BEHIND THAT NEWSPAPER."
"AND THE WOMAN TO YOUR RIGHT. THAT'S AGENT RUDOLPH. SHE'S A BLOODY CRACK SHOT. SHE HAS AN AMERICAN COLT THIRTY-EIGHT INSIDE HER CLUTCH."
NOW THE THING I ASSUME YOU CAME FOR IS SEALED AWAY IN A PLACE WHERE YOU'LL NEVER BE ABLE TO REACH IT.
SO WHY DON'T YOU TELL ME IF THERE'S SOME OTHER REASON YOU ASKED TO MEET, BECAUSE IF THERE ISN'T, I'D LIKE TO HAVE YOU KILLED, LIKE ALL THE ONES BEFORE YOU, SO I CAN GO GET A PROPER LUNCH AT THE PUB OVER THERE.
HUH. AND HERE I THOUGHT YOU ENGLISH WERE ALL ABOUT MANNERS. COLOR ME CORRECTED, I GUESS.

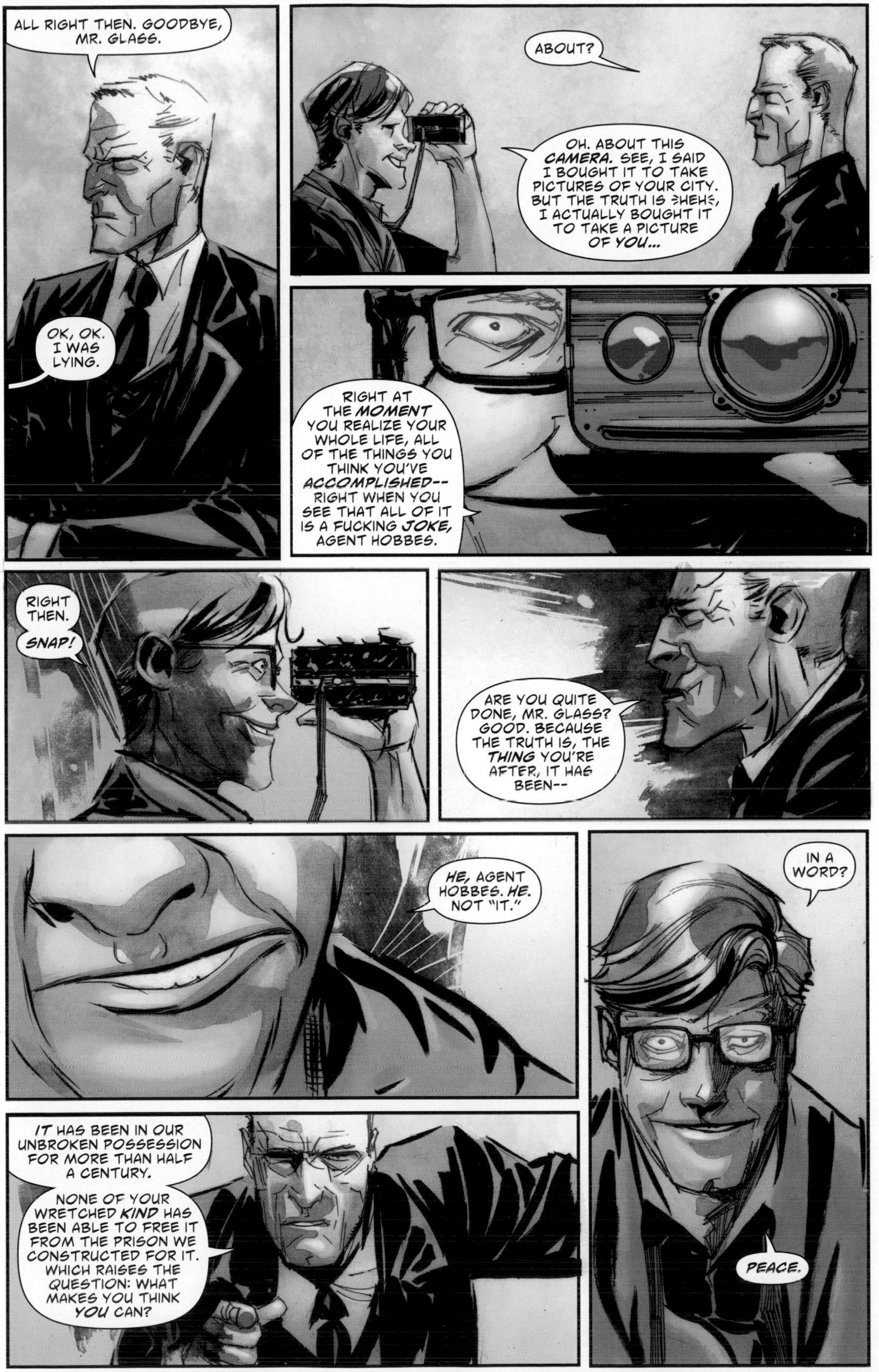
ALL RIGHT THEN. GOODBYE, MR. GLASS.
OK, OK. I WAS LYING.
ABOUT?
OH. ABOUT THIS CAMERA. SEE, I SAID I BOUGHT IT TO TAKE PICTURES OF YOUR CITY. BUT THE TRUTH IS HEH, I ACTUALLY BOUGHT IT TO TAKE A PICTURE OF YOU...
RIGHT AT THE MOMENT YOU REALIZE YOUR WHOLE LIFE, ALL OF THE THINGS YOU THINK YOU'VE ACCOMPLISHED-- RIGHT WHEN YOU SEE THAT ALL OF IT IS A FUCKING JOKE, AGENT HOBBES.
RIGHT THEN.
SNAP!
ARE YOU QUITE DONE, MR. GLASS? GOOD. BECAUSE THE TRUTH IS, THE THING YOU'RE AFTER, IT HAS BEEN--
HE, AGENT HOBBES. HE. NOT "IT."
IT HAS BEEN IN OUR UNBROKEN POSSESSION FOR MORE THAN HALF A CENTURY.
NONE OF YOUR WRETCHED KIND HAS BEEN ABLE TO FREE IT FROM THE PRISON WE CONSTRUCTED FOR IT. WHICH RAISES THE QUESTION: WHAT MAKES YOU THINK YOU CAN?
IN A WORD?
PEACE.

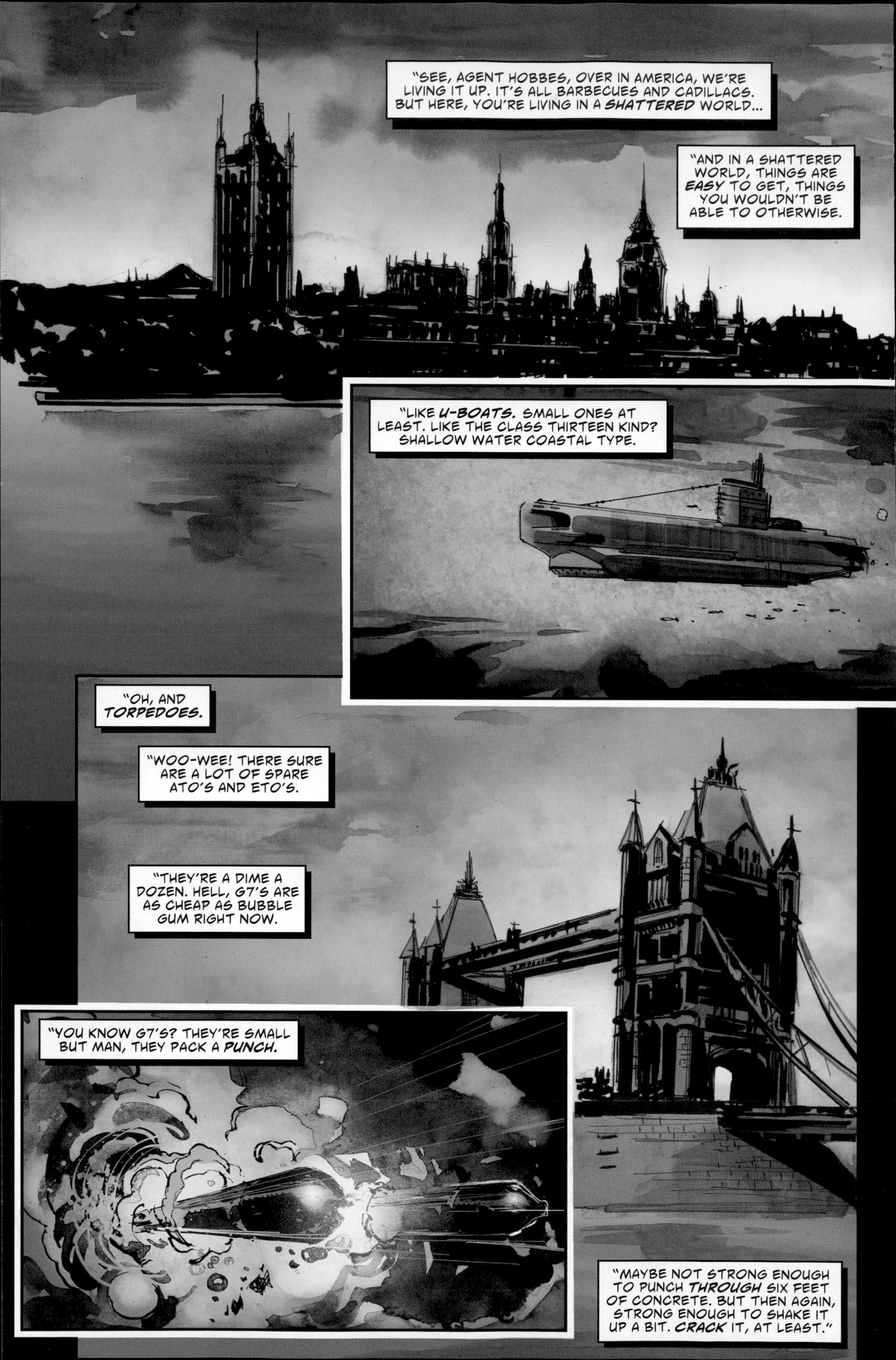
"SEE, AGENT HOBBES, OVER IN AMERICA, WE'RE LIVING IT UP. IT'S ALL BARBECUES AND CADILLACS. BUT HERE, YOU'RE LIVING IN A *SHATTERED* WORLD...
"AND IN A SHATTERED WORLD, THINGS ARE *EASY* TO GET, THINGS YOU WOULDN'T BE ABLE TO OTHERWISE.
"LIKE *U-BOATS.* SMALL ONES AT LEAST. LIKE THE CLASS THIRTEEN KIND? SHALLOW WATER COASTAL TYPE.
"OH, AND *TORPEDOES.*
"WOO-WEE! THERE SURE ARE A LOT OF SPARE ATO'S AND ETO'S.
"THEY'RE A DIME A DOZEN. HELL, G7'S ARE AS CHEAP AS BUBBLE GUM RIGHT NOW.
"YOU KNOW G7'S? THEY'RE SMALL BUT MAN, THEY PACK A *PUNCH.*
"MAYBE NOT STRONG ENOUGH TO PUNCH *THROUGH* SIX FEET OF CONCRETE. BUT THEN AGAIN, STRONG ENOUGH TO SHAKE IT UP A BIT. *CRACK* IT, AT LEAST."

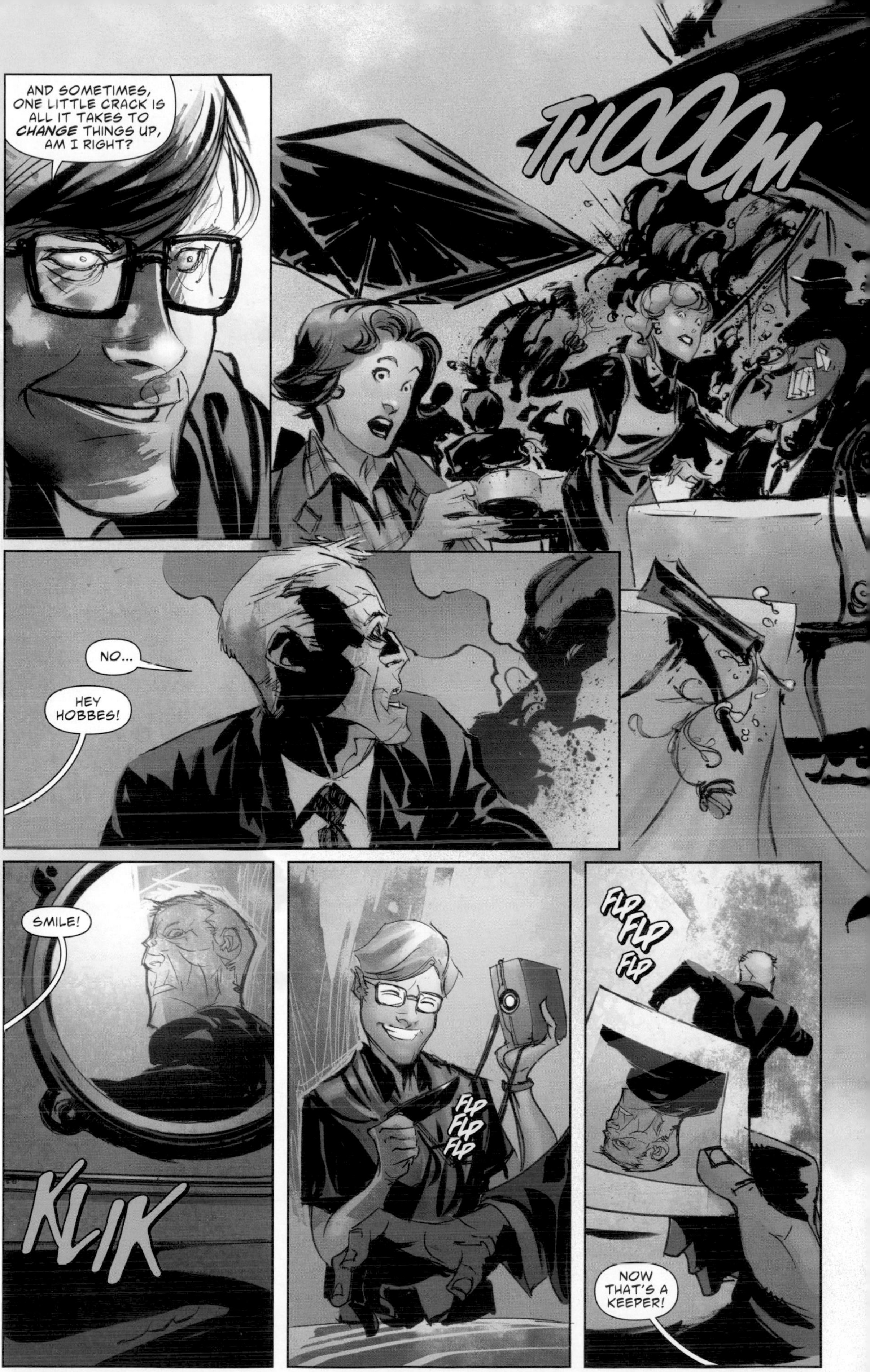
AND SOMETIMES, ONE LITTLE CRACK IS ALL IT TAKES TO CHANGE THINGS UP, AM I RIGHT?
THOOOM
NO...
HEY HOBBES!
SMILE!
KLIK
FLP FLP FLP
FLP FLP FLP
NOW THAT'S A KEEPER!

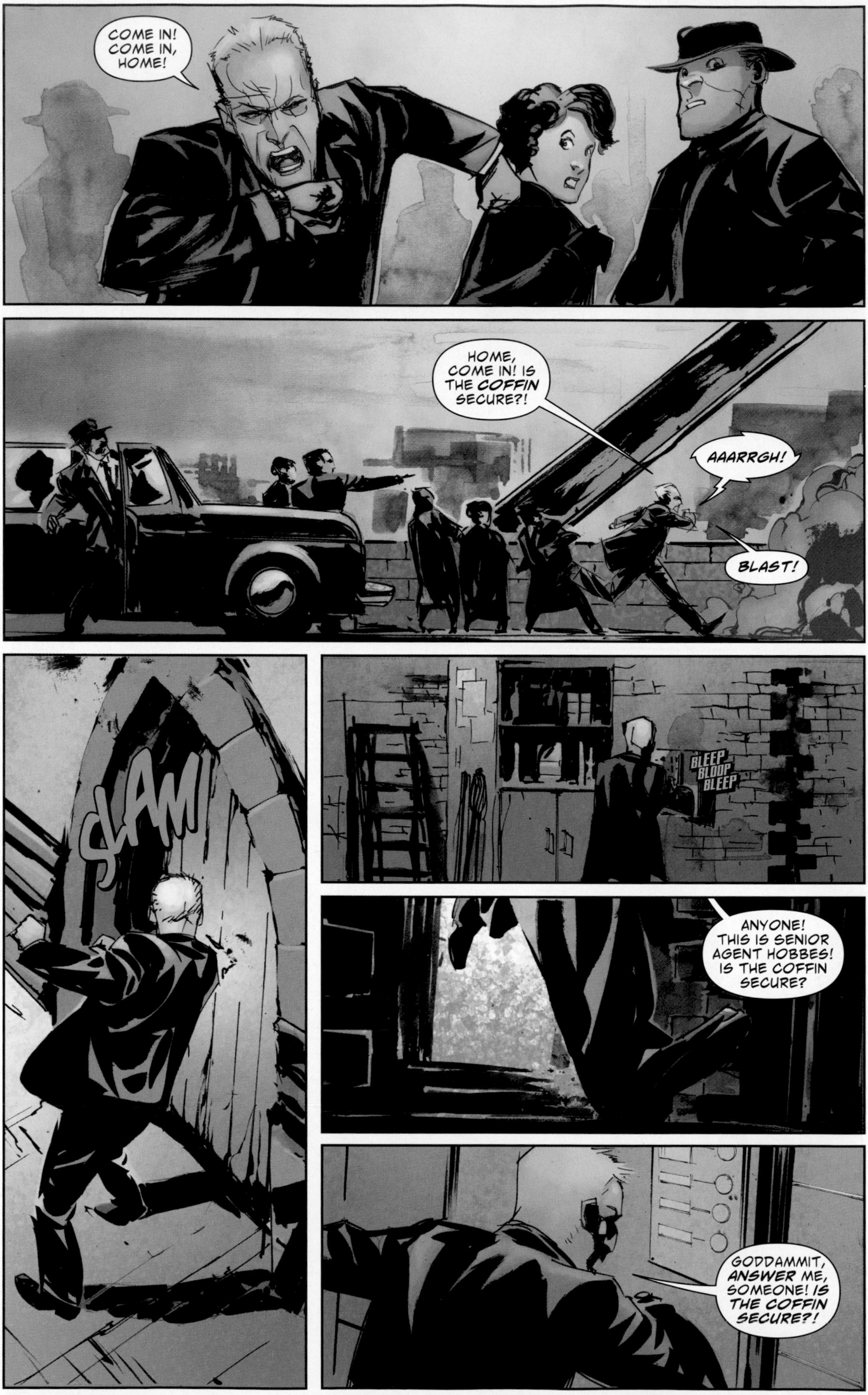
COME IN! COME IN, HOME!
HOME, COME IN! IS THE COFFIN SECURE?!
AAARRGH!
BLAST!
SLAM
BLEEP BLOOP BLEEP
ANYONE! THIS IS SENIOR AGENT HOBBES! IS THE COFFIN SECURE?
GODDAMMIT, ANSWER ME, SOMEONE! IS THE COFFIN SECURE?!

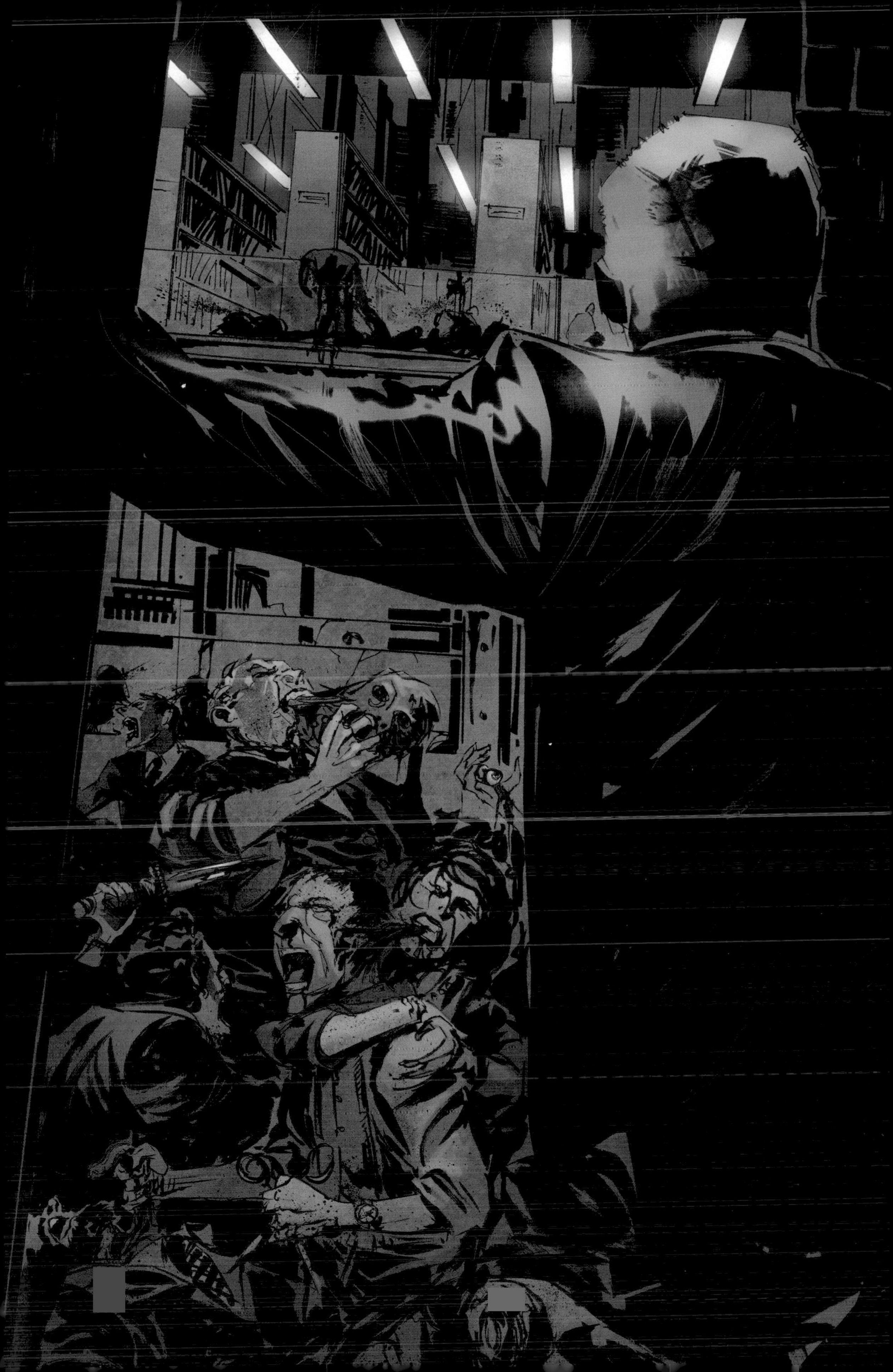

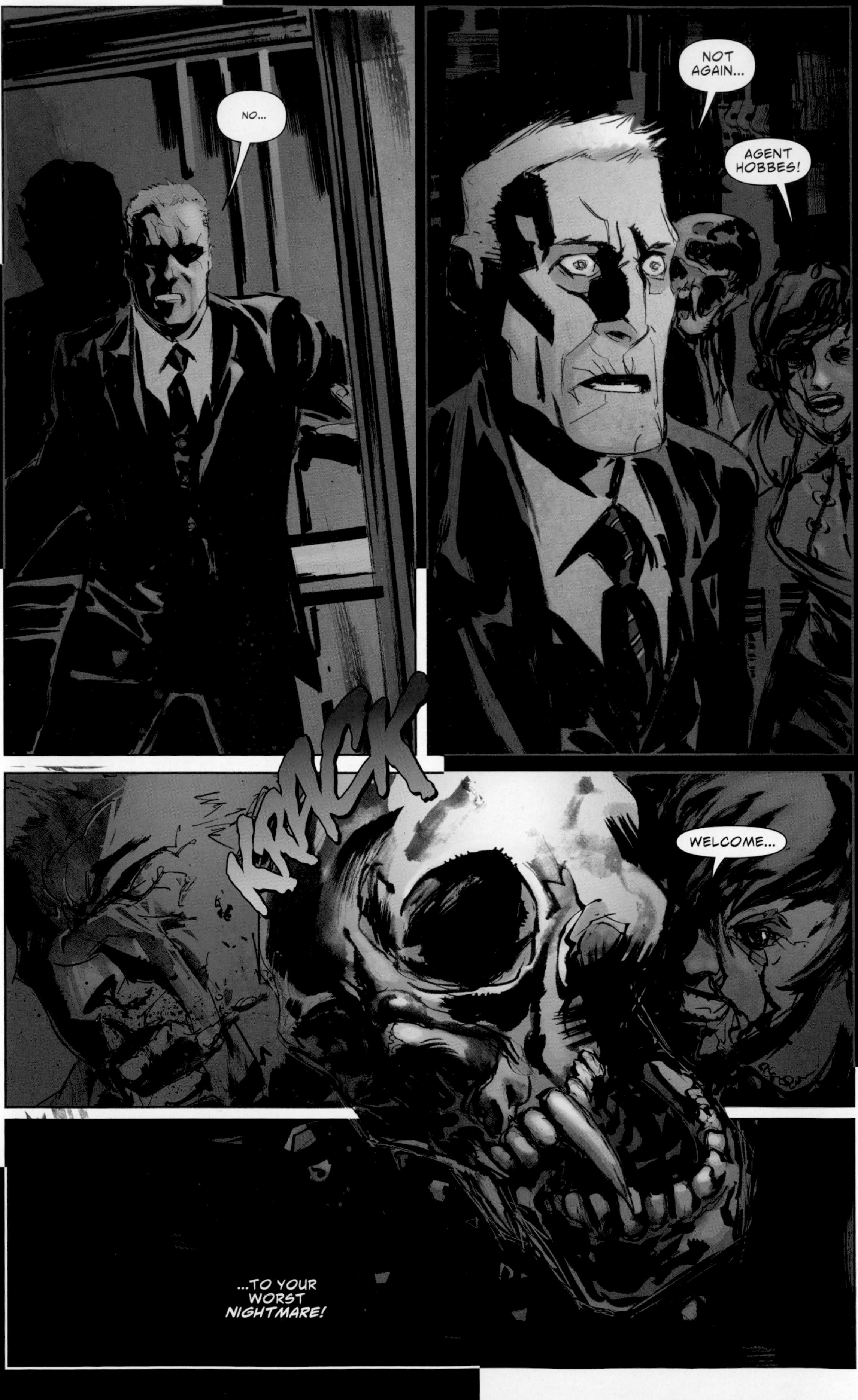
NO...
NOT AGAIN...
AGENT HOBBES!
KRACK
WELCOME...
...TO YOUR WORST NIGHTMARE!

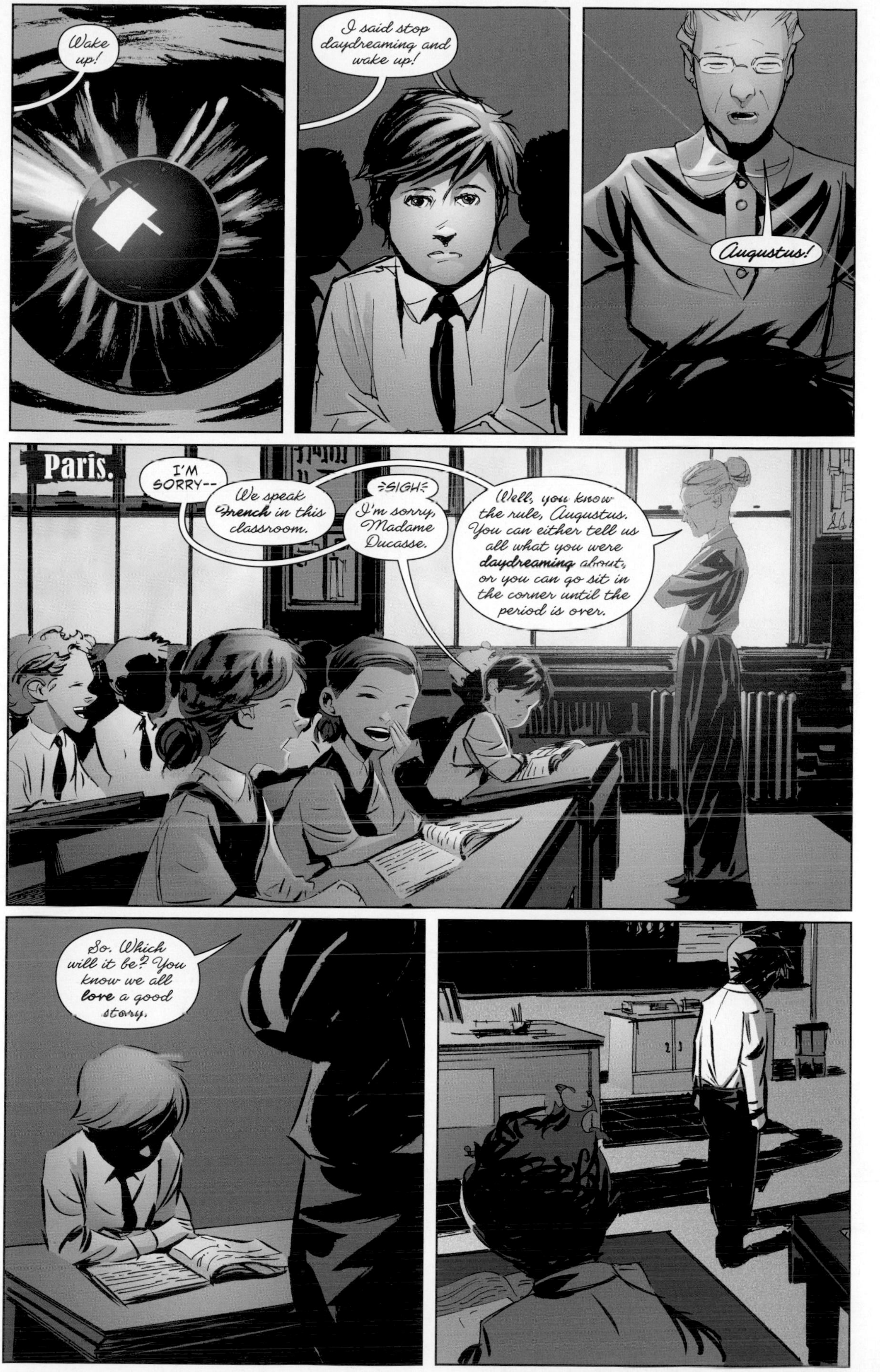
Wake up!
I said stop daydreaming and wake up!
Augustus!
Paris.
I'M SORRY--
We speak French in this classroom.
SIGH
I'm sorry, Madame Ducasse.
Well, you know the rule, Augustus. You can either tell us all what you were daydreaming about, or you can go sit in the corner until the period is over.
So. Which will it be? You know we all love a good story.

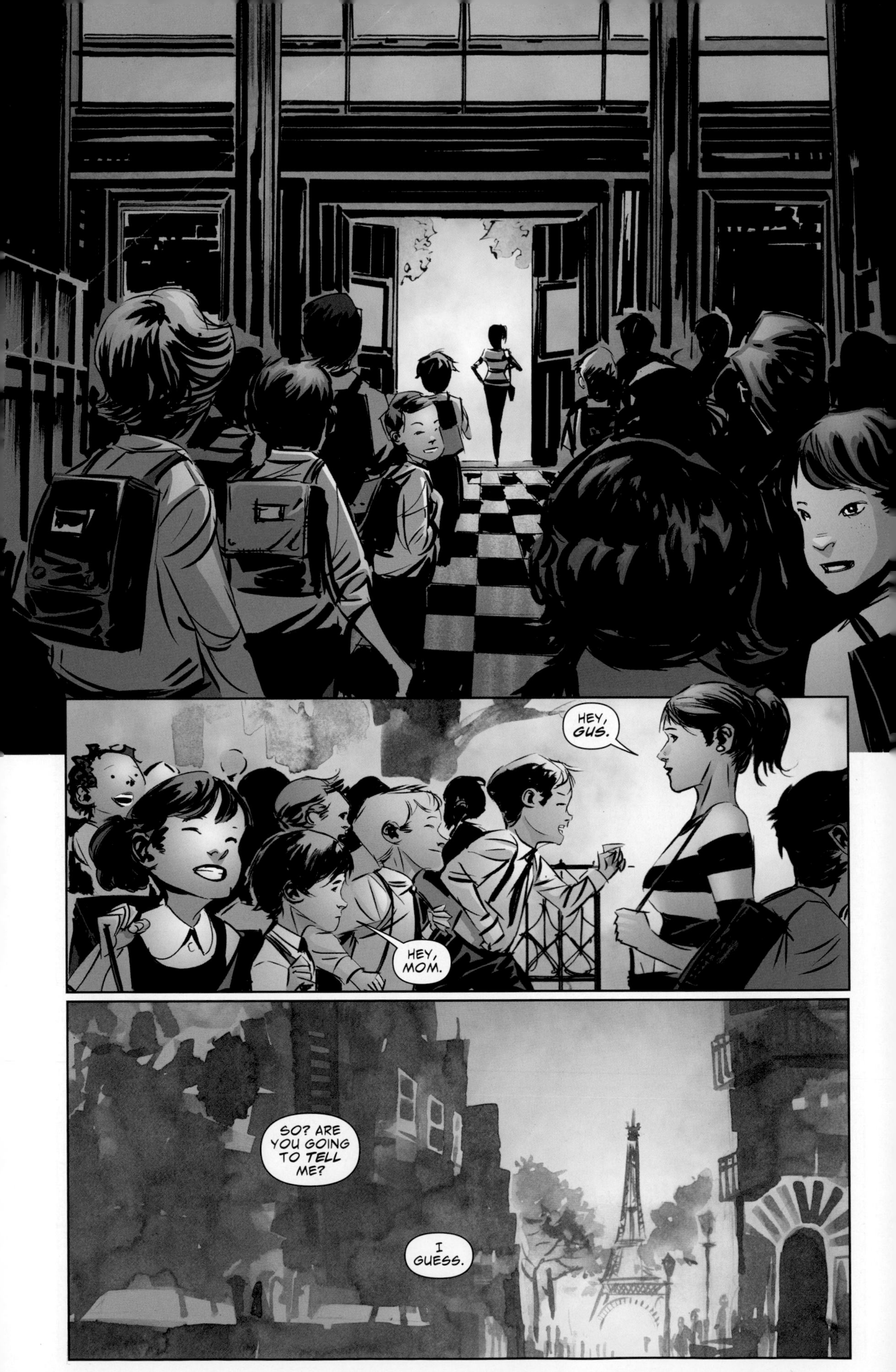
HEY, GUS.
HEY, MOM.
SO? ARE YOU GOING TO TELL ME?
I GUESS.

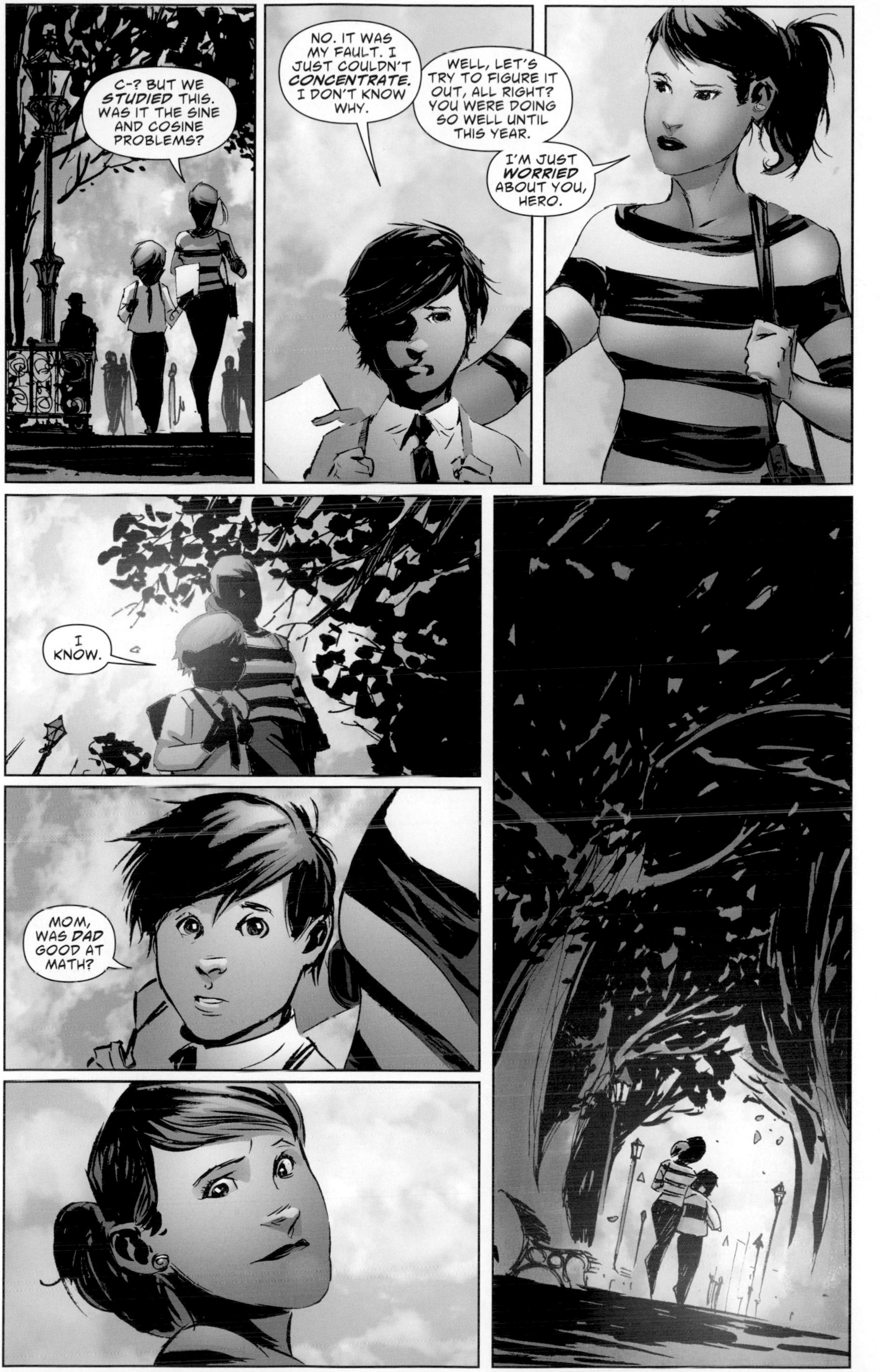
C-? BUT WE *STUDIED* THIS. WAS IT THE SINE AND COSINE PROBLEMS?
NO. IT WAS MY FAULT. I JUST COULDN'T *CONCENTRATE.* I DON'T KNOW WHY.
WELL, LET'S TRY TO FIGURE IT OUT, ALL RIGHT? YOU WERE DOING SO WELL UNTIL THIS YEAR.
I'M JUST *WORRIED* ABOUT YOU, HERO.
I KNOW.
MOM, WAS *DAD* GOOD AT MATH?

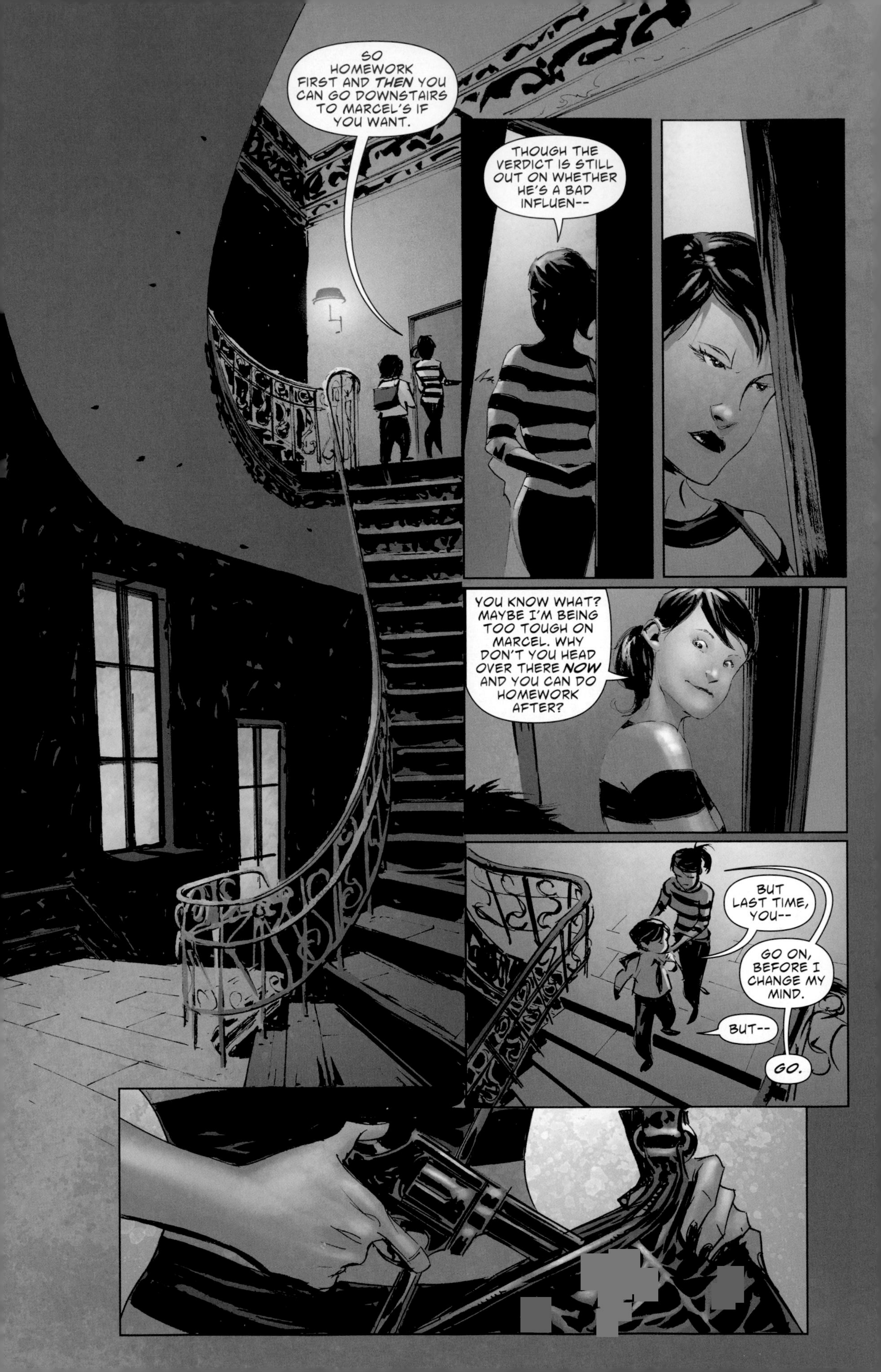
SO HOMEWORK FIRST AND THEN YOU CAN GO DOWNSTAIRS TO MARCEL'S IF YOU WANT.
THOUGH THE VERDICT IS STILL OUT ON WHETHER HE'S A BAD INFLUEN--
YOU KNOW WHAT? MAYBE I'M BEING TOO TOUGH ON MARCEL. WHY DON'T YOU HEAD OVER THERE NOW AND YOU CAN DO HOMEWORK AFTER?
BUT LAST TIME, YOU--
GO ON, BEFORE I CHANGE MY MIND.
BUT--
GO.

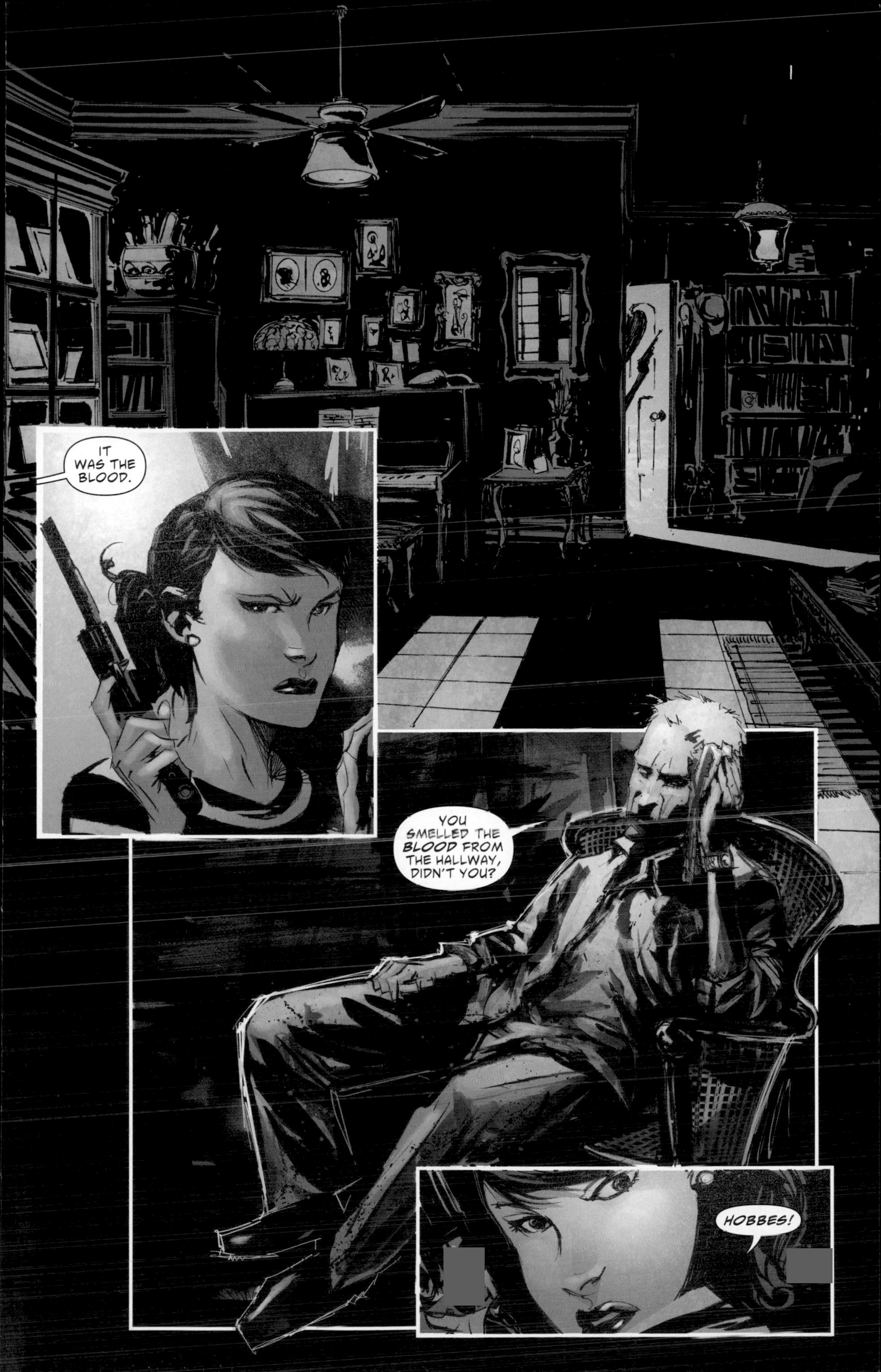
IT WAS THE BLOOD.
YOU SMELLED THE BLOOD FROM THE HALLWAY, DIDN'T YOU?
HOBBES!

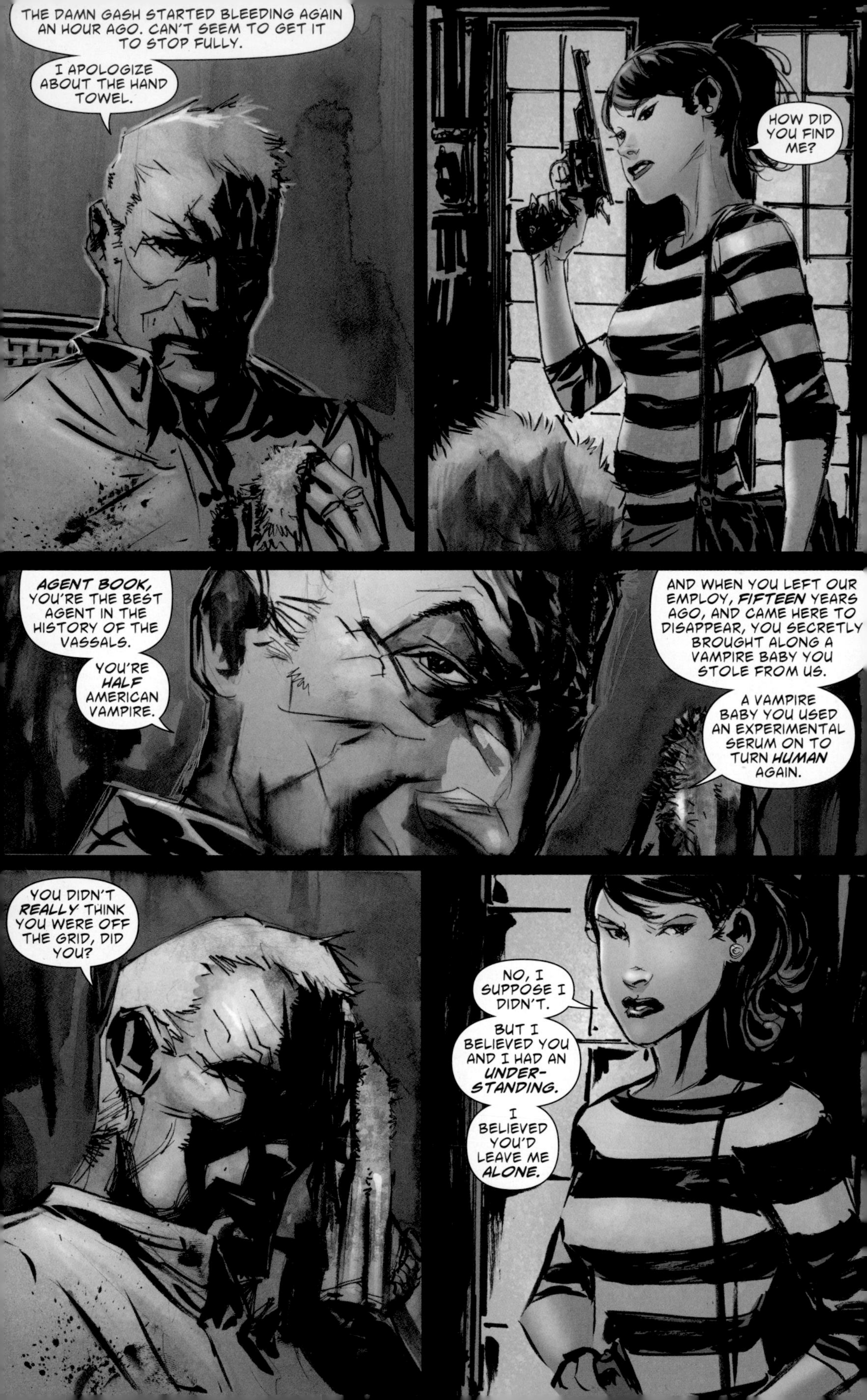
THE DAMN GASH STARTED BLEEDING AGAIN AN HOUR AGO. CAN'T SEEM TO GET IT TO STOP FULLY.
I APOLOGIZE ABOUT THE HAND TOWEL.
HOW DID YOU FIND ME?
AGENT BOOK, YOU'RE THE BEST AGENT IN THE HISTORY OF THE VASSALS.
YOU'RE HALF AMERICAN VAMPIRE.
AND WHEN YOU LEFT OUR EMPLOY, FIFTEEN YEARS AGO, AND CAME HERE TO DISAPPEAR, YOU SECRETLY BROUGHT ALONG A VAMPIRE BABY YOU STOLE FROM US.
A VAMPIRE BABY YOU USED AN EXPERIMENTAL SERUM ON TO TURN HUMAN AGAIN.
YOU DIDN'T REALLY THINK YOU WERE OFF THE GRID, DID YOU?
NO, I SUPPOSE I DIDN'T.
BUT I BELIEVED YOU AND I HAD AN UNDER-STANDING.
I BELIEVED YOU'D LEAVE ME ALONE.

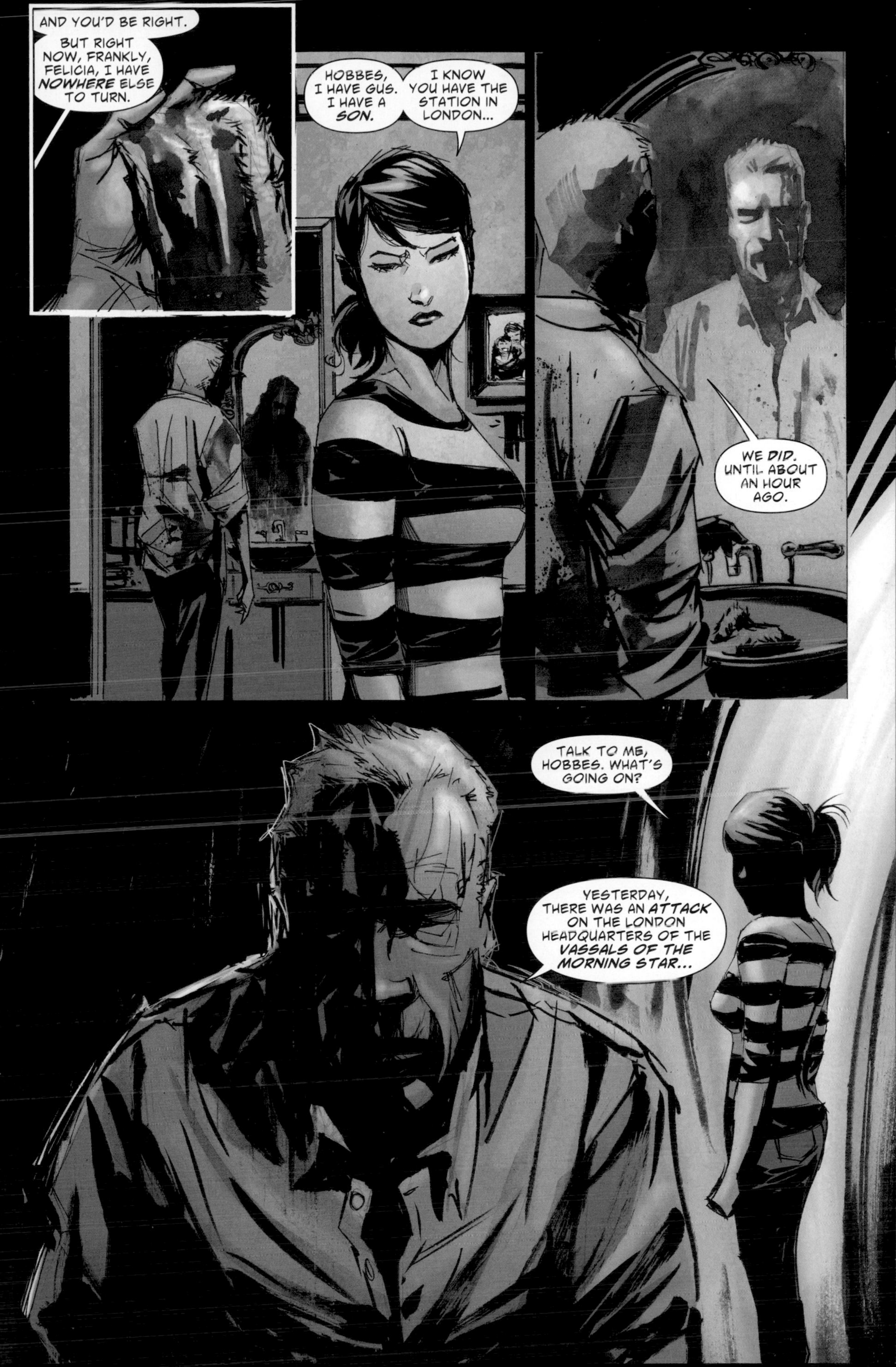
AND YOU'D BE RIGHT.
BUT RIGHT NOW, FRANKLY, FELICIA, I HAVE NOWHERE ELSE TO TURN.
HOBBES, I HAVE GUS. I HAVE A SON.
I KNOW YOU HAVE THE STATION IN LONDON...
WE DID. UNTIL ABOUT AN HOUR AGO.
TALK TO ME, HOBBES. WHAT'S GOING ON?
YESTERDAY, THERE WAS AN ATTACK ON THE LONDON HEADQUARTERS OF THE VASSALS OF THE MORNING STAR...

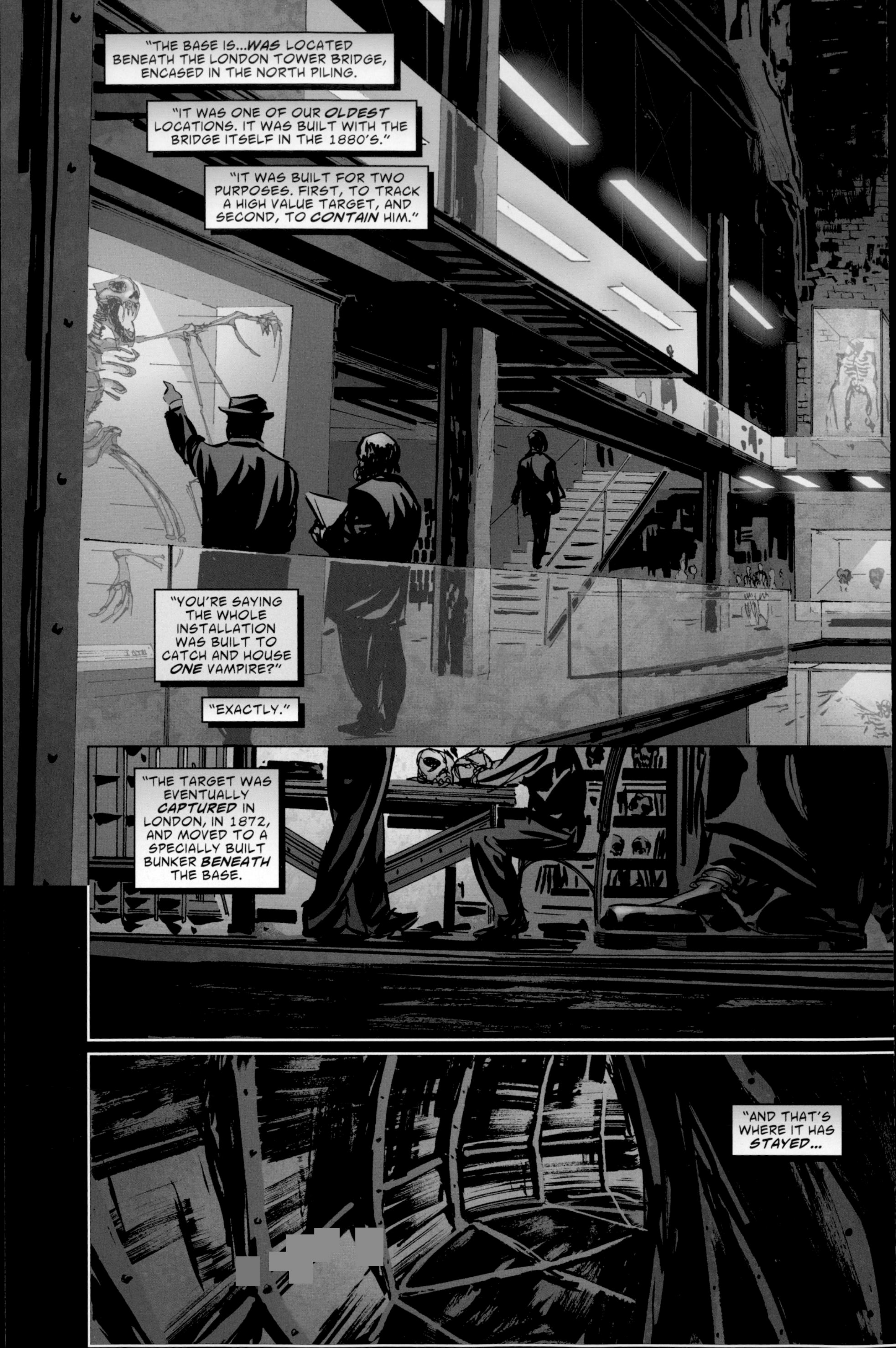
"THE BASE IS...WAS LOCATED BENEATH THE LONDON TOWER BRIDGE, ENCASED IN THE NORTH PILING.
"IT WAS ONE OF OUR OLDEST LOCATIONS. IT WAS BUILT WITH THE BRIDGE ITSELF IN THE 1880'S."
"IT WAS BUILT FOR TWO PURPOSES. FIRST, TO TRACK A HIGH VALUE TARGET, AND SECOND, TO CONTAIN HIM."
"YOU'RE SAYING THE WHOLE INSTALLATION WAS BUILT TO CATCH AND HOUSE ONE VAMPIRE?"
"EXACTLY."
"THE TARGET WAS EVENTUALLY CAPTURED IN LONDON, IN 1872, AND MOVED TO A SPECIALLY BUILT BUNKER BENEATH THE BASE.
"AND THAT'S WHERE IT HAS STAYED...

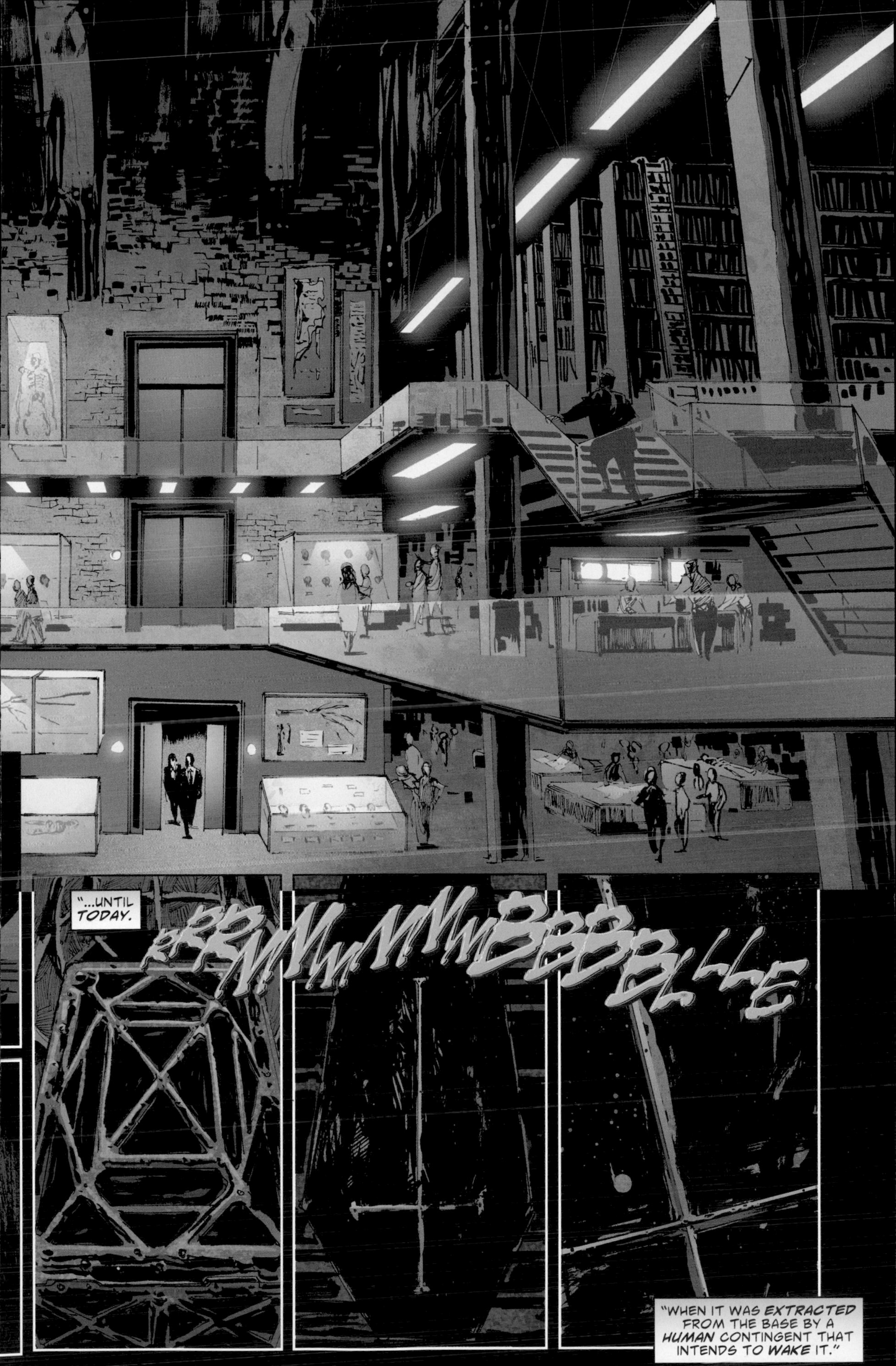
"...UNTIL TODAY.
RRRRMMMMMMBBBBLLLE
"WHEN IT WAS EXTRACTED FROM THE BASE BY A HUMAN CONTINGENT THAT INTENDS TO WAKE IT."

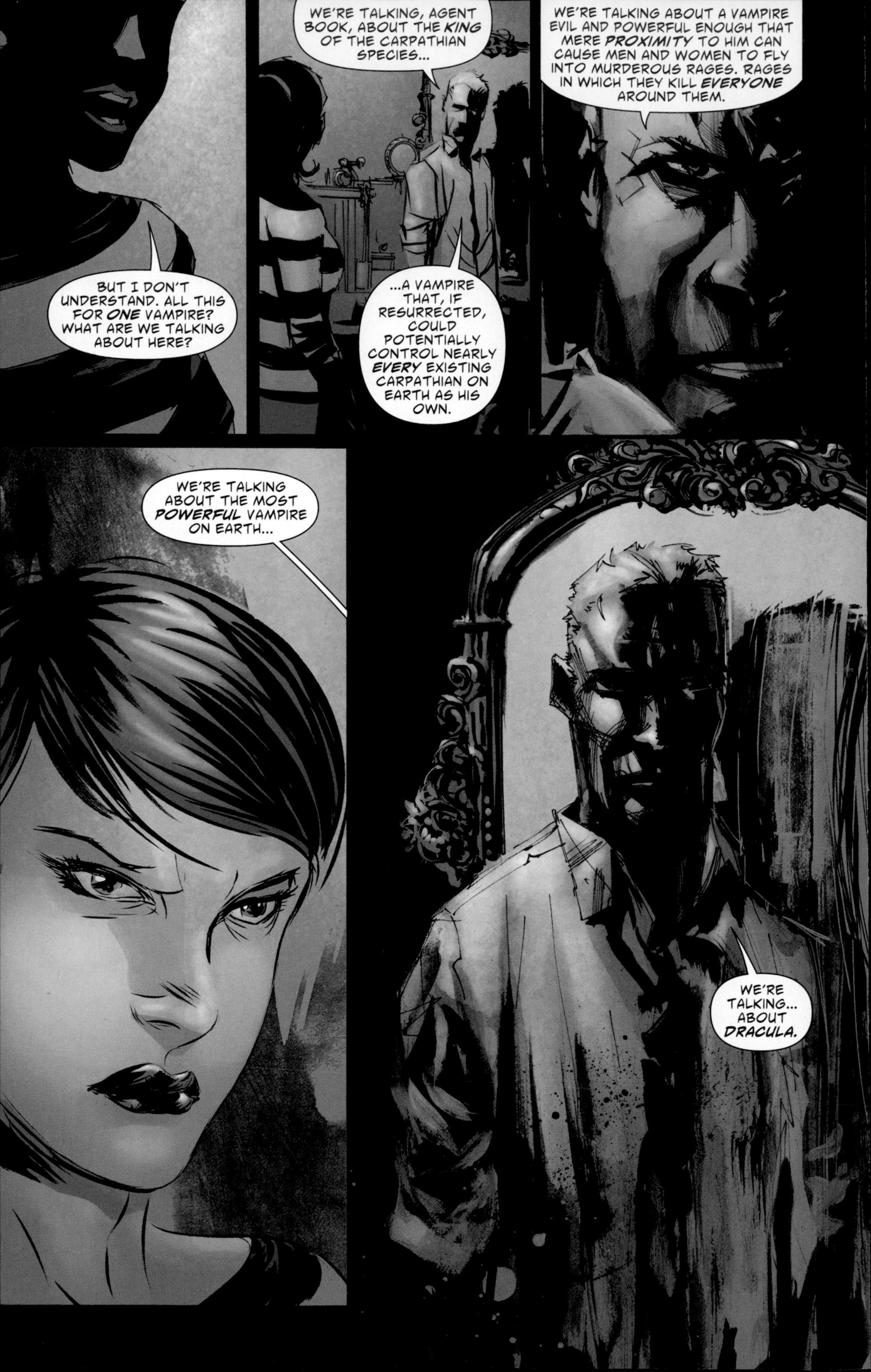

BUT I DON'T UNDERSTAND. ALL THIS FOR ONE VAMPIRE? WHAT ARE WE TALKING ABOUT HERE?
WE'RE TALKING, AGENT BOOK, ABOUT THE KING OF THE CARPATHIAN SPECIES...
...A VAMPIRE THAT, IF RESURRECTED, COULD POTENTIALLY CONTROL NEARLY EVERY EXISTING CARPATHIAN ON EARTH AS HIS OWN.
WE'RE TALKING ABOUT A VAMPIRE EVIL AND POWERFUL ENOUGH THAT MERE PROXIMITY TO HIM CAN CAUSE MEN AND WOMEN TO FLY INTO MURDEROUS RAGES. RAGES IN WHICH THEY KILL EVERYONE AROUND THEM.
WE'RE TALKING ABOUT THE MOST POWERFUL VAMPIRE ON EARTH...
WE'RE TALKING... ABOUT DRACULA.

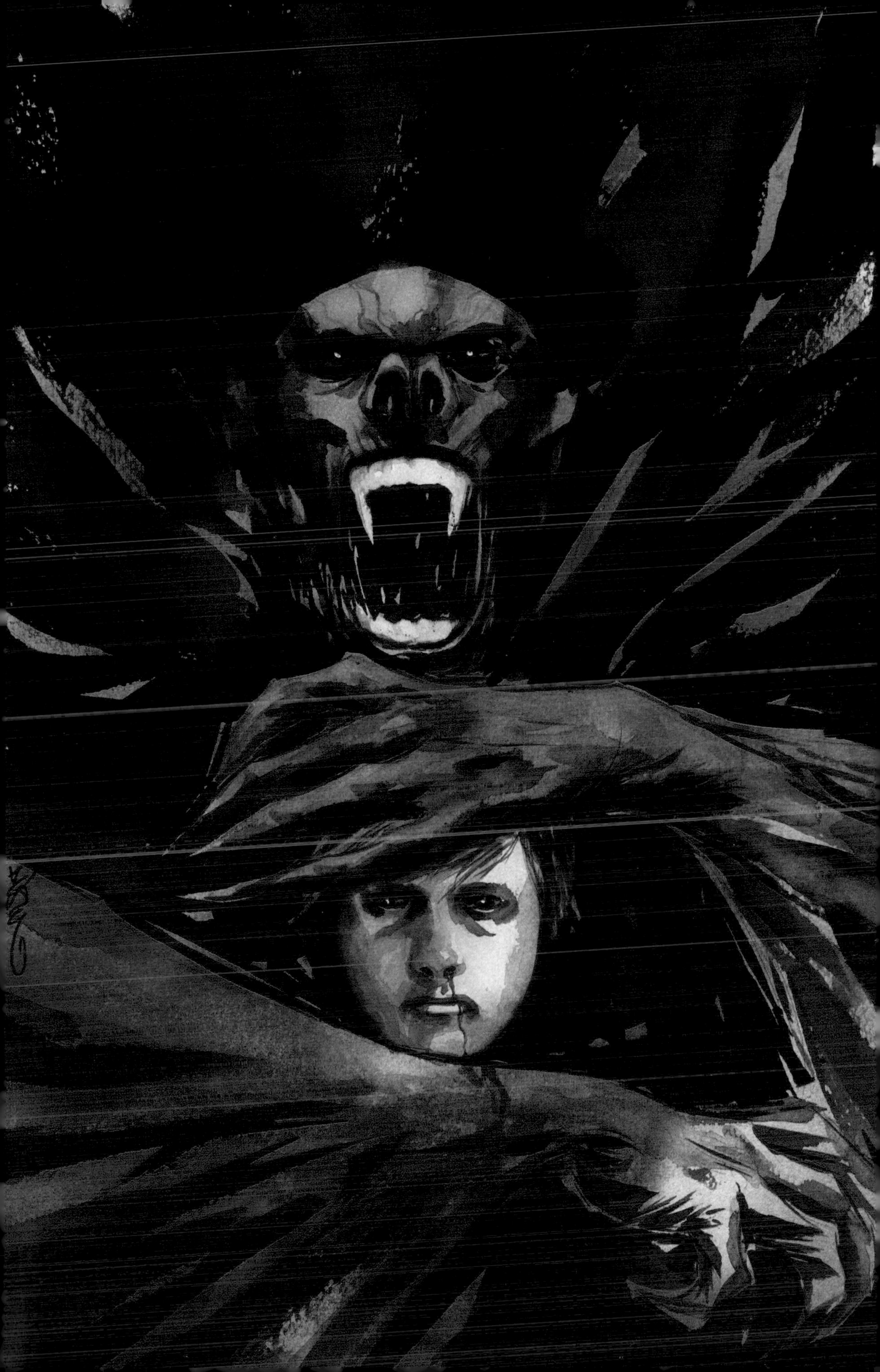

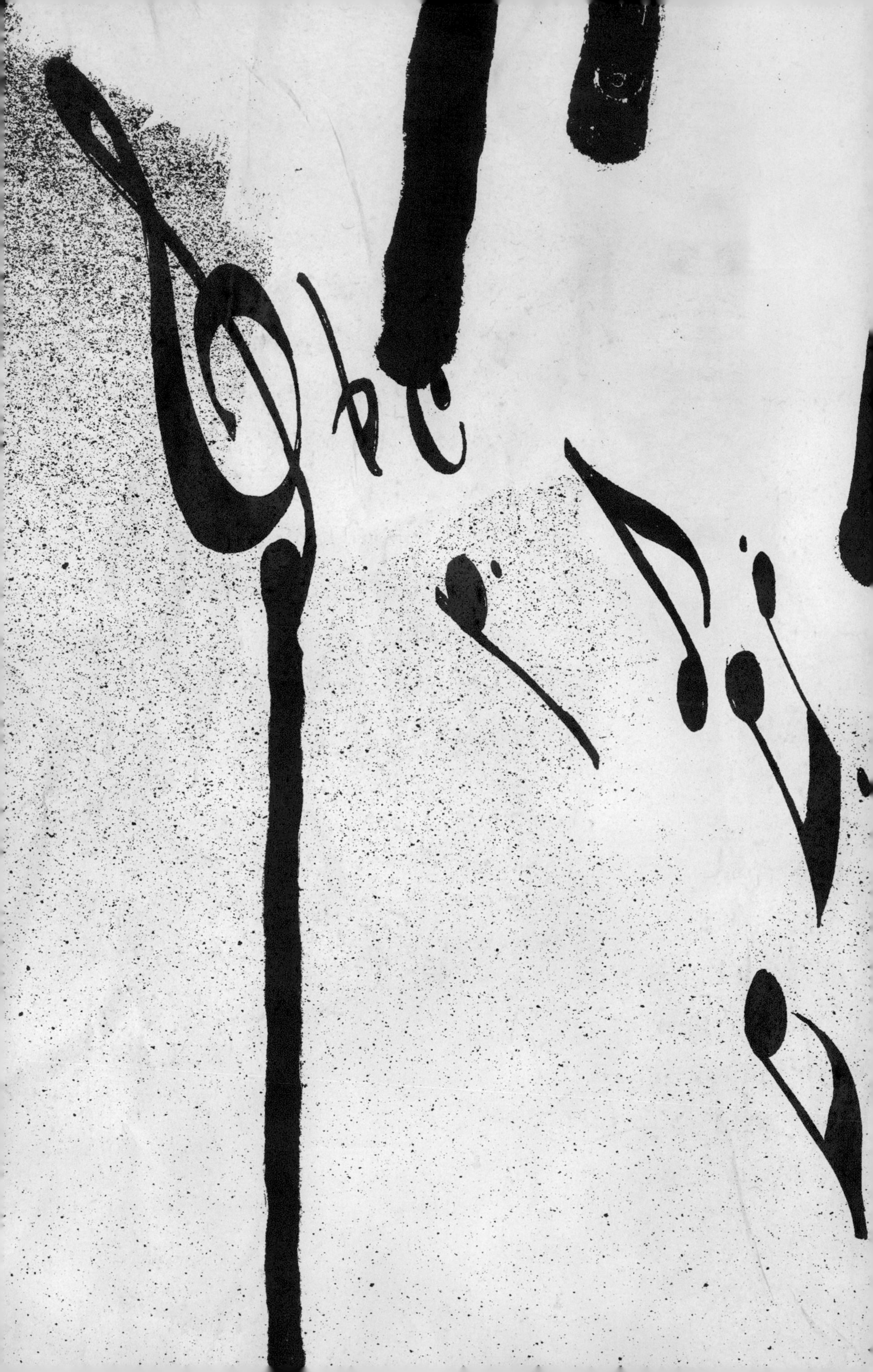

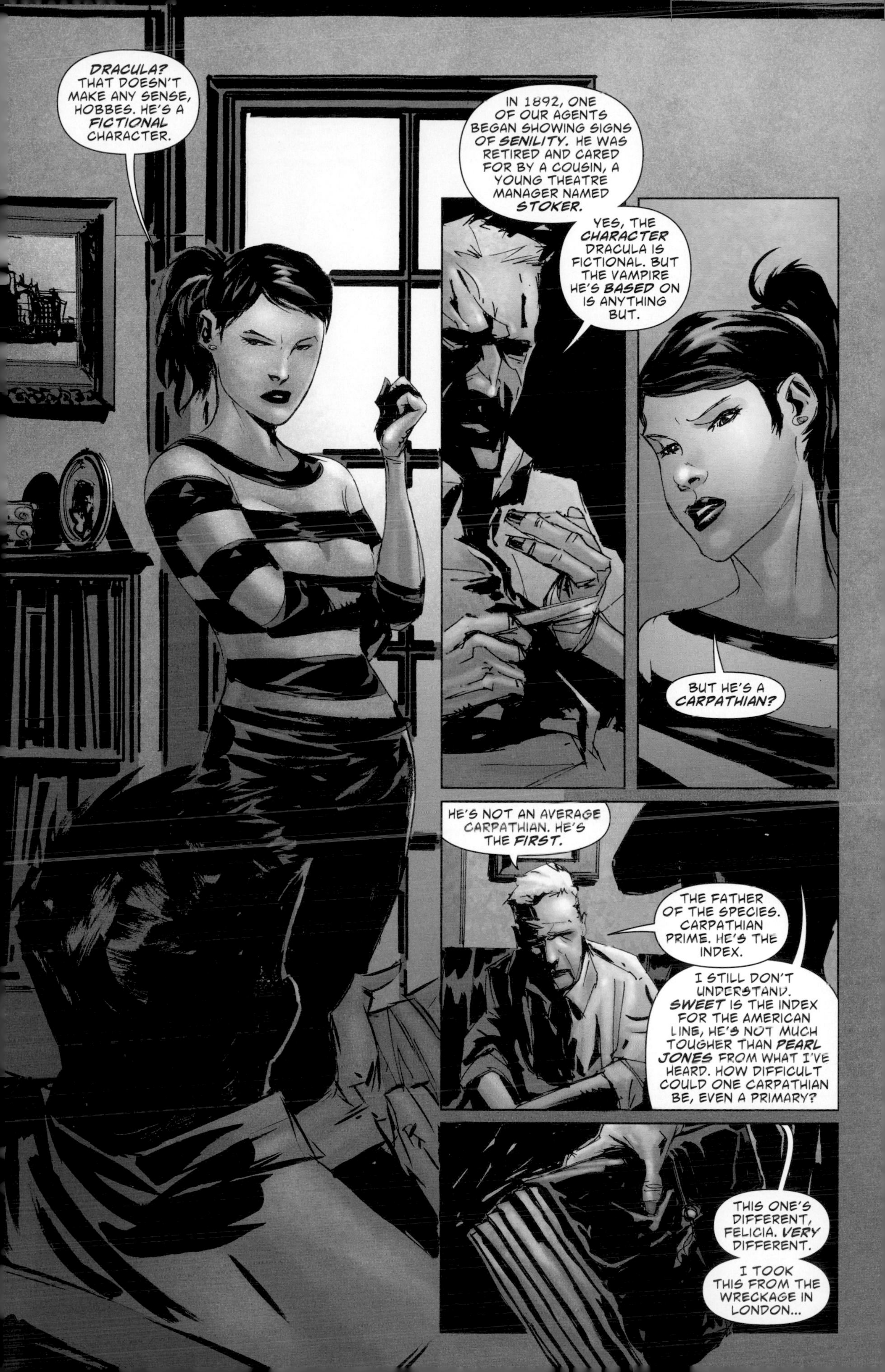
DRACULA? THAT DOESN'T MAKE ANY SENSE, HOBBES. HE'S A FICTIONAL CHARACTER.
IN 1892, ONE OF OUR AGENTS BEGAN SHOWING SIGNS OF SENILITY. HE WAS RETIRED AND CARED FOR BY A COUSIN, A YOUNG THEATRE MANAGER NAMED STOKER.
YES, THE CHARACTER DRACULA IS FICTIONAL. BUT THE VAMPIRE HE'S BASED ON IS ANYTHING BUT.
BUT HE'S A CARPATHIAN?
HE'S NOT AN AVERAGE CARPATHIAN. HE'S THE FIRST.
THE FATHER OF THE SPECIES. CARPATHIAN PRIME. HE'S THE INDEX.
I STILL DON'T UNDERSTAND. SWEET IS THE INDEX FOR THE AMERICAN LINE, HE'S NOT MUCH TOUGHER THAN PEARL JONES FROM WHAT I'VE HEARD. HOW DIFFICULT COULD ONE CARPATHIAN BE, EVEN A PRIMARY?
THIS ONE'S DIFFERENT, FELICIA. VERY DIFFERENT.
I TOOK THIS FROM THE WRECKAGE IN LONDON...

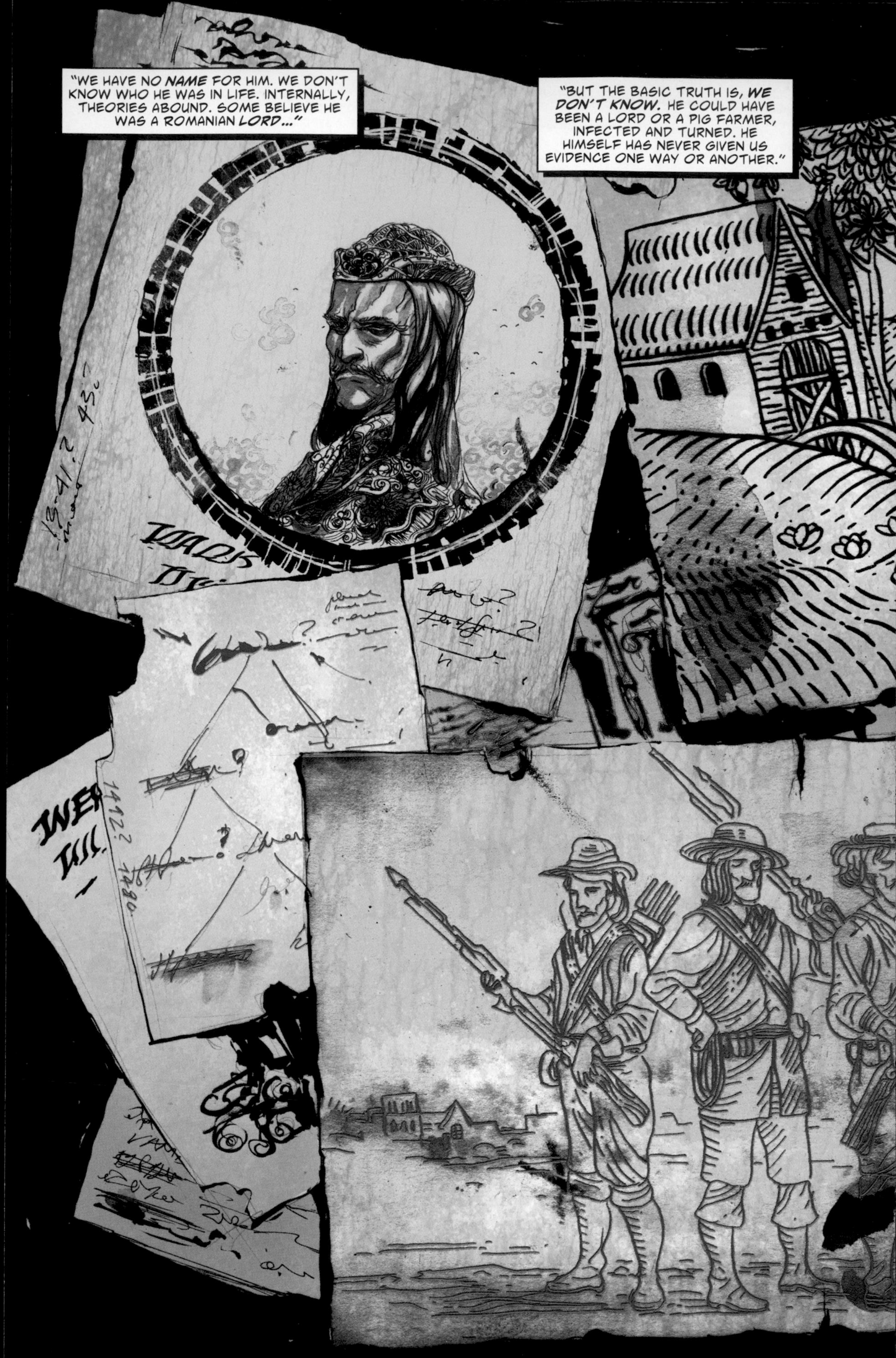
"WE HAVE NO NAME FOR HIM. WE DON'T KNOW WHO HE WAS IN LIFE. INTERNALLY, THEORIES ABOUND. SOME BELIEVE HE WAS A ROMANIAN LORD..."
"BUT THE BASIC TRUTH IS, WE DON'T KNOW. HE COULD HAVE BEEN A LORD OR A PIG FARMER, INFECTED AND TURNED. HE HIMSELF HAS NEVER GIVEN US EVIDENCE ONE WAY OR ANOTHER."

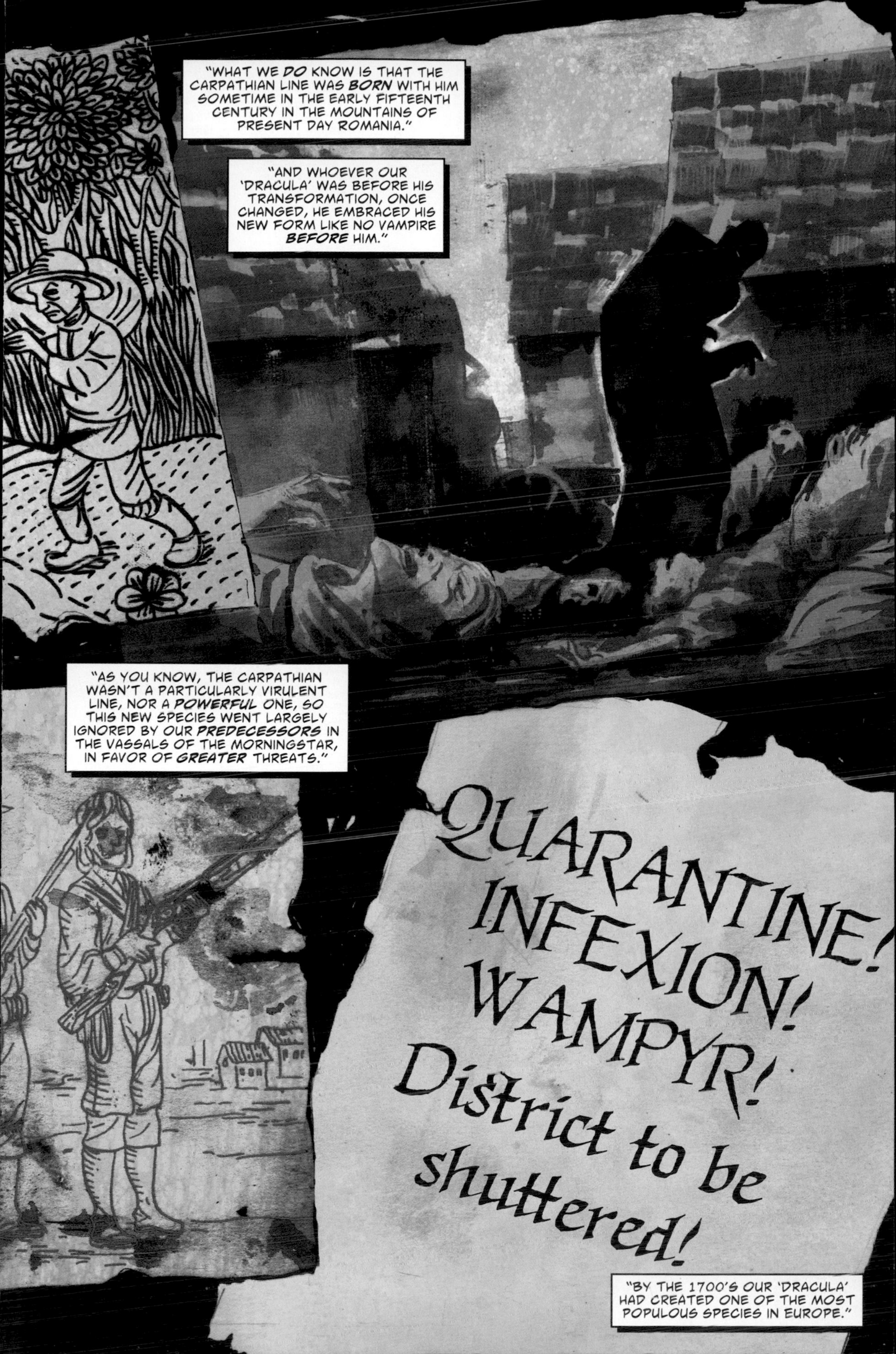
"WHAT WE DO KNOW IS THAT THE CARPATHIAN LINE WAS BORN WITH HIM SOMETIME IN THE EARLY FIFTEENTH CENTURY IN THE MOUNTAINS OF PRESENT DAY ROMANIA."
"AND WHOEVER OUR 'DRACULA' WAS BEFORE HIS TRANSFORMATION, ONCE CHANGED, HE EMBRACED HIS NEW FORM LIKE NO VAMPIRE BEFORE HIM."
"AS YOU KNOW, THE CARPATHIAN WASN'T A PARTICULARLY VIRULENT LINE, NOR A POWERFUL ONE, SO THIS NEW SPECIES WENT LARGELY IGNORED BY OUR PREDECESSORS IN THE VASSALS OF THE MORNINGSTAR, IN FAVOR OF GREATER THREATS."
QUARANTINE! INFEXION! WAMPYR! District to be shuttered!
"BY THE 1700'S OUR 'DRACULA' HAD CREATED ONE OF THE MOST POPULOUS SPECIES IN EUROPE."

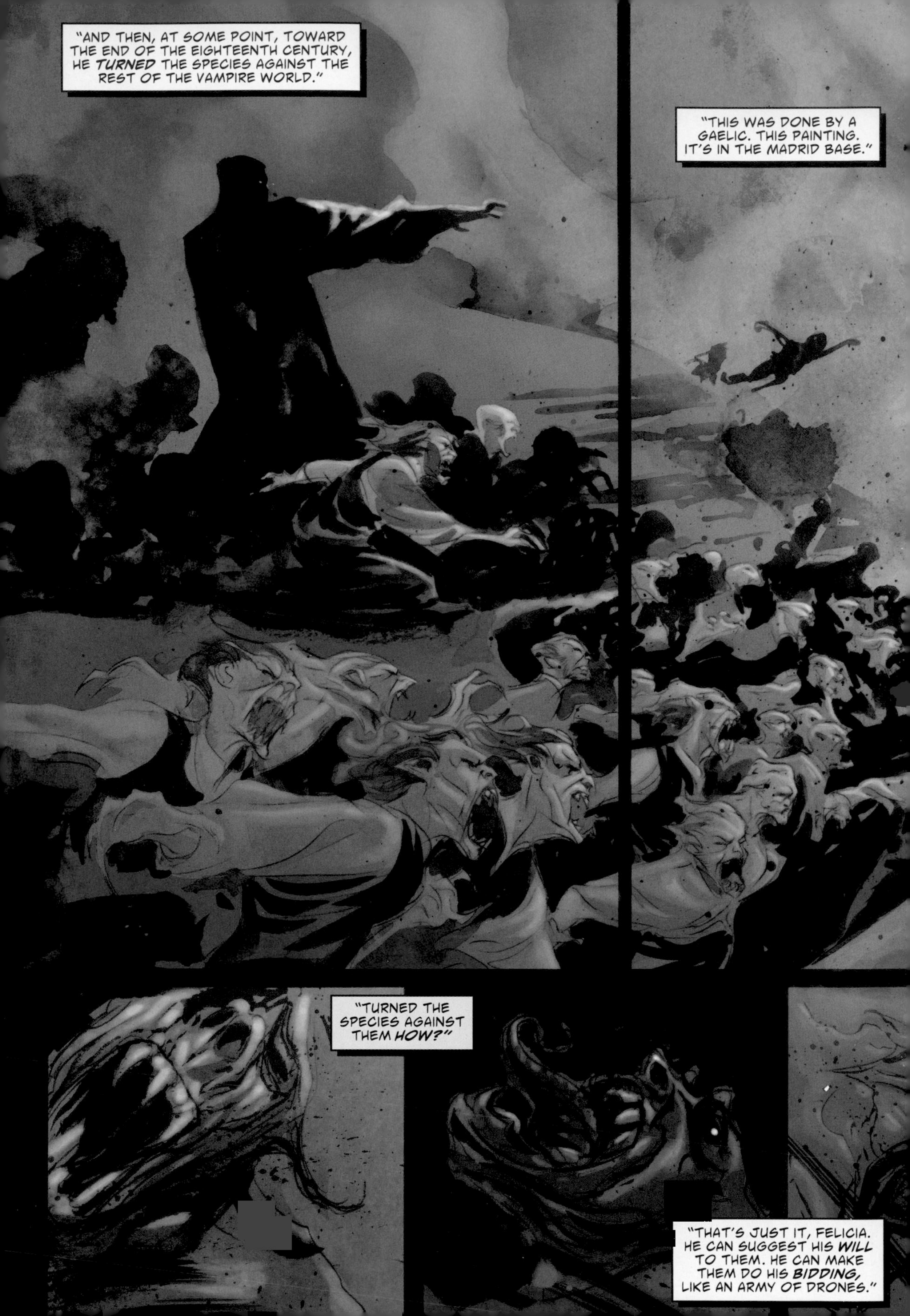

"AND THEN, AT SOME POINT, TOWARD THE END OF THE EIGHTEENTH CENTURY, HE *TURNED* THE SPECIES AGAINST THE REST OF THE VAMPIRE WORLD."
"THIS WAS DONE BY A GAELIC. THIS PAINTING. IT'S IN THE MADRID BASE."
"TURNED THE SPECIES AGAINST THEM *HOW?*"
"THAT'S JUST IT, FELICIA. HE CAN SUGGEST HIS *WILL* TO THEM. HE CAN MAKE THEM DO HIS *BIDDING,* LIKE AN ARMY OF DRONES."

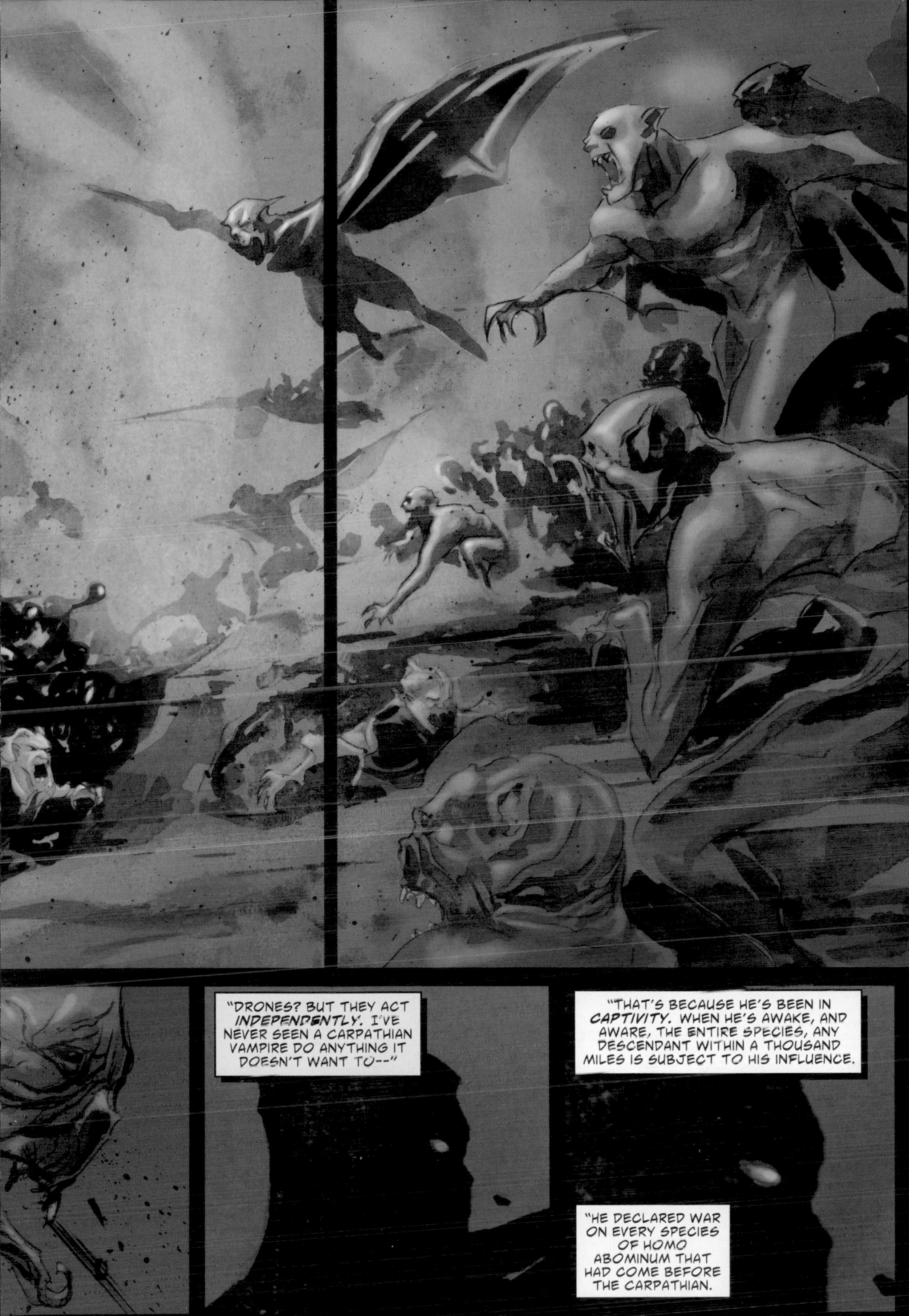
"DRONES? BUT THEY ACT INDEPENDENTLY. I'VE NEVER SEEN A CARPATHIAN VAMPIRE DO ANYTHING IT DOESN'T WANT TO--"
"THAT'S BECAUSE HE'S BEEN IN CAPTIVITY. WHEN HE'S AWAKE, AND AWARE, THE ENTIRE SPECIES, ANY DESCENDANT WITHIN A THOUSAND MILES IS SUBJECT TO HIS INFLUENCE.
"HE DECLARED WAR ON EVERY SPECIES OF HOMO ABOMINUM THAT HAD COME BEFORE THE CARPATHIAN.

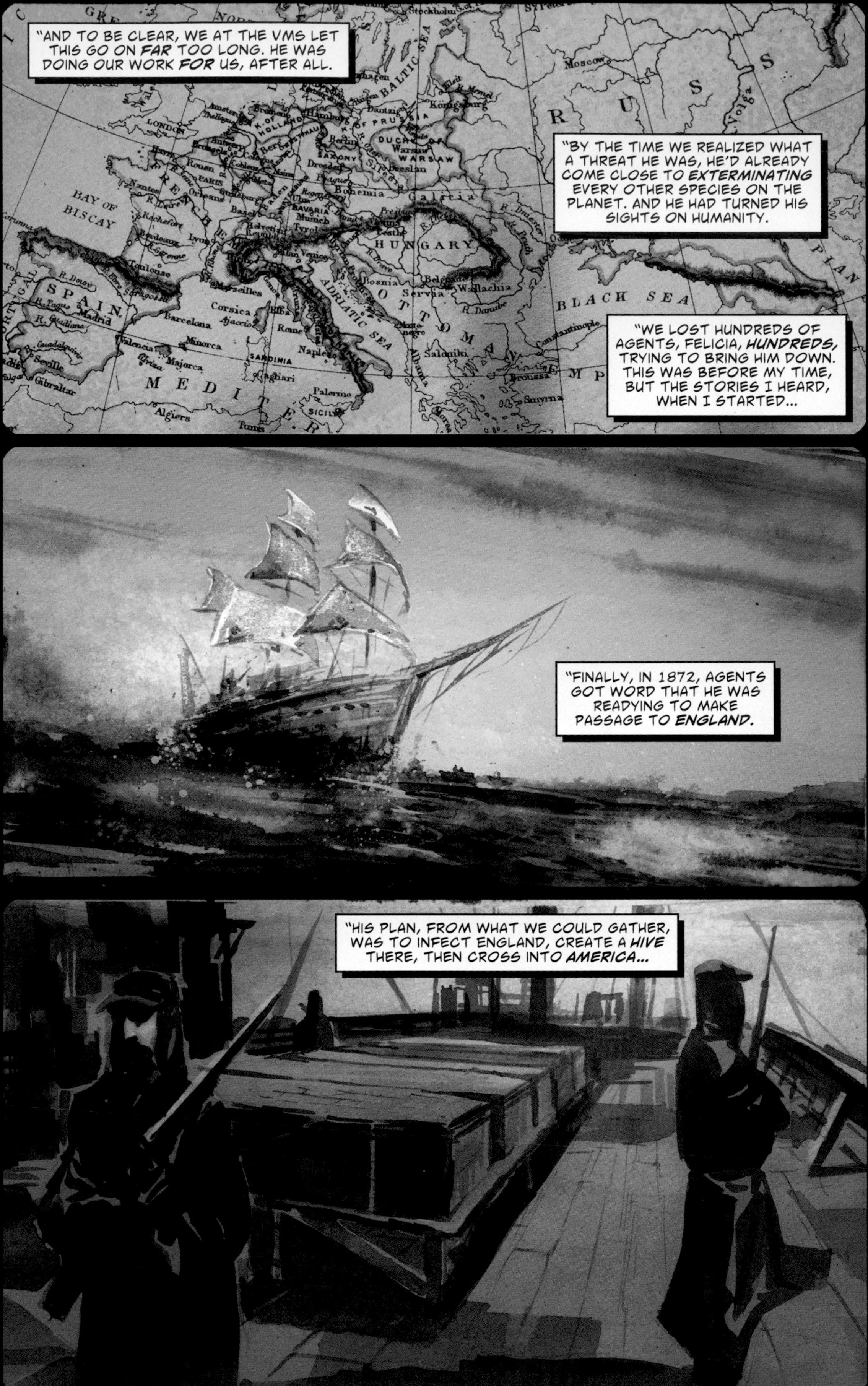
"AND TO BE CLEAR, WE AT THE VMS LET THIS GO ON *FAR* TOO LONG. HE WAS DOING OUR WORK *FOR* US, AFTER ALL.
"BY THE TIME WE REALIZED WHAT A THREAT HE WAS, HE'D ALREADY COME CLOSE TO *EXTERMINATING* EVERY OTHER SPECIES ON THE PLANET. AND HE HAD TURNED HIS SIGHTS ON HUMANITY.
"WE LOST HUNDREDS OF AGENTS, FELICIA, *HUNDREDS,* TRYING TO BRING HIM DOWN. THIS WAS BEFORE MY TIME, BUT THE STORIES I HEARD, WHEN I STARTED...
BAY OF BISCAY
SPAIN
HUNGARY
BLACK SEA
ADRIATIC SEA
"FINALLY, IN 1872, AGENTS GOT WORD THAT HE WAS READYING TO MAKE PASSAGE TO *ENGLAND.*
"HIS PLAN, FROM WHAT WE COULD GATHER, WAS TO INFECT ENGLAND, CREATE A *HIVE* THERE, THEN CROSS INTO *AMERICA*...

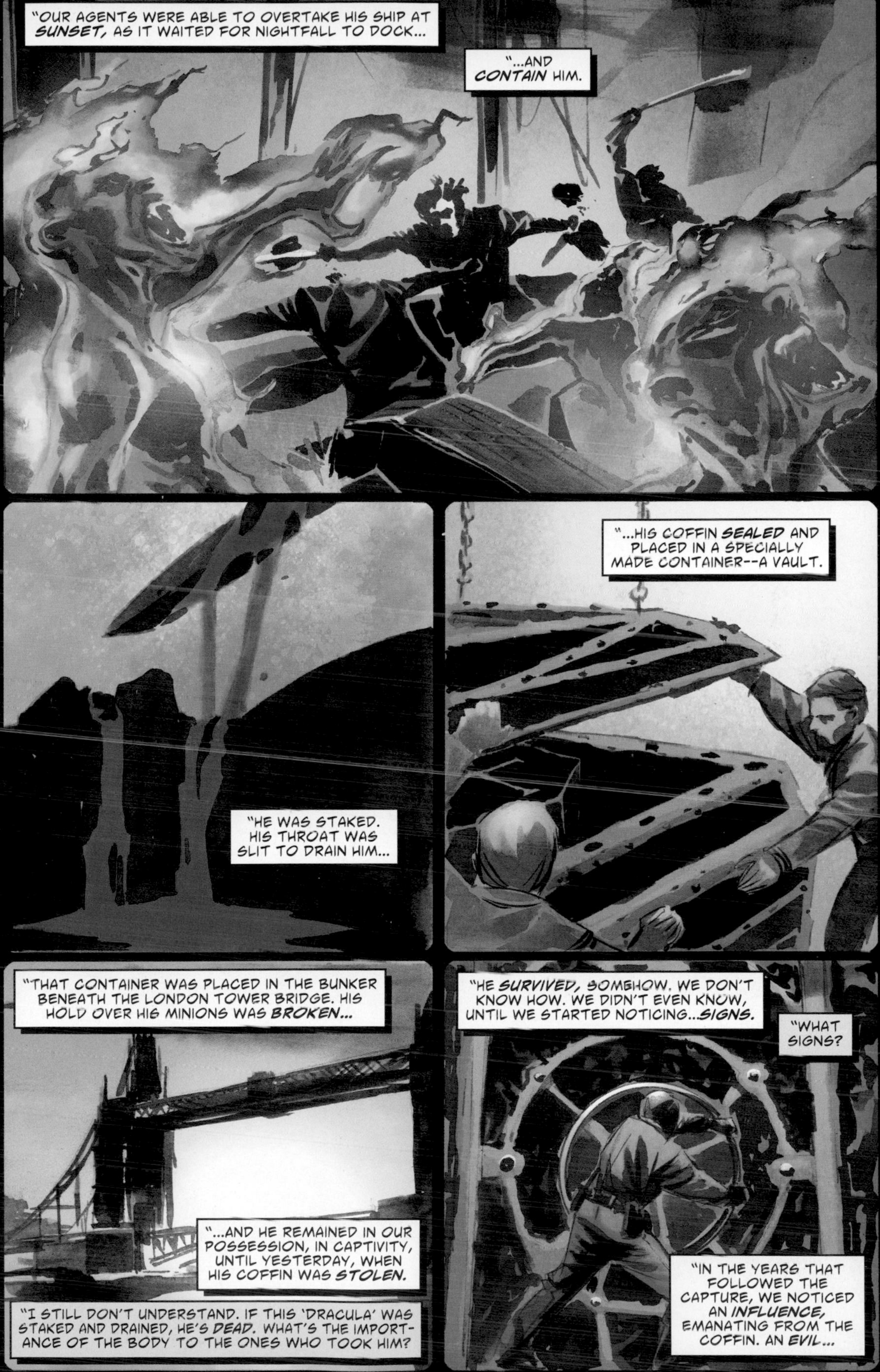
"OUR AGENTS WERE ABLE TO OVERTAKE HIS SHIP AT SUNSET, AS IT WAITED FOR NIGHTFALL TO DOCK...
"...AND CONTAIN HIM.
"HE WAS STAKED. HIS THROAT WAS SLIT TO DRAIN HIM...
"...HIS COFFIN SEALED AND PLACED IN A SPECIALLY MADE CONTAINER--A VAULT.
"THAT CONTAINER WAS PLACED IN THE BUNKER BENEATH THE LONDON TOWER BRIDGE. HIS HOLD OVER HIS MINIONS WAS BROKEN...
"...AND HE REMAINED IN OUR POSSESSION, IN CAPTIVITY, UNTIL YESTERDAY, WHEN HIS COFFIN WAS STOLEN.
"I STILL DON'T UNDERSTAND. IF THIS 'DRACULA' WAS STAKED AND DRAINED, HE'S DEAD. WHAT'S THE IMPORTANCE OF THE BODY TO THE ONES WHO TOOK HIM?
"HE SURVIVED, SOMEHOW. WE DON'T KNOW HOW. WE DIDN'T EVEN KNOW, UNTIL WE STARTED NOTICING...SIGNS.
"WHAT SIGNS?
"IN THE YEARS THAT FOLLOWED THE CAPTURE, WE NOTICED AN INFLUENCE, EMANATING FROM THE COFFIN. AN EVIL...

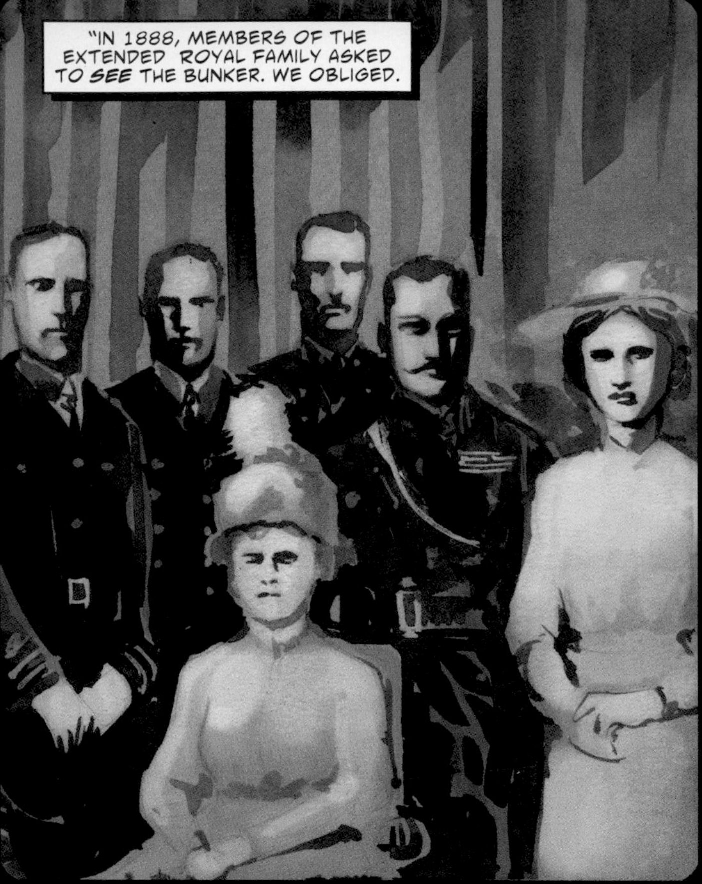
"IN 1888, MEMBERS OF THE EXTENDED ROYAL FAMILY ASKED TO *SEE* THE BUNKER. WE OBLIGED.
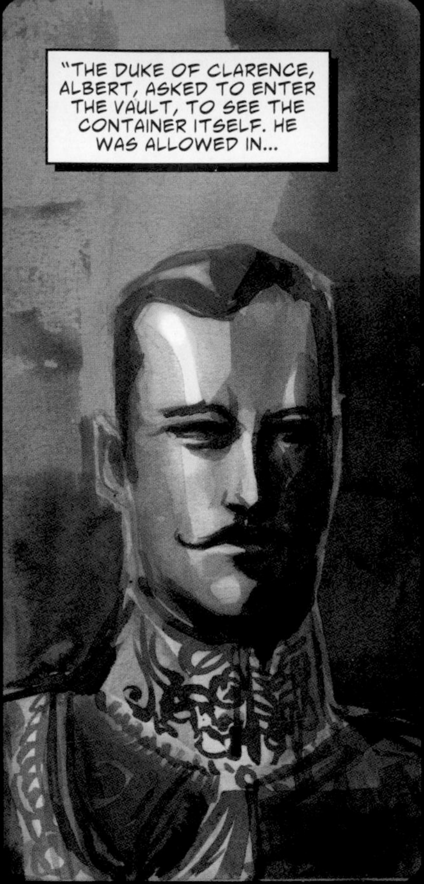
"THE DUKE OF CLARENCE, ALBERT, ASKED TO ENTER THE VAULT, TO SEE THE CONTAINER ITSELF. HE WAS ALLOWED IN...
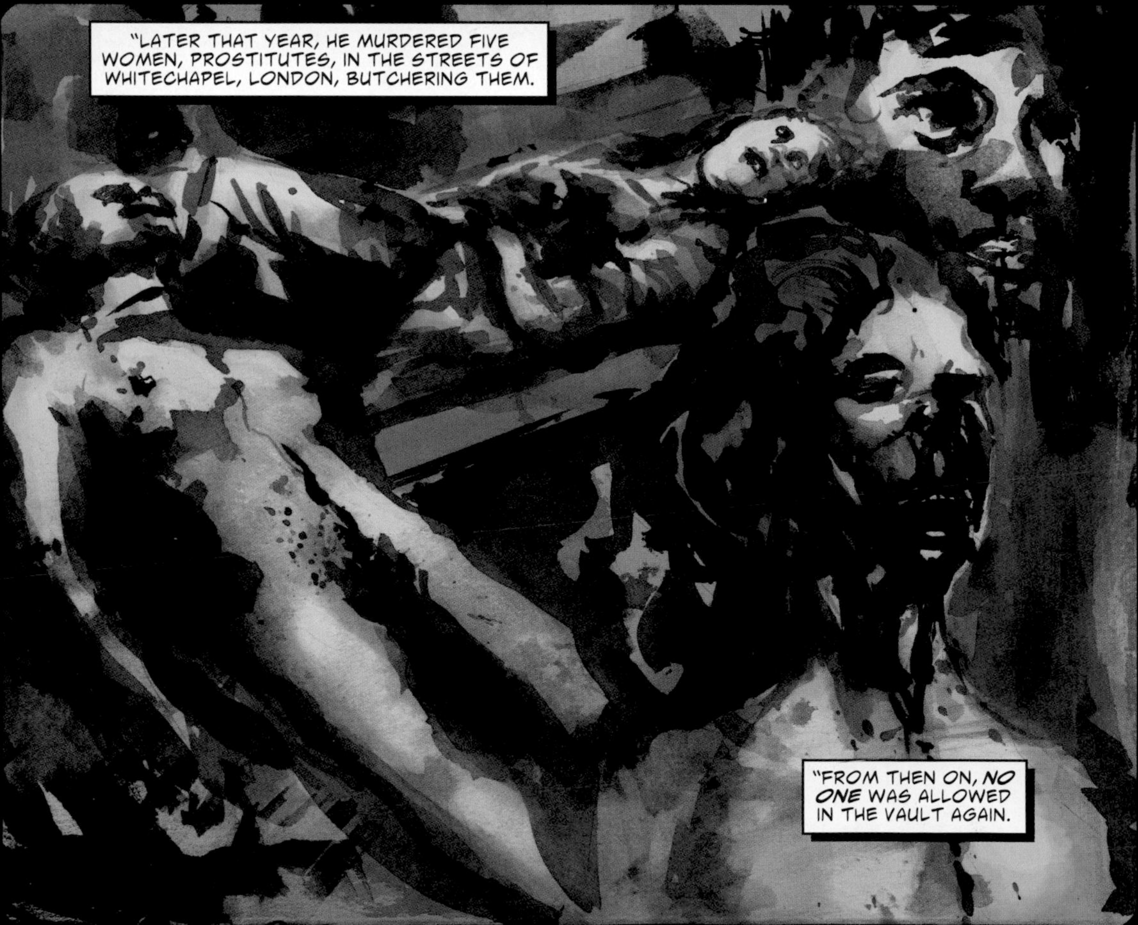
"LATER THAT YEAR, HE MURDERED FIVE WOMEN, PROSTITUTES, IN THE STREETS OF WHITECHAPEL, LONDON, BUTCHERING THEM.
"FROM THEN ON, *NO ONE* WAS ALLOWED IN THE VAULT AGAIN.

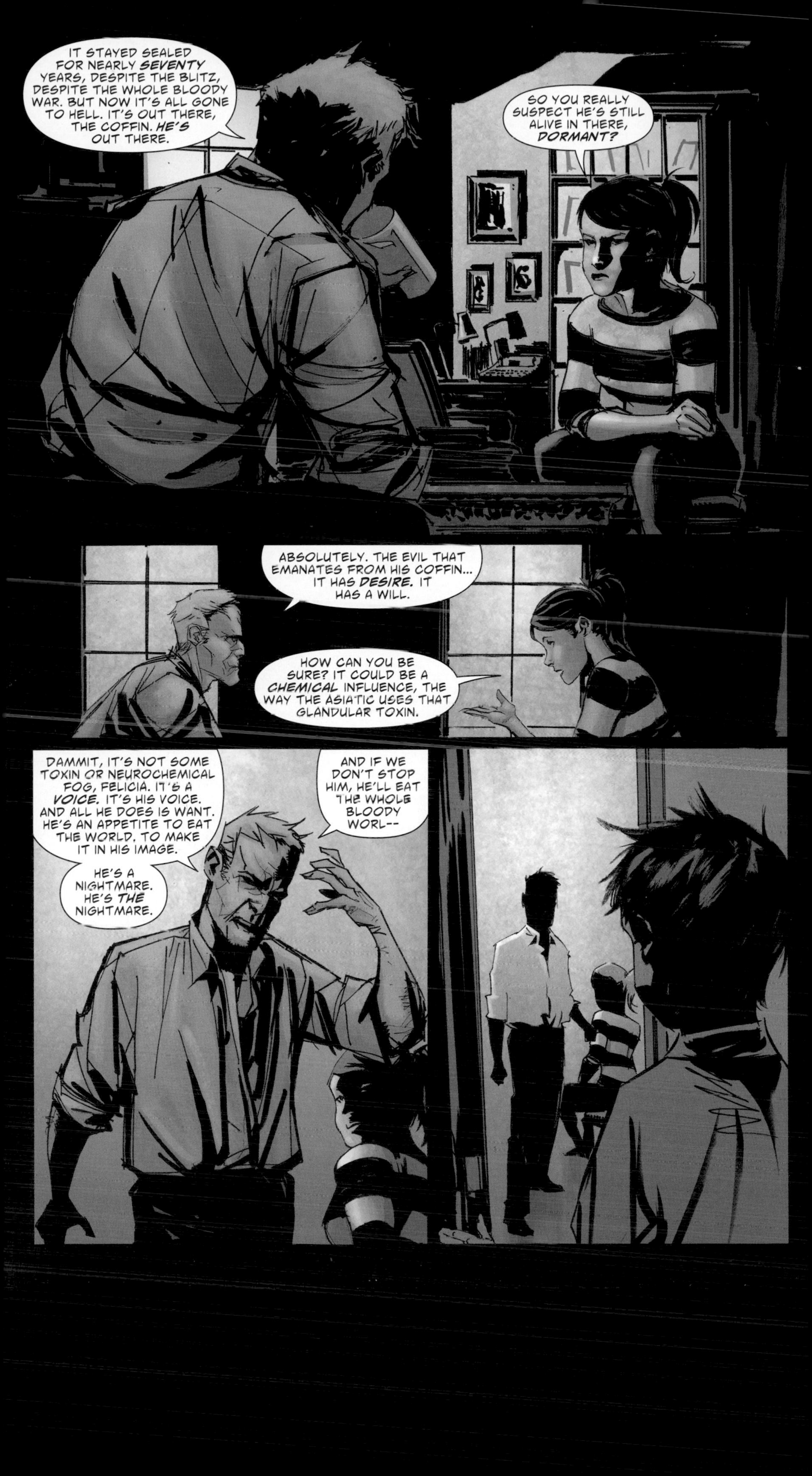
IT STAYED SEALED FOR NEARLY SEVENTY YEARS, DESPITE THE BLITZ, DESPITE THE WHOLE BLOODY WAR. BUT NOW IT'S ALL GONE TO HELL. IT'S OUT THERE, THE COFFIN. HE'S OUT THERE.
SO YOU REALLY SUSPECT HE'S STILL ALIVE IN THERE, DORMANT?
ABSOLUTELY. THE EVIL THAT EMANATES FROM HIS COFFIN... IT HAS DESIRE. IT HAS A WILL.
HOW CAN YOU BE SURE? IT COULD BE A CHEMICAL INFLUENCE, THE WAY THE ASIATIC USES THAT GLANDULAR TOXIN.
DAMMIT, IT'S NOT SOME TOXIN OR NEUROCHEMICAL FOG, FELICIA. IT'S A VOICE. IT'S HIS VOICE. AND ALL HE DOES IS WANT. HE'S AN APPETITE TO EAT THE WORLD. TO MAKE IT IN HIS IMAGE.
HE'S A NIGHTMARE. HE'S THE NIGHTMARE.
AND IF WE DON'T STOP HIM, HE'LL EAT THE WHOLE BLOODY WORL--

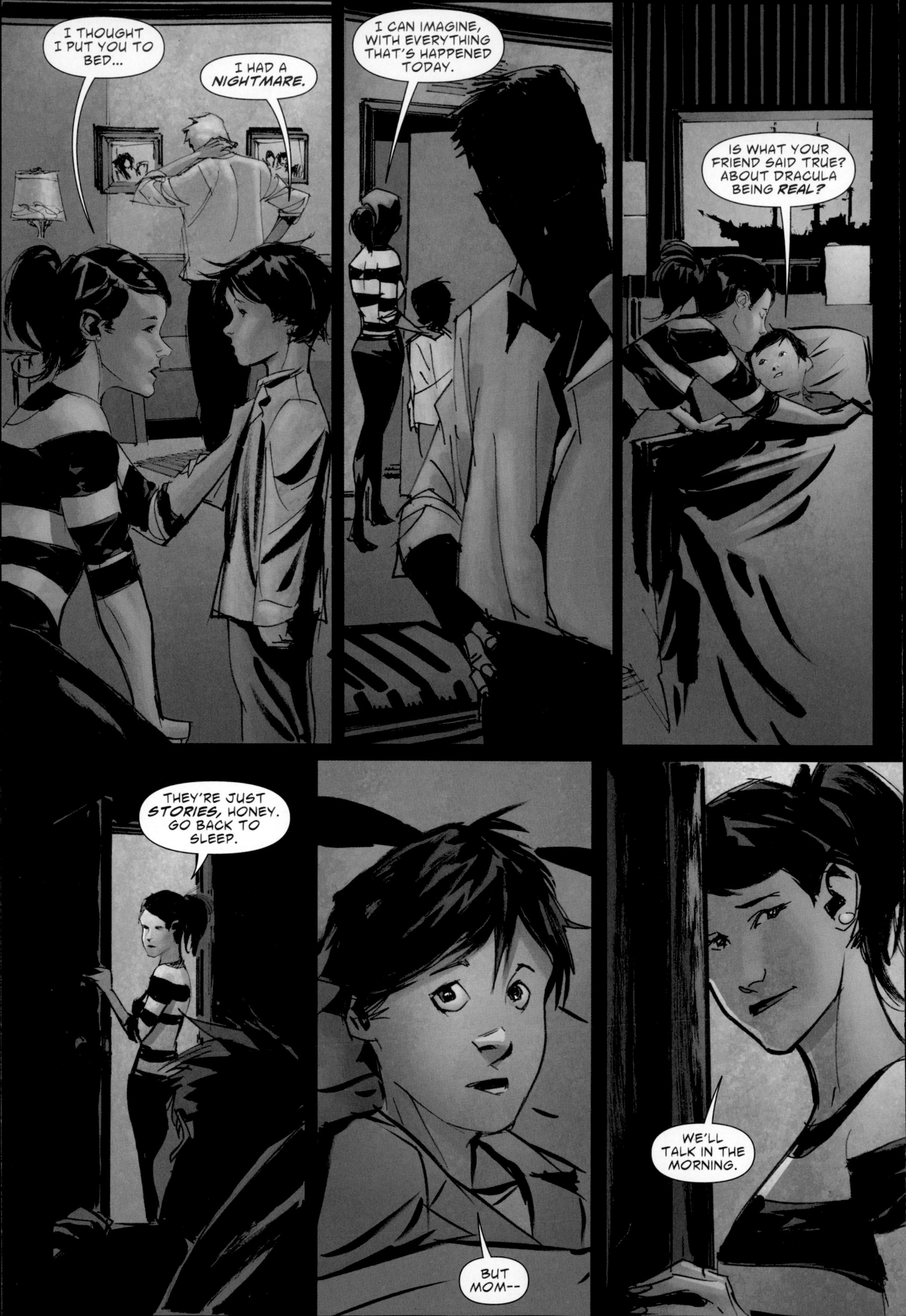

I THOUGHT I PUT YOU TO BED...
I HAD A *NIGHTMARE.*
I CAN IMAGINE, WITH EVERYTHING THAT'S HAPPENED TODAY.
IS WHAT YOUR FRIEND SAID TRUE? ABOUT DRACULA BEING *REAL?*
THEY'RE JUST *STORIES,* HONEY. GO BACK TO SLEEP.
BUT MOM--
WE'LL TALK IN THE MORNING.

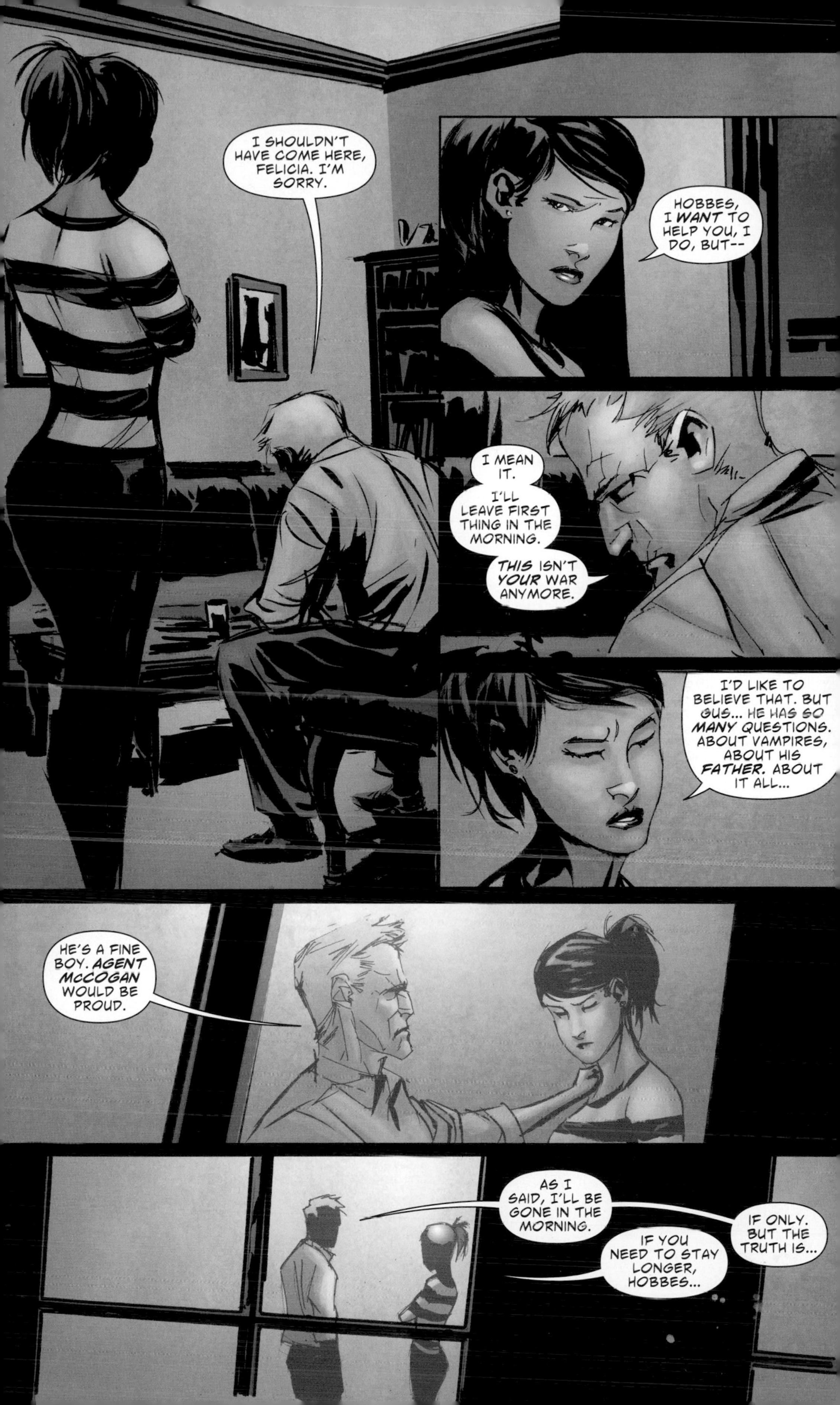
I SHOULDN'T HAVE COME HERE, FELICIA. I'M SORRY.
HOBBES, I *WANT* TO HELP YOU, I DO, BUT--
I MEAN IT.
I'LL LEAVE FIRST THING IN THE MORNING.
THIS ISN'T *YOUR* WAR ANYMORE.
I'D LIKE TO BELIEVE THAT. BUT GUS... HE HAS SO *MANY* QUESTIONS. ABOUT VAMPIRES, ABOUT HIS *FATHER.* ABOUT IT ALL...
HE'S A FINE BOY. *AGENT McCOGAN* WOULD BE PROUD.
AS I SAID, I'LL BE GONE IN THE MORNING.
IF YOU NEED TO STAY LONGER, HOBBES...
IF ONLY. BUT THE TRUTH IS...

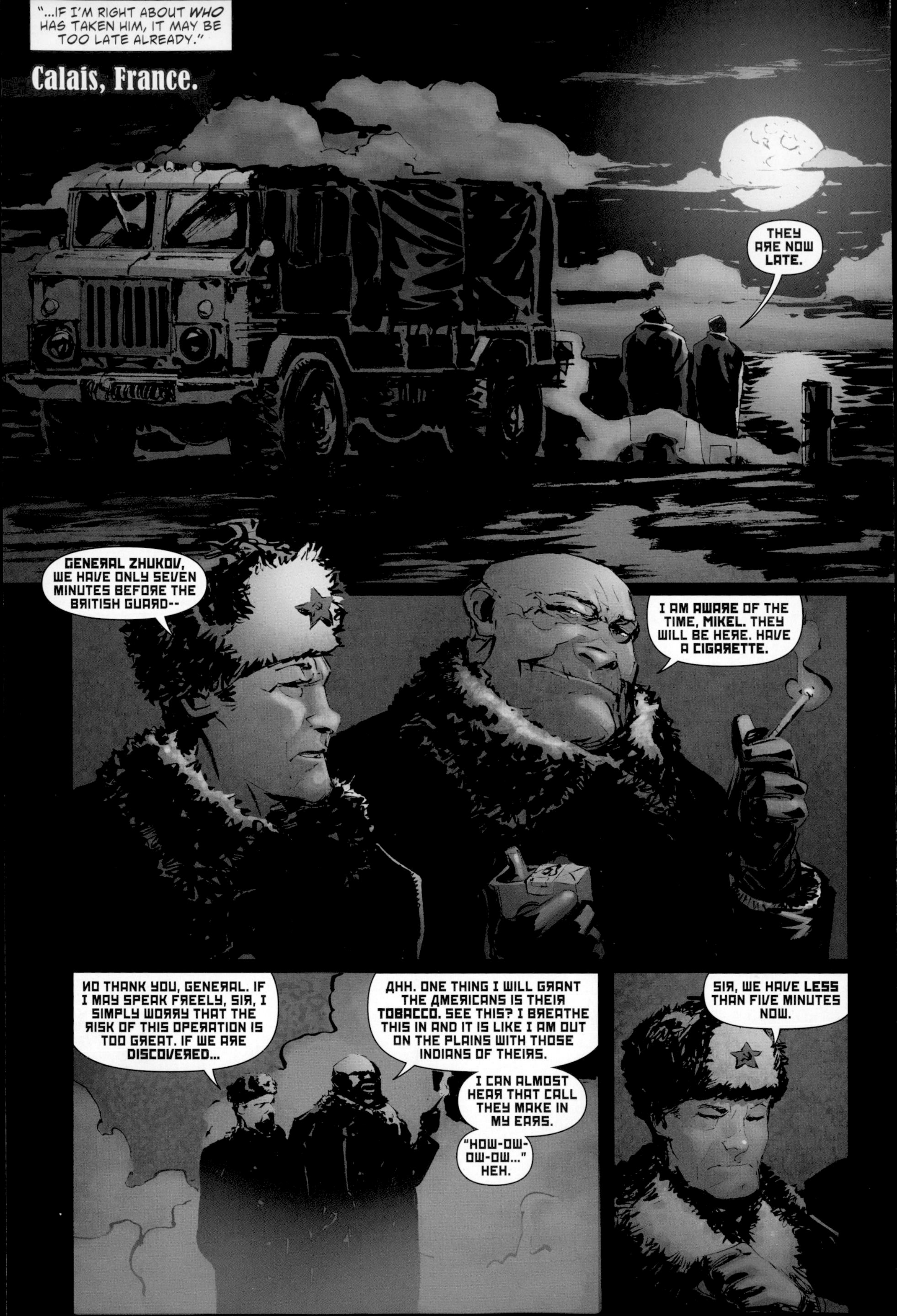
"...IF I'M RIGHT ABOUT WHO HAS TAKEN HIM, IT MAY BE TOO LATE ALREADY."
Calais, France.
THEY ARE NOW LATE.
GENERAL ZHUKOV, WE HAVE ONLY SEVEN MINUTES BEFORE THE BRITISH GUARD--
I AM AWARE OF THE TIME, MIKEL. THEY WILL BE HERE. HAVE A CIGARETTE.
NO THANK YOU, GENERAL. IF I MAY SPEAK FREELY, SIR, I SIMPLY WORRY THAT THE RISK OF THIS OPERATION IS TOO GREAT. IF WE ARE DISCOVERED...
AHH. ONE THING I WILL GRANT THE AMERICANS IS THEIR TOBACCO. SEE THIS? I BREATHE THIS IN AND IT IS LIKE I AM OUT ON THE PLAINS WITH THOSE INDIANS OF THEIRS.
I CAN ALMOST HEAR THAT CALL THEY MAKE IN MY EARS.
"HOW-OW-OW-OW..." HEH.
SIR, WE HAVE LESS THAN FIVE MINUTES NOW.

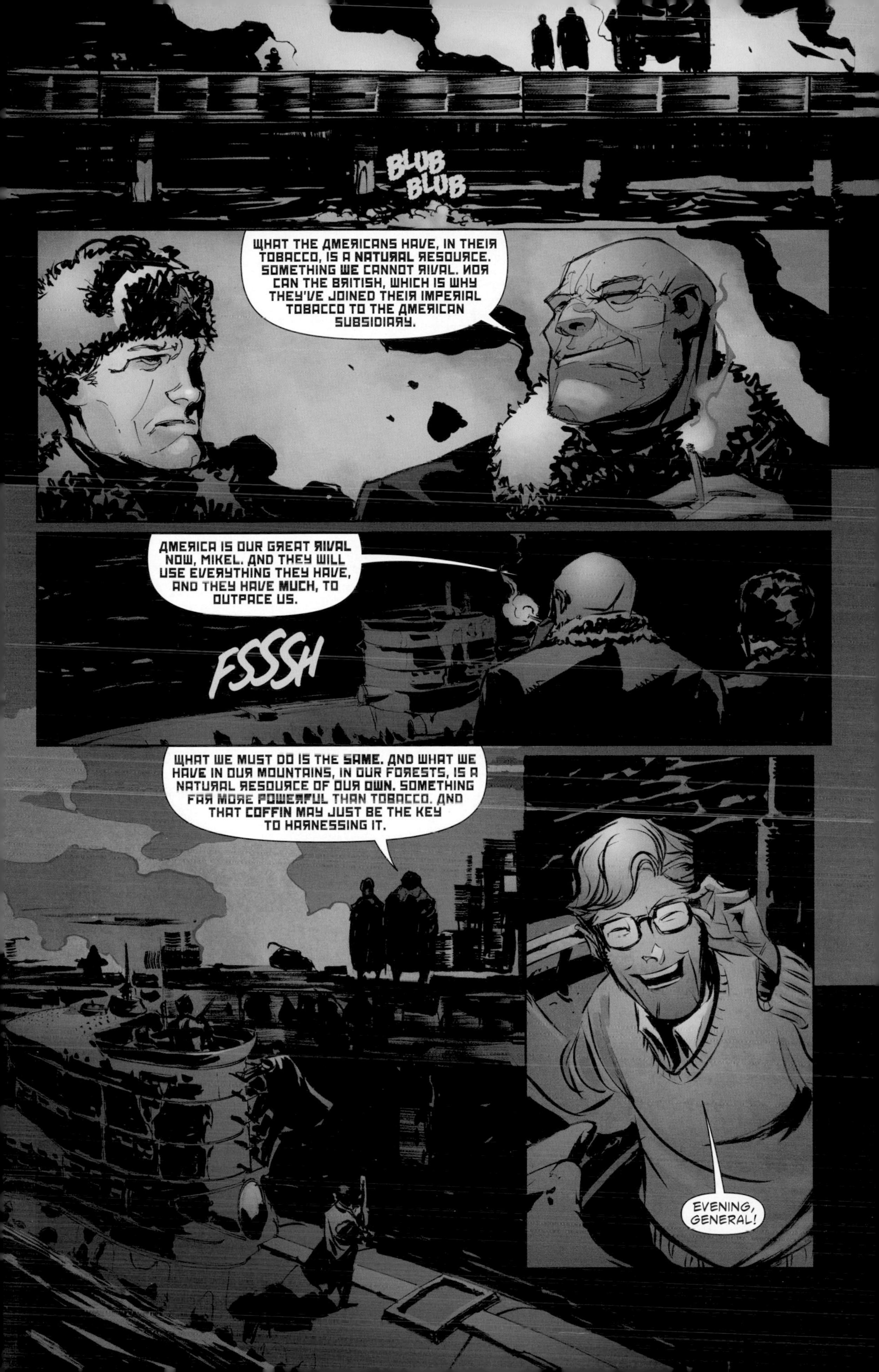

BLUB BLUB
WHAT THE AMERICANS HAVE, IN THEIR TOBACCO, IS A NATURAL RESOURCE. SOMETHING WE CANNOT RIVAL. NOR CAN THE BRITISH, WHICH IS WHY THEY'VE JOINED THEIR IMPERIAL TOBACCO TO THE AMERICAN SUBSIDIARY.
AMERICA IS OUR GREAT RIVAL NOW, MIKEL. AND THEY WILL USE EVERYTHING THEY HAVE, AND THEY HAVE MUCH, TO OUTPACE US.
FSSSH
WHAT WE MUST DO IS THE SAME. AND WHAT WE HAVE IN OUR MOUNTAINS, IN OUR FORESTS, IS A NATURAL RESOURCE OF OUR OWN. SOMETHING FAR MORE POWERFUL THAN TOBACCO. AND THAT COFFIN MAY JUST BE THE KEY TO HARNESSING IT.
EVENING, GENERAL!

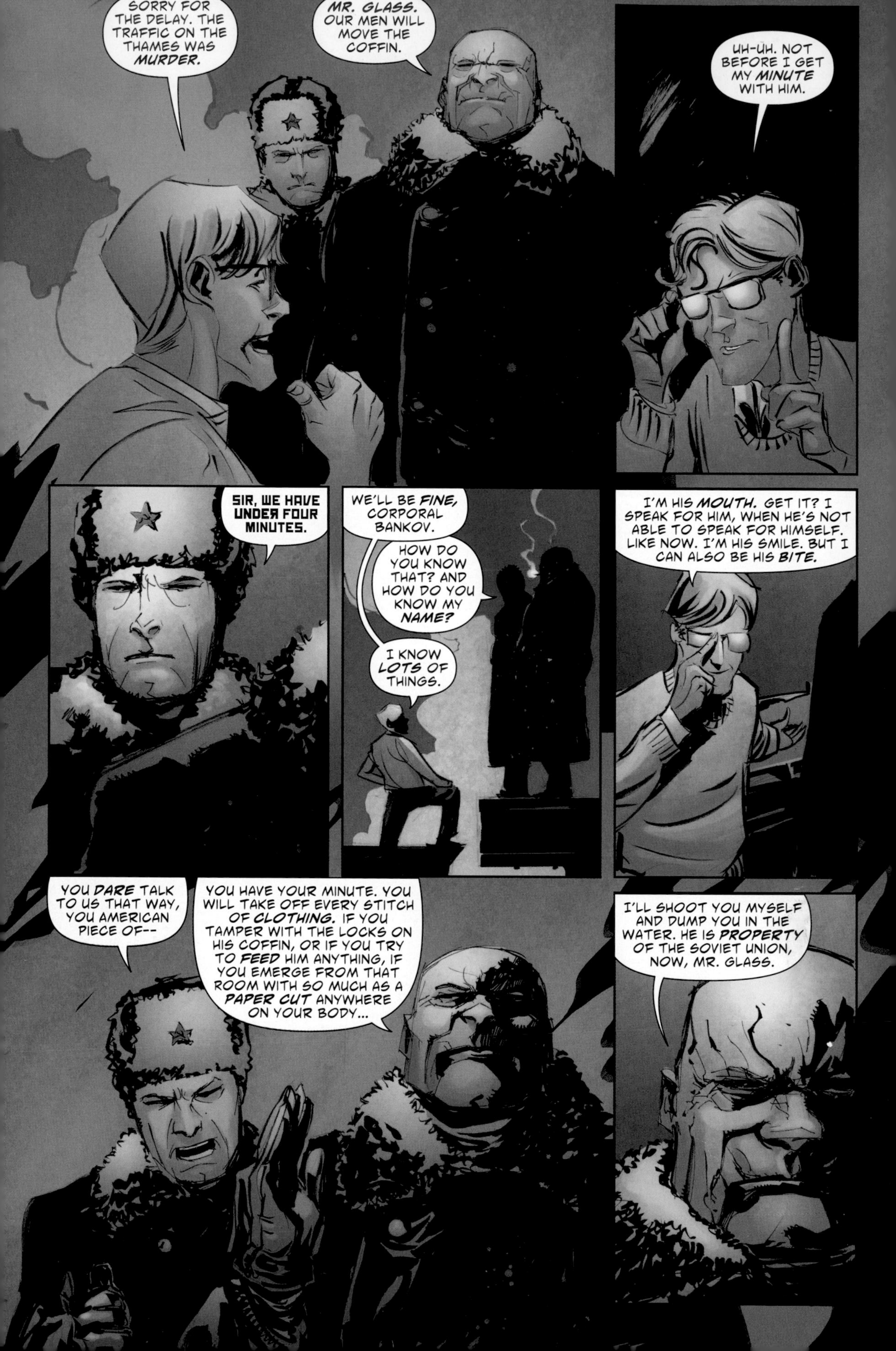
SORRY FOR THE DELAY. THE TRAFFIC ON THE THAMES WAS MURDER.
MR. GLASS. OUR MEN WILL MOVE THE COFFIN.
UH-UH. NOT BEFORE I GET MY MINUTE WITH HIM.
SIR, WE HAVE UNDER FOUR MINUTES.
WE'LL BE FINE, CORPORAL BANKOV.
HOW DO YOU KNOW THAT? AND HOW DO YOU KNOW MY NAME?
I KNOW LOTS OF THINGS.
I'M HIS MOUTH. GET IT? I SPEAK FOR HIM, WHEN HE'S NOT ABLE TO SPEAK FOR HIMSELF. LIKE NOW. I'M HIS SMILE. BUT I CAN ALSO BE HIS BITE.
YOU DARE TALK TO US THAT WAY, YOU AMERICAN PIECE OF--
YOU HAVE YOUR MINUTE. YOU WILL TAKE OFF EVERY STITCH OF CLOTHING. IF YOU TAMPER WITH THE LOCKS ON HIS COFFIN, OR IF YOU TRY TO FEED HIM ANYTHING, IF YOU EMERGE FROM THAT ROOM WITH SO MUCH AS A PAPER CUT ANYWHERE ON YOUR BODY...
I'LL SHOOT YOU MYSELF AND DUMP YOU IN THE WATER. HE IS PROPERTY OF THE SOVIET UNION, NOW, MR. GLASS.

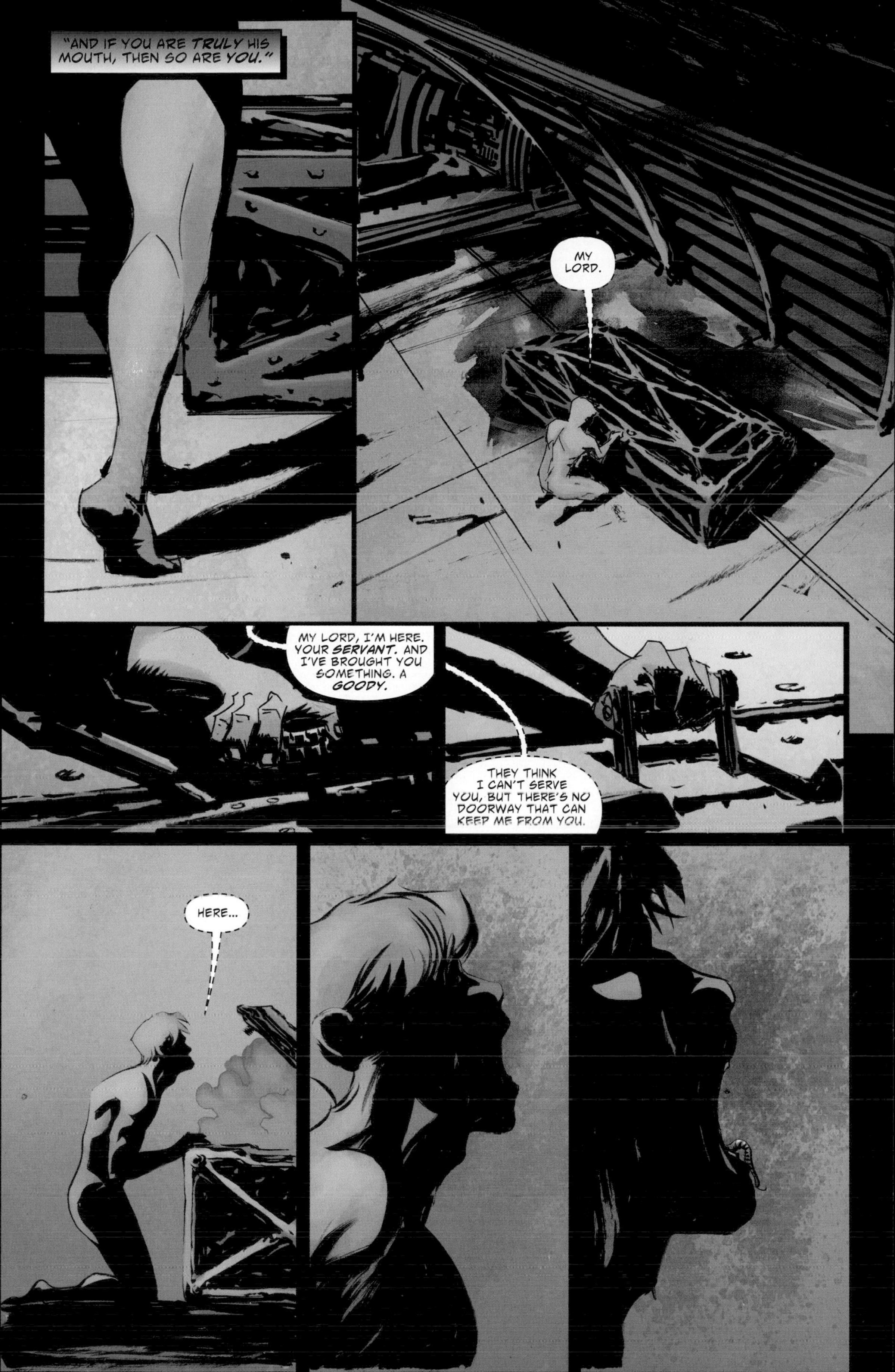
"AND IF YOU ARE TRULY HIS MOUTH, THEN SO ARE YOU."
MY LORD.
MY LORD, I'M HERE. YOUR SERVANT. AND I'VE BROUGHT YOU SOMETHING. A GOODY.
THEY THINK I CAN'T SERVE YOU, BUT THERE'S NO DOORWAY THAT CAN KEEP ME FROM YOU.
HERE...

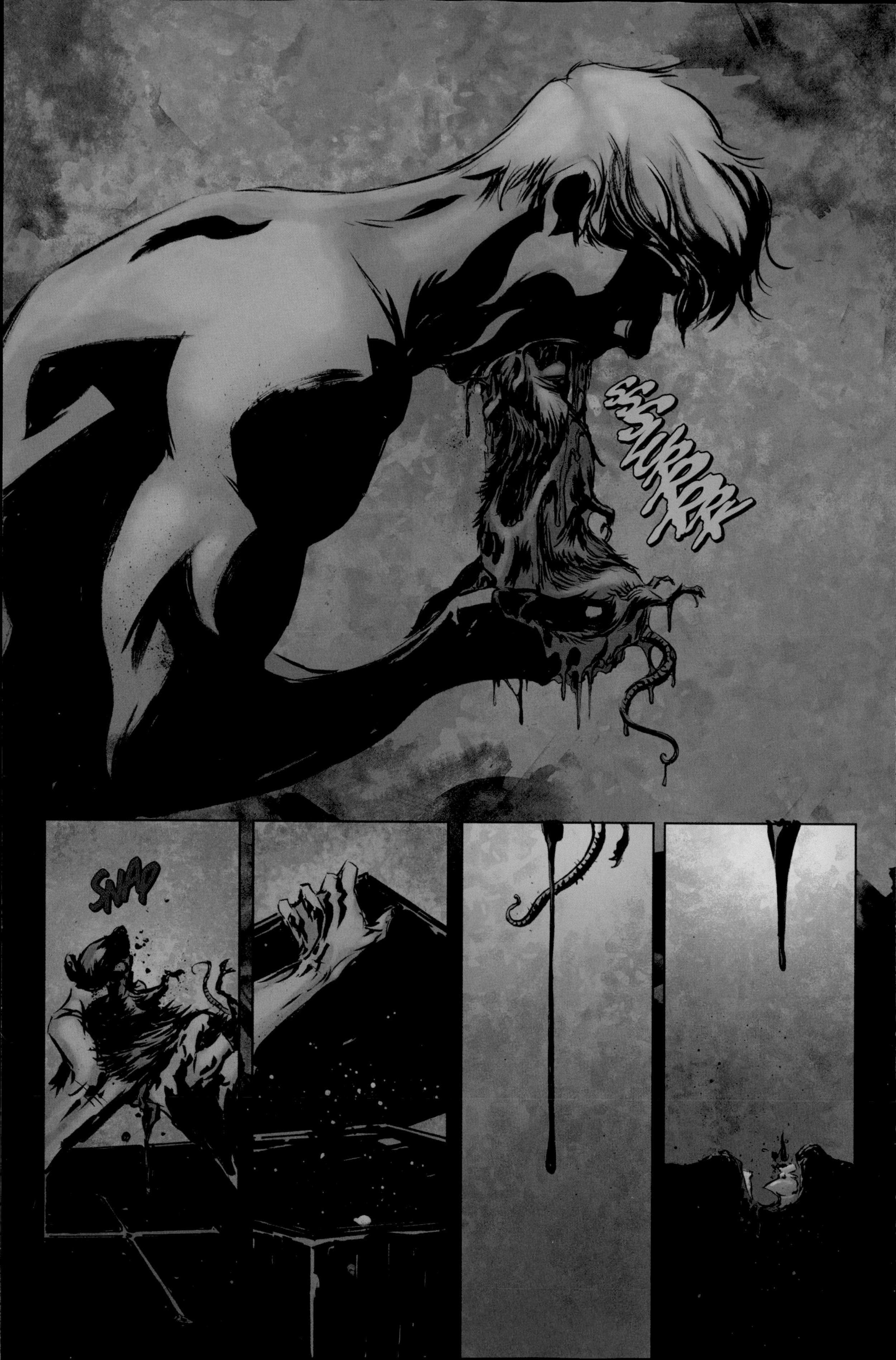
SSSLURRRRK
SNAP

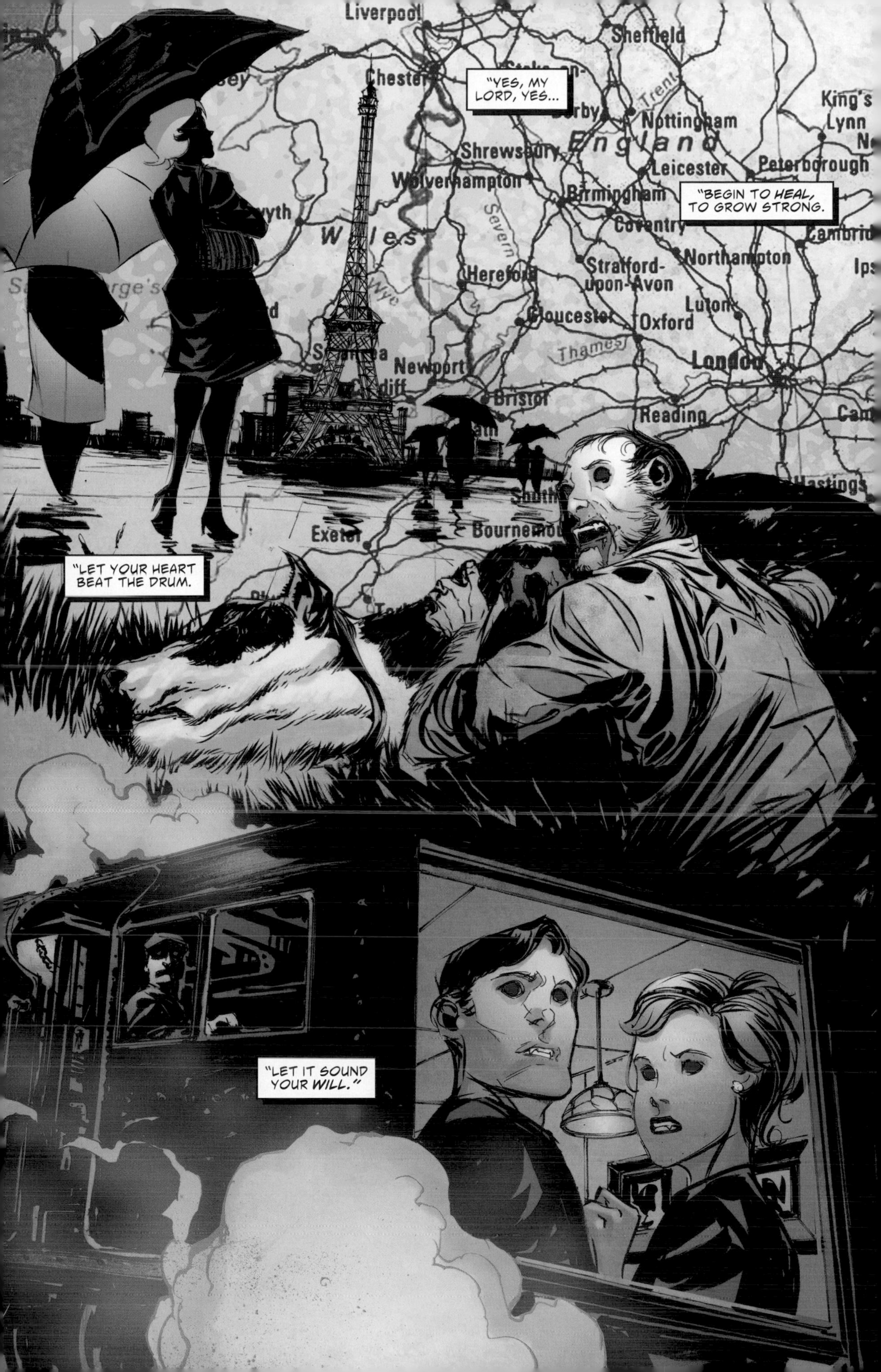

"YES, MY LORD, YES...
"BEGIN TO HEAL, TO GROW STRONG.
"LET YOUR HEART BEAT THE DRUM.
"LET IT SOUND YOUR WILL."
Liverpool
Sheffield
Chester
Nottingham
England
Shrewsbury
Leicester
Peterborough
Wolverhampton
Birmingham
Wales
Coventry
Northampton
Hereford
Stratford-upon-Avon
Gloucester
Oxford
Thames
London
Newport
Bristol
Reading
Exeter
Hastings

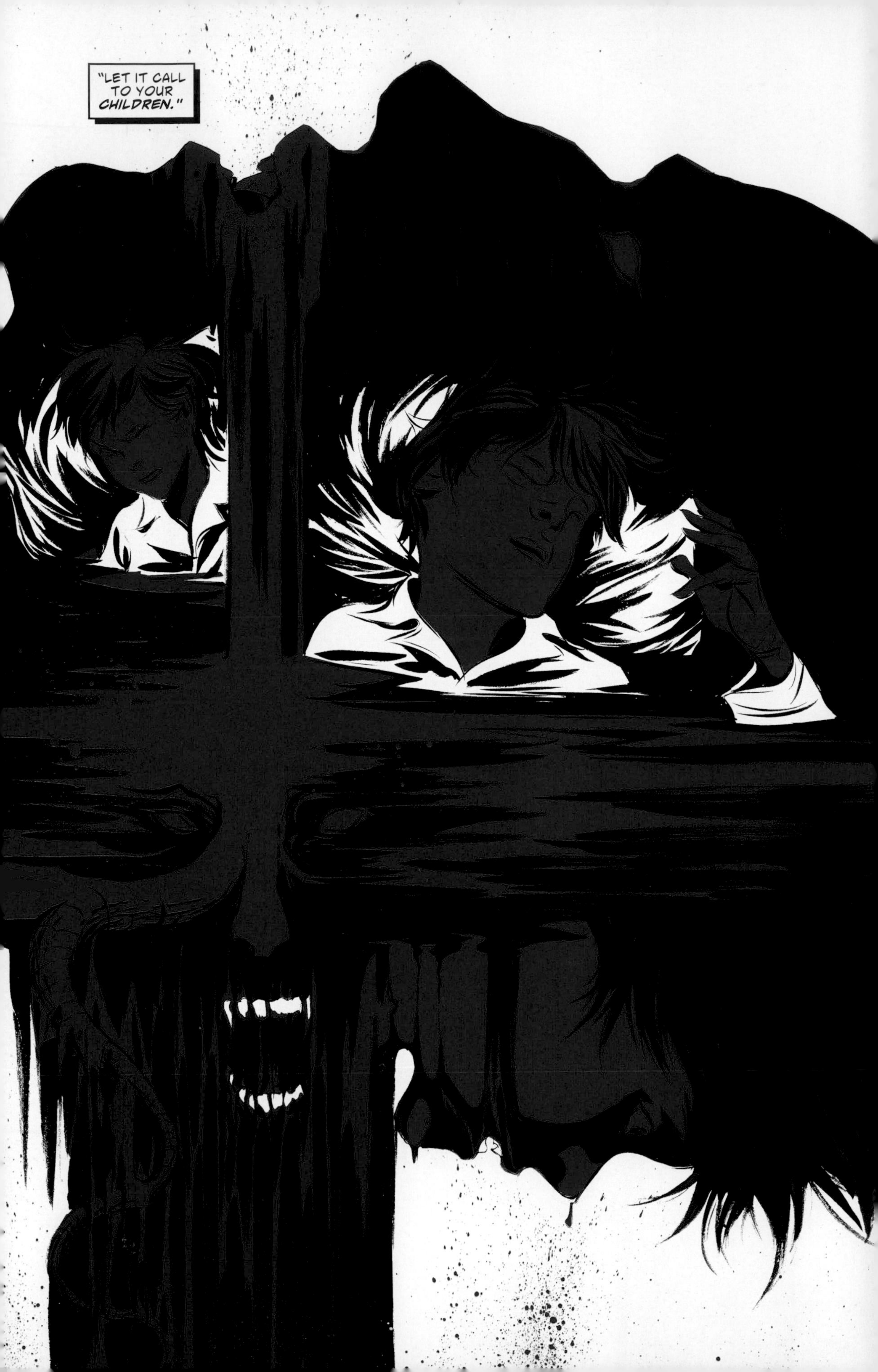
"LET IT CALL TO YOUR CHILDREN."

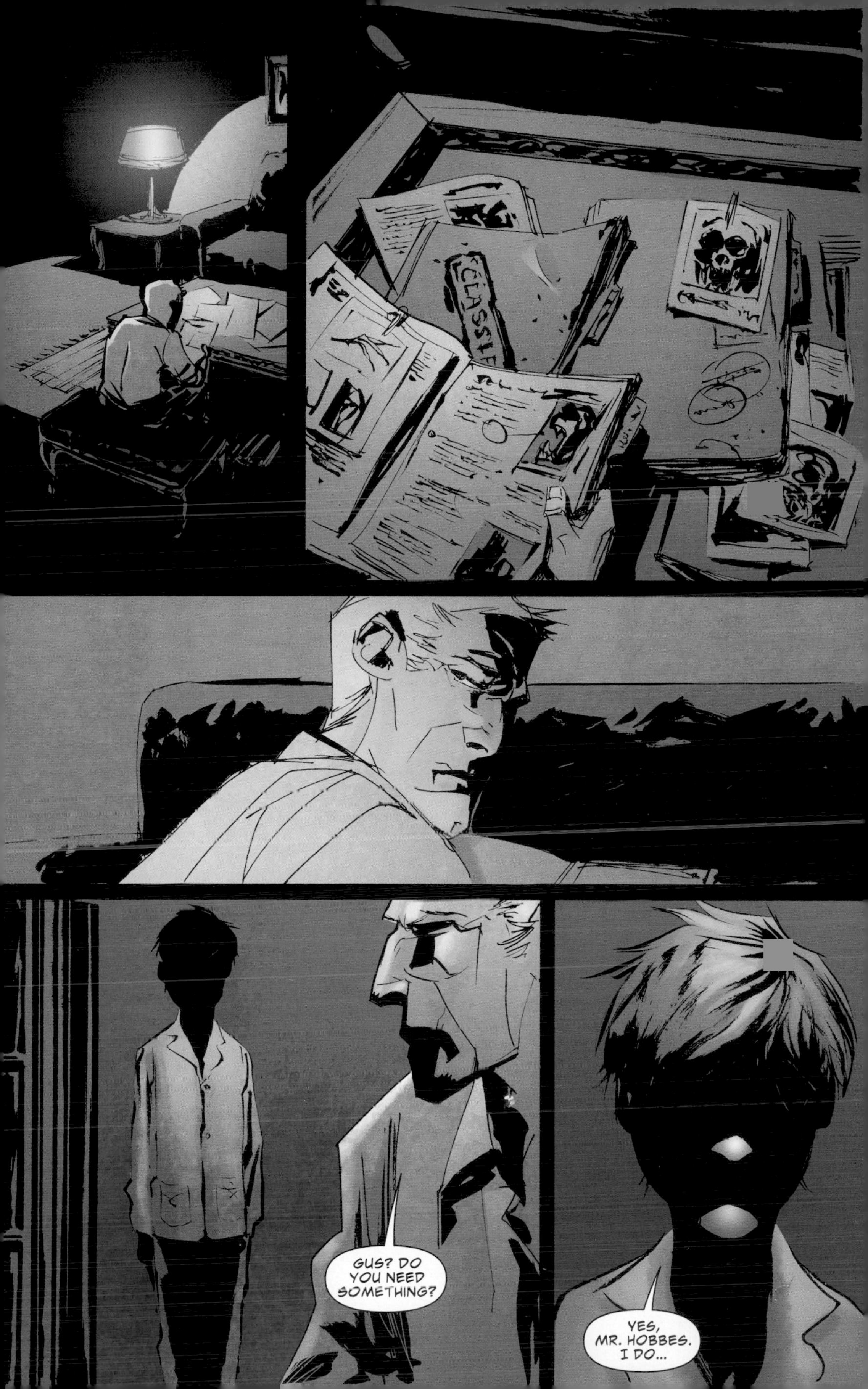
GUS? DO YOU NEED SOMETHING?
YES, MR. HOBBES. I DO...

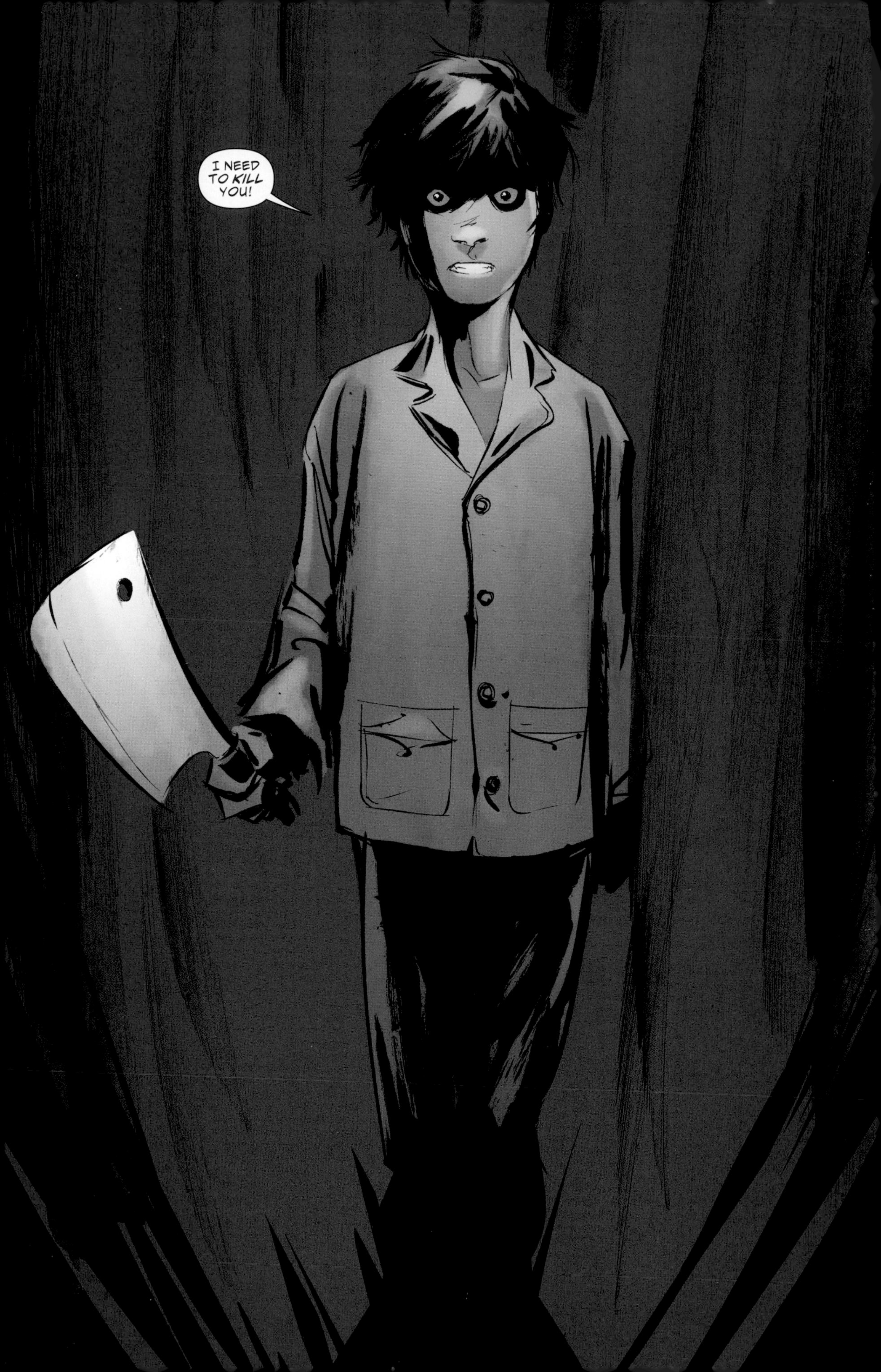
I NEED TO KILL YOU!

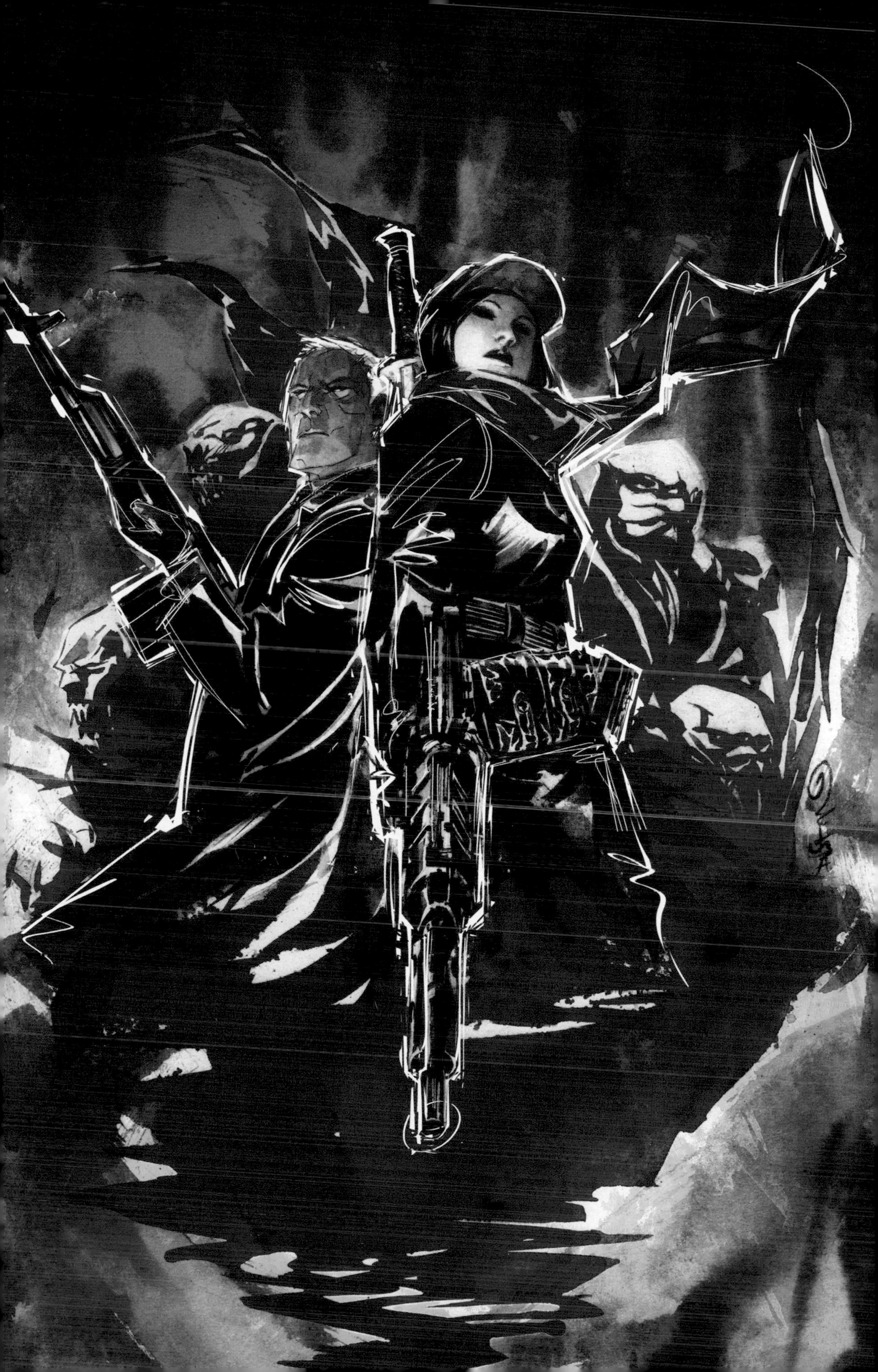

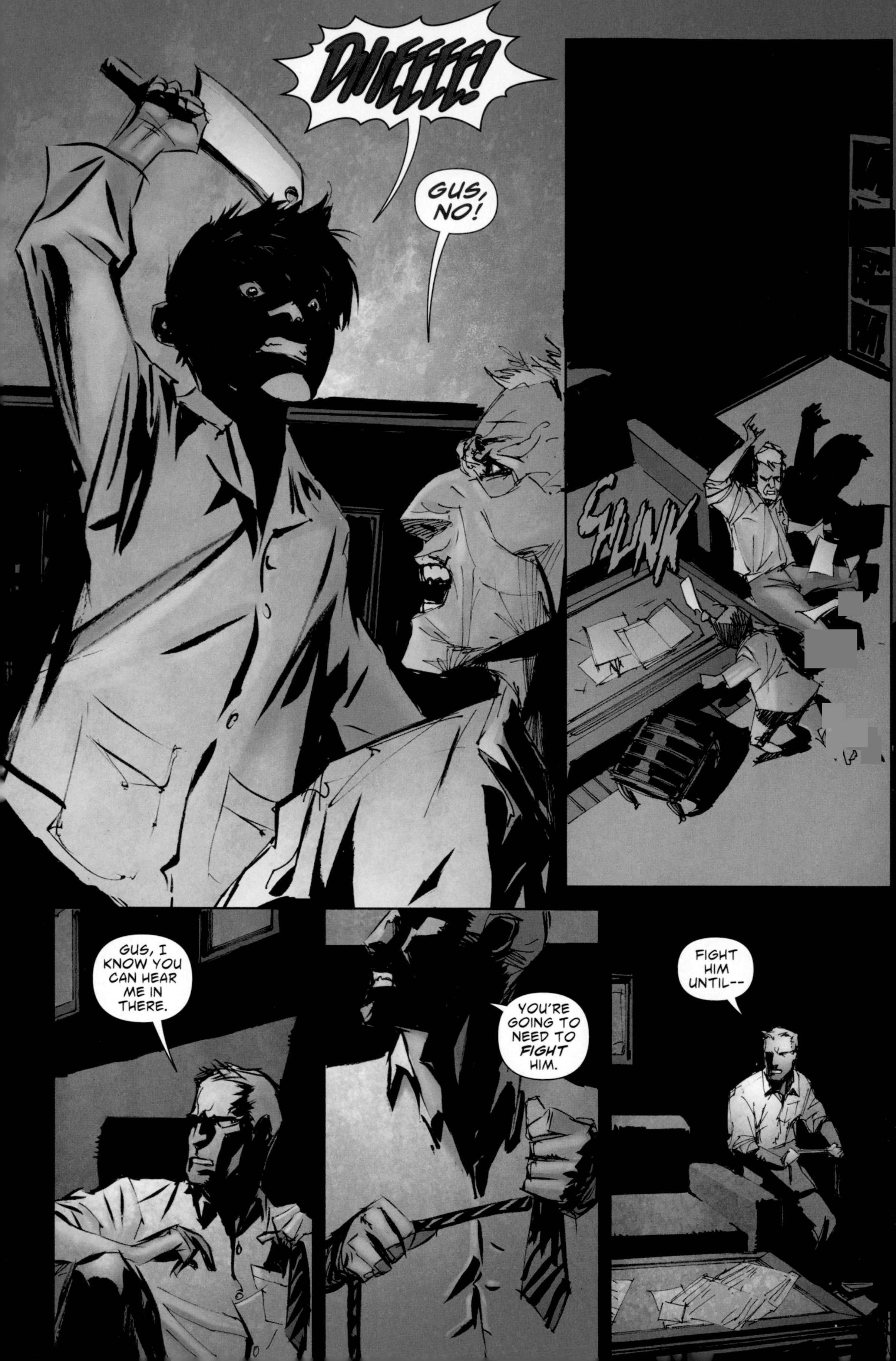

DIEEEE!
GUS, NO!
CHUNK
GUS, I KNOW YOU CAN HEAR ME IN THERE.
YOU'RE GOING TO NEED TO *FIGHT* HIM.
FIGHT HIM UNTIL--

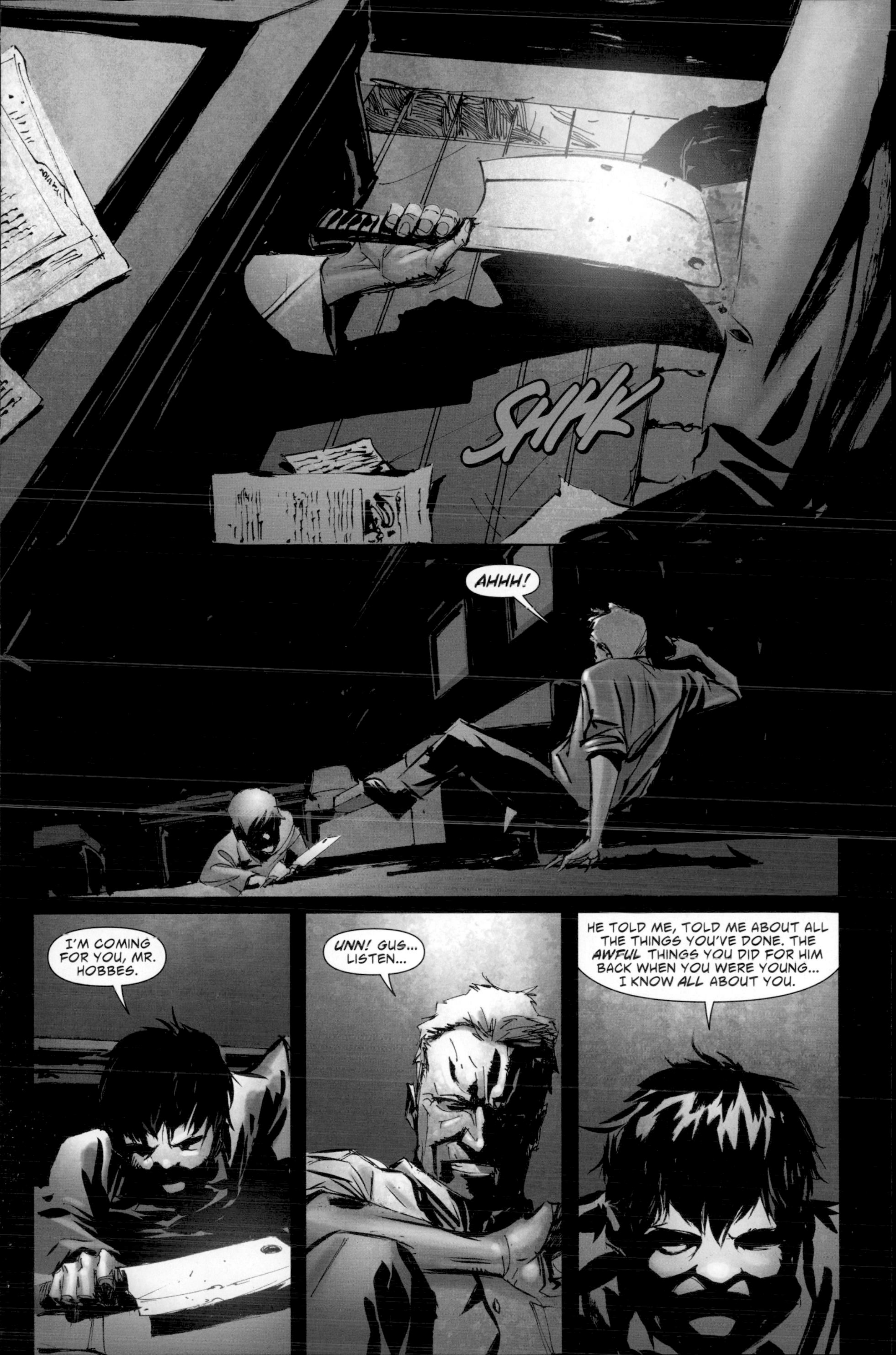
SHNK
AHHH!
I'M COMING FOR YOU, MR. HOBBES.
UNN! GUS... LISTEN...
HE TOLD ME, TOLD ME ABOUT ALL THE THINGS YOU'VE DONE. THE AWFUL THINGS YOU DID FOR HIM BACK WHEN YOU WERE YOUNG... I KNOW ALL ABOUT YOU.

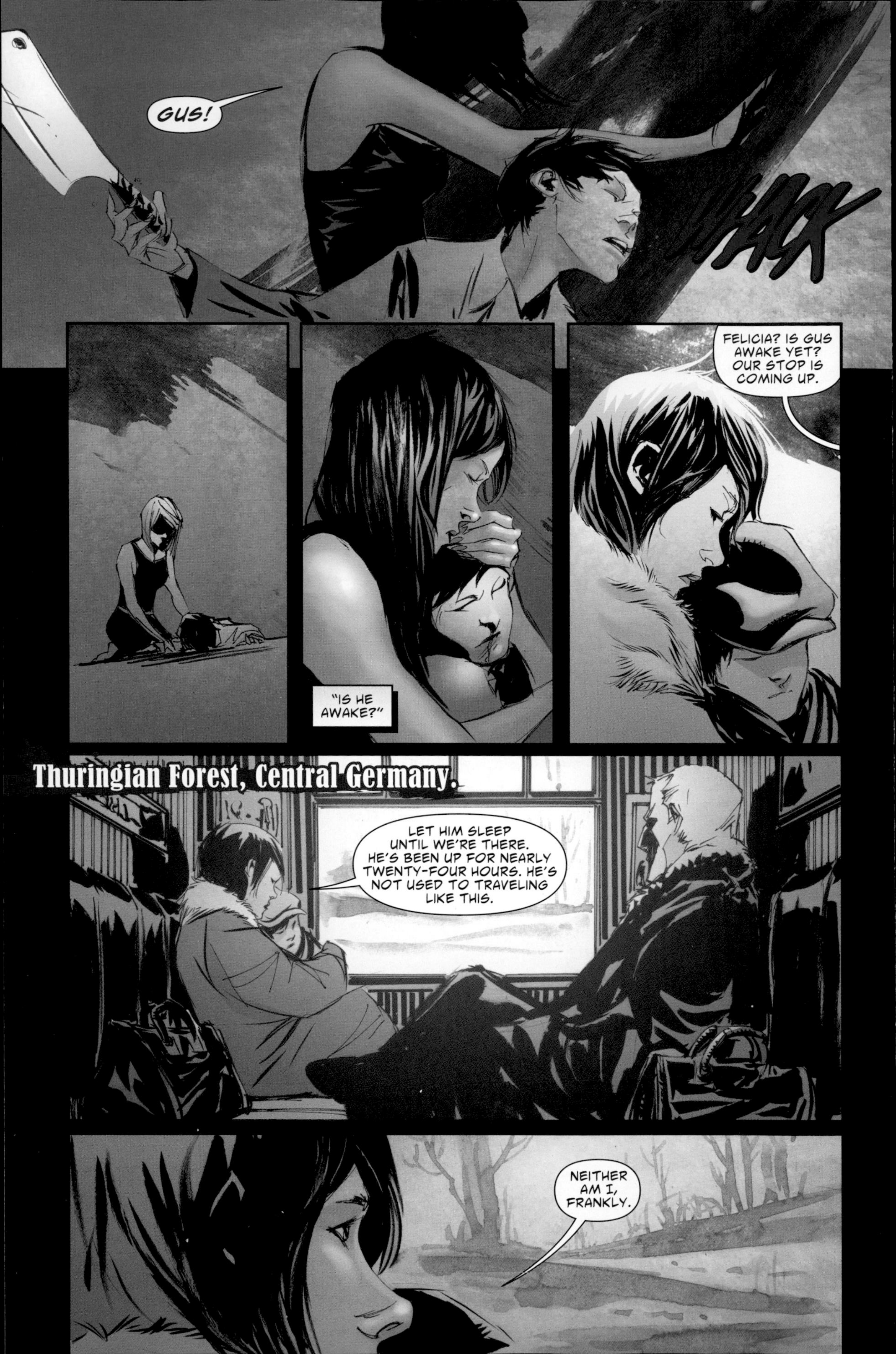
GUS!
WHACK
FELICIA? IS GUS AWAKE YET? OUR STOP IS COMING UP.
"IS HE AWAKE?"
Thuringian Forest, Central Germany.
LET HIM SLEEP UNTIL WE'RE THERE. HE'S BEEN UP FOR NEARLY TWENTY-FOUR HOURS. HE'S NOT USED TO TRAVELING LIKE THIS.
NEITHER AM I, FRANKLY.

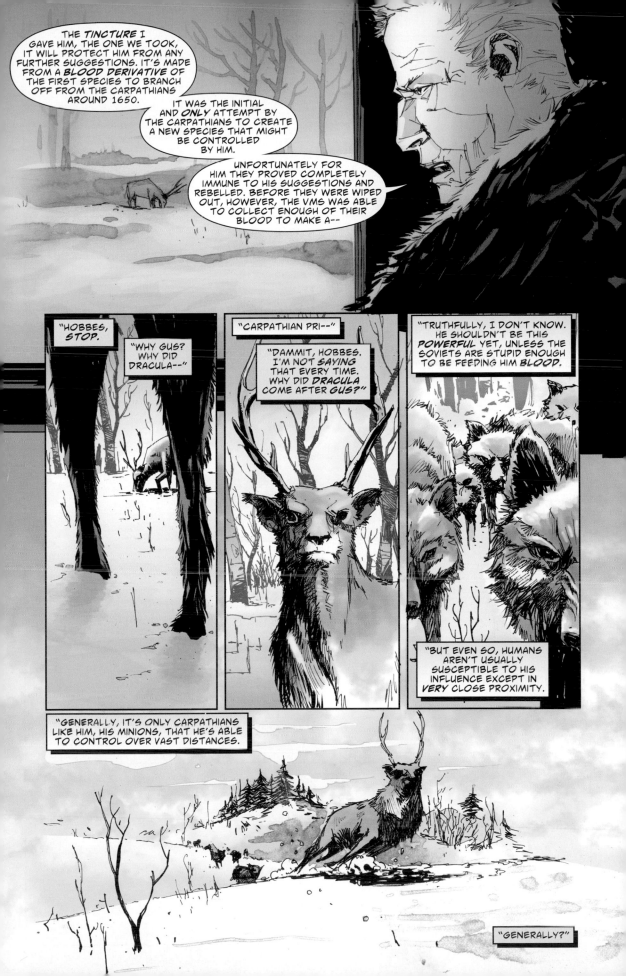

THE *TINCTURE* I GAVE HIM, THE ONE WE TOOK, IT WILL PROTECT HIM FROM ANY FURTHER SUGGESTIONS. IT'S MADE FROM A *BLOOD DERIVATIVE* OF THE FIRST SPECIES TO BRANCH OFF FROM THE CARPATHIANS AROUND 1650.

IT WAS THE INITIAL AND *ONLY* ATTEMPT BY THE CARPATHIANS TO CREATE A NEW SPECIES THAT MIGHT BE CONTROLLED BY HIM.

UNFORTUNATELY FOR HIM THEY PROVED COMPLETELY IMMUNE TO HIS SUGGESTIONS AND REBELLED. BEFORE THEY WERE WIPED OUT, HOWEVER, THE VMS WAS ABLE TO COLLECT ENOUGH OF THEIR BLOOD TO MAKE A--

"HOBBES, *STOP.*

"WHY GUS? WHY DID DRACULA--"

"CARPATHIAN PRI--"

"DAMMIT, HOBBES. I'M NOT *SAYING* THAT EVERY TIME. WHY DID *DRACULA* COME AFTER *GUS?*"

"TRUTHFULLY, I DON'T KNOW. HE SHOULDN'T BE THIS *POWERFUL* YET, UNLESS THE SOVIETS ARE STUPID ENOUGH TO BE FEEDING HIM *BLOOD.*

"BUT EVEN SO, HUMANS AREN'T USUALLY SUSCEPTIBLE TO HIS INFLUENCE EXCEPT IN *VERY* CLOSE PROXIMITY.

"GENERALLY, IT'S ONLY CARPATHIANS LIKE HIM, HIS MINIONS, THAT HE'S ABLE TO CONTROL OVER VAST DISTANCES.

"GENERALLY?"

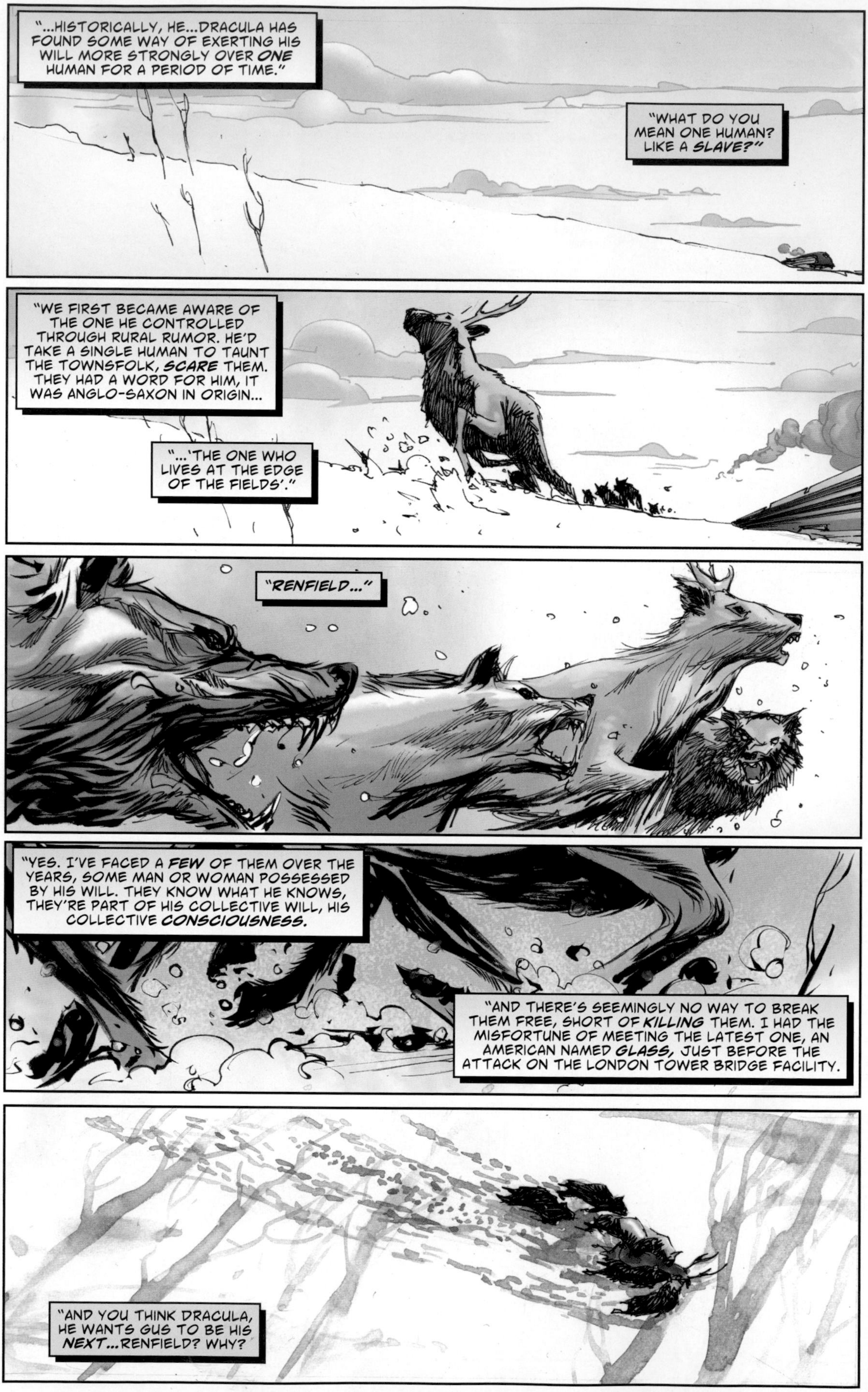
"...HISTORICALLY, HE...DRACULA HAS FOUND SOME WAY OF EXERTING HIS WILL MORE STRONGLY OVER ONE HUMAN FOR A PERIOD OF TIME."
"WHAT DO YOU MEAN ONE HUMAN? LIKE A SLAVE?"
"WE FIRST BECAME AWARE OF THE ONE HE CONTROLLED THROUGH RURAL RUMOR. HE'D TAKE A SINGLE HUMAN TO TAUNT THE TOWNSFOLK, SCARE THEM. THEY HAD A WORD FOR HIM, IT WAS ANGLO-SAXON IN ORIGIN...
"...'THE ONE WHO LIVES AT THE EDGE OF THE FIELDS'."
"RENFIELD..."
"YES. I'VE FACED A FEW OF THEM OVER THE YEARS, SOME MAN OR WOMAN POSSESSED BY HIS WILL. THEY KNOW WHAT HE KNOWS, THEY'RE PART OF HIS COLLECTIVE WILL, HIS COLLECTIVE CONSCIOUSNESS.
"AND THERE'S SEEMINGLY NO WAY TO BREAK THEM FREE, SHORT OF KILLING THEM. I HAD THE MISFORTUNE OF MEETING THE LATEST ONE, AN AMERICAN NAMED GLASS, JUST BEFORE THE ATTACK ON THE LONDON TOWER BRIDGE FACILITY.
"AND YOU THINK DRACULA, HE WANTS GUS TO BE HIS NEXT...RENFIELD? WHY?"

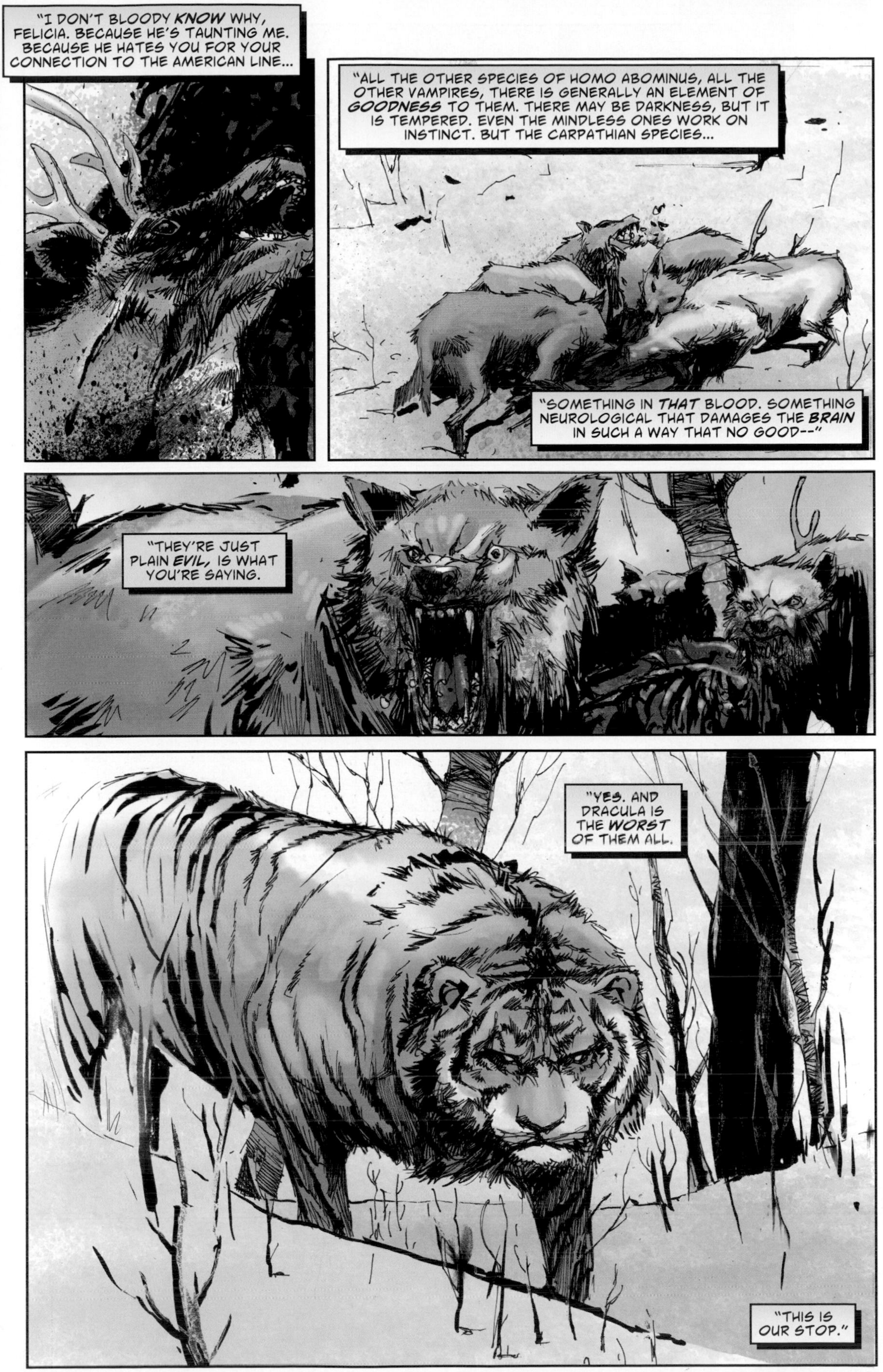
"I DON'T BLOODY KNOW WHY, FELICIA. BECAUSE HE'S TAUNTING ME. BECAUSE HE HATES YOU FOR YOUR CONNECTION TO THE AMERICAN LINE...
"ALL THE OTHER SPECIES OF HOMO ABOMINUS, ALL THE OTHER VAMPIRES, THERE IS GENERALLY AN ELEMENT OF GOODNESS TO THEM. THERE MAY BE DARKNESS, BUT IT IS TEMPERED. EVEN THE MINDLESS ONES WORK ON INSTINCT. BUT THE CARPATHIAN SPECIES...
"SOMETHING IN THAT BLOOD. SOMETHING NEUROLOGICAL THAT DAMAGES THE BRAIN IN SUCH A WAY THAT NO GOOD--"
"THEY'RE JUST PLAIN EVIL, IS WHAT YOU'RE SAYING.
"YES. AND DRACULA IS THE WORST OF THEM ALL.
"THIS IS OUR STOP."

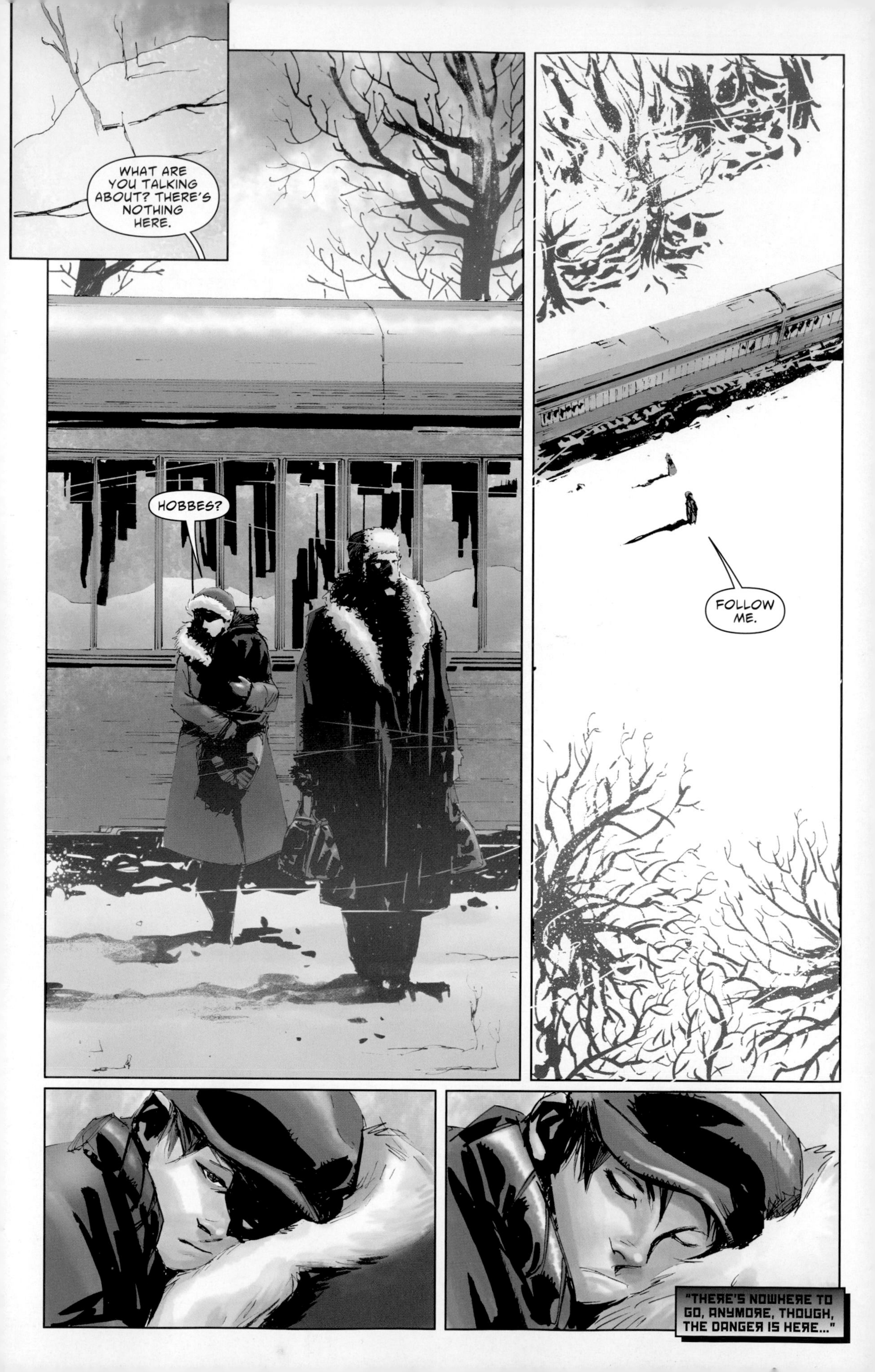
WHAT ARE YOU TALKING ABOUT? THERE'S NOTHING HERE.
HOBBES?
FOLLOW ME.
"THERE'S NOWHERE TO GO, ANYMORE, THOUGH, THE DANGER IS HERE..."

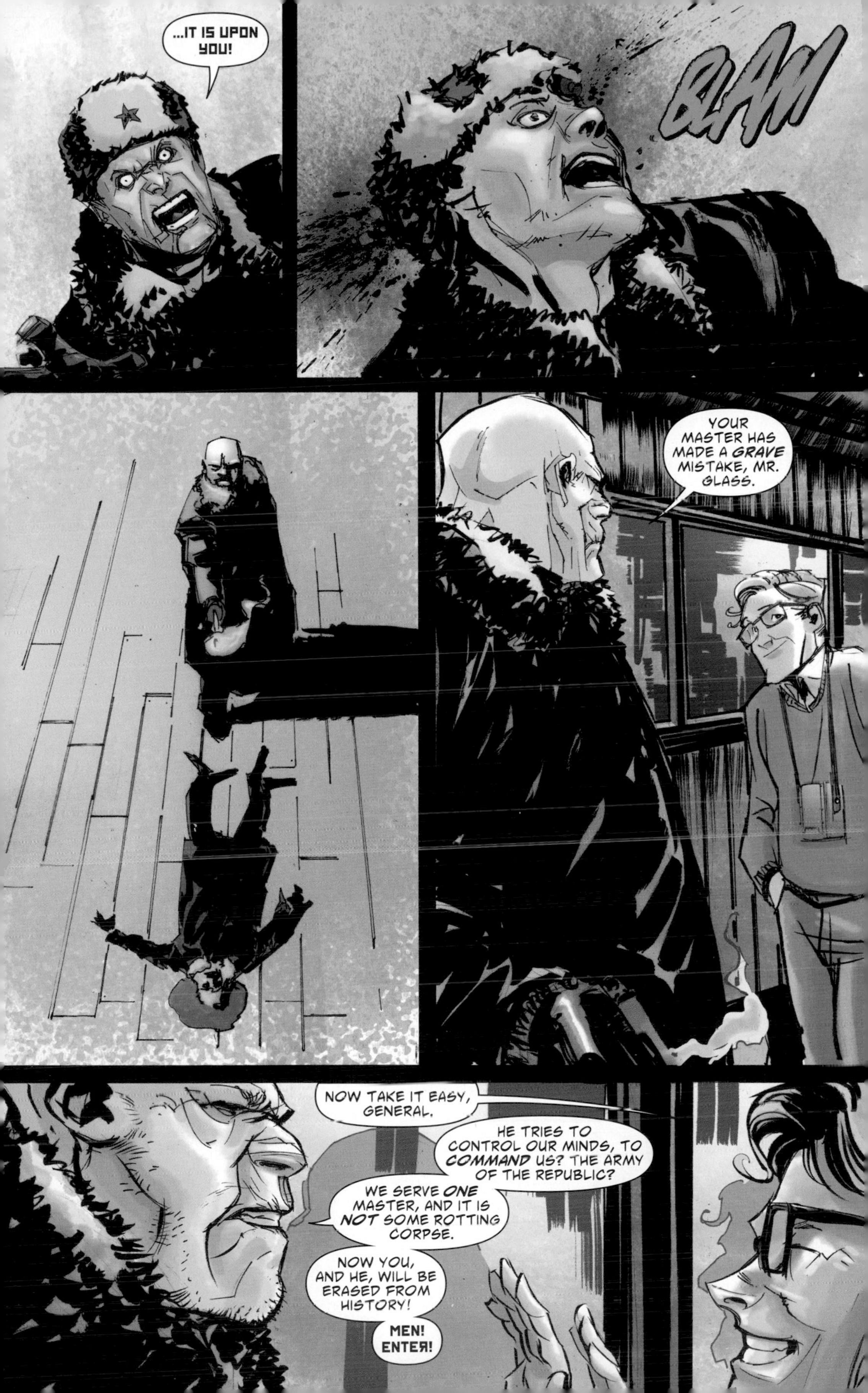
...IT IS UPON YOU!
BLAM
YOUR MASTER HAS MADE A GRAVE MISTAKE, MR. GLASS.
NOW TAKE IT EASY, GENERAL.
HE TRIES TO CONTROL OUR MINDS, TO COMMAND US? THE ARMY OF THE REPUBLIC?
WE SERVE ONE MASTER, AND IT IS NOT SOME ROTTING CORPSE.
NOW YOU, AND HE, WILL BE ERASED FROM HISTORY!
MEN! ENTEЯ!

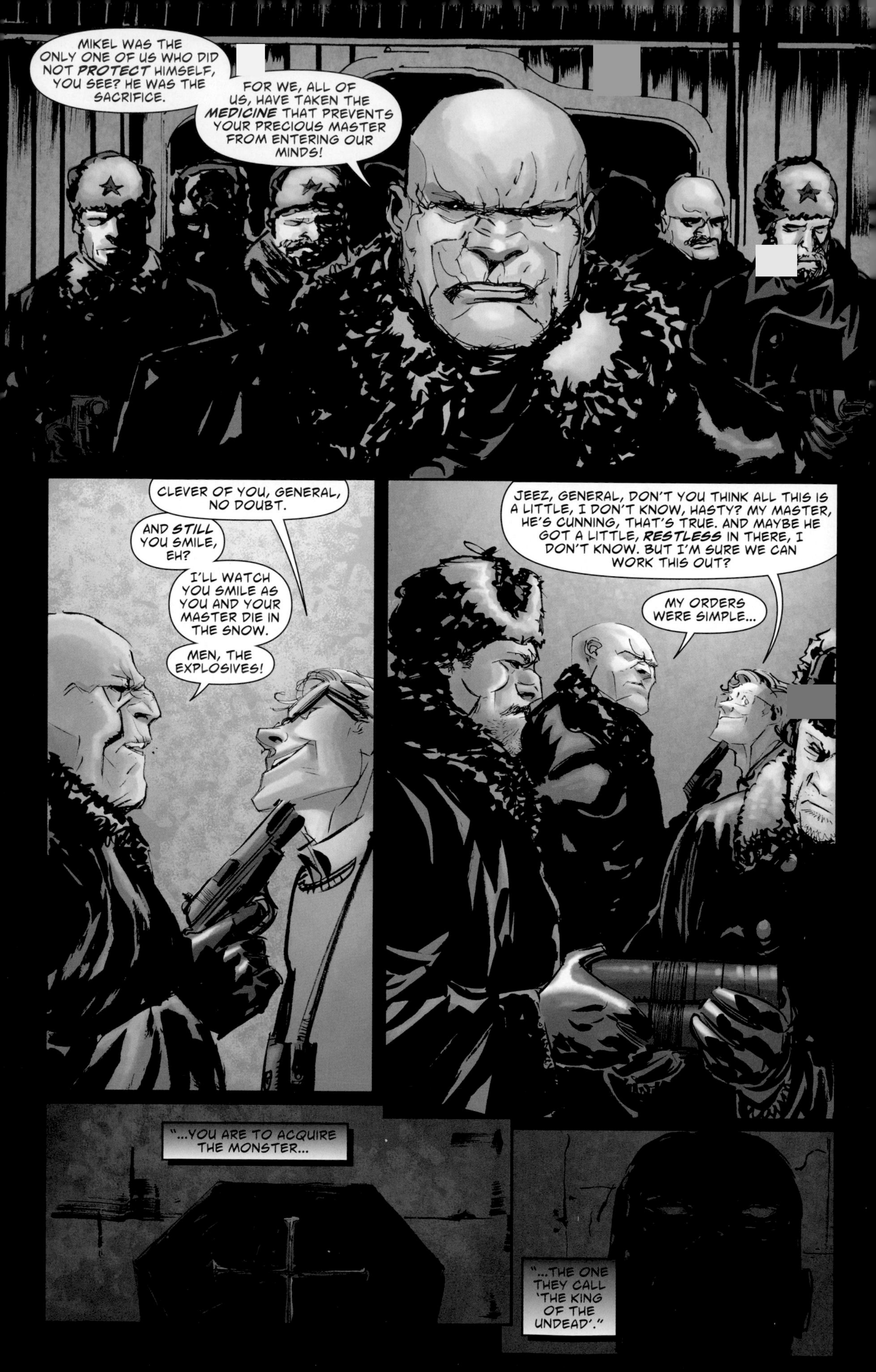
MIKEL WAS THE ONLY ONE OF US WHO DID NOT PROTECT HIMSELF, YOU SEE? HE WAS THE SACRIFICE.
FOR WE, ALL OF US, HAVE TAKEN THE MEDICINE THAT PREVENTS YOUR PRECIOUS MASTER FROM ENTERING OUR MINDS!
CLEVER OF YOU, GENERAL, NO DOUBT.
AND STILL YOU SMILE, EH?
I'LL WATCH YOU SMILE AS YOU AND YOUR MASTER DIE IN THE SNOW.
MEN, THE EXPLOSIVES!
JEEZ, GENERAL, DON'T YOU THINK ALL THIS IS A LITTLE, I DON'T KNOW, HASTY? MY MASTER, HE'S CUNNING, THAT'S TRUE. AND MAYBE HE GOT A LITTLE RESTLESS IN THERE, I DON'T KNOW. BUT I'M SURE WE CAN WORK THIS OUT?
MY ORDERS WERE SIMPLE...
"...YOU ARE TO ACQUIRE THE MONSTER...
"...THE ONE THEY CALL 'THE KING OF THE UNDEAD'."

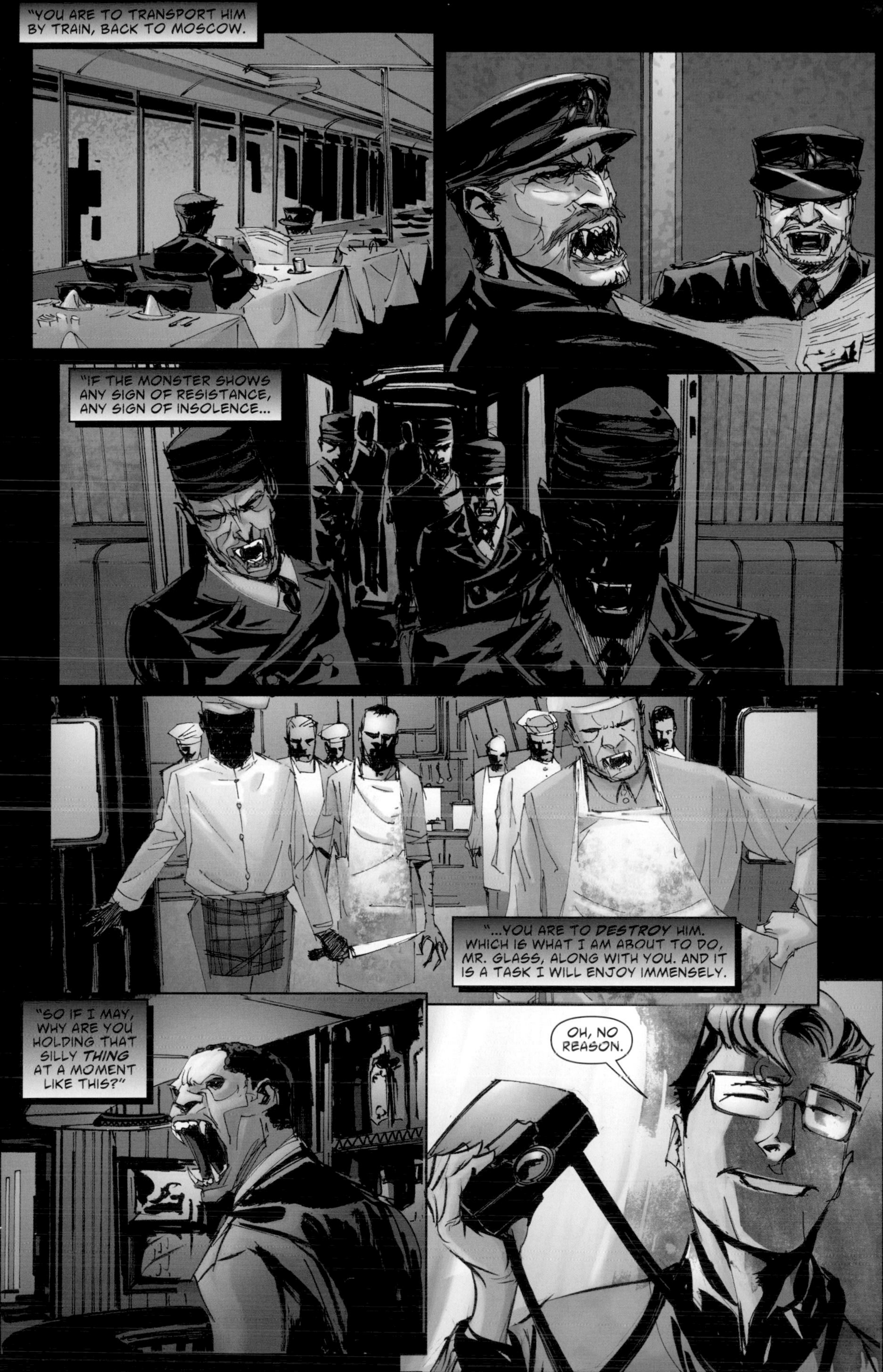
"YOU ARE TO TRANSPORT HIM BY TRAIN, BACK TO MOSCOW.
"IF THE MONSTER SHOWS ANY SIGN OF RESISTANCE, ANY SIGN OF INSOLENCE...
"...YOU ARE TO *DESTROY* HIM. WHICH IS WHAT I AM ABOUT TO DO, MR. GLASS, ALONG WITH YOU. AND IT IS A TASK I WILL ENJOY IMMENSELY.
"SO IF I MAY, WHY ARE YOU HOLDING THAT SILLY *THING* AT A MOMENT LIKE THIS?"
OH, NO REASON.

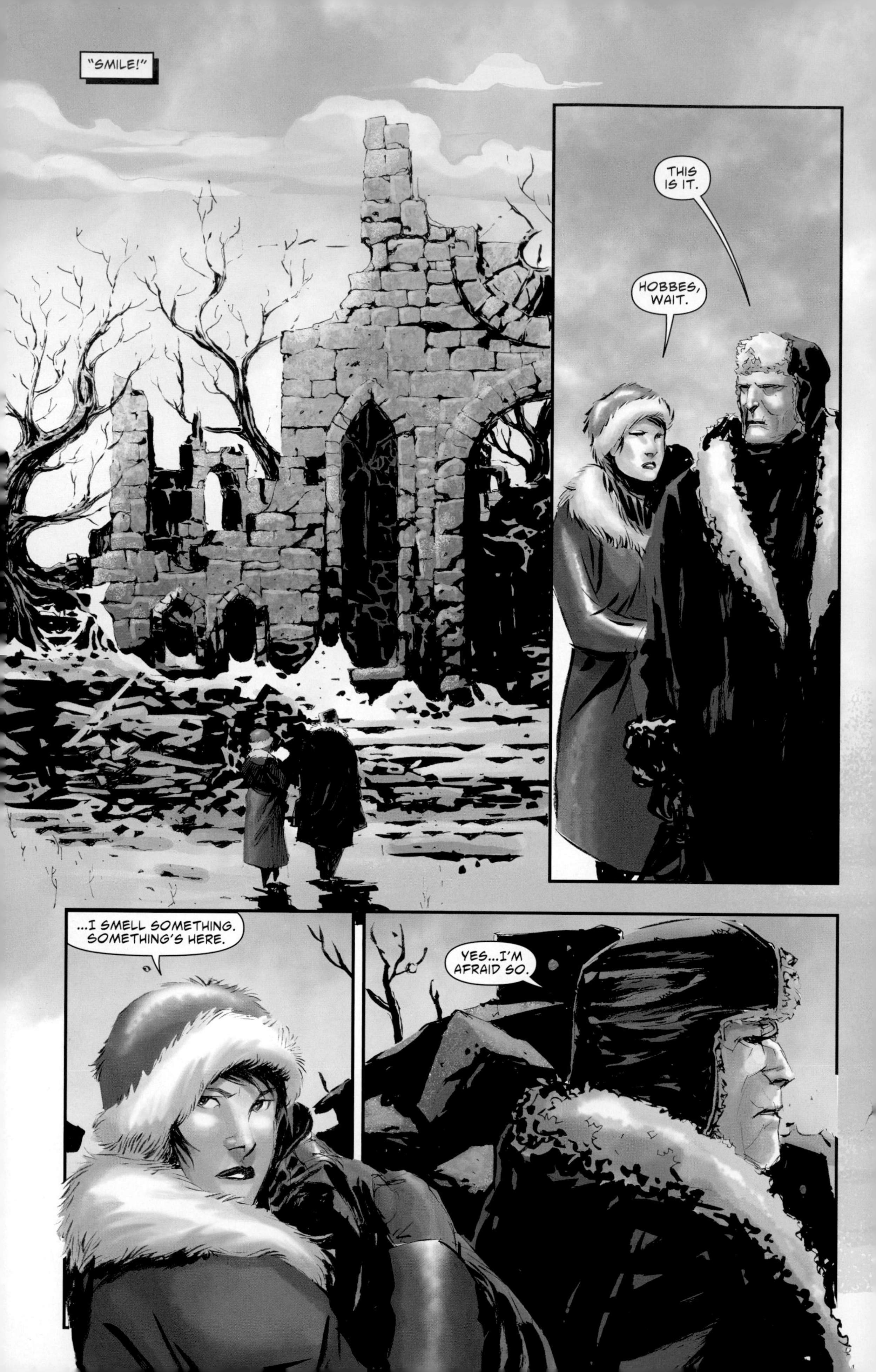
"SMILE!"
THIS IS IT.
HOBBES, WAIT.
...I SMELL SOMETHING. SOMETHING'S HERE.
YES...I'M AFRAID SO.

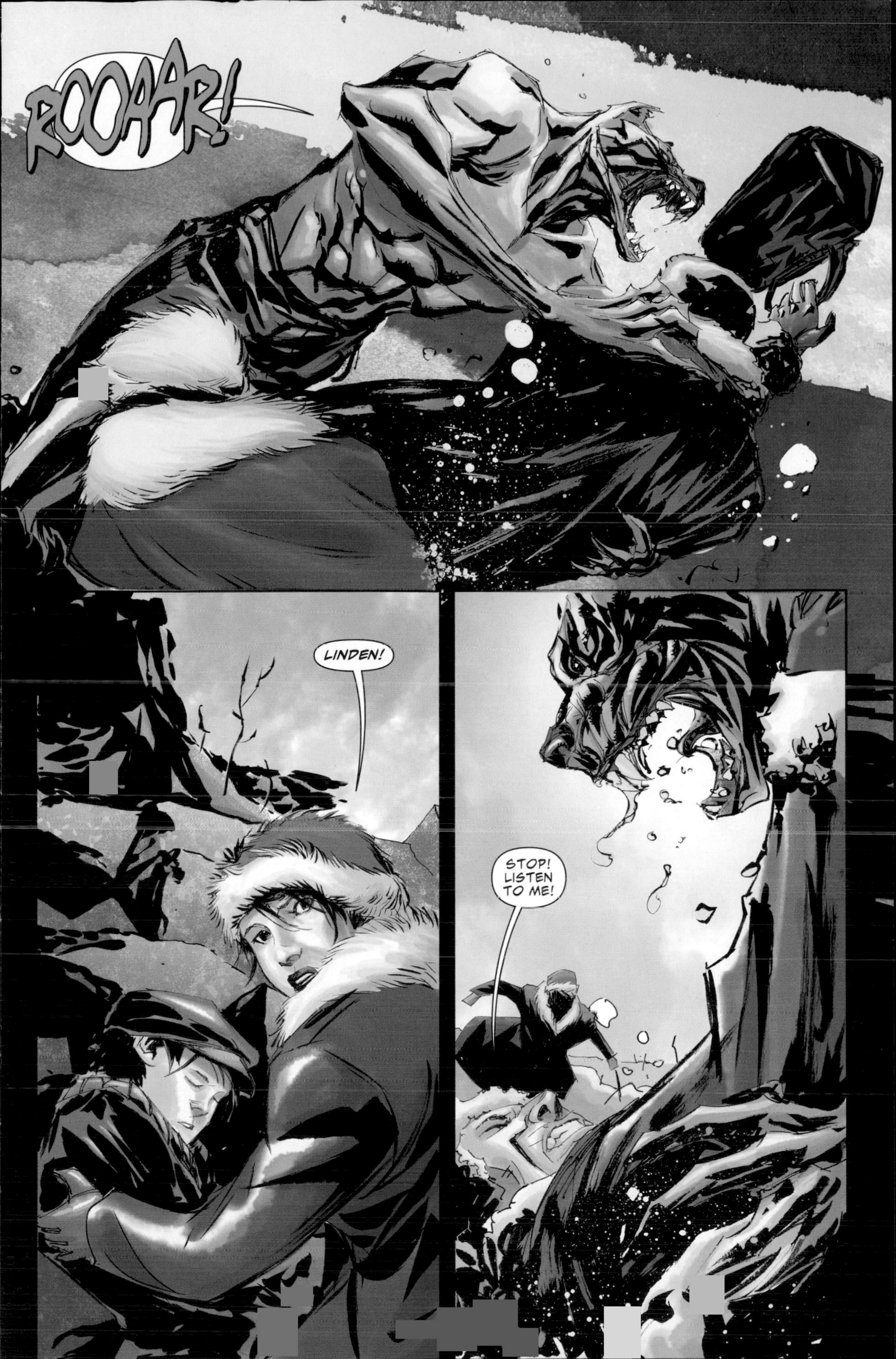
ROOAAR!
LINDEN!
STOP! LISTEN TO ME!

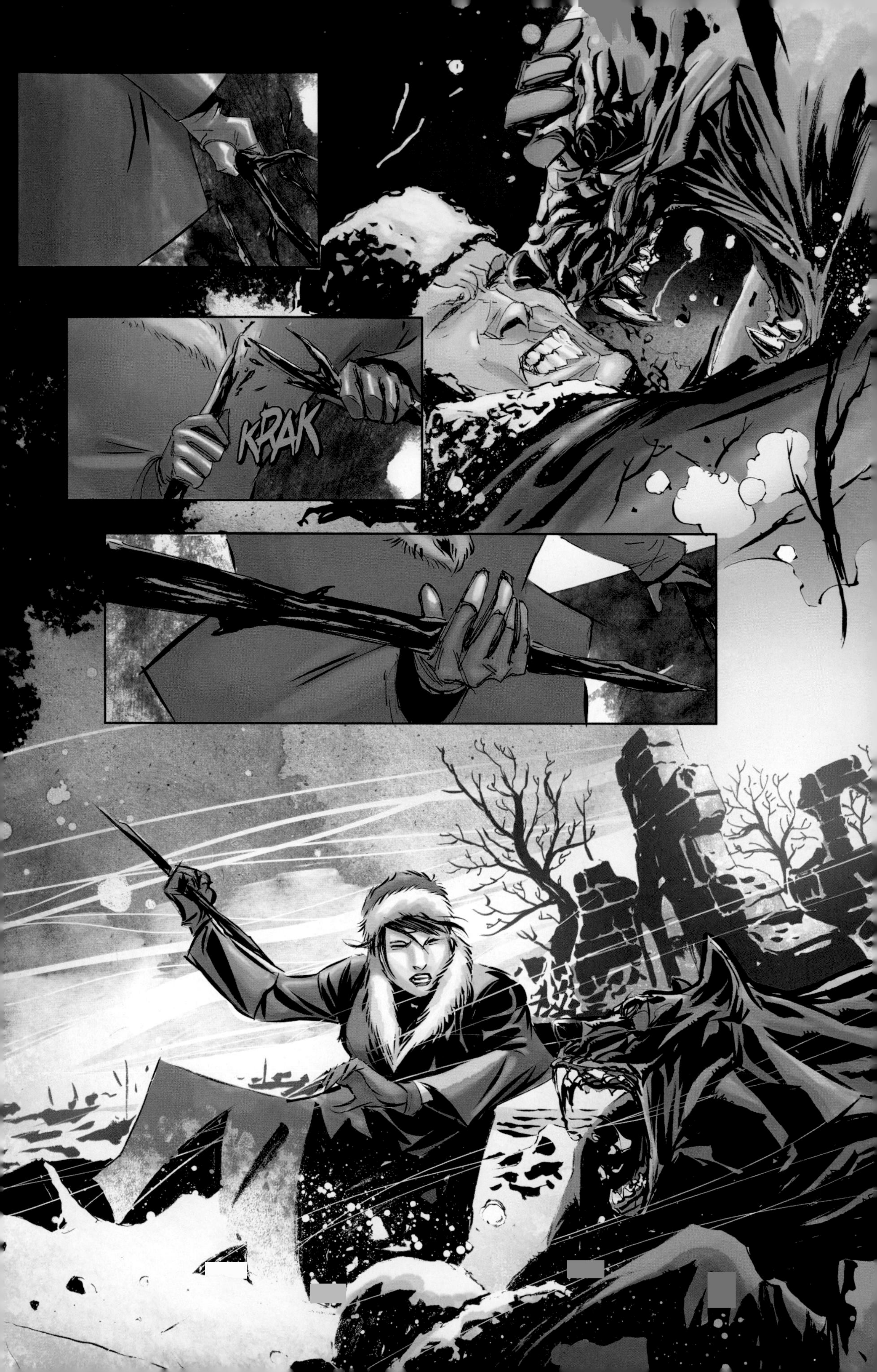
KRAK

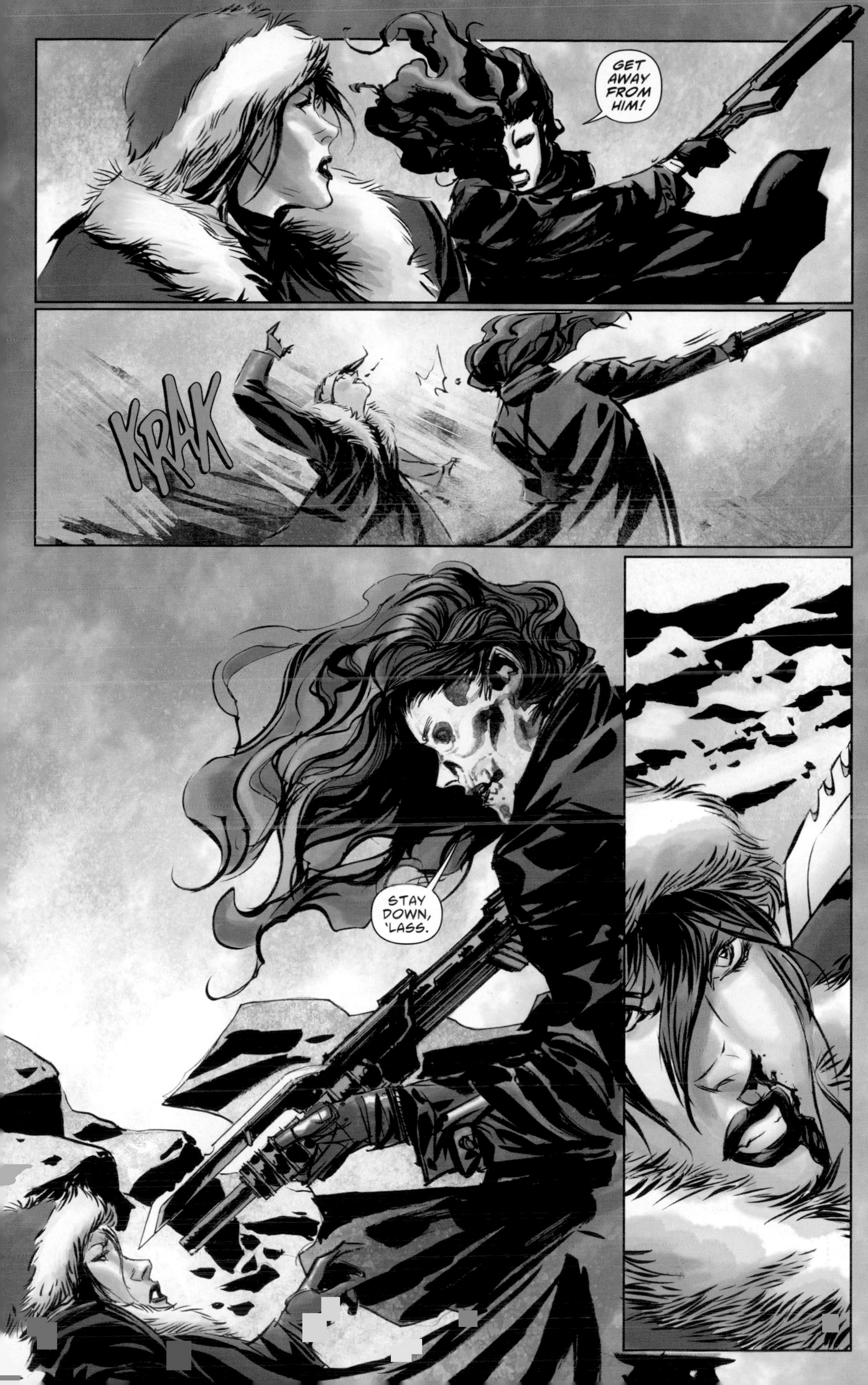
GET AWAY FROM HIM!
KRAK
STAY DOWN, 'LASS.

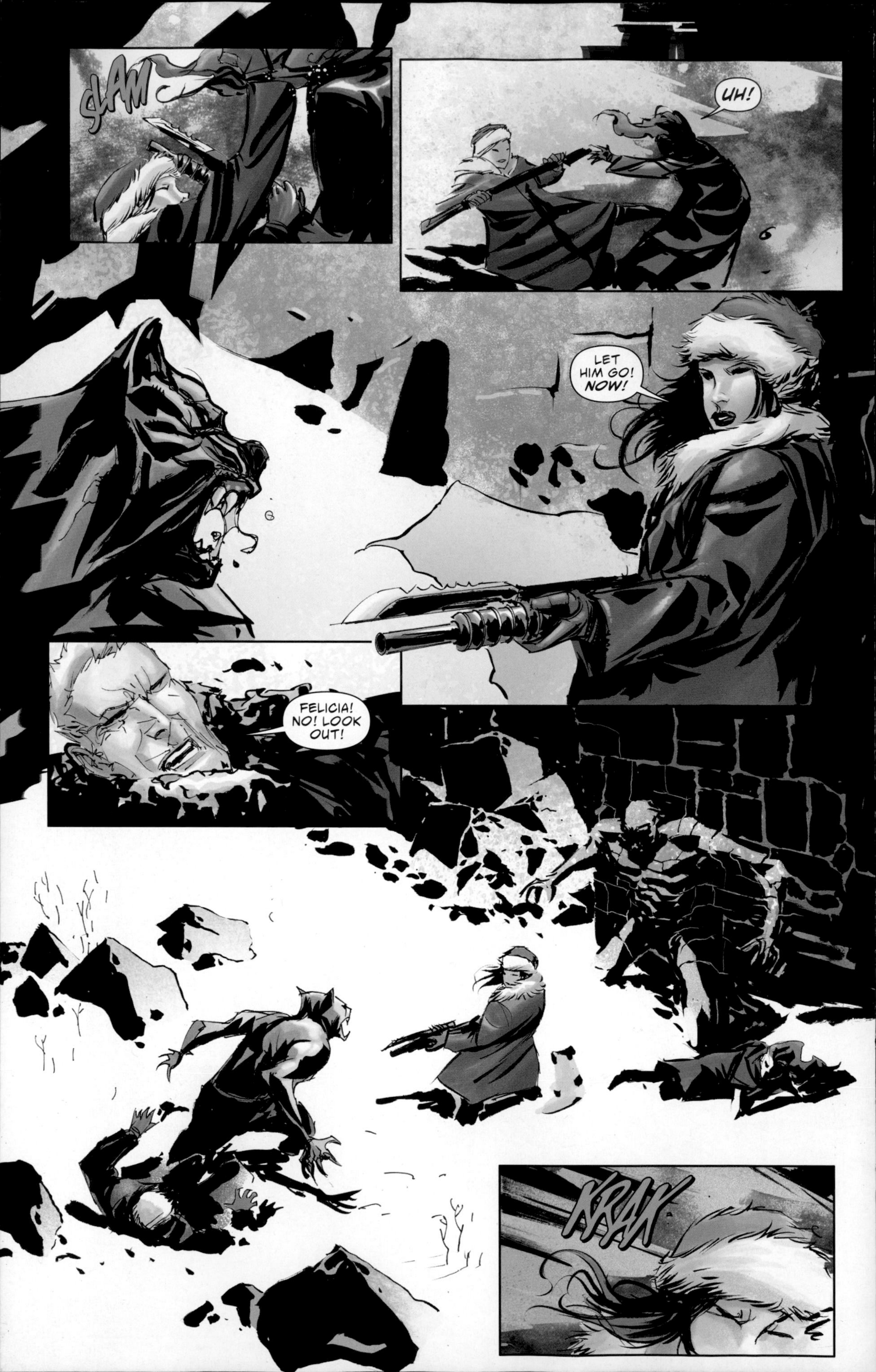
SLAM
UH!
LET HIM GO! NOW!
FELICIA! NO! LOOK OUT!
KRAK

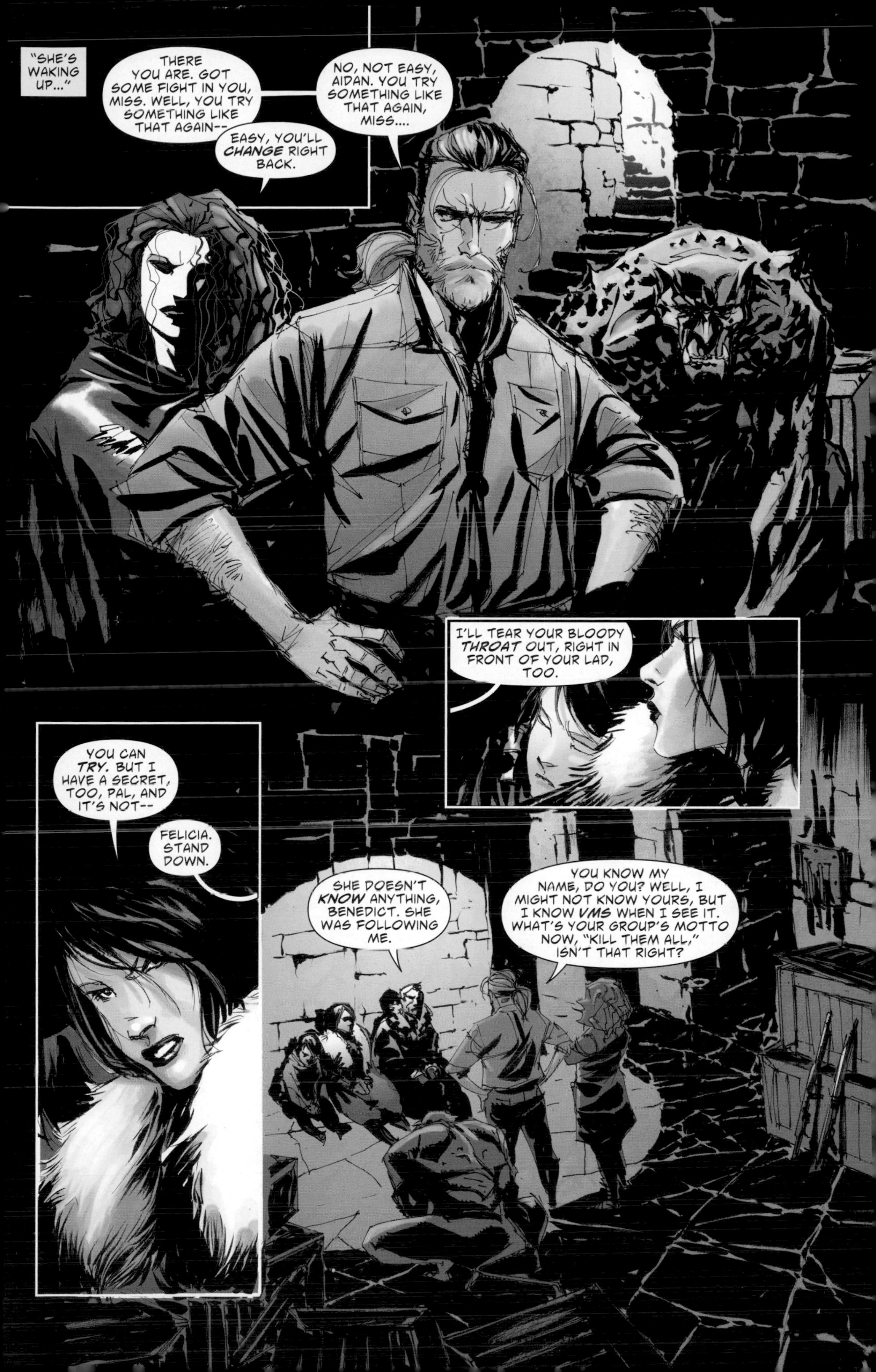
"SHE'S WAKING UP..."
THERE YOU ARE. GOT SOME FIGHT IN YOU, MISS. WELL, YOU TRY SOMETHING LIKE THAT AGAIN--
EASY, YOU'LL CHANGE RIGHT BACK.
NO, NOT EASY, AIDAN. YOU TRY SOMETHING LIKE THAT AGAIN, MISS....
I'LL TEAR YOUR BLOODY THROAT OUT, RIGHT IN FRONT OF YOUR LAD, TOO.
YOU CAN TRY. BUT I HAVE A SECRET, TOO, PAL, AND IT'S NOT--
FELICIA. STAND DOWN.
SHE DOESN'T KNOW ANYTHING, BENEDICT. SHE WAS FOLLOWING ME.
YOU KNOW MY NAME, DO YOU? WELL, I MIGHT NOT KNOW YOURS, BUT I KNOW VMS WHEN I SEE IT. WHAT'S YOUR GROUP'S MOTTO NOW, "KILL THEM ALL," ISN'T THAT RIGHT?

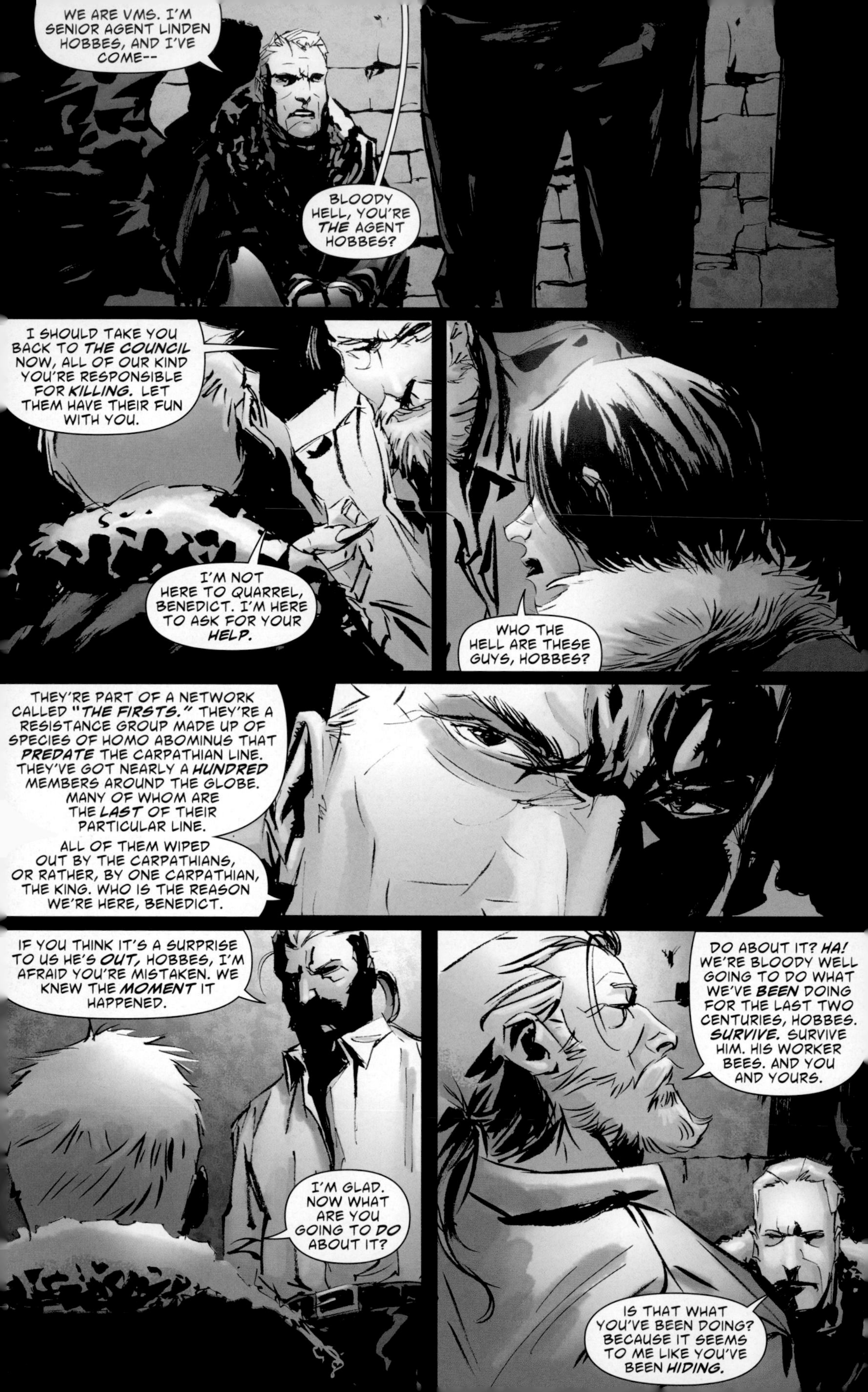
WE ARE VMS. I'M SENIOR AGENT LINDEN HOBBES, AND I'VE COME--
BLOODY HELL, YOU'RE THE AGENT HOBBES?
I SHOULD TAKE YOU BACK TO THE COUNCIL NOW, ALL OF OUR KIND YOU'RE RESPONSIBLE FOR KILLING. LET THEM HAVE THEIR FUN WITH YOU.
I'M NOT HERE TO QUARREL, BENEDICT. I'M HERE TO ASK FOR YOUR HELP.
WHO THE HELL ARE THESE GUYS, HOBBES?
THEY'RE PART OF A NETWORK CALLED "THE FIRSTS." THEY'RE A RESISTANCE GROUP MADE UP OF SPECIES OF HOMO ABOMINUS THAT PREDATE THE CARPATHIAN LINE. THEY'VE GOT NEARLY A HUNDRED MEMBERS AROUND THE GLOBE. MANY OF WHOM ARE THE LAST OF THEIR PARTICULAR LINE.
ALL OF THEM WIPED OUT BY THE CARPATHIANS, OR RATHER, BY ONE CARPATHIAN, THE KING. WHO IS THE REASON WE'RE HERE, BENEDICT.
IF YOU THINK IT'S A SURPRISE TO US HE'S OUT, HOBBES, I'M AFRAID YOU'RE MISTAKEN. WE KNEW THE MOMENT IT HAPPENED.
I'M GLAD. NOW WHAT ARE YOU GOING TO DO ABOUT IT?
DO ABOUT IT? HA! WE'RE BLOODY WELL GOING TO DO WHAT WE'VE BEEN DOING FOR THE LAST TWO CENTURIES, HOBBES. SURVIVE. SURVIVE HIM. HIS WORKER BEES. AND YOU AND YOURS.
IS THAT WHAT YOU'VE BEEN DOING? BECAUSE IT SEEMS TO ME LIKE YOU'VE BEEN HIDING.

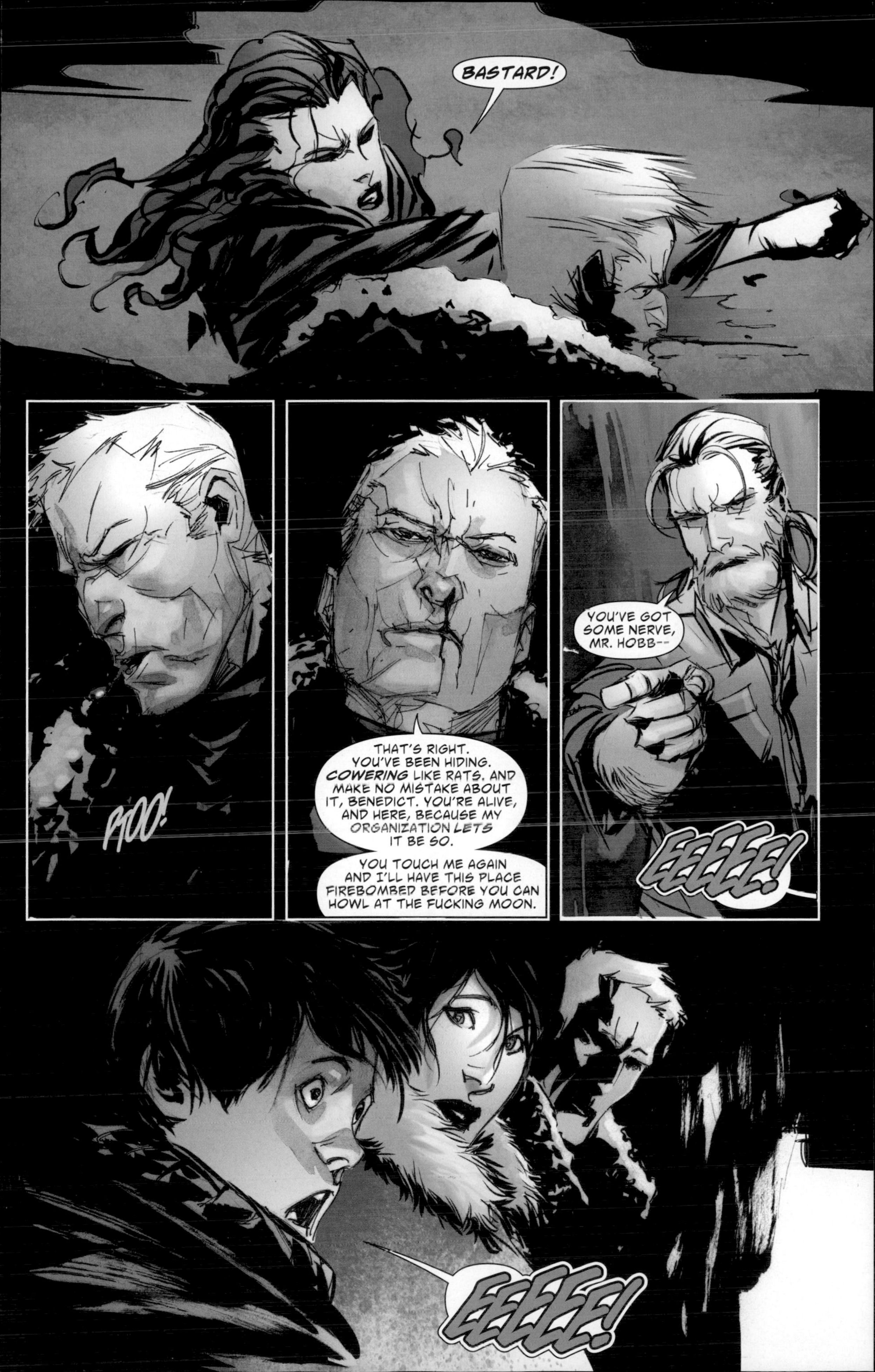
BASTARD!
PTOO!
THAT'S RIGHT. YOU'VE BEEN HIDING. COWERING LIKE RATS. AND MAKE NO MISTAKE ABOUT IT, BENEDICT. YOU'RE ALIVE, AND HERE, BECAUSE MY ORGANIZATION LETS IT BE SO.
YOU TOUCH ME AGAIN AND I'LL HAVE THIS PLACE FIREBOMBED BEFORE YOU CAN HOWL AT THE FUCKING MOON.
YOU'VE GOT SOME NERVE, MR. HOBB--
EEEEE!
EEEEE!

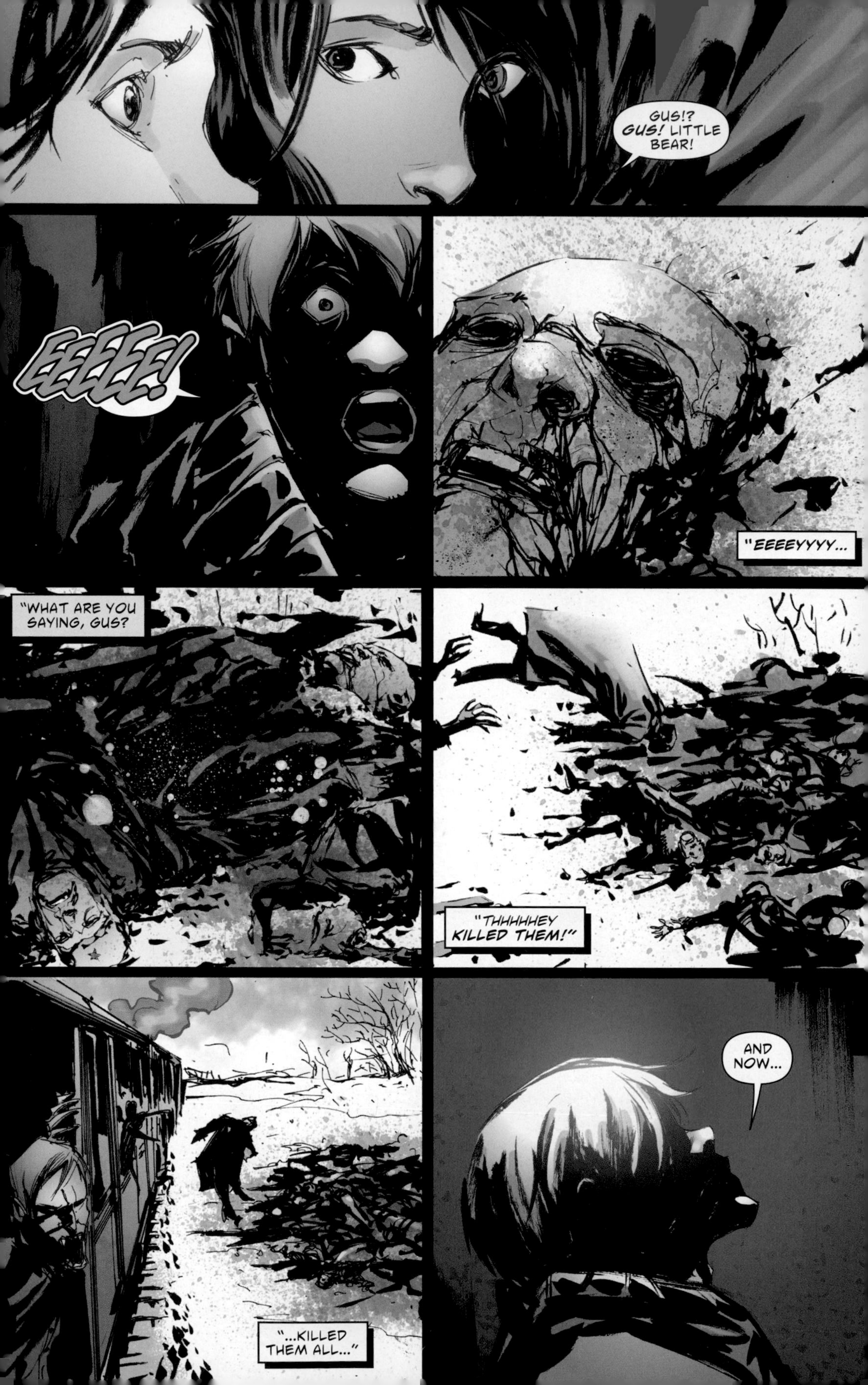
GUS!? GUS! LITTLE BEAR!
EEEEE!
"EEEEYYYY...
"WHAT ARE YOU SAYING, GUS?
"THHHHHEY KILLED THEM!"
"...KILLED THEM ALL..."
AND NOW...

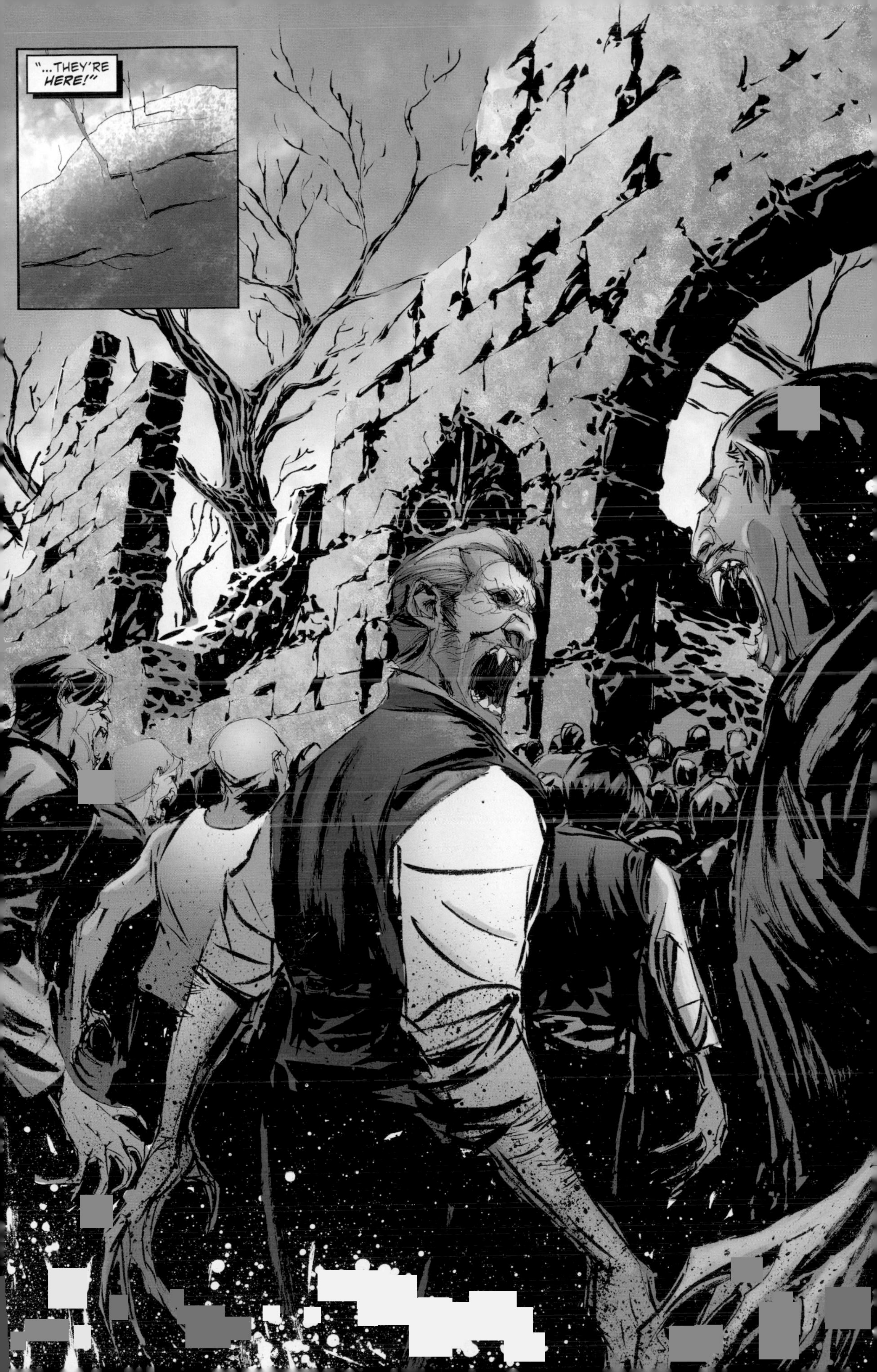
"...THEY'RE HERE!"

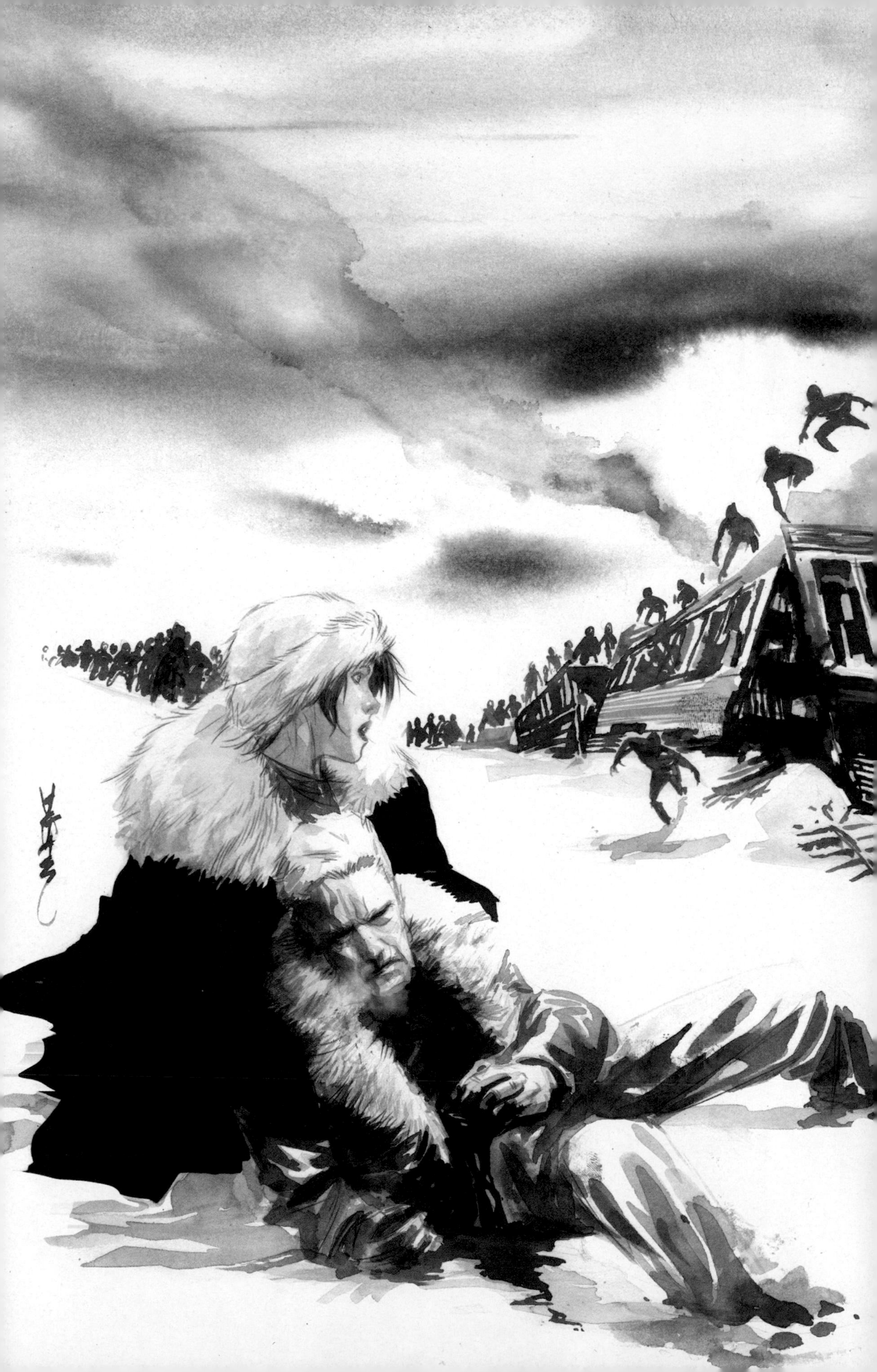

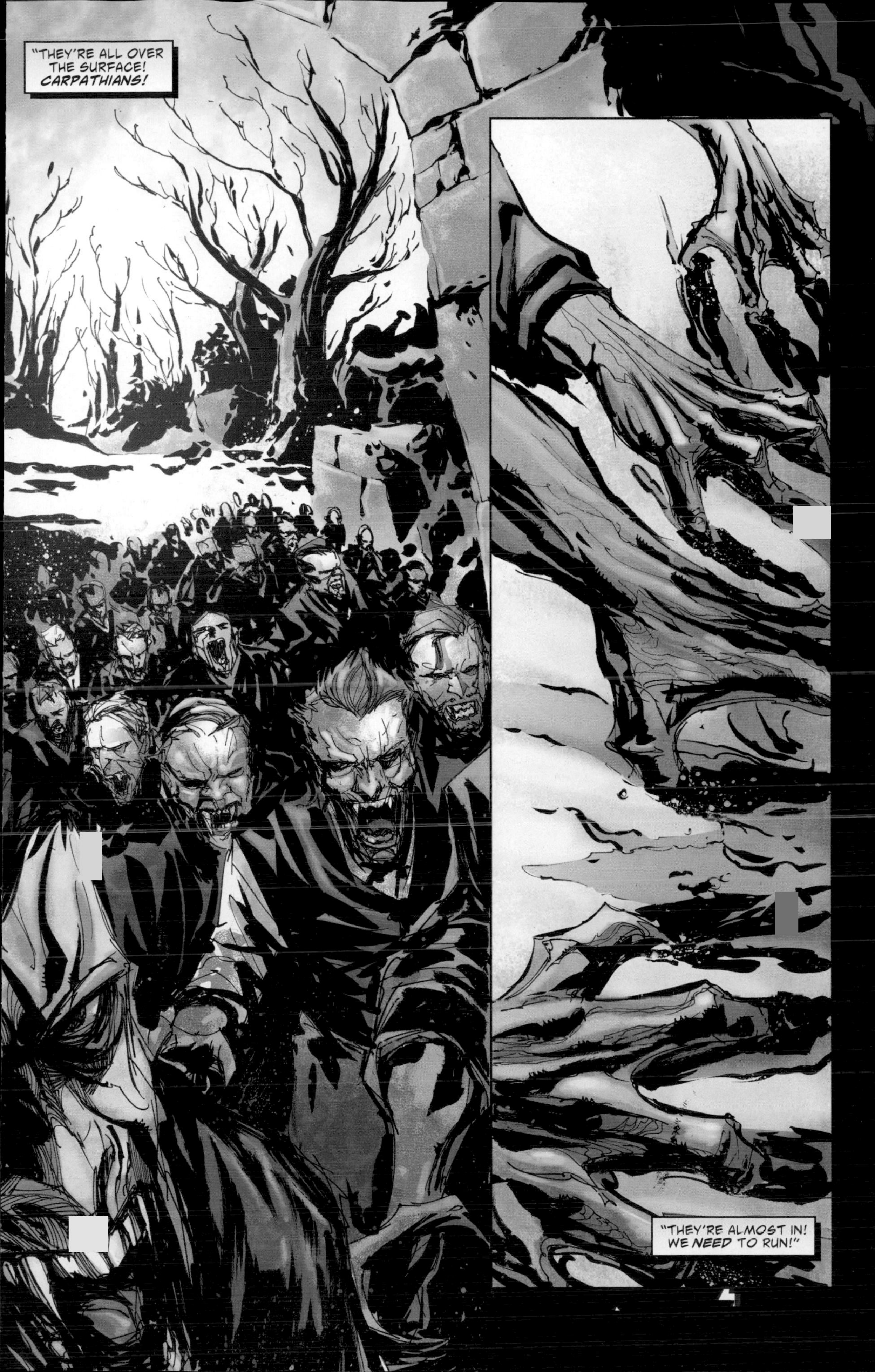
"THEY'RE ALL OVER THE SURFACE! CARPATHIANS!
"THEY'RE ALMOST IN! WE NEED TO RUN!"

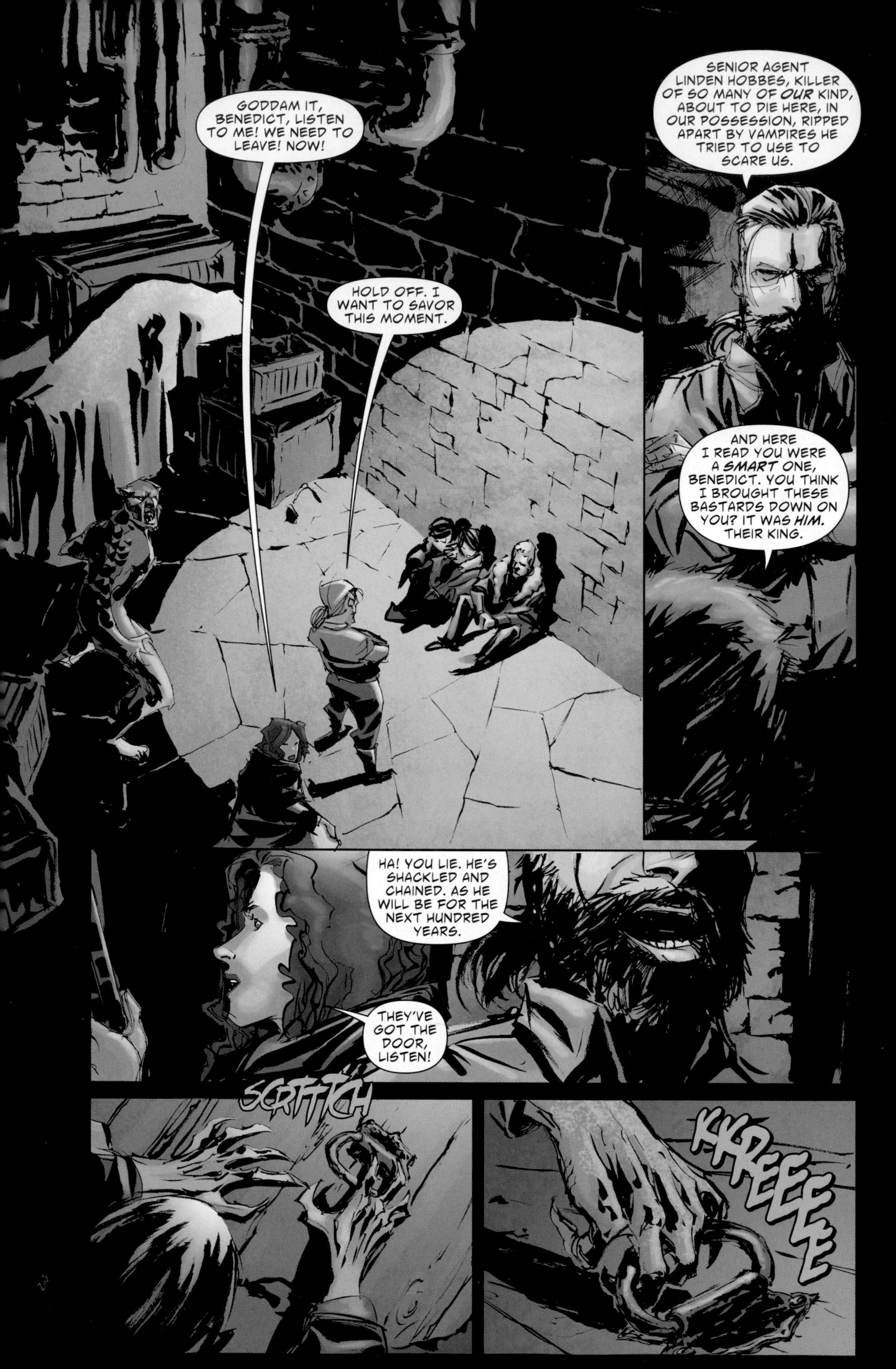
GODDAM IT, BENEDICT, LISTEN TO ME! WE NEED TO LEAVE! NOW!
HOLD OFF. I WANT TO SAVOR THIS MOMENT.
SENIOR AGENT LINDEN HOBBES, KILLER OF SO MANY OF OUR KIND, ABOUT TO DIE HERE, IN OUR POSSESSION, RIPPED APART BY VAMPIRES HE TRIED TO USE TO SCARE US.
AND HERE I READ YOU WERE A SMART ONE, BENEDICT. YOU THINK I BROUGHT THESE BASTARDS DOWN ON YOU? IT WAS HIM. THEIR KING.
HA! YOU LIE. HE'S SHACKLED AND CHAINED. AS HE WILL BE FOR THE NEXT HUNDRED YEARS.
THEY'VE GOT THE DOOR, LISTEN!
SCRTTTCH
KKREEEEE

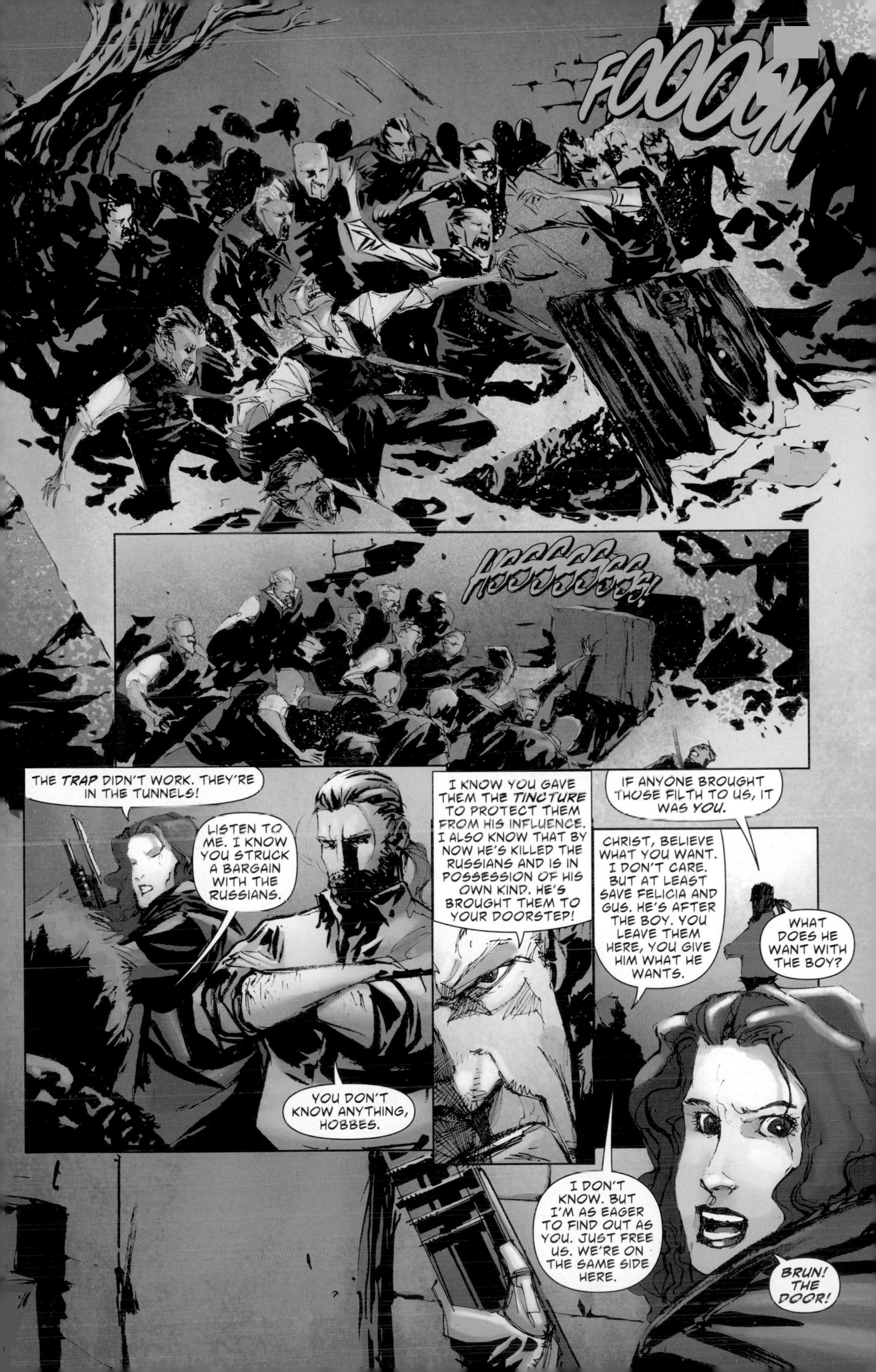
FOOOOM
HSSSSSSS!
THE *TRAP* DIDN'T WORK. THEY'RE IN THE TUNNELS!
LISTEN TO ME. I KNOW YOU STRUCK A BARGAIN WITH THE RUSSIANS.
YOU DON'T KNOW ANYTHING, HOBBES.
I KNOW YOU GAVE THEM THE *TINCTURE* TO PROTECT THEM FROM HIS INFLUENCE. I ALSO KNOW THAT BY NOW HE'S KILLED THE RUSSIANS AND IS IN POSSESSION OF HIS OWN KIND. HE'S BROUGHT THEM TO YOUR DOORSTEP!
IF ANYONE BROUGHT THOSE FILTH TO US, IT WAS *YOU*.
CHRIST, BELIEVE WHAT YOU WANT. I DON'T CARE. BUT AT LEAST SAVE FELICIA AND GUS. HE'S AFTER THE BOY. YOU LEAVE THEM HERE, YOU GIVE HIM WHAT HE WANTS.
WHAT DOES HE WANT WITH THE BOY?
I DON'T KNOW. BUT I'M AS EAGER TO FIND OUT AS YOU. JUST FREE US. WE'RE ON THE SAME SIDE HERE.
BRUN! THE DOOR!

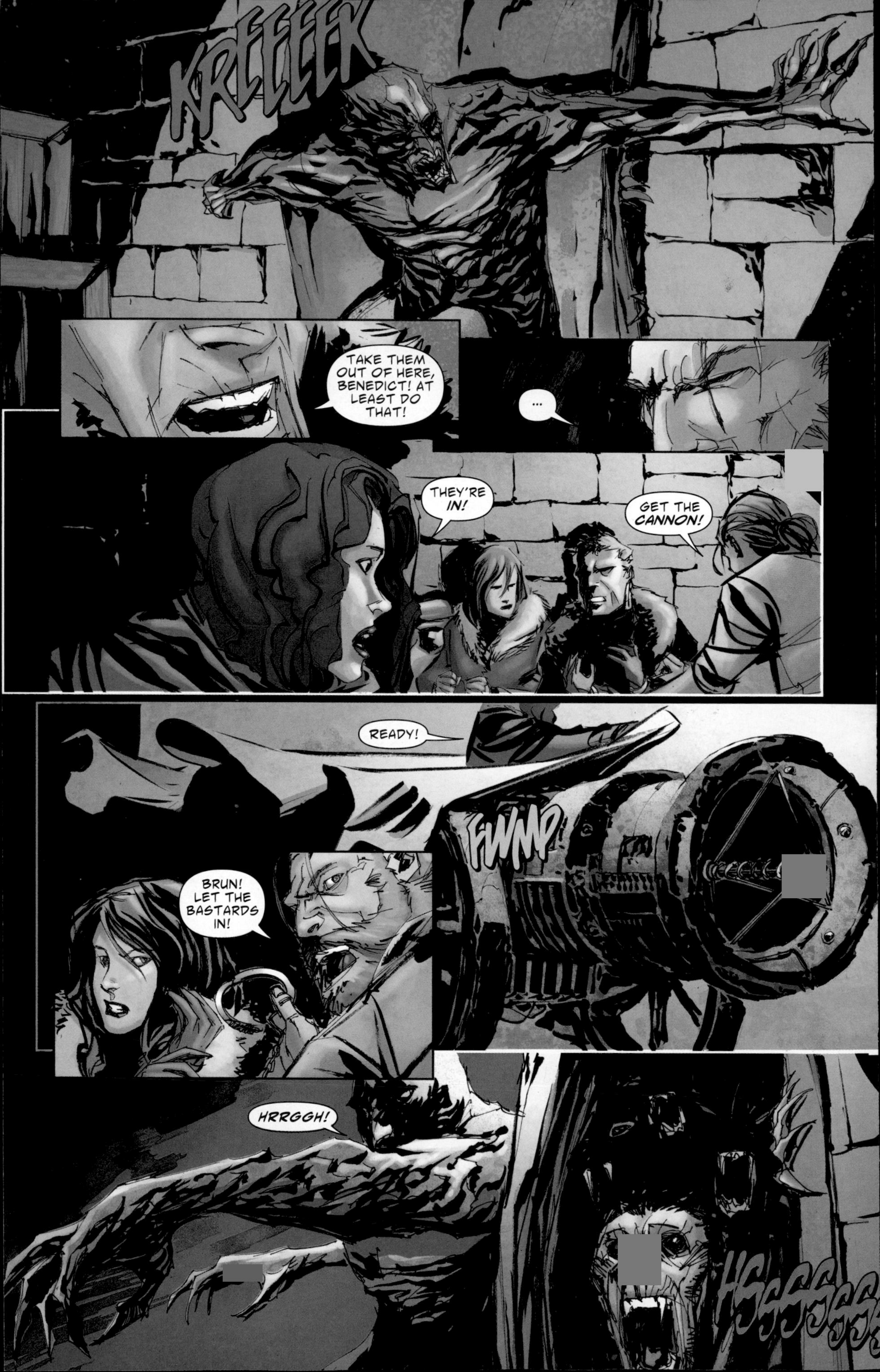
KREEEEK
TAKE THEM OUT OF HERE, BENEDICT! AT LEAST DO THAT!
...
THEY'RE IN!
GET THE CANNON!
READY!
FWMP
BRUN! LET THE BASTARDS IN!
HRRGGH!

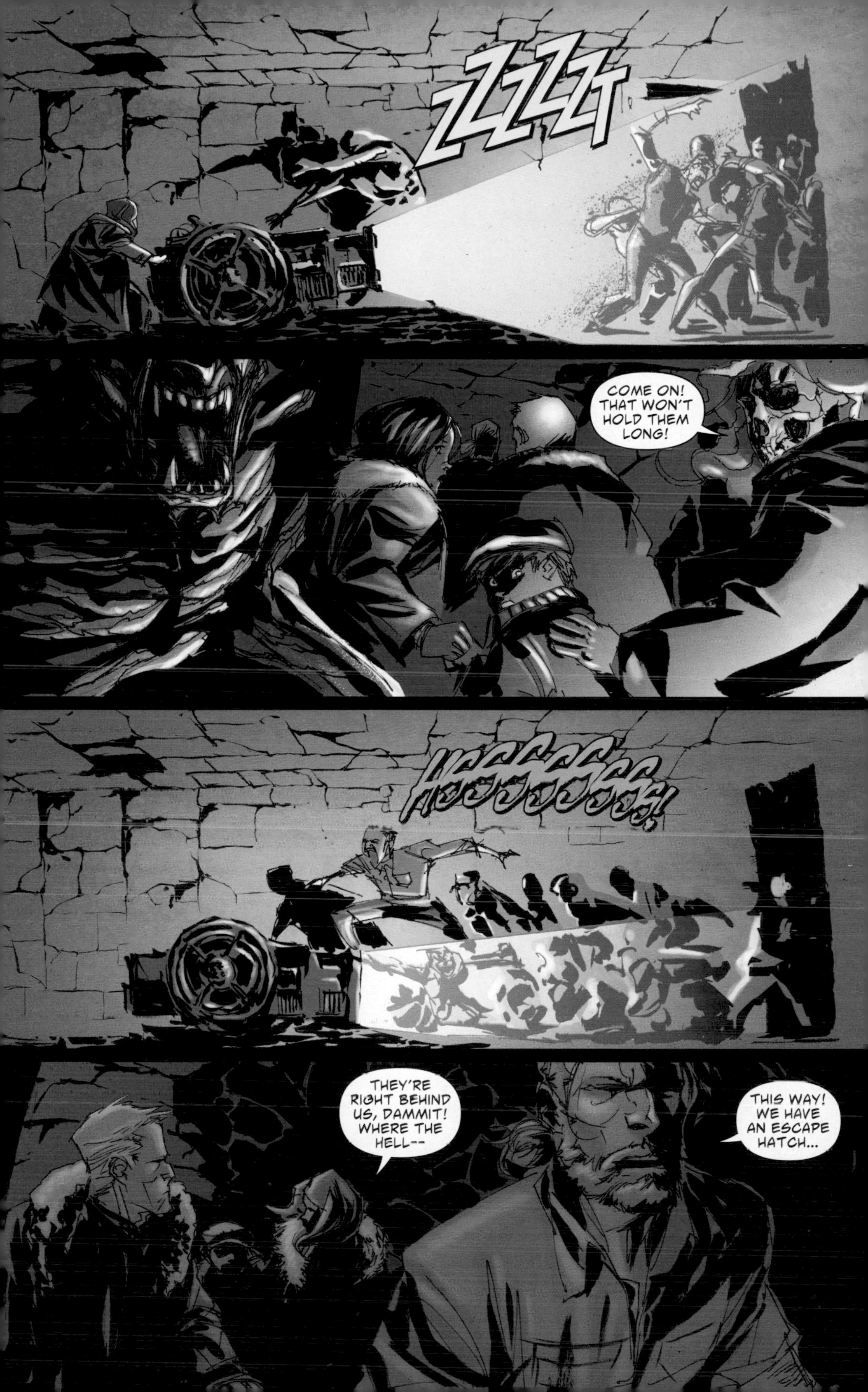
ZZZZZT
COME ON! THAT WON'T HOLD THEM LONG!
HSSSSSSS!
THEY'RE RIGHT BEHIND US, DAMMIT! WHERE THE HELL--
THIS WAY! WE HAVE AN ESCAPE HATCH...

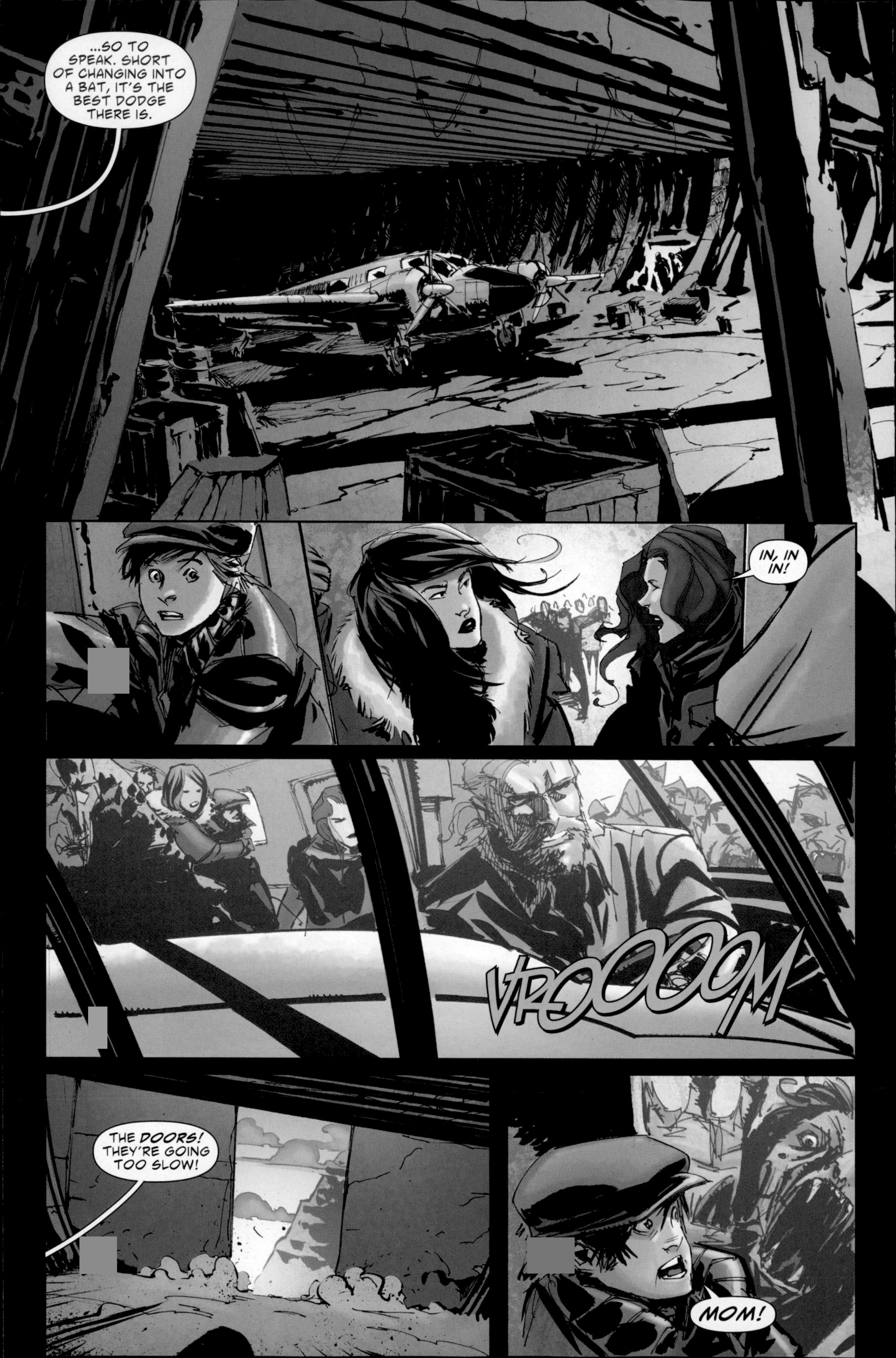
...SO TO SPEAK. SHORT OF CHANGING INTO A BAT, IT'S THE BEST DODGE THERE IS.
IN, IN IN!
VROOOOOM
THE *DOORS!* THEY'RE GOING TOO SLOW!
MOM!

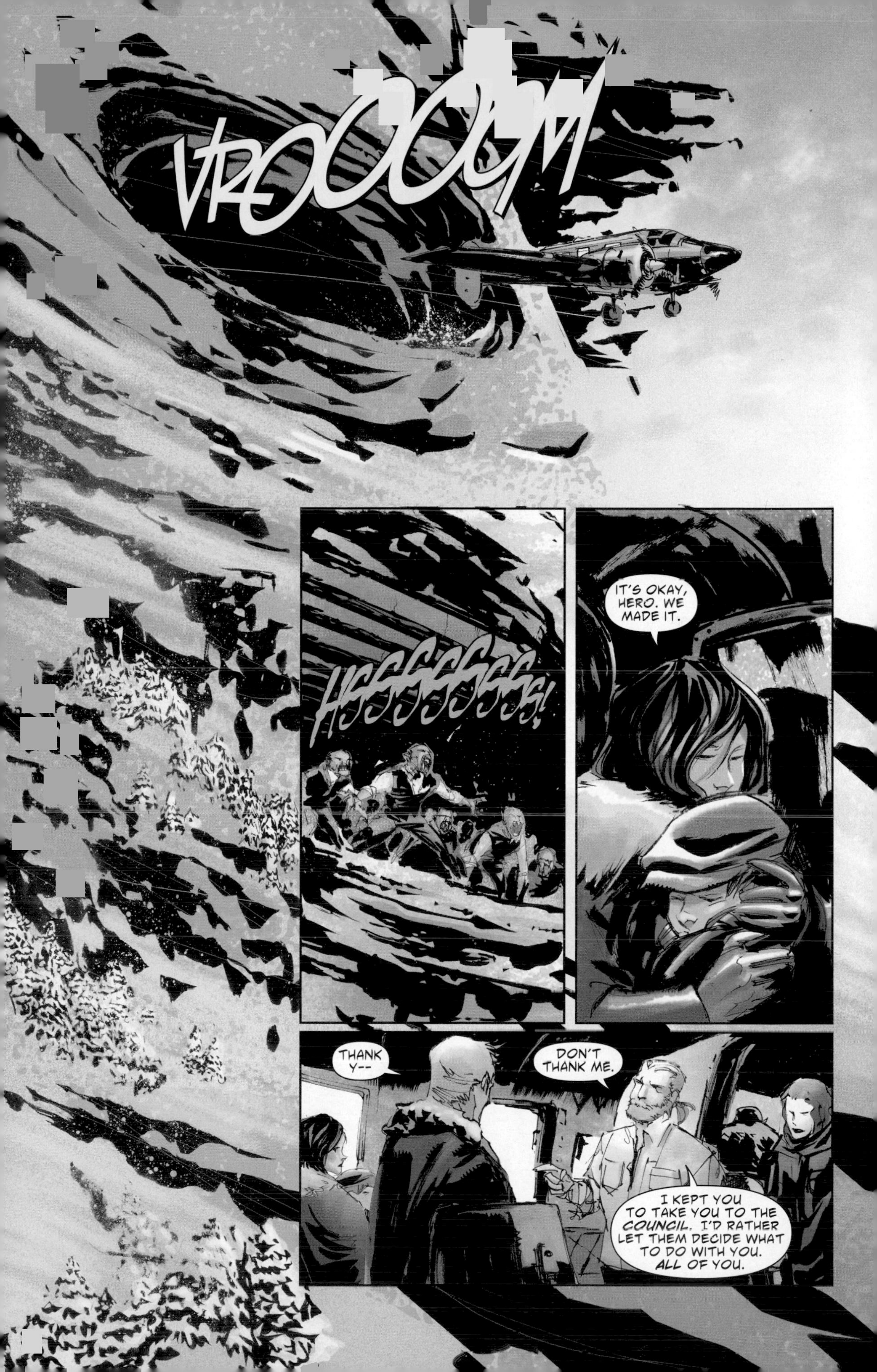
VROOOM
HSSSSSSS!
IT'S OKAY, HERO. WE MADE IT.
THANK Y--
DON'T THANK ME.
I KEPT YOU TO TAKE YOU TO THE COUNCIL. I'D RATHER LET THEM DECIDE WHAT TO DO WITH YOU. ALL OF YOU.

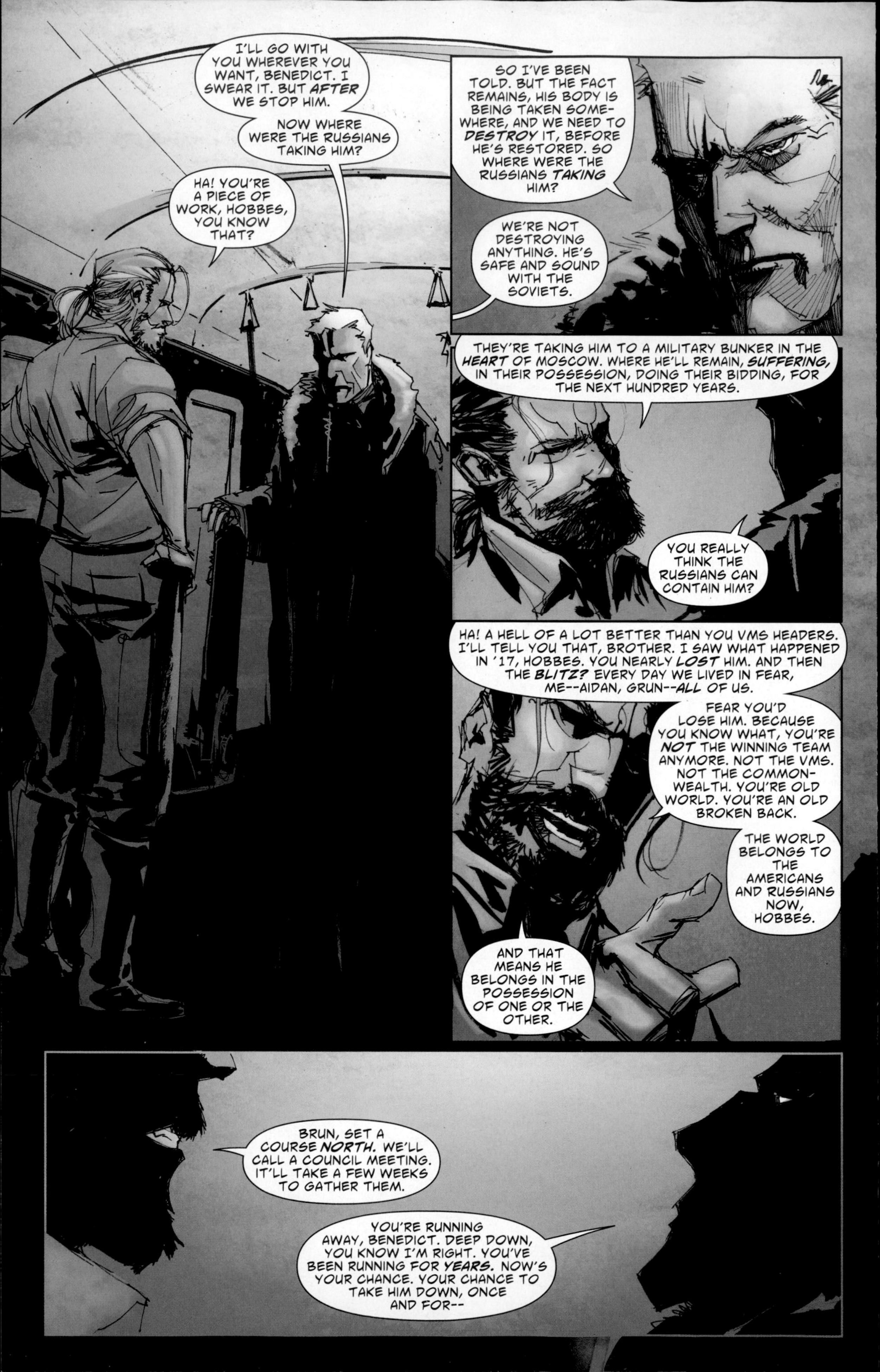
I'LL GO WITH YOU WHEREVER YOU WANT, BENEDICT. I SWEAR IT. BUT AFTER WE STOP HIM.
NOW WHERE WERE THE RUSSIANS TAKING HIM?
HA! YOU'RE A PIECE OF WORK, HOBBES, YOU KNOW THAT?
SO I'VE BEEN TOLD. BUT THE FACT REMAINS, HIS BODY IS BEING TAKEN SOME-WHERE, AND WE NEED TO DESTROY IT, BEFORE HE'S RESTORED. SO WHERE WERE THE RUSSIANS TAKING HIM?
WE'RE NOT DESTROYING ANYTHING. HE'S SAFE AND SOUND WITH THE SOVIETS.
THEY'RE TAKING HIM TO A MILITARY BUNKER IN THE HEART OF MOSCOW. WHERE HE'LL REMAIN, SUFFERING, IN THEIR POSSESSION, DOING THEIR BIDDING, FOR THE NEXT HUNDRED YEARS.
YOU REALLY THINK THE RUSSIANS CAN CONTAIN HIM?
HA! A HELL OF A LOT BETTER THAN YOU VMS HEADERS. I'LL TELL YOU THAT, BROTHER. I SAW WHAT HAPPENED IN '17, HOBBES. YOU NEARLY LOST HIM. AND THEN THE BLITZ? EVERY DAY WE LIVED IN FEAR, ME--AIDAN, GRUN--ALL OF US.
FEAR YOU'D LOSE HIM. BECAUSE YOU KNOW WHAT, YOU'RE NOT THE WINNING TEAM ANYMORE. NOT THE VMS. NOT THE COMMON-WEALTH. YOU'RE OLD WORLD. YOU'RE AN OLD BROKEN BACK.
THE WORLD BELONGS TO THE AMERICANS AND RUSSIANS NOW, HOBBES.
AND THAT MEANS HE BELONGS IN THE POSSESSION OF ONE OR THE OTHER.
BRUN, SET A COURSE NORTH. WE'LL CALL A COUNCIL MEETING. IT'LL TAKE A FEW WEEKS TO GATHER THEM.
YOU'RE RUNNING AWAY, BENEDICT. DEEP DOWN, YOU KNOW I'M RIGHT. YOU'VE BEEN RUNNING FOR YEARS. NOW'S YOUR CHANCE. YOUR CHANCE TO TAKE HIM DOWN, ONCE AND FOR--

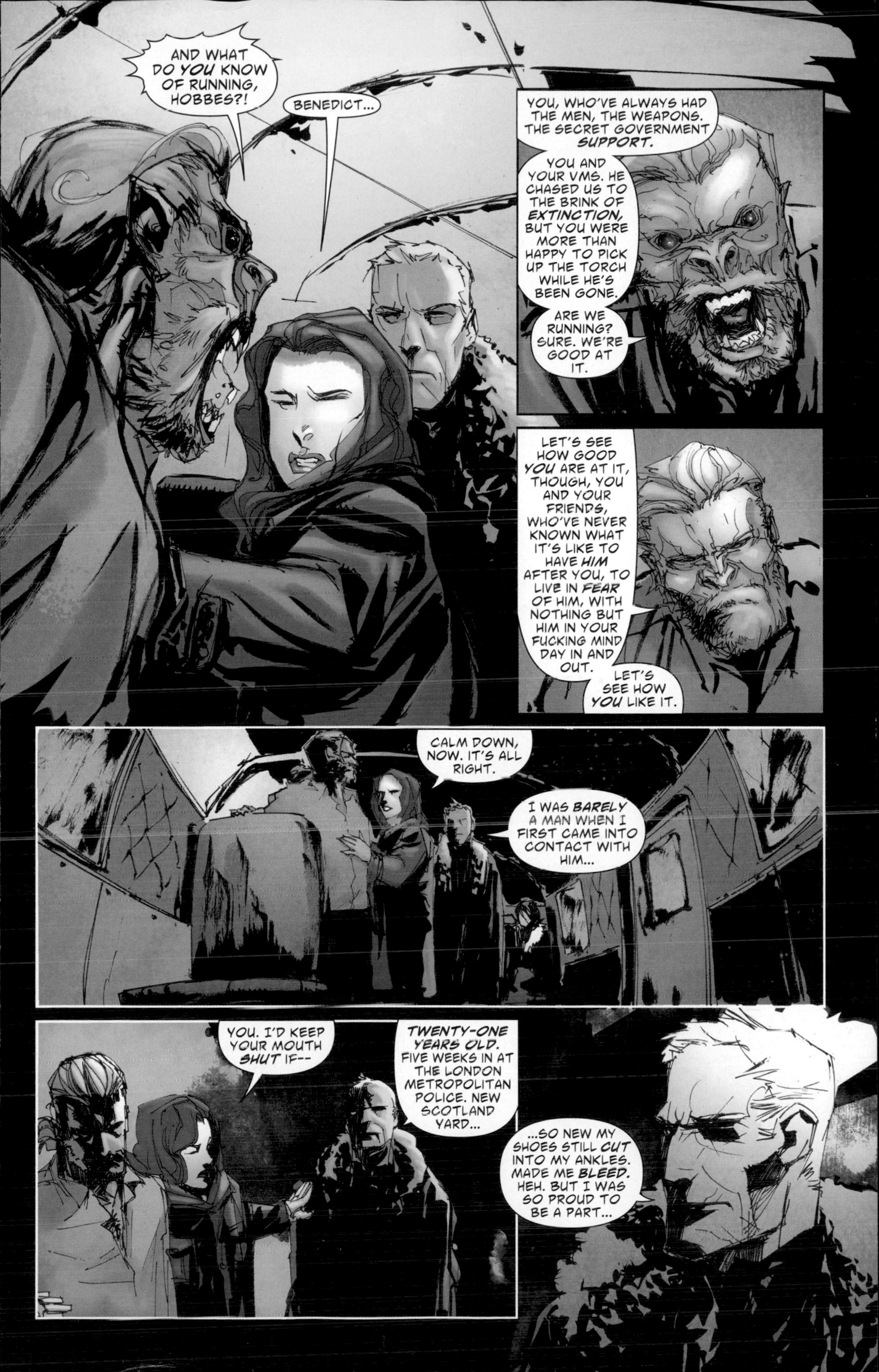
AND WHAT DO YOU KNOW OF RUNNING, HOBBES?!
BENEDICT...
YOU, WHO'VE ALWAYS HAD THE MEN, THE WEAPONS. THE SECRET GOVERNMENT SUPPORT.
YOU AND YOUR VMS. HE CHASED US TO THE BRINK OF EXTINCTION, BUT YOU WERE MORE THAN HAPPY TO PICK UP THE TORCH WHILE HE'S BEEN GONE.
ARE WE RUNNING? SURE. WE'RE GOOD AT IT.
LET'S SEE HOW GOOD YOU ARE AT IT, THOUGH, YOU AND YOUR FRIENDS, WHO'VE NEVER KNOWN WHAT IT'S LIKE TO HAVE HIM AFTER YOU, TO LIVE IN FEAR OF HIM, WITH NOTHING BUT HIM IN YOUR FUCKING MIND DAY IN AND OUT.
LET'S SEE HOW YOU LIKE IT.
CALM DOWN, NOW. IT'S ALL RIGHT.
I WAS BARELY A MAN WHEN I FIRST CAME INTO CONTACT WITH HIM...
YOU. I'D KEEP YOUR MOUTH SHUT IF--
TWENTY-ONE YEARS OLD. FIVE WEEKS IN AT THE LONDON METROPOLITAN POLICE. NEW SCOTLAND YARD...
...SO NEW MY SHOES STILL CUT INTO MY ANKLES. MADE ME BLEED. HEH. BUT I WAS SO PROUD TO BE A PART...

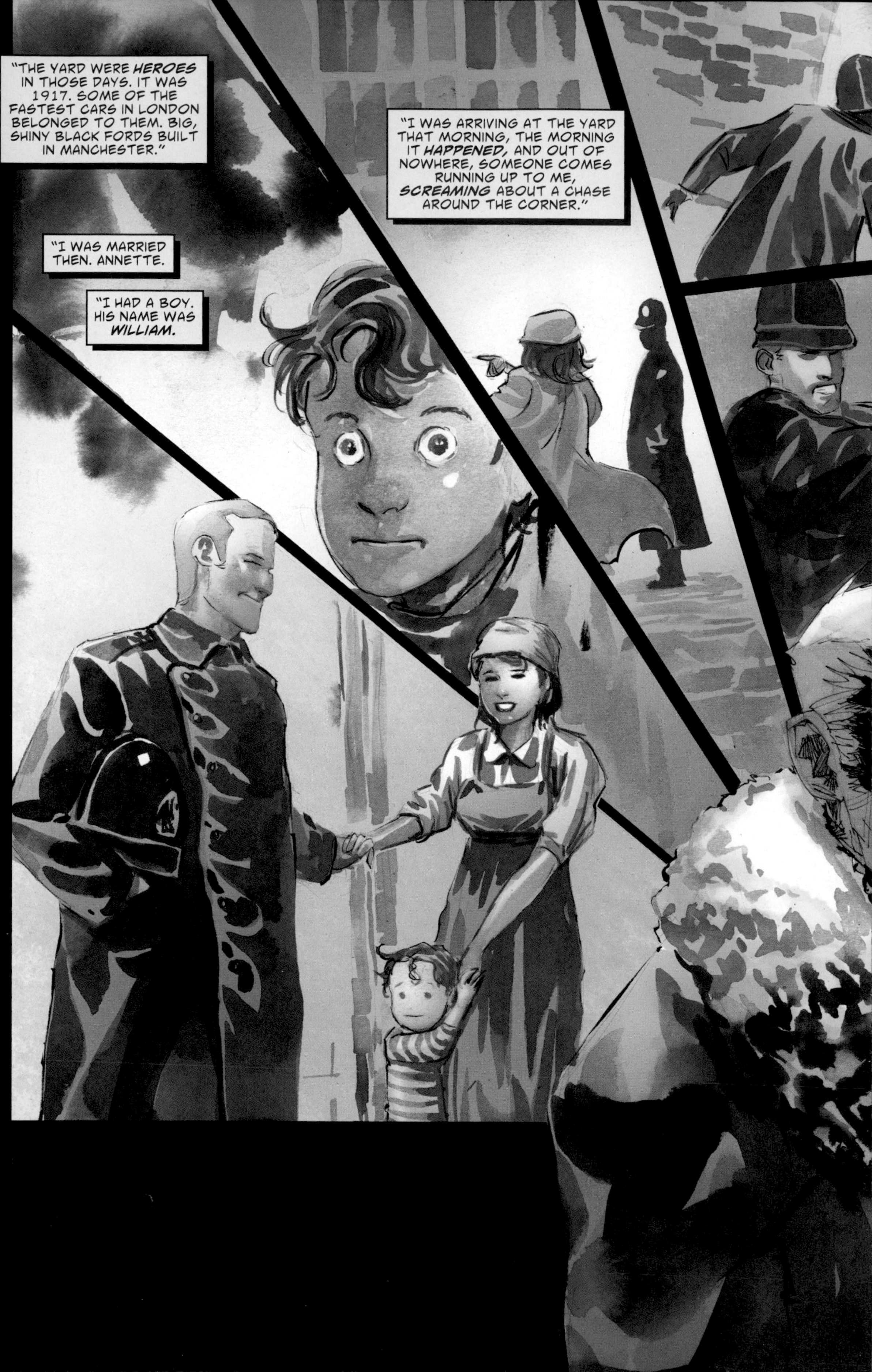
"THE YARD WERE HEROES IN THOSE DAYS. IT WAS 1917. SOME OF THE FASTEST CARS IN LONDON BELONGED TO THEM. BIG, SHINY BLACK FORDS BUILT IN MANCHESTER."
"I WAS MARRIED THEN. ANNETTE.
"I HAD A BOY. HIS NAME WAS WILLIAM.
"I WAS ARRIVING AT THE YARD THAT MORNING, THE MORNING IT HAPPENED, AND OUT OF NOWHERE, SOMEONE COMES RUNNING UP TO ME, SCREAMING ABOUT A CHASE AROUND THE CORNER."

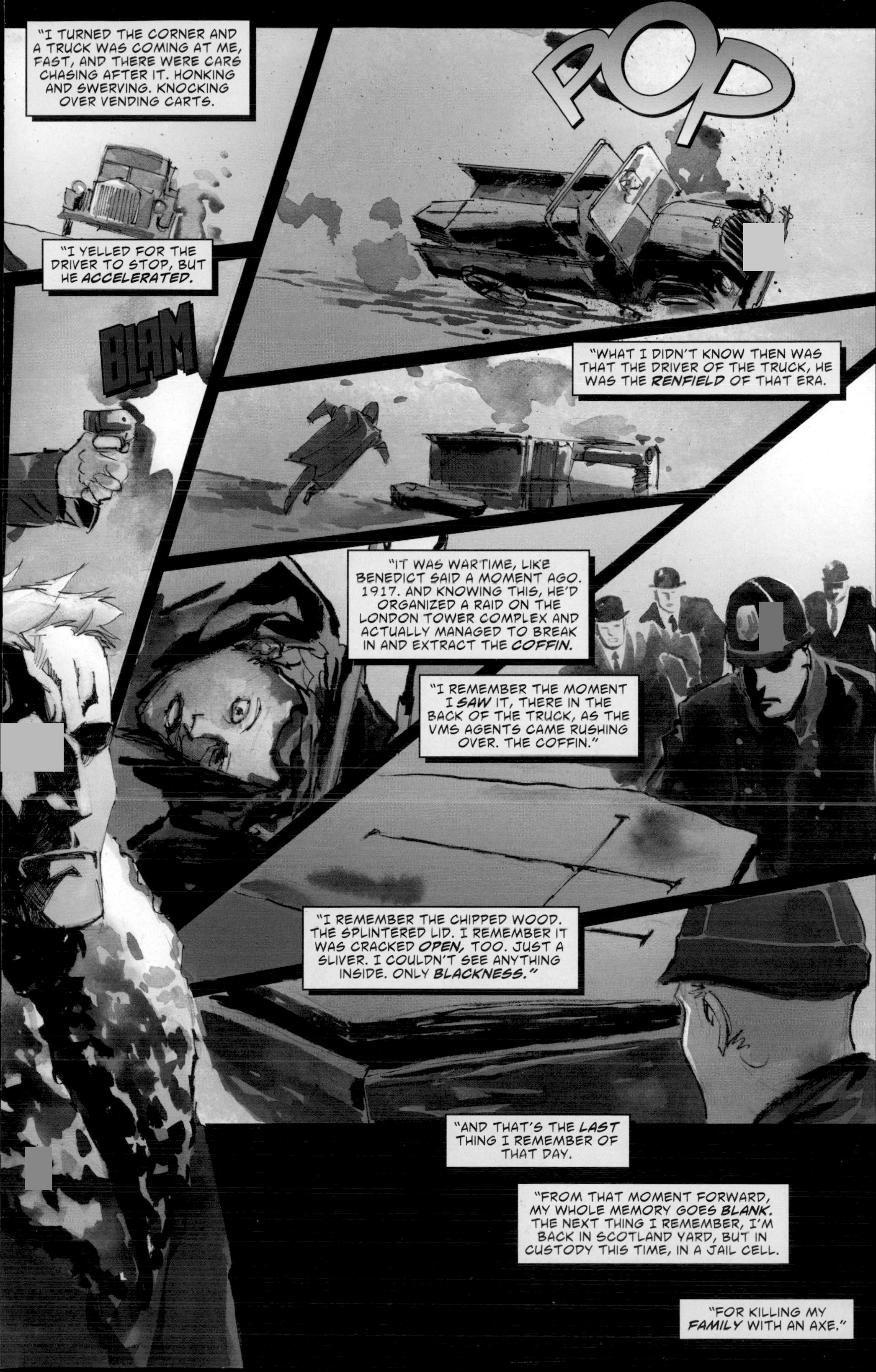
"I TURNED THE CORNER AND A TRUCK WAS COMING AT ME, FAST, AND THERE WERE CARS CHASING AFTER IT. HONKING AND SWERVING. KNOCKING OVER VENDING CARTS.
POP
"I YELLED FOR THE DRIVER TO STOP, BUT HE ACCELERATED.
BLAM
"WHAT I DIDN'T KNOW THEN WAS THAT THE DRIVER OF THE TRUCK, HE WAS THE RENFIELD OF THAT ERA.
"IT WAS WARTIME, LIKE BENEDICT SAID A MOMENT AGO. 1917. AND KNOWING THIS, HE'D ORGANIZED A RAID ON THE LONDON TOWER COMPLEX AND ACTUALLY MANAGED TO BREAK IN AND EXTRACT THE COFFIN.
"I REMEMBER THE MOMENT I SAW IT, THERE IN THE BACK OF THE TRUCK, AS THE VMS AGENTS CAME RUSHING OVER. THE COFFIN."
"I REMEMBER THE CHIPPED WOOD. THE SPLINTERED LID. I REMEMBER IT WAS CRACKED OPEN, TOO. JUST A SLIVER. I COULDN'T SEE ANYTHING INSIDE. ONLY BLACKNESS."
"AND THAT'S THE LAST THING I REMEMBER OF THAT DAY.
"FROM THAT MOMENT FORWARD, MY WHOLE MEMORY GOES BLANK. THE NEXT THING I REMEMBER, I'M BACK IN SCOTLAND YARD, BUT IN CUSTODY THIS TIME, IN A JAIL CELL.
"FOR KILLING MY FAMILY WITH AN AXE."

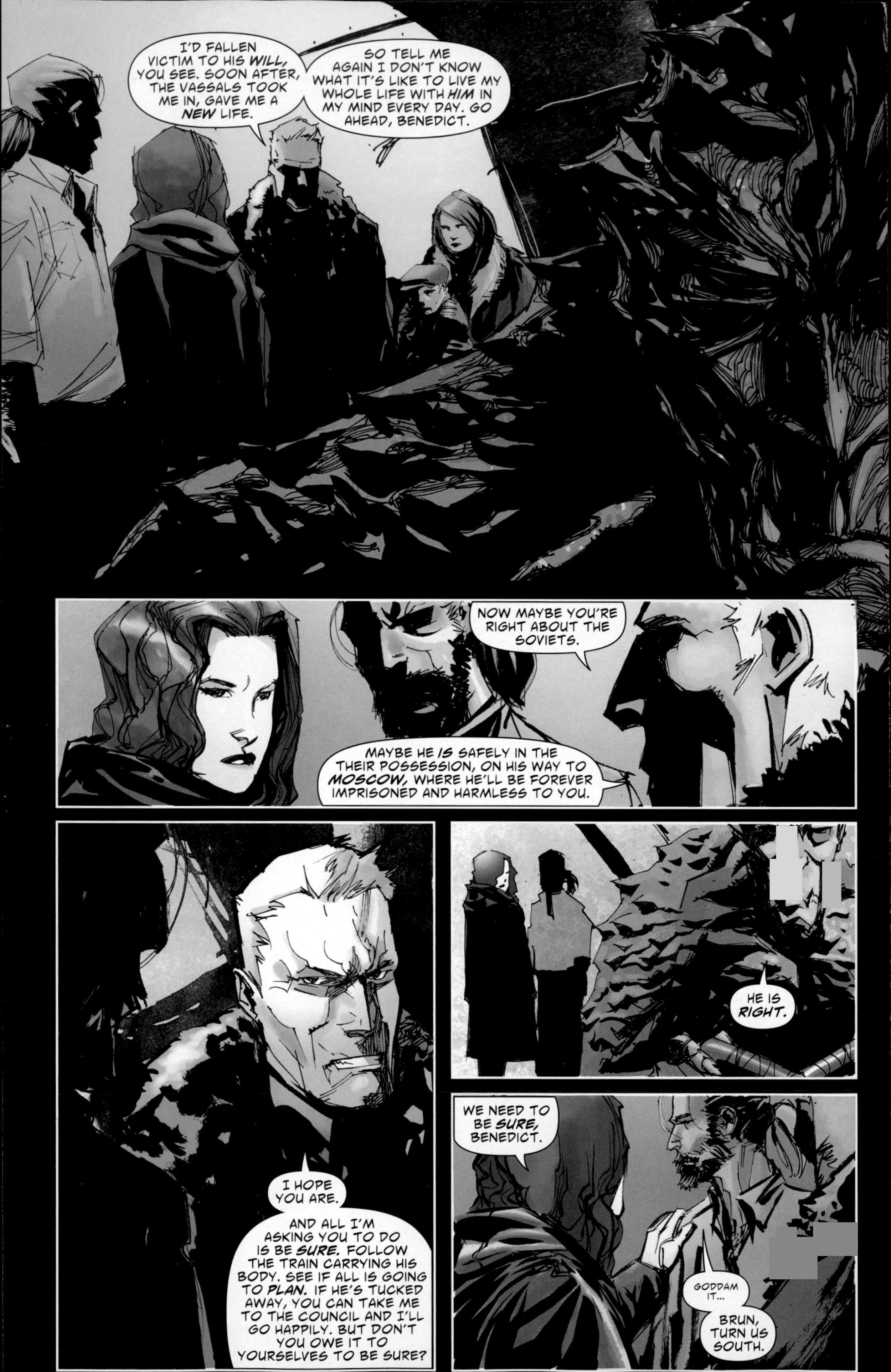

I'D FALLEN VICTIM TO HIS WILL, YOU SEE. SOON AFTER, THE VASSALS TOOK ME IN, GAVE ME A NEW LIFE.
SO TELL ME AGAIN I DON'T KNOW WHAT IT'S LIKE TO LIVE MY WHOLE LIFE WITH HIM IN MY MIND EVERY DAY. GO AHEAD, BENEDICT.
NOW MAYBE YOU'RE RIGHT ABOUT THE SOVIETS.
MAYBE HE IS SAFELY IN THE THEIR POSSESSION, ON HIS WAY TO MOSCOW, WHERE HE'LL BE FOREVER IMPRISONED AND HARMLESS TO YOU.
HE IS RIGHT.
I HOPE YOU ARE.
AND ALL I'M ASKING YOU TO DO IS BE SURE. FOLLOW THE TRAIN CARRYING HIS BODY. SEE IF ALL IS GOING TO PLAN. IF HE'S TUCKED AWAY, YOU CAN TAKE ME TO THE COUNCIL AND I'LL GO HAPPILY. BUT DON'T YOU OWE IT TO YOURSELVES TO BE SURE?
WE NEED TO BE SURE, BENEDICT.
GODDAM IT...
BRUN, TURN US SOUTH.

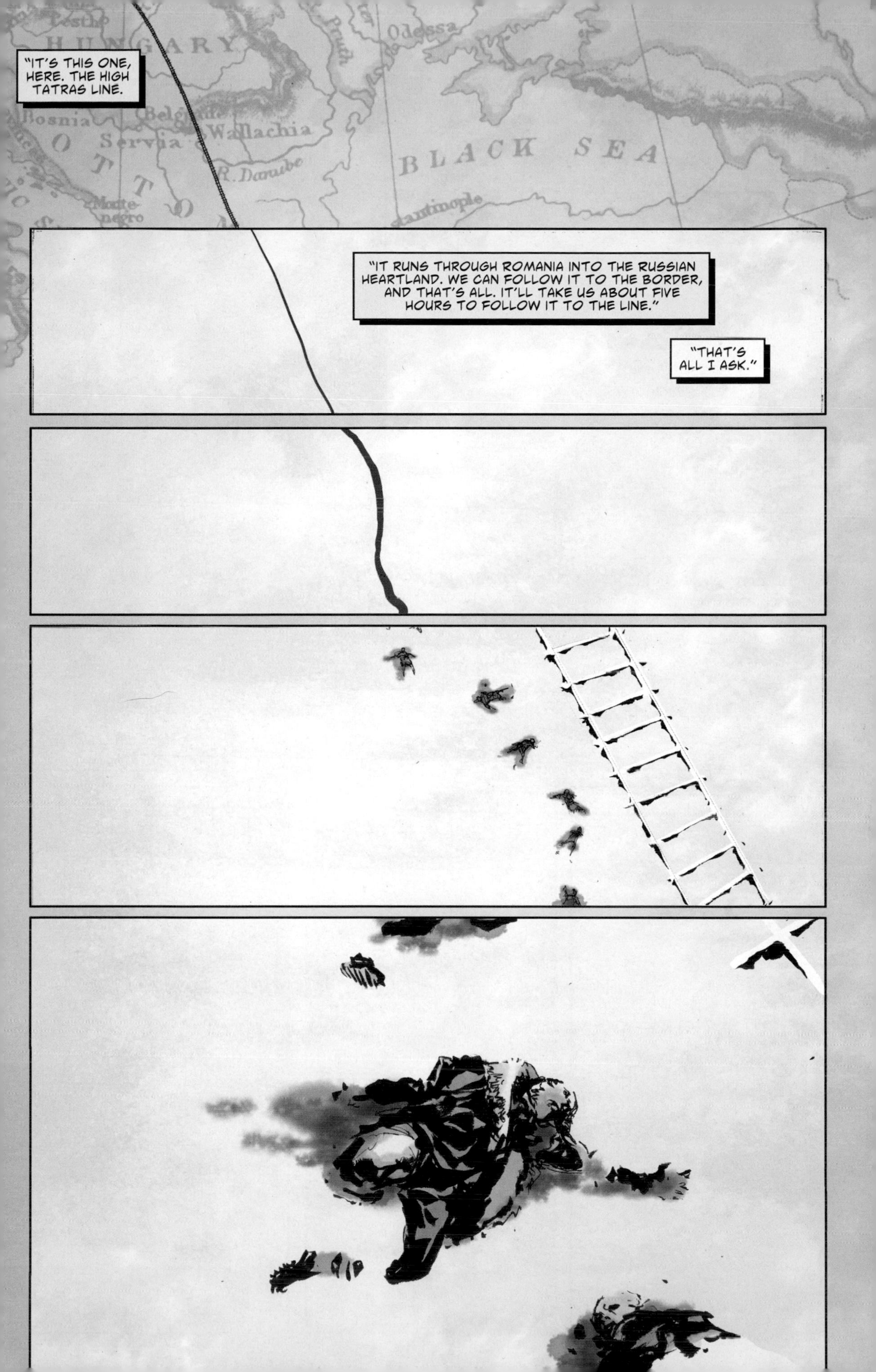
"IT'S THIS ONE, HERE. THE HIGH TATRAS LINE.
HUNGARY
Odessa
Bosnia
Servia
Wallachia
BLACK SEA
R. Danube
"IT RUNS THROUGH ROMANIA INTO THE RUSSIAN HEARTLAND. WE CAN FOLLOW IT TO THE BORDER, AND THAT'S ALL. IT'LL TAKE US ABOUT FIVE HOURS TO FOLLOW IT TO THE LINE."
"THAT'S ALL I ASK."

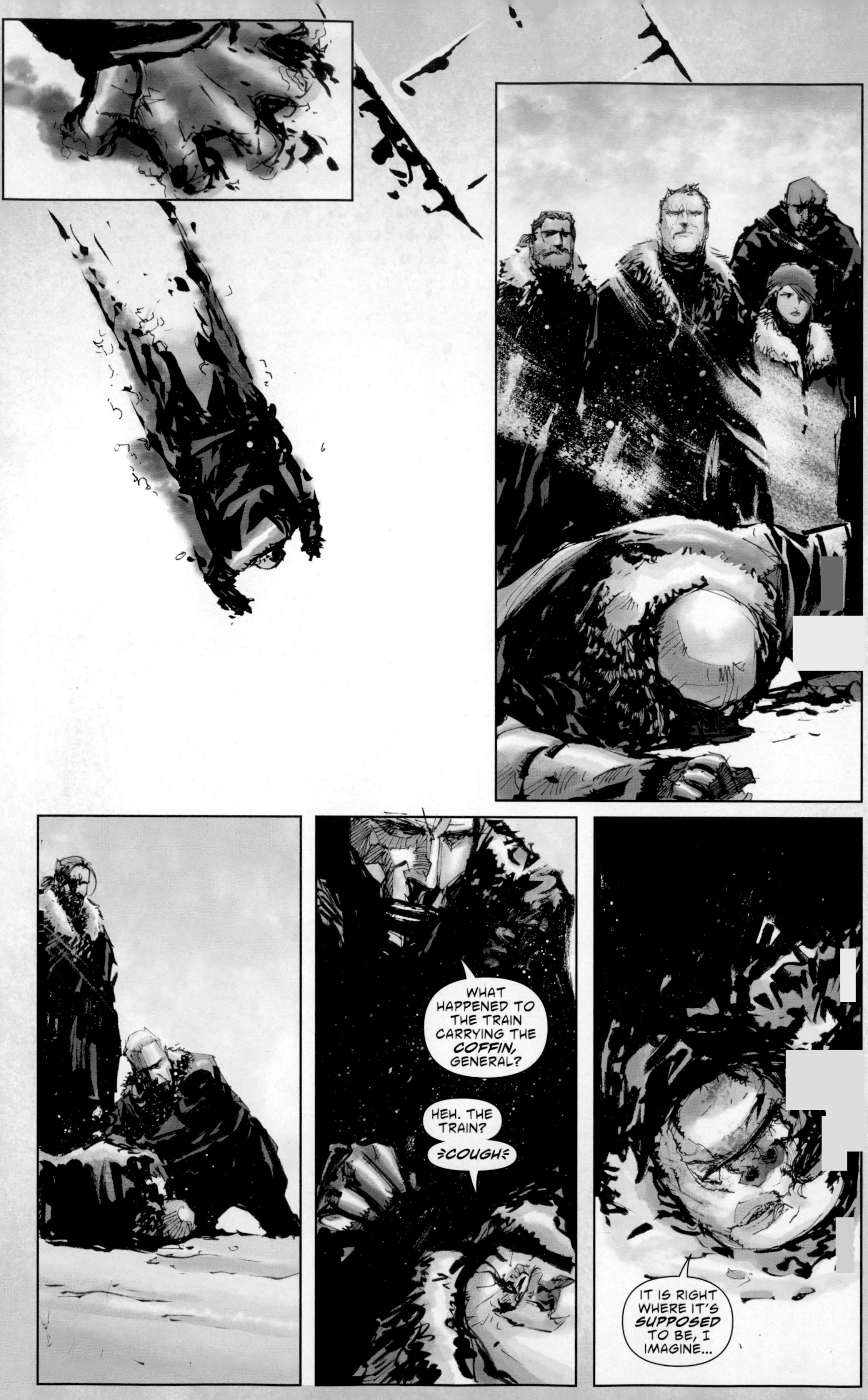
WHAT HAPPENED TO THE TRAIN CARRYING THE COFFIN, GENERAL?
HEH. THE TRAIN?
COUGH
IT IS RIGHT WHERE IT'S SUPPOSED TO BE, I IMAGINE...

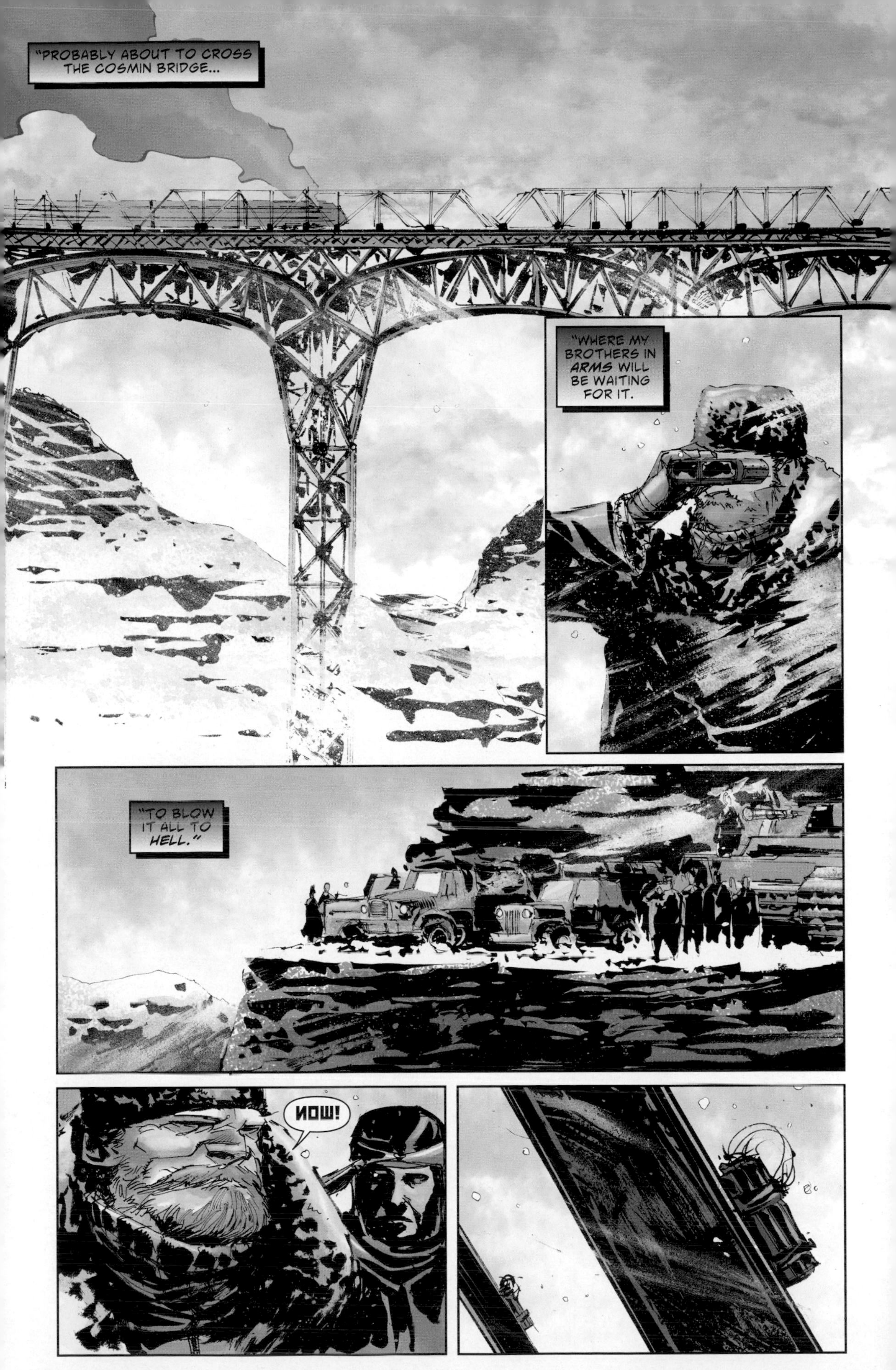
"PROBABLY ABOUT TO CROSS THE COSMIN BRIDGE...
"WHERE MY BROTHERS IN ARMS WILL BE WAITING FOR IT.
"TO BLOW IT ALL TO HELL."
NOW!

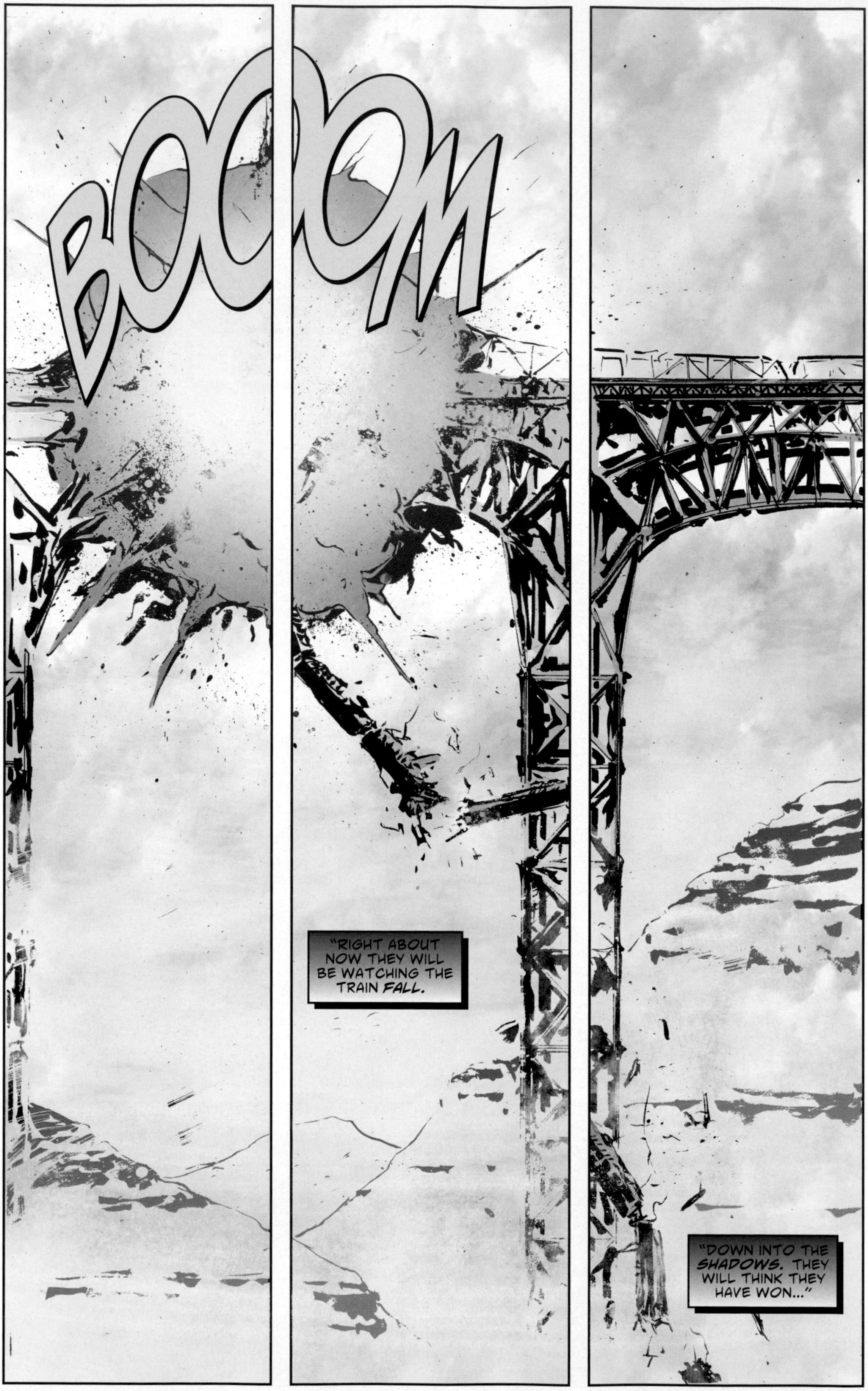
BOOOM
"RIGHT ABOUT NOW THEY WILL BE WATCHING THE TRAIN FALL.
"DOWN INTO THE SHADOWS. THEY WILL THINK THEY HAVE WON..."

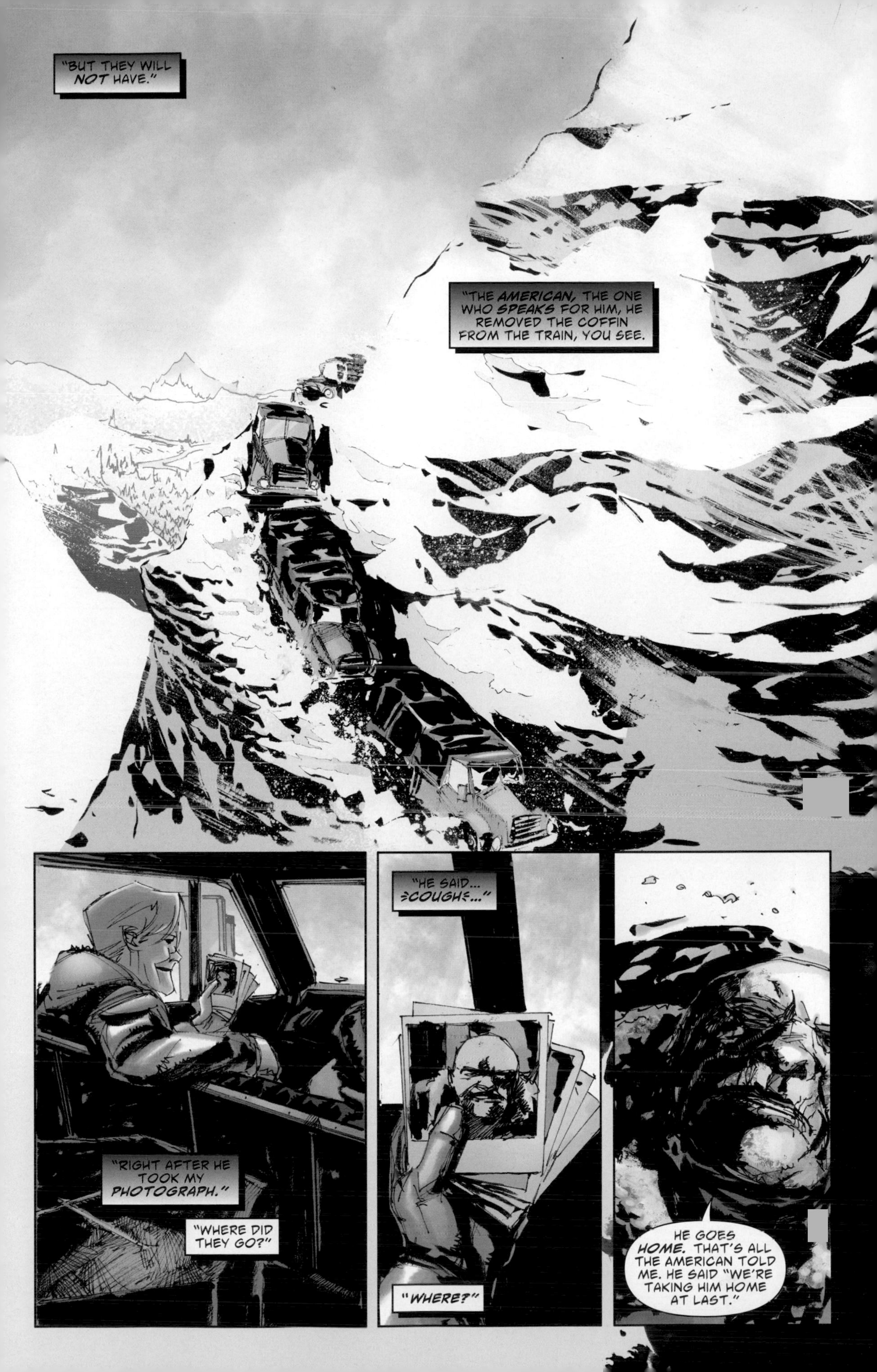
"BUT THEY WILL NOT HAVE."
"THE AMERICAN, THE ONE WHO SPEAKS FOR HIM, HE REMOVED THE COFFIN FROM THE TRAIN, YOU SEE.
"RIGHT AFTER HE TOOK MY PHOTOGRAPH."
"WHERE DID THEY GO?"
"HE SAID... *COUGH*..."
"WHERE?"
HE GOES HOME. THAT'S ALL THE AMERICAN TOLD ME. HE SAID "WE'RE TAKING HIM HOME AT LAST."

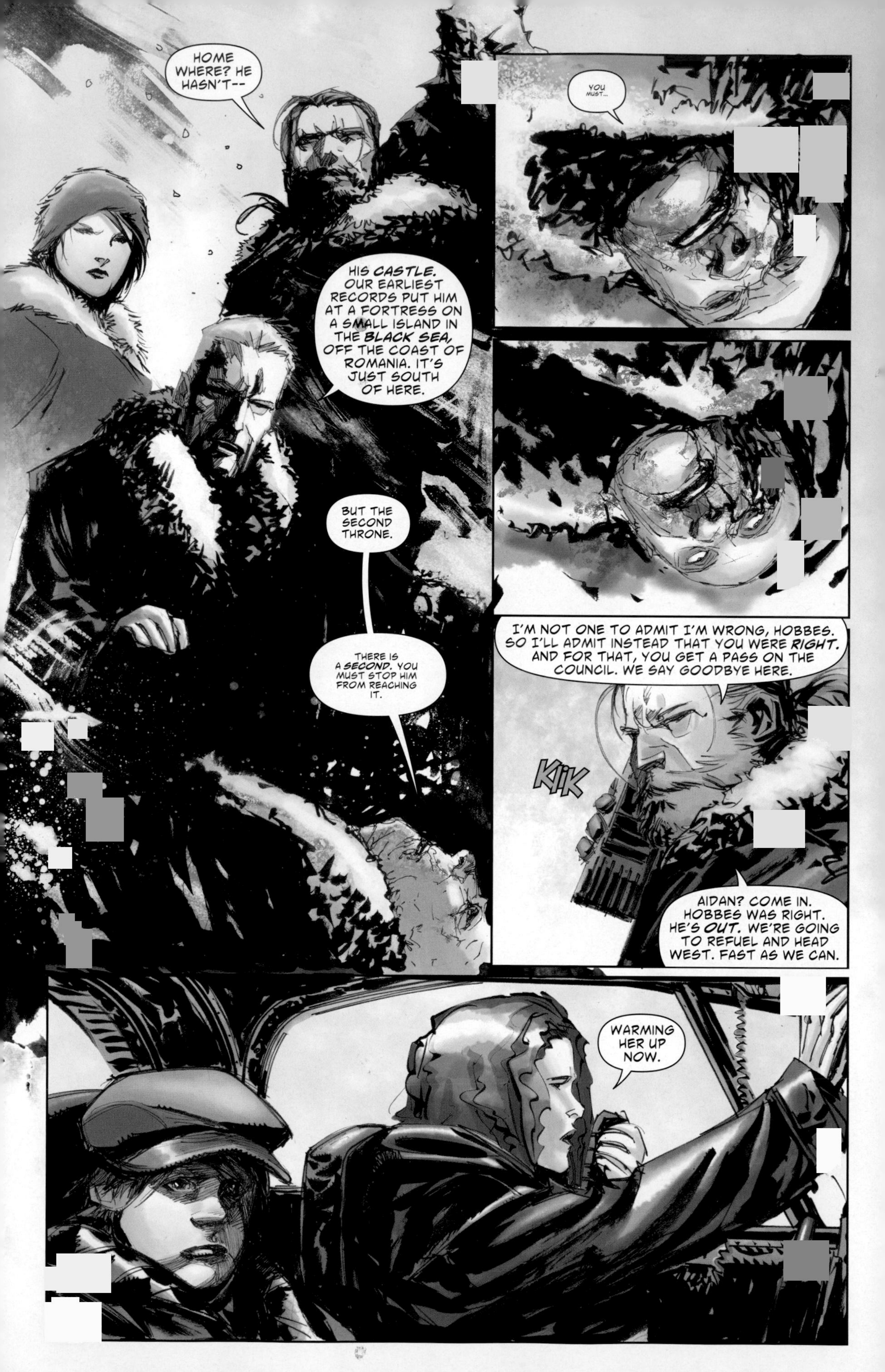
HOME WHERE? HE HASN'T--
HIS CASTLE. OUR EARLIEST RECORDS PUT HIM AT A FORTRESS ON A SMALL ISLAND IN THE BLACK SEA, OFF THE COAST OF ROMANIA. IT'S JUST SOUTH OF HERE.
BUT THE SECOND THRONE.
THERE IS A SECOND. YOU MUST STOP HIM FROM REACHING IT.
YOU MUST...
I'M NOT ONE TO ADMIT I'M WRONG, HOBBES. SO I'LL ADMIT INSTEAD THAT YOU WERE RIGHT. AND FOR THAT, YOU GET A PASS ON THE COUNCIL. WE SAY GOODBYE HERE.
KLIK
AIDAN? COME IN. HOBBES WAS RIGHT. HE'S OUT. WE'RE GOING TO REFUEL AND HEAD WEST. FAST AS WE CAN.
WARMING HER UP NOW.

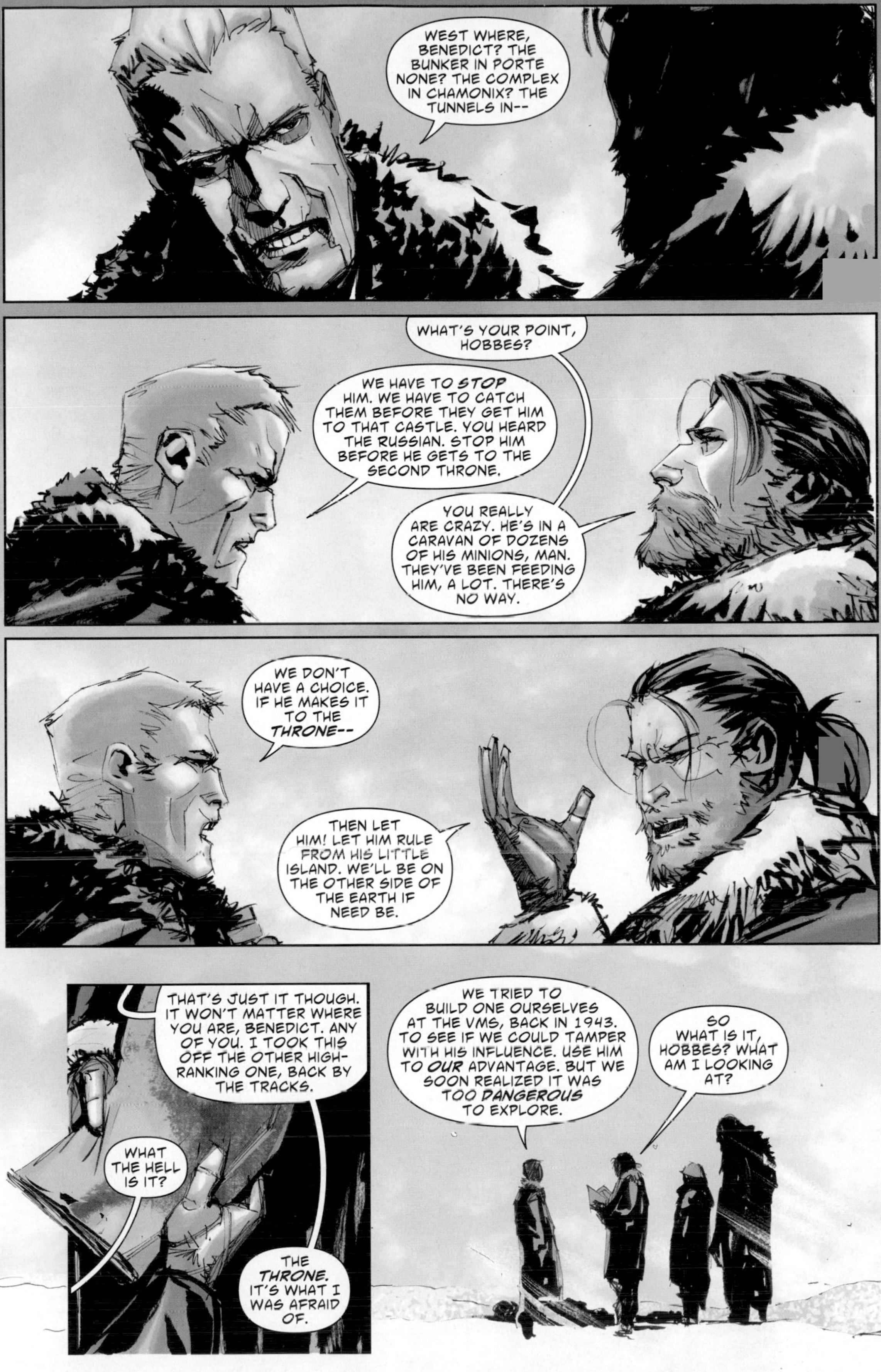
WEST WHERE, BENEDICT? THE BUNKER IN PORTE NONE? THE COMPLEX IN CHAMONIX? THE TUNNELS IN--
WHAT'S YOUR POINT, HOBBES?
WE HAVE TO STOP HIM. WE HAVE TO CATCH THEM BEFORE THEY GET HIM TO THAT CASTLE. YOU HEARD THE RUSSIAN. STOP HIM BEFORE HE GETS TO THE SECOND THRONE.
YOU REALLY ARE CRAZY. HE'S IN A CARAVAN OF DOZENS OF HIS MINIONS, MAN. THEY'VE BEEN FEEDING HIM, A LOT. THERE'S NO WAY.
WE DON'T HAVE A CHOICE. IF HE MAKES IT TO THE THRONE--
THEN LET HIM! LET HIM RULE FROM HIS LITTLE ISLAND. WE'LL BE ON THE OTHER SIDE OF THE EARTH IF NEED BE.
THAT'S JUST IT THOUGH. IT WON'T MATTER WHERE YOU ARE, BENEDICT. ANY OF YOU. I TOOK THIS OFF THE OTHER HIGH-RANKING ONE, BACK BY THE TRACKS.
WHAT THE HELL IS IT?
THE THRONE. IT'S WHAT I WAS AFRAID OF.
WE TRIED TO BUILD ONE OURSELVES AT THE VMS, BACK IN 1943. TO SEE IF WE COULD TAMPER WITH HIS INFLUENCE. USE HIM TO OUR ADVANTAGE. BUT WE SOON REALIZED IT WAS TOO DANGEROUS TO EXPLORE.
SO WHAT IS IT, HOBBES? WHAT AM I LOOKING AT?

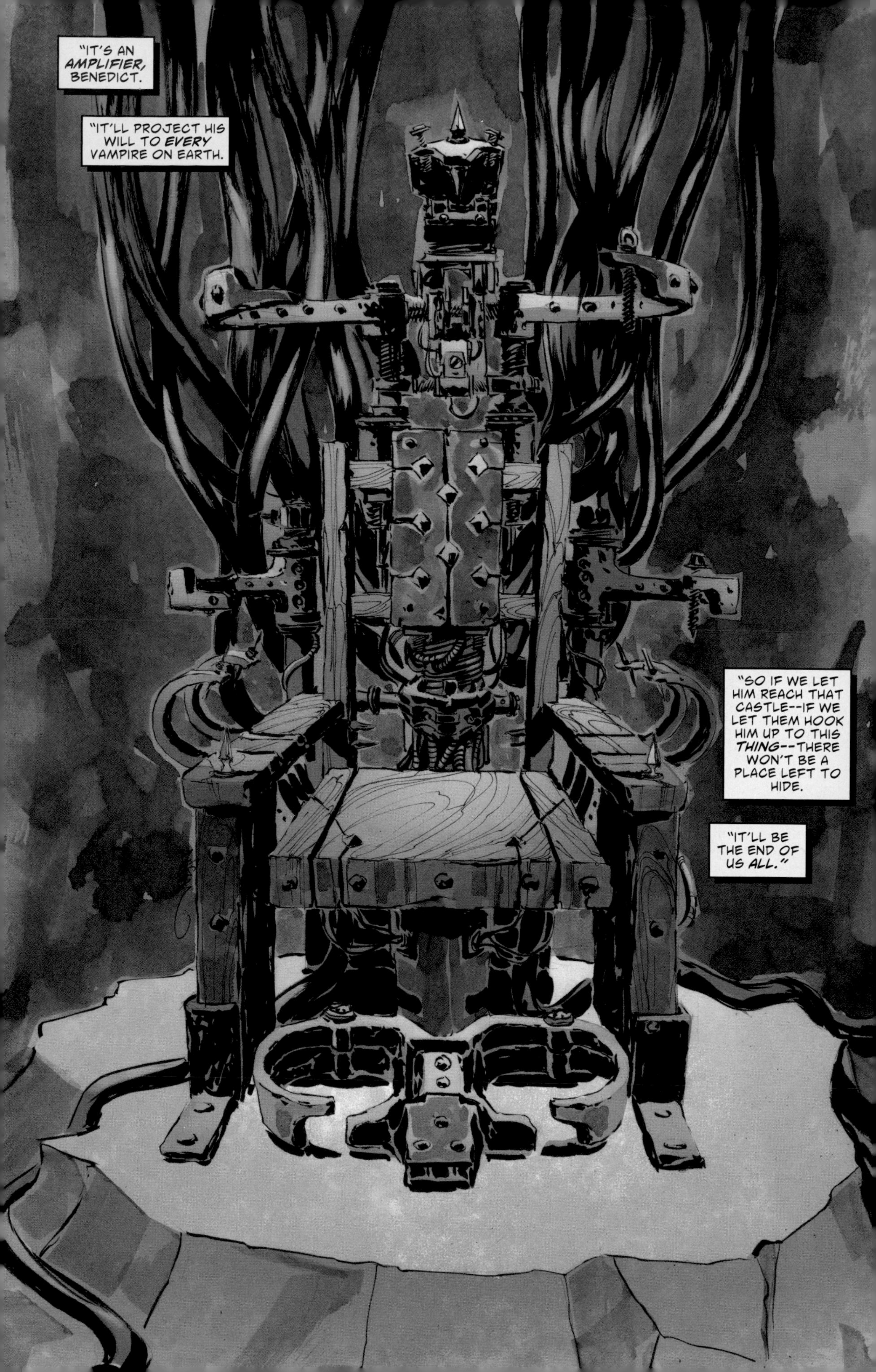
"IT'S AN AMPLIFIER, BENEDICT.
"IT'LL PROJECT HIS WILL TO EVERY VAMPIRE ON EARTH.
"SO IF WE LET HIM REACH THAT CASTLE--IF WE LET THEM HOOK HIM UP TO THIS THING--THERE WON'T BE A PLACE LEFT TO HIDE.
"IT'LL BE THE END OF US ALL."

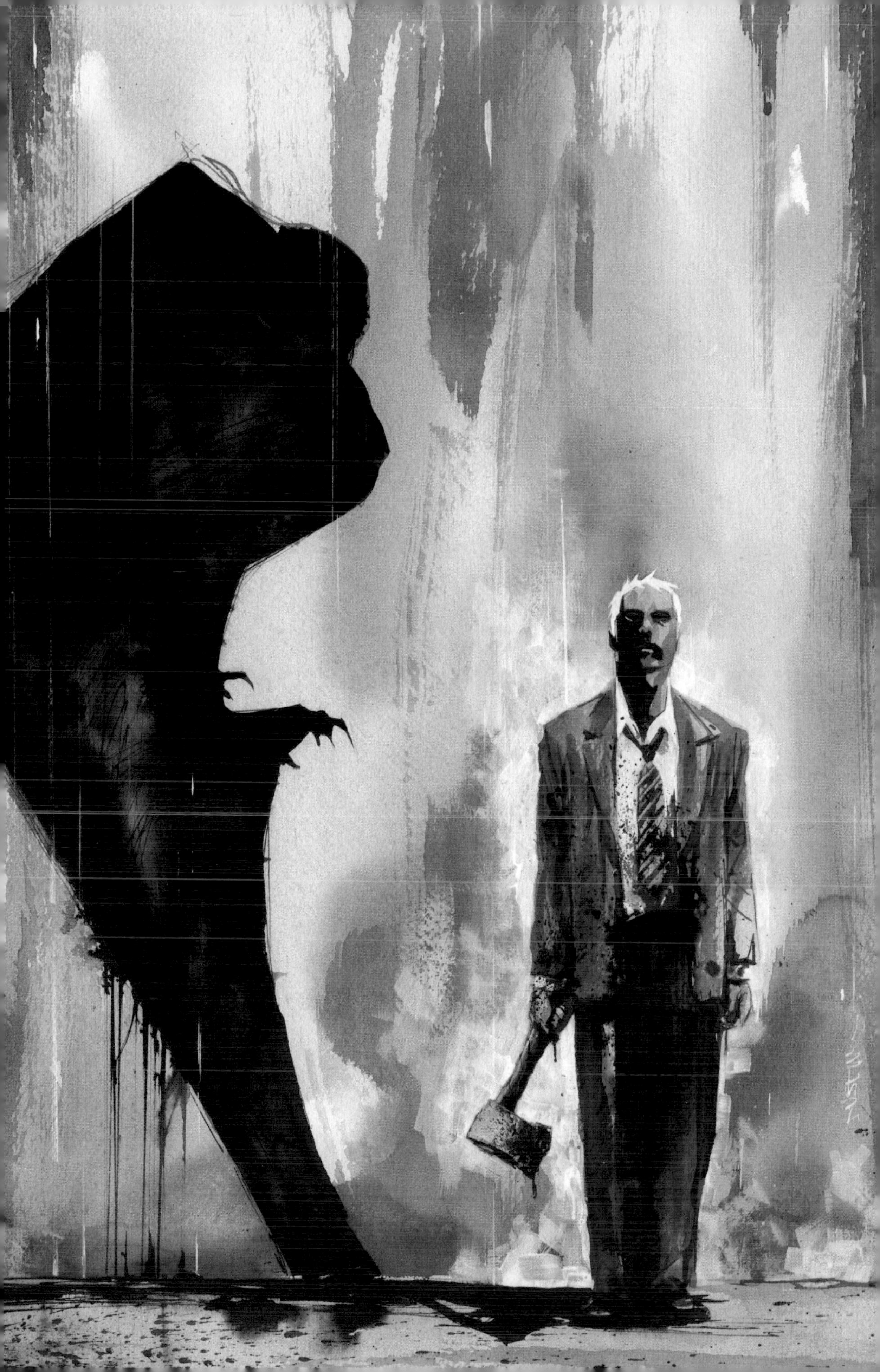

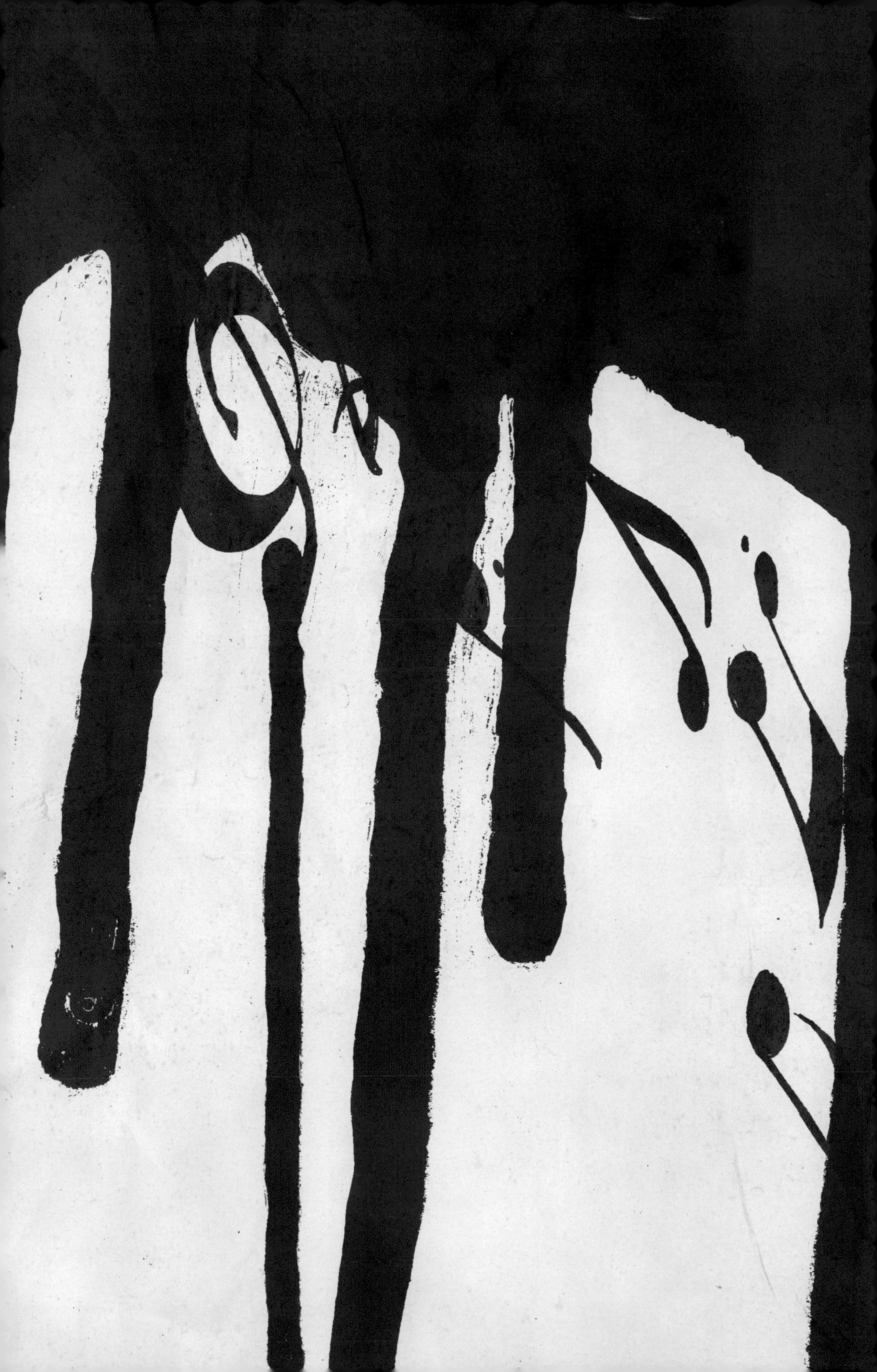

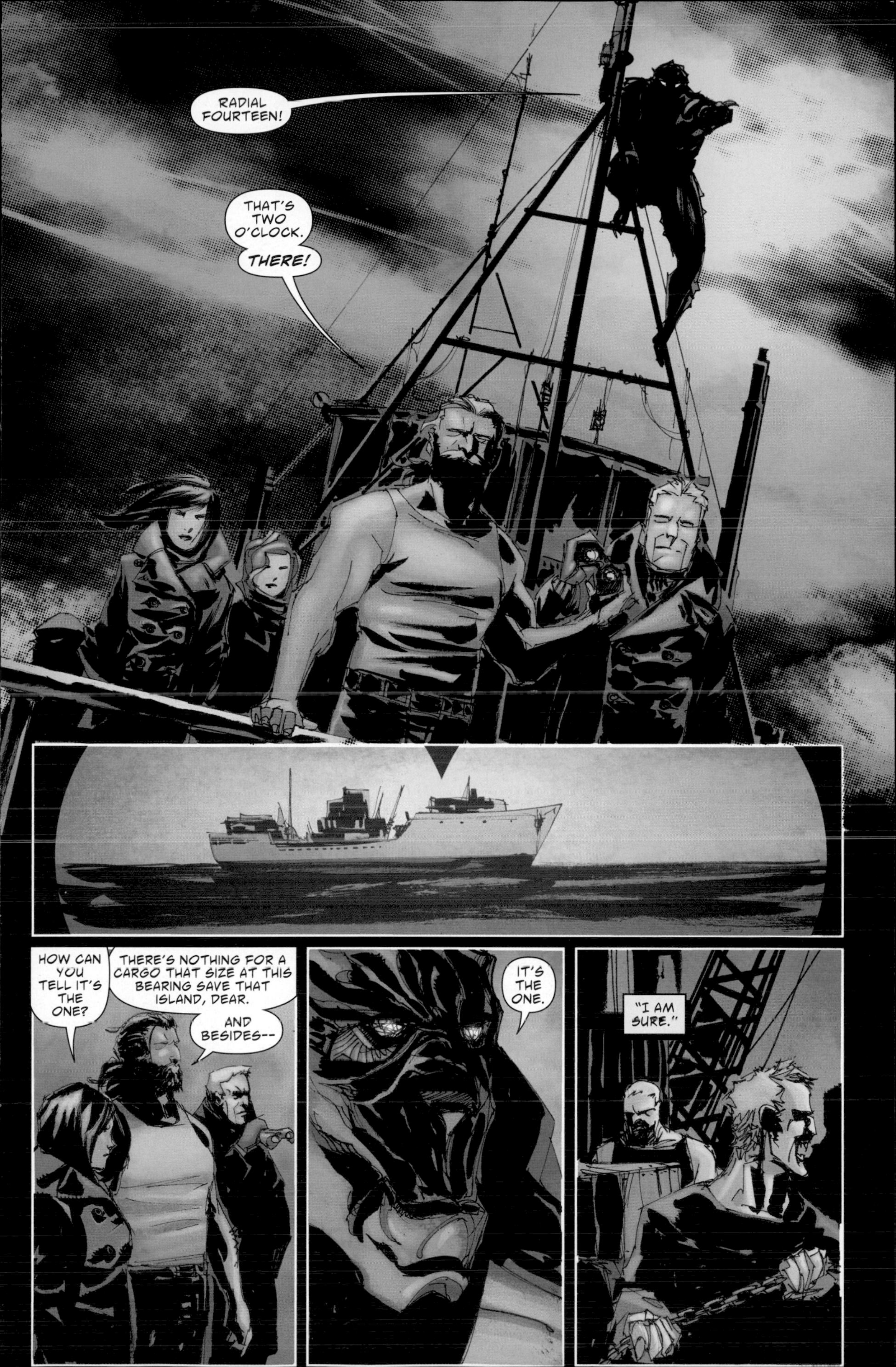
RADIAL FOURTEEN!
THAT'S TWO O'CLOCK.
THERE!
HOW CAN YOU TELL IT'S THE ONE?
THERE'S NOTHING FOR A CARGO THAT SIZE AT THIS BEARING SAVE THAT ISLAND, DEAR.
AND BESIDES--
IT'S THE ONE.
"I AM SURE."

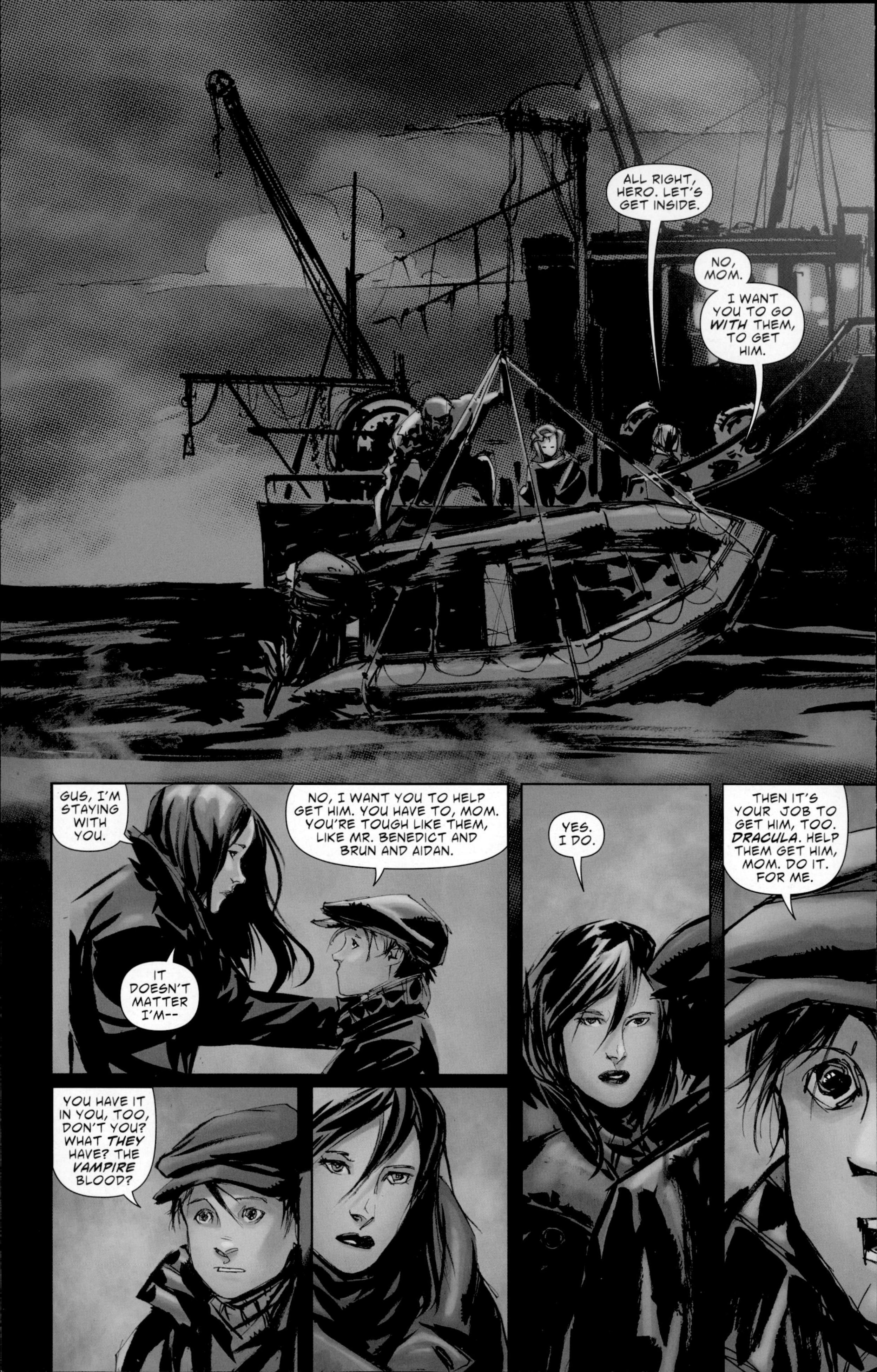
ALL RIGHT, HERO. LET'S GET INSIDE.
NO, MOM.
I WANT YOU TO GO WITH THEM, TO GET HIM.
GUS, I'M STAYING WITH YOU.
NO, I WANT YOU TO HELP GET HIM. YOU HAVE TO, MOM. YOU'RE TOUGH LIKE THEM, LIKE MR. BENEDICT AND BRUN AND AIDAN.
IT DOESN'T MATTER I'M--
YOU HAVE IT IN YOU, TOO, DON'T YOU? WHAT THEY HAVE? THE VAMPIRE BLOOD?
YES. I DO.
THEN IT'S YOUR JOB TO GET HIM, TOO. DRACULA. HELP THEM GET HIM, MOM. DO IT. FOR ME.

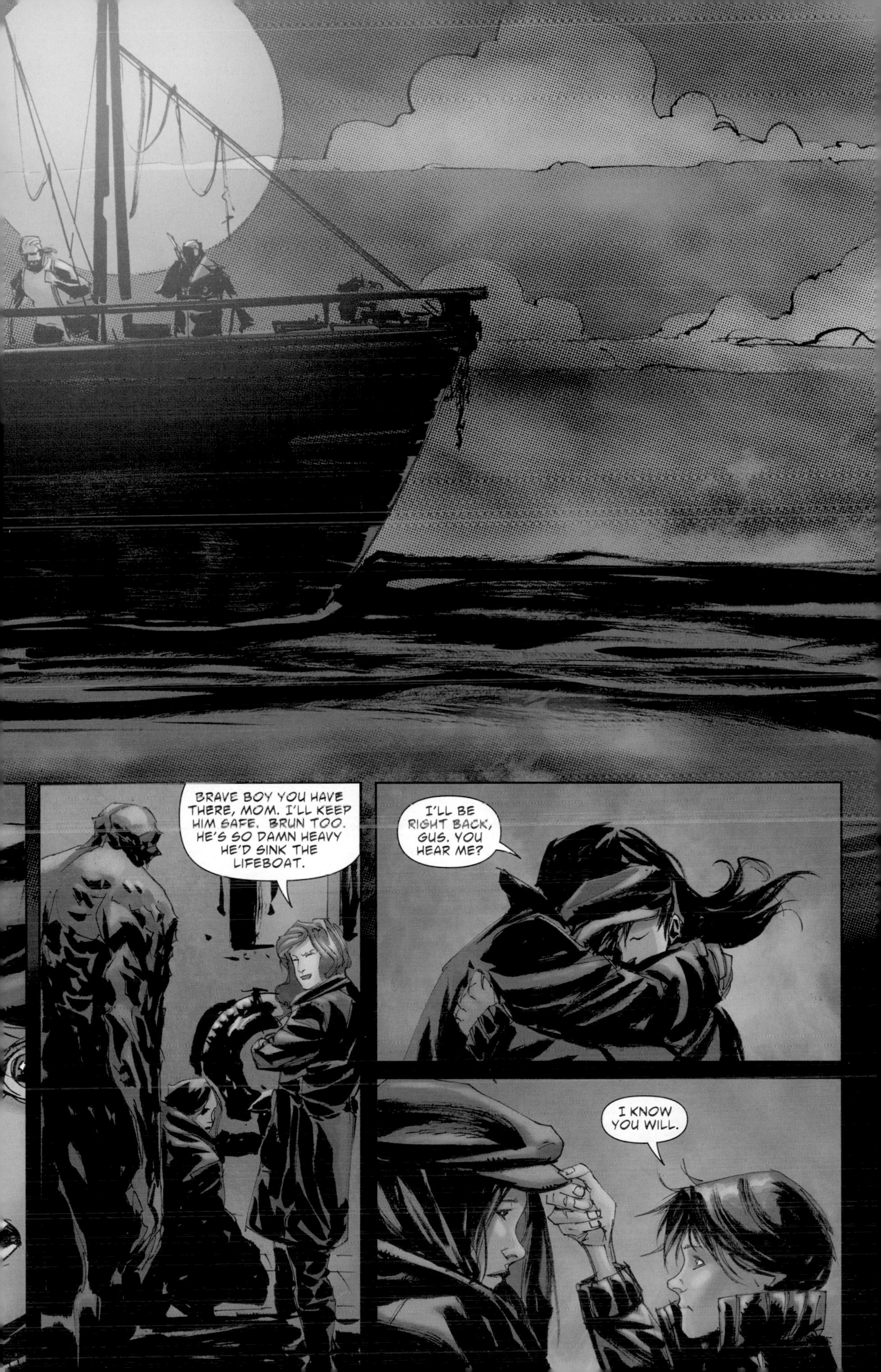
BRAVE BOY YOU HAVE THERE, MOM. I'LL KEEP HIM SAFE. BRUN TOO. HE'S SO DAMN HEAVY HE'D SINK THE LIFEBOAT.
I'LL BE RIGHT BACK, GUS. YOU HEAR ME?
I KNOW YOU WILL.

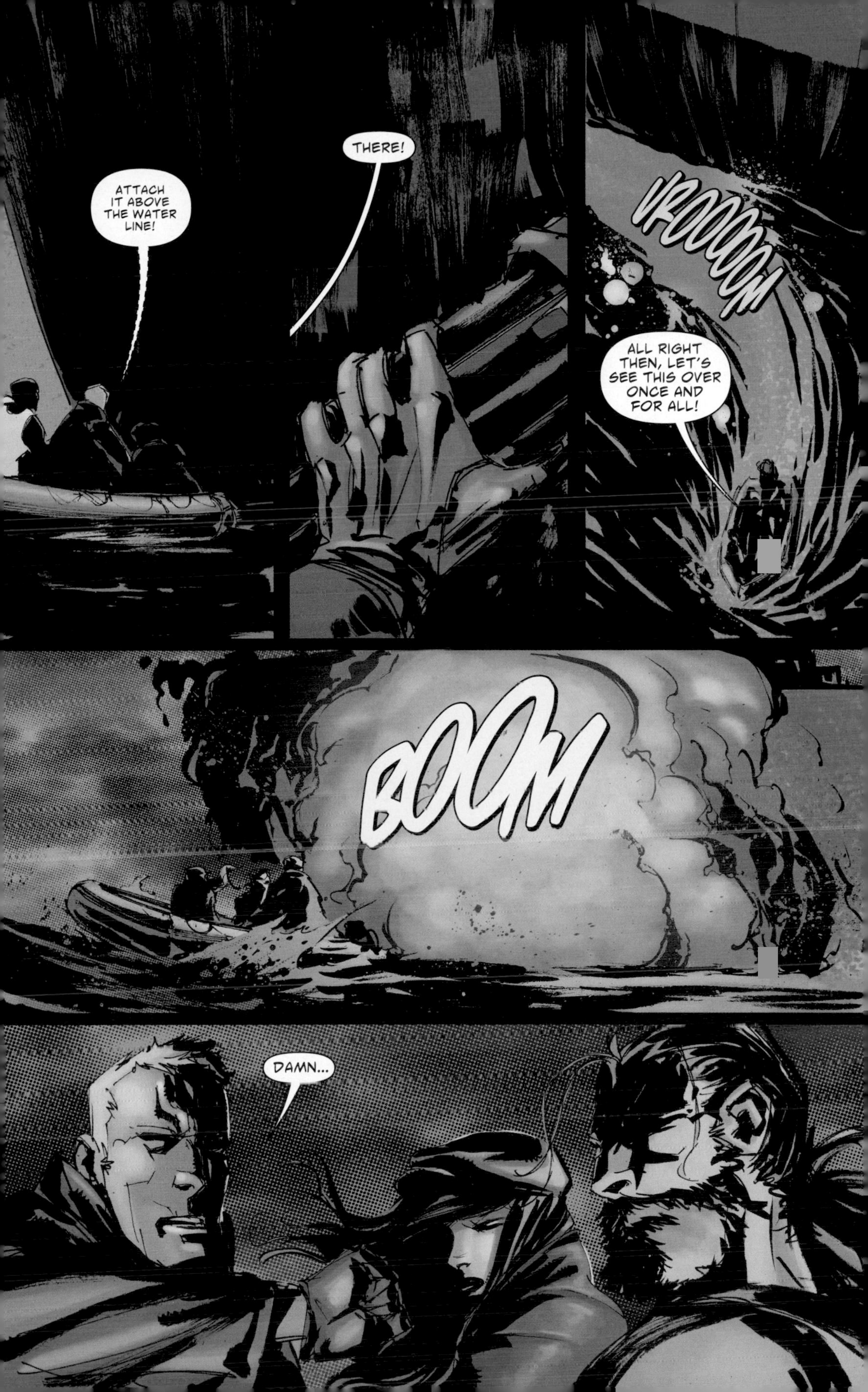
ATTACH IT ABOVE THE WATER LINE!
THERE!
VROOOOOM
ALL RIGHT THEN, LET'S SEE THIS OVER ONCE AND FOR ALL!
BOOM
DAMN...

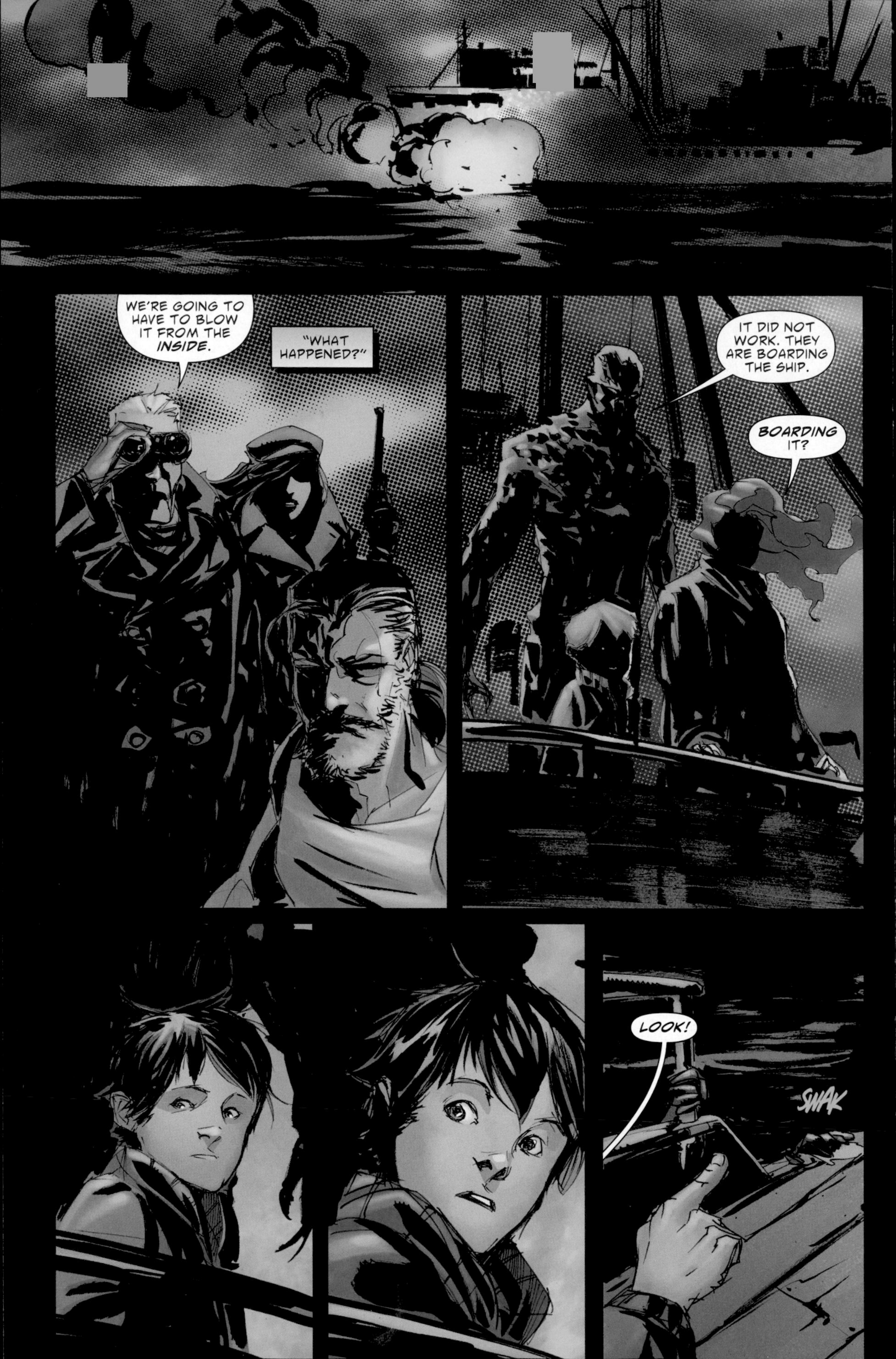
WE'RE GOING TO HAVE TO BLOW IT FROM THE INSIDE.
"WHAT HAPPENED?"
IT DID NOT WORK. THEY ARE BOARDING THE SHIP.
BOARDING IT?
LOOK!
SWAK

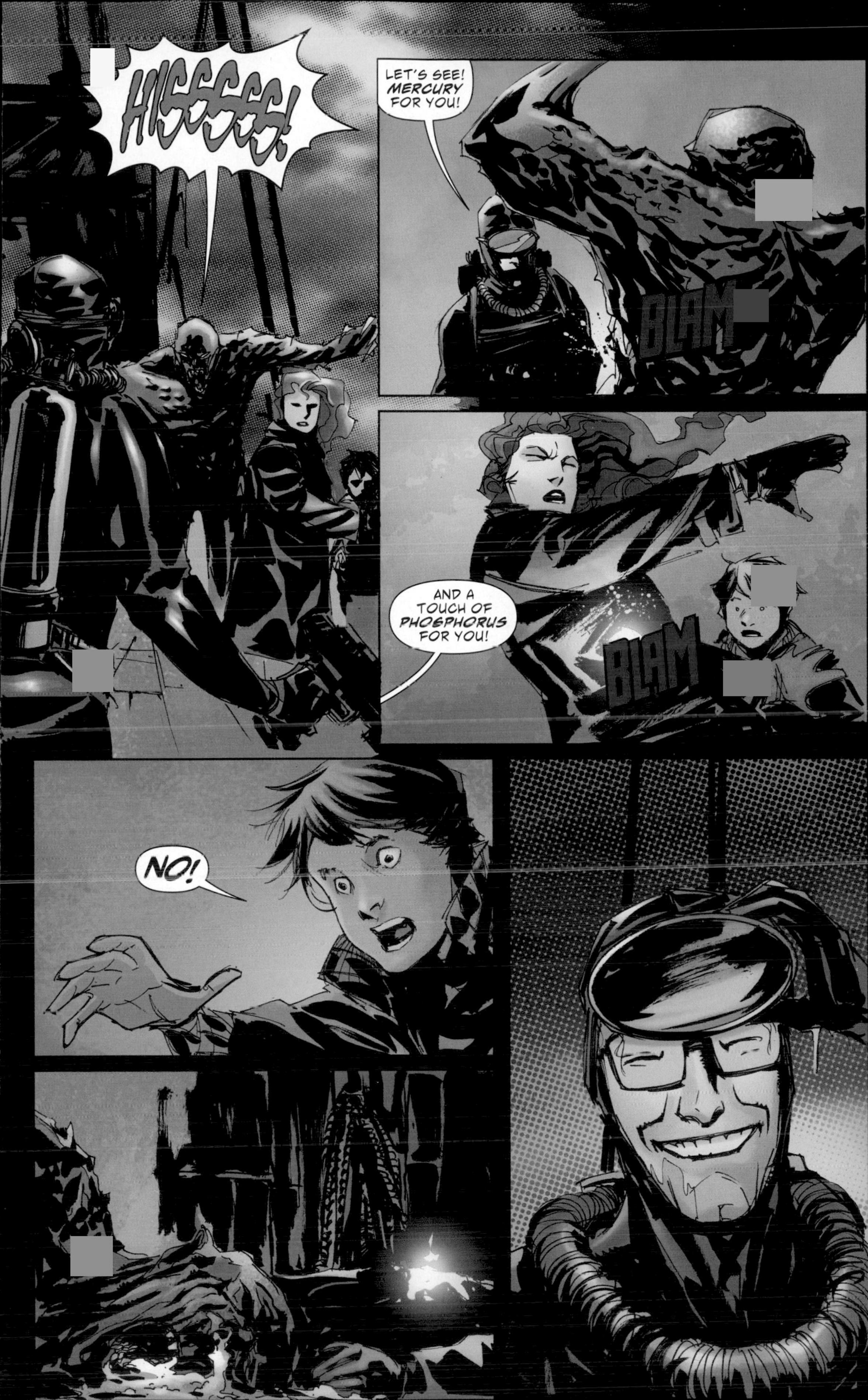
HISSSSS!
LET'S SEE! MERCURY FOR YOU!
BLAM
AND A TOUCH OF PHOSPHORUS FOR YOU!
BLAM
NO!

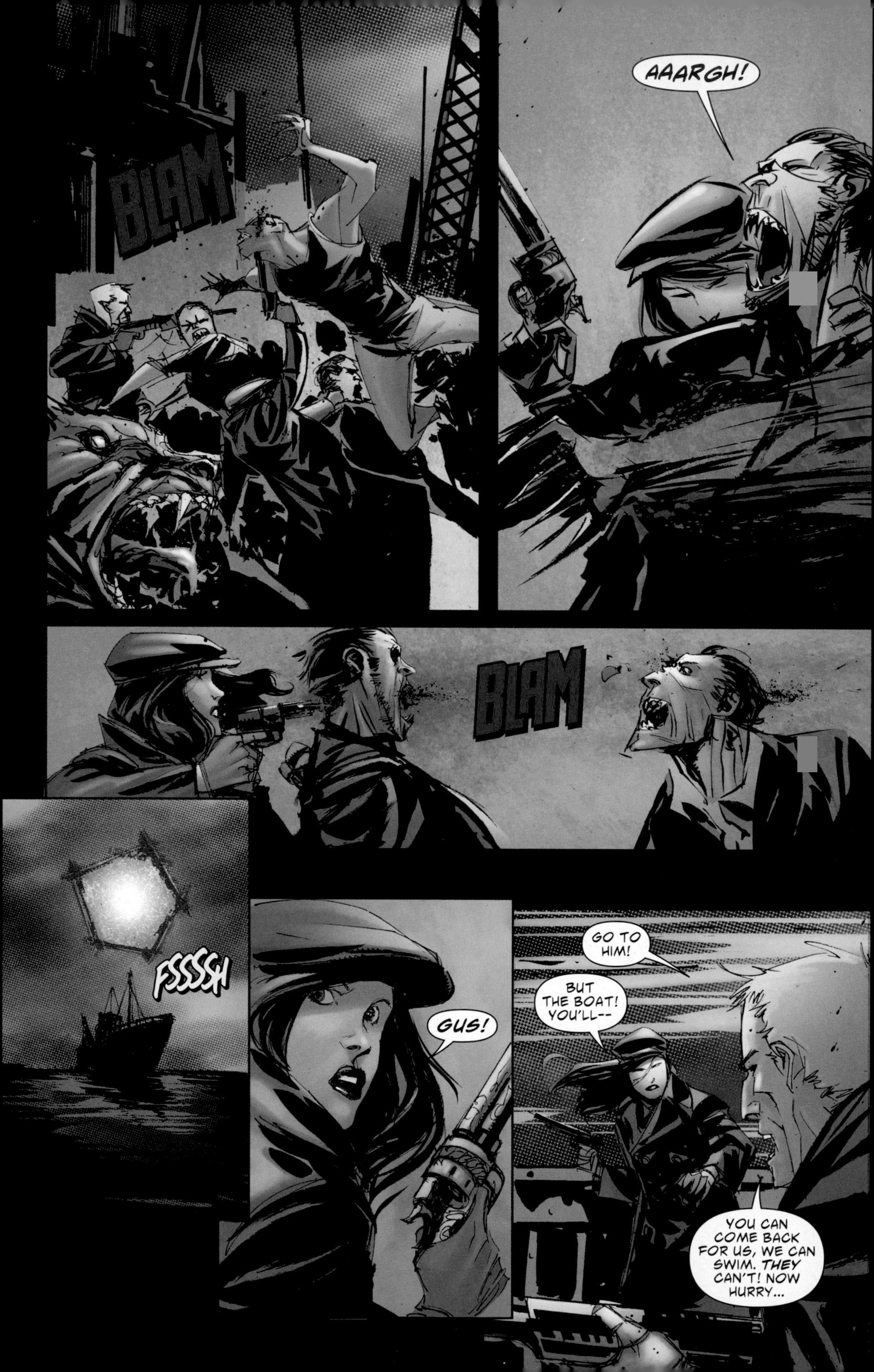
BLAM
AAARGH!
BLAM
FSSSSH
GUS!
GO TO HIM!
BUT THE BOAT! YOU'LL--
YOU CAN COME BACK FOR US, WE CAN SWIM. THEY CAN'T! NOW HURRY...

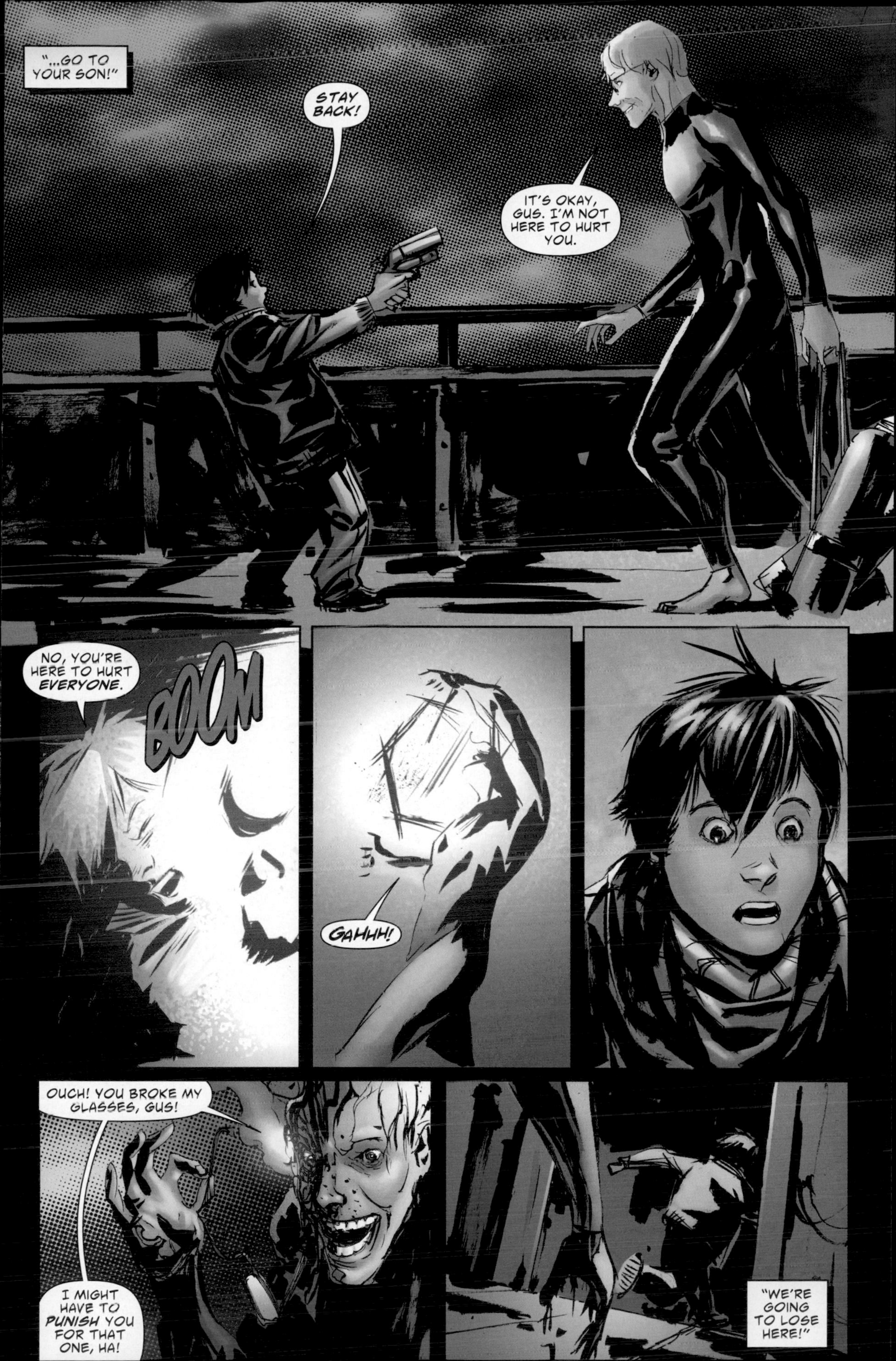
"...GO TO YOUR SON!"
STAY BACK!
IT'S OKAY, GUS. I'M NOT HERE TO HURT YOU.
NO, YOU'RE HERE TO HURT *EVERYONE*.
BOOM
GAHHH!
OUCH! YOU BROKE MY GLASSES, GUS!
I MIGHT HAVE TO *PUNISH* YOU FOR THAT ONE, HA!
"WE'RE GOING TO LOSE HERE!"

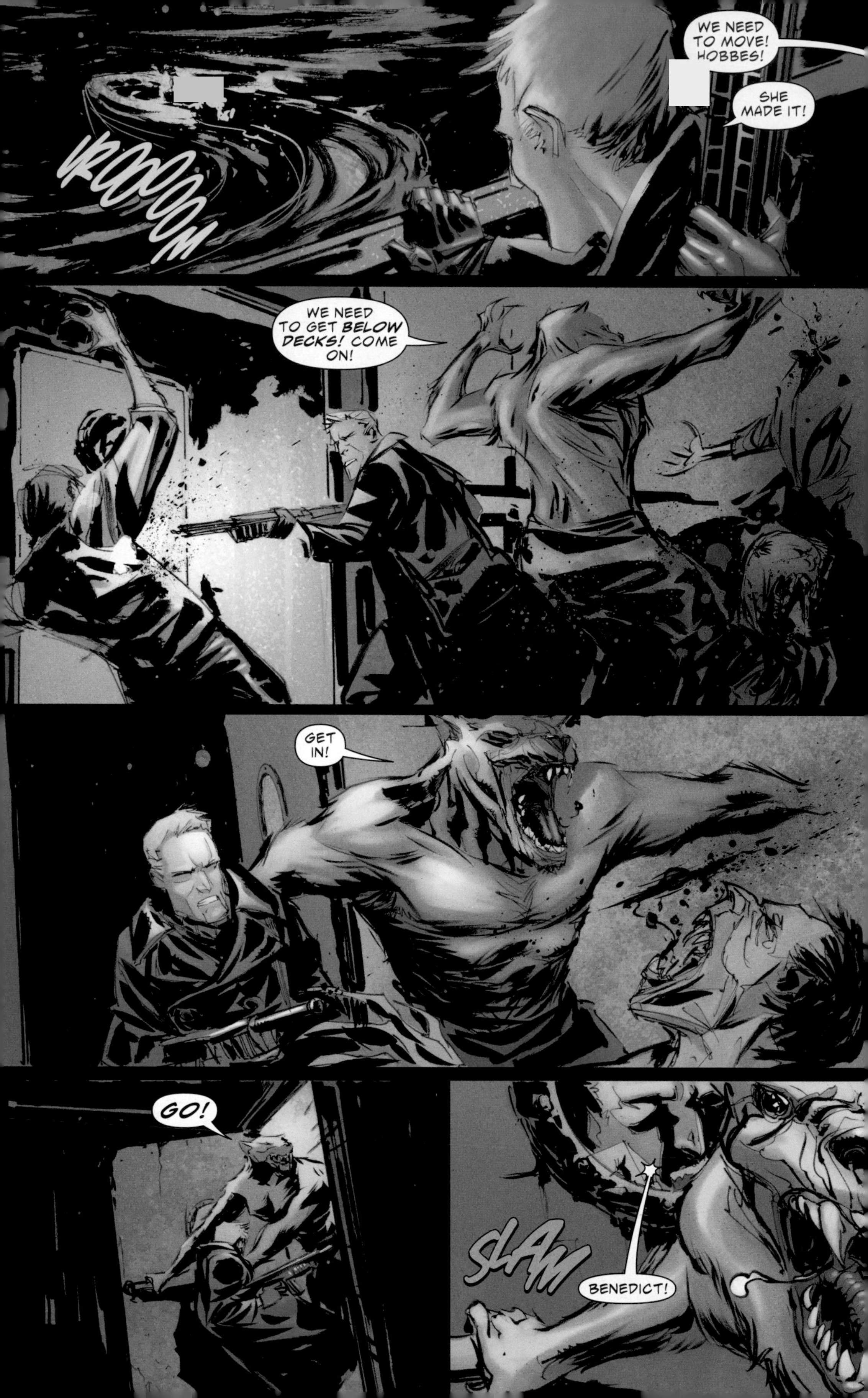
VROOOOOM
WE NEED TO MOVE! HOBBES!
SHE MADE IT!
WE NEED TO GET BELOW DECKS! COME ON!
GET IN!
GO!
SLAM
BENEDICT!

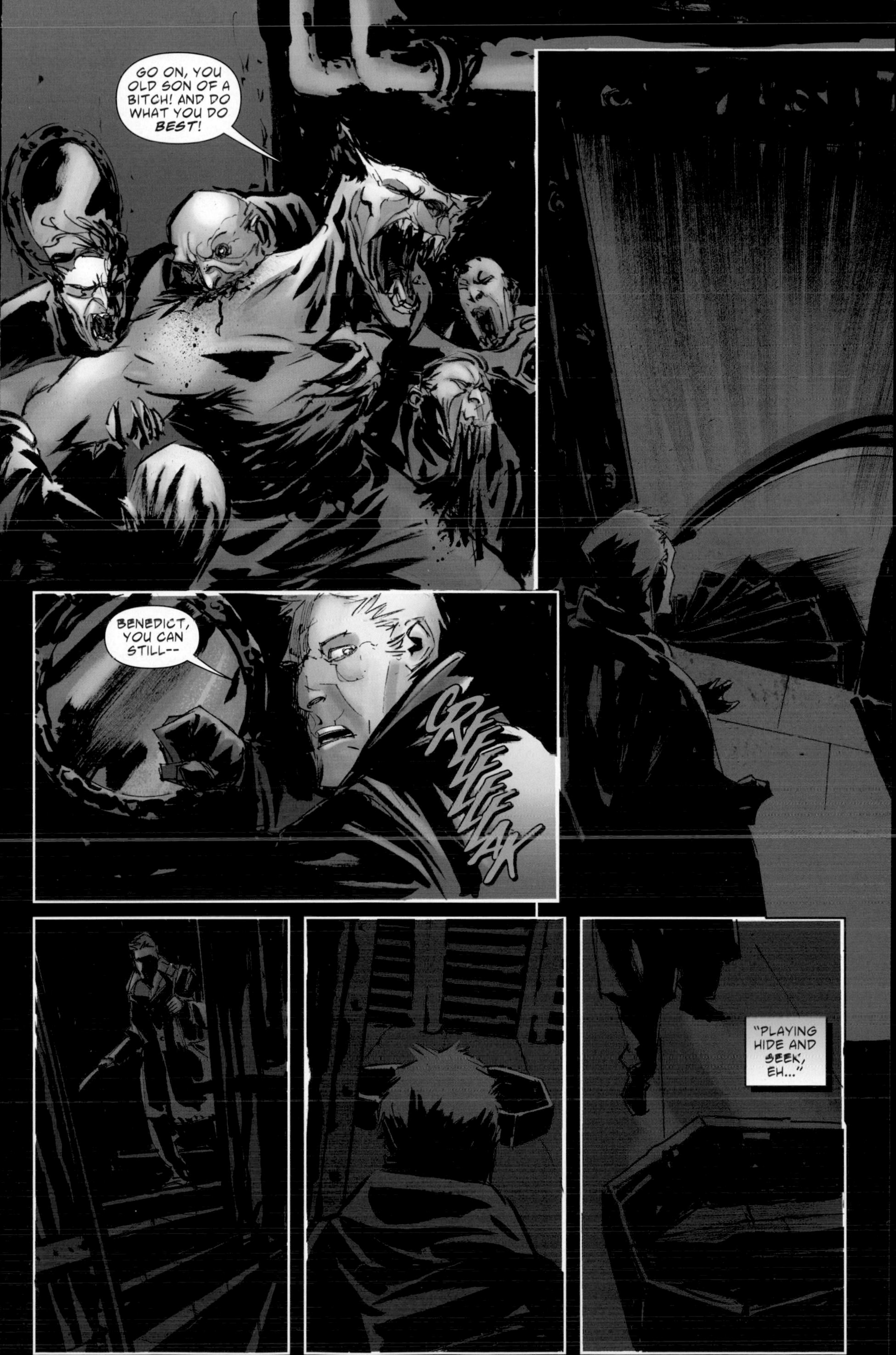
GO ON, YOU OLD SON OF A BITCH! AND DO WHAT YOU DO BEST!
BENEDICT, YOU CAN STILL--
CREEEAAAK
"PLAYING HIDE AND SEEK, EH..."

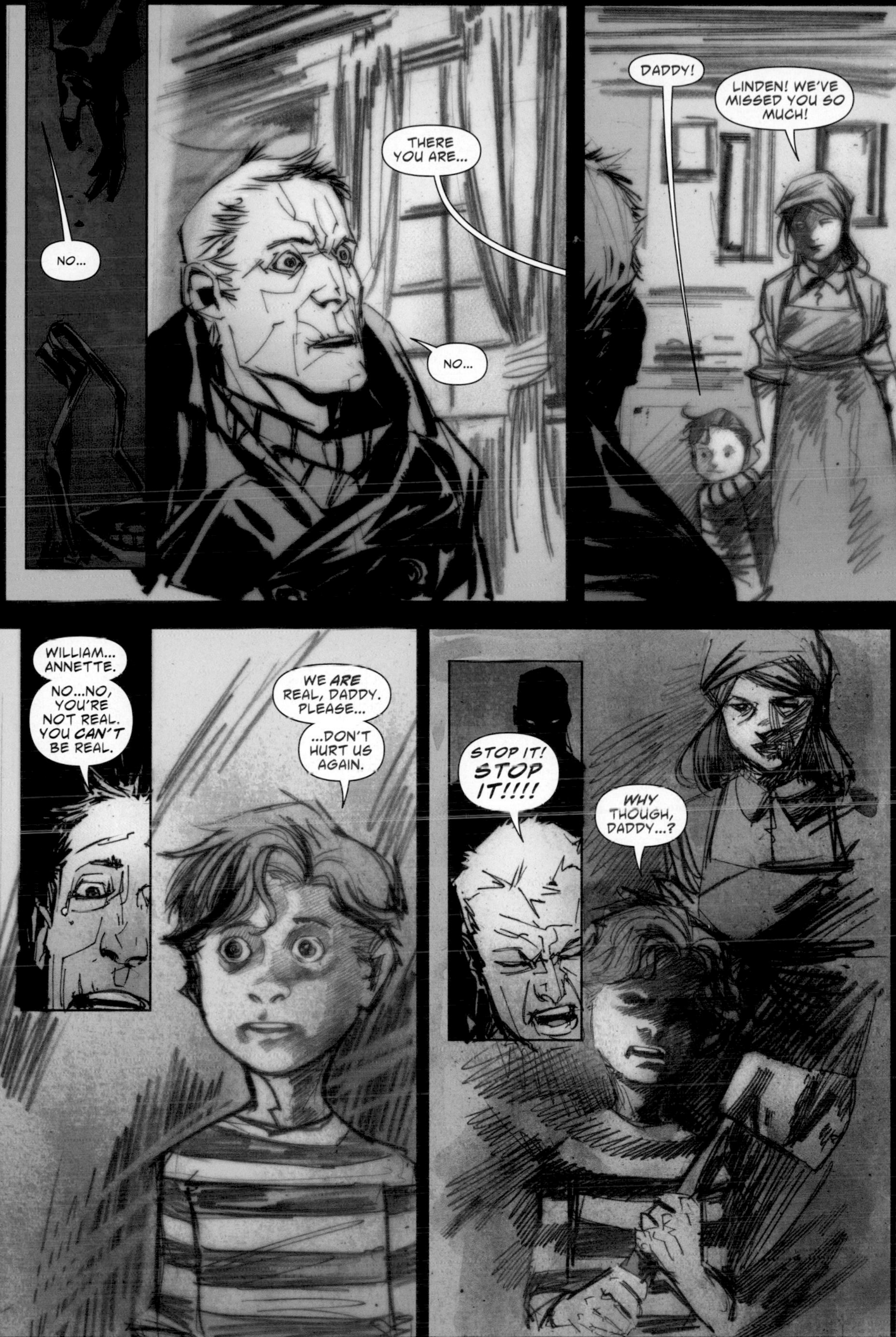
NO...
THERE YOU ARE...
NO...
DADDY!
LINDEN! WE'VE MISSED YOU SO MUCH!
WILLIAM... ANNETTE.
NO...NO, YOU'RE NOT REAL. YOU *CAN'T* BE REAL.
WE *ARE* REAL, DADDY. PLEASE...
...DON'T HURT US AGAIN.
STOP IT! STOP IT!!!!
WHY THOUGH, DADDY...?

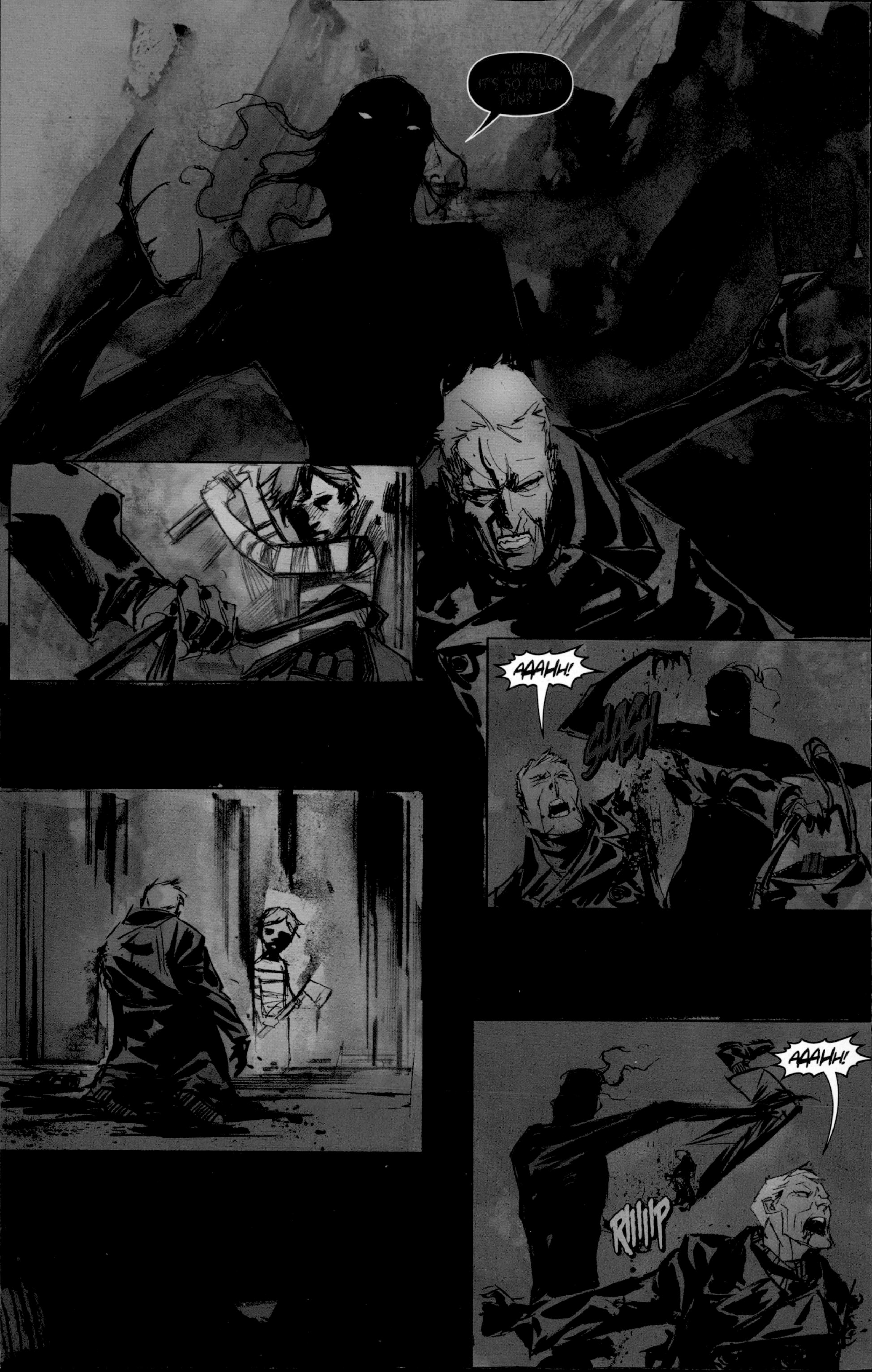
...WHEN IT'S SO MUCH FUN? !
AAAHH!
AAAHH!
RIIIIP

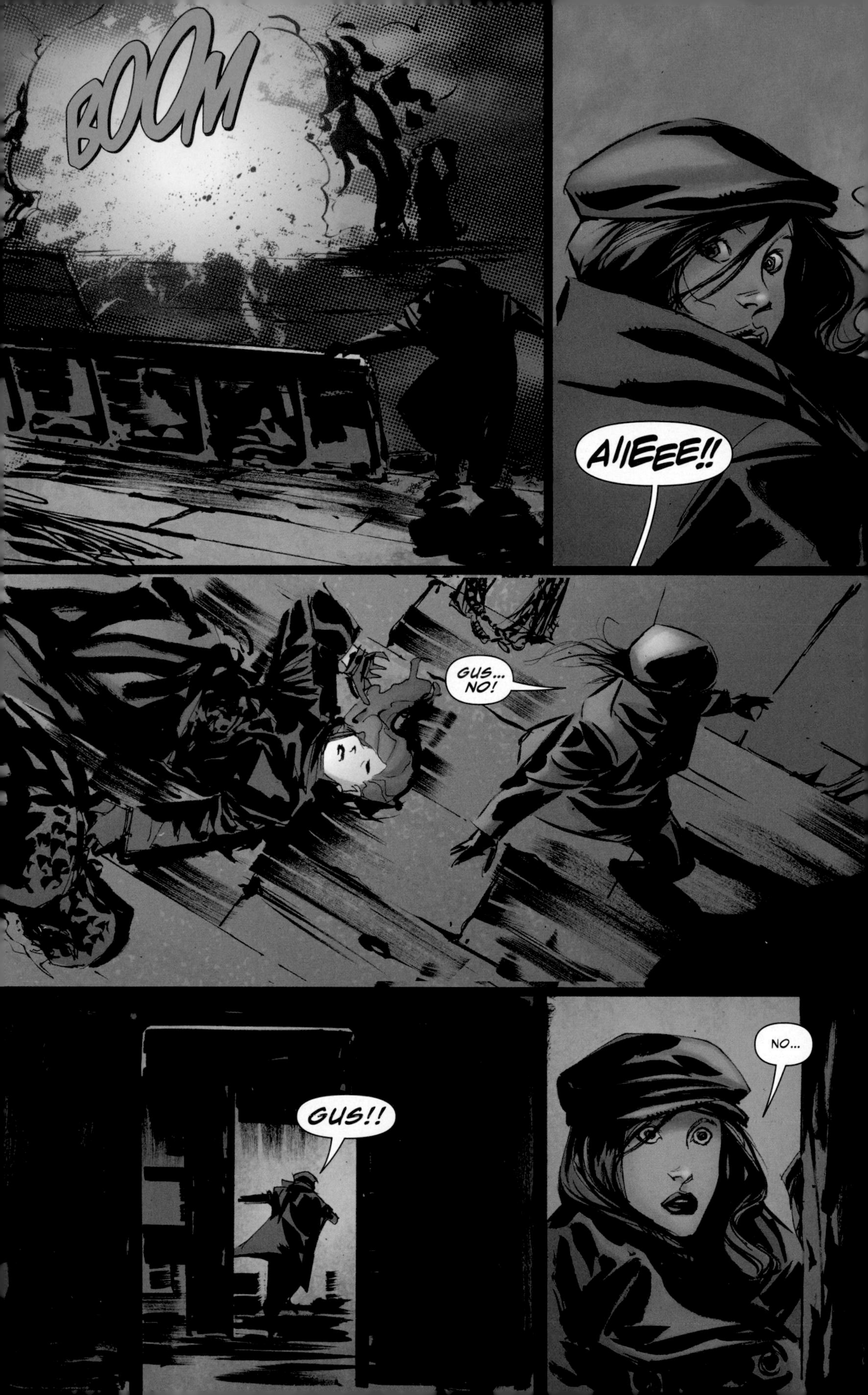
BOOM
AIIEEE!!
GUS... NO!
GUS!!
NO...

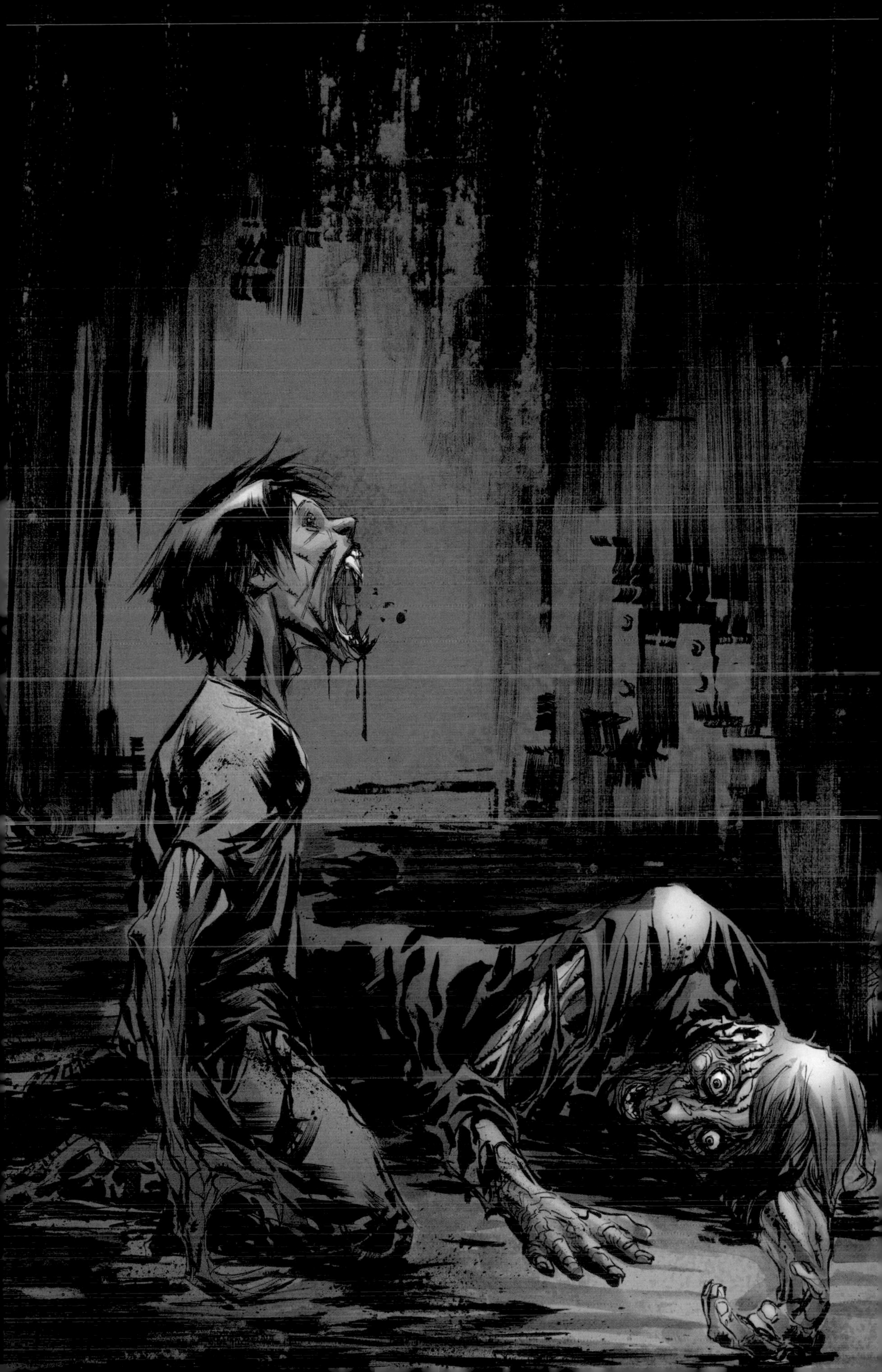

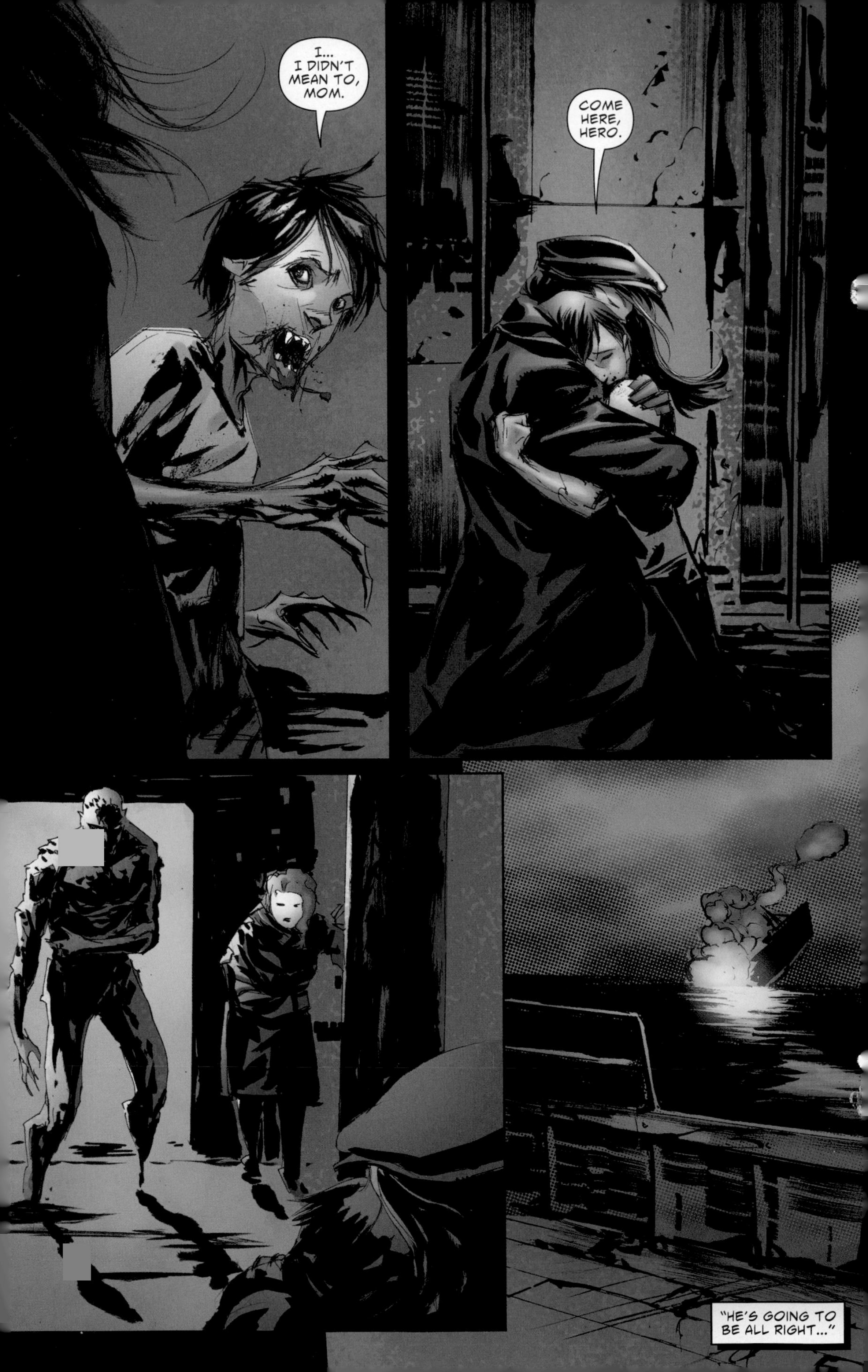
I... I DIDN'T MEAN TO, MOM.
COME HERE, HERO.
"HE'S GOING TO BE ALL RIGHT..."

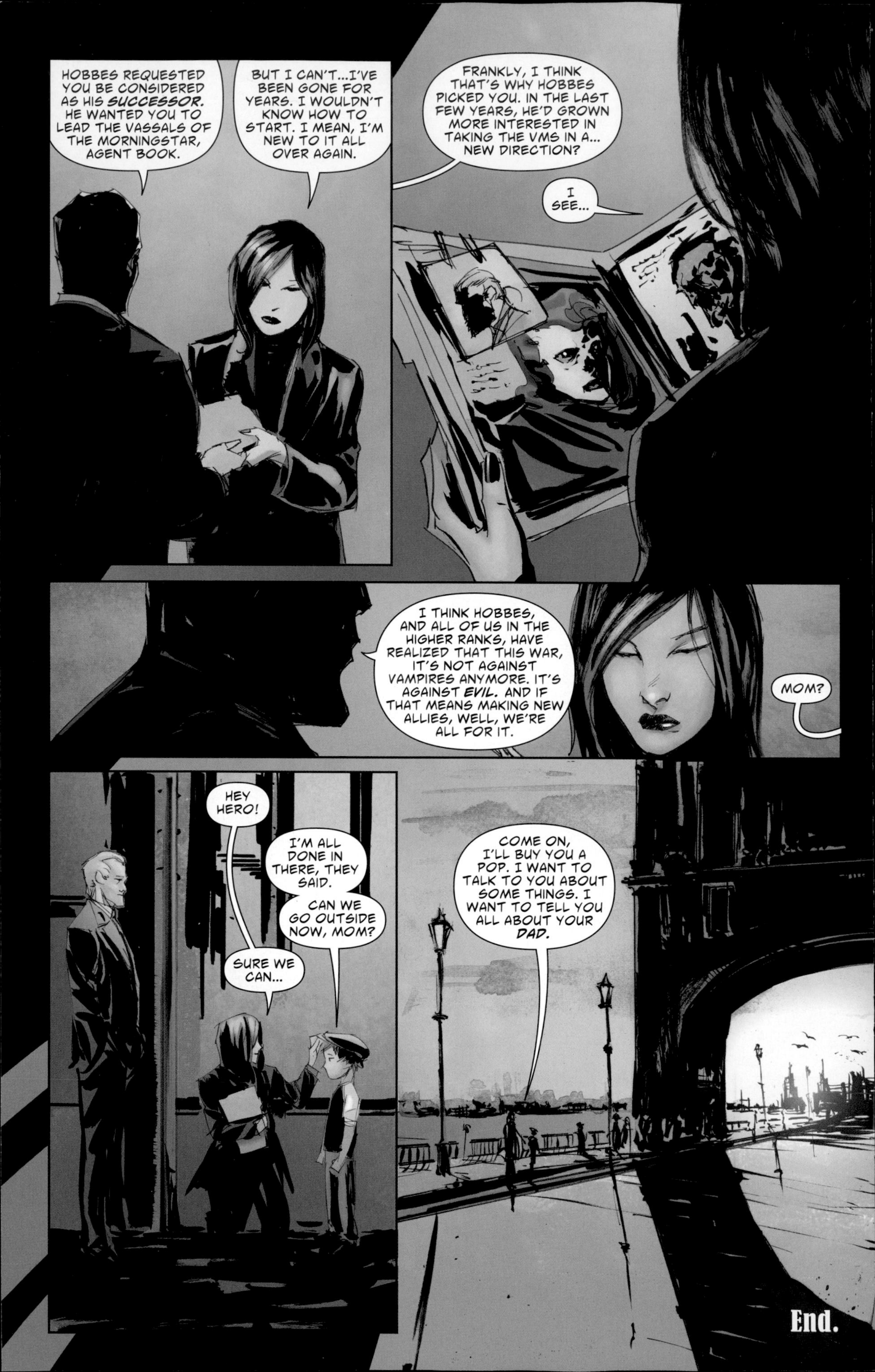
HOBBES REQUESTED YOU BE CONSIDERED AS HIS *SUCCESSOR.* HE WANTED YOU TO LEAD THE VASSALS OF THE MORNINGSTAR, AGENT BOOK.
BUT I CAN'T...I'VE BEEN GONE FOR YEARS. I WOULDN'T KNOW HOW TO START. I MEAN, I'M NEW TO IT ALL OVER AGAIN.
FRANKLY, I THINK THAT'S WHY HOBBES PICKED YOU. IN THE LAST FEW YEARS, HE'D GROWN MORE INTERESTED IN TAKING THE VMS IN A... NEW DIRECTION?
I SEE...
I THINK HOBBES, AND ALL OF US IN THE HIGHER RANKS, HAVE REALIZED THAT THIS WAR, IT'S NOT AGAINST VAMPIRES ANYMORE. IT'S AGAINST *EVIL.* AND IF THAT MEANS MAKING NEW ALLIES, WELL, WE'RE ALL FOR IT.
MOM?
HEY HERO!
I'M ALL DONE IN THERE, THEY SAID.
CAN WE GO OUTSIDE NOW, MOM?
SURE WE CAN...
COME ON, I'LL BUY YOU A POP. I WANT TO TALK TO YOU ABOUT SOME THINGS. I WANT TO TELL YOU ALL ABOUT YOUR *DAD.*
End.

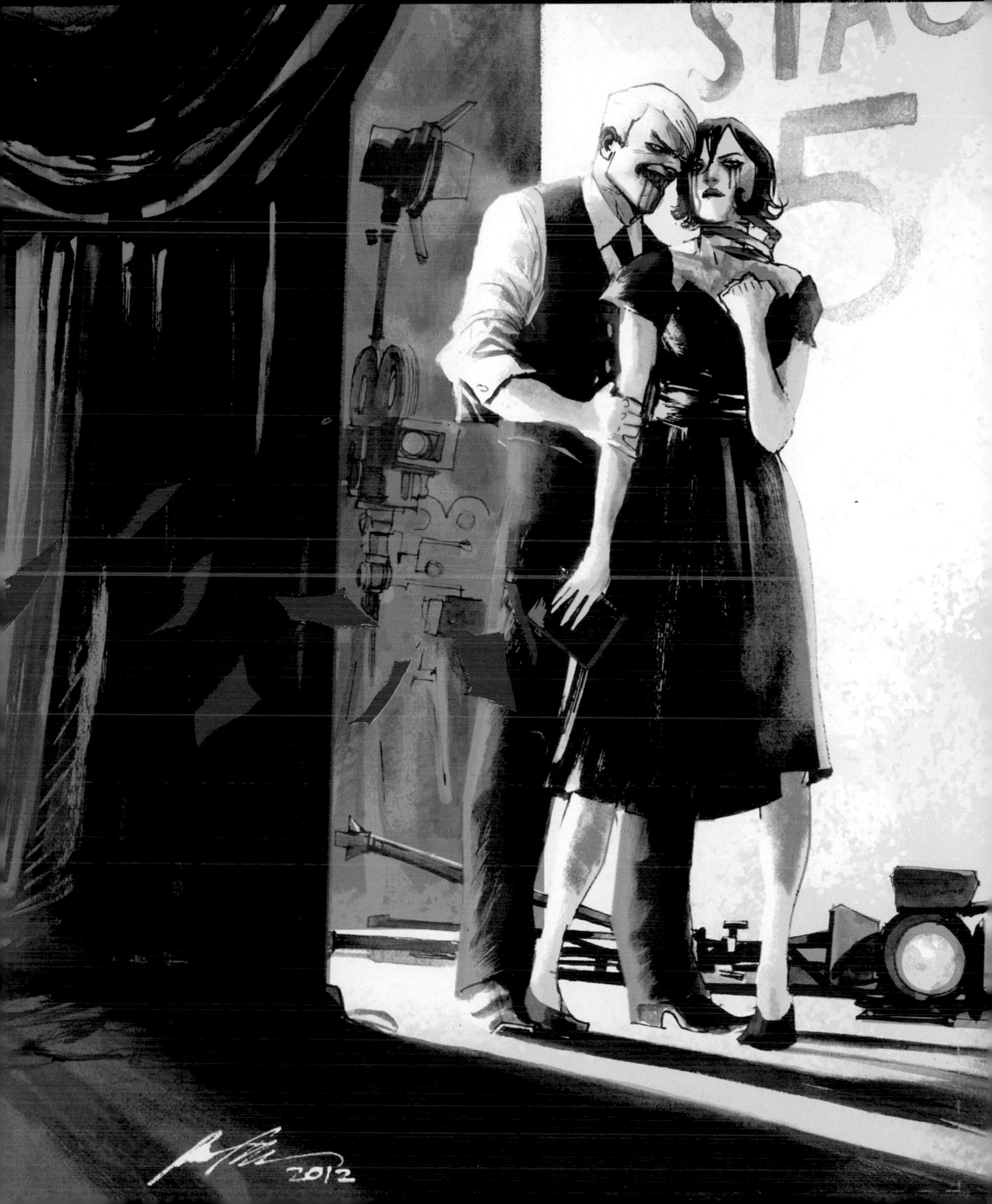
2012

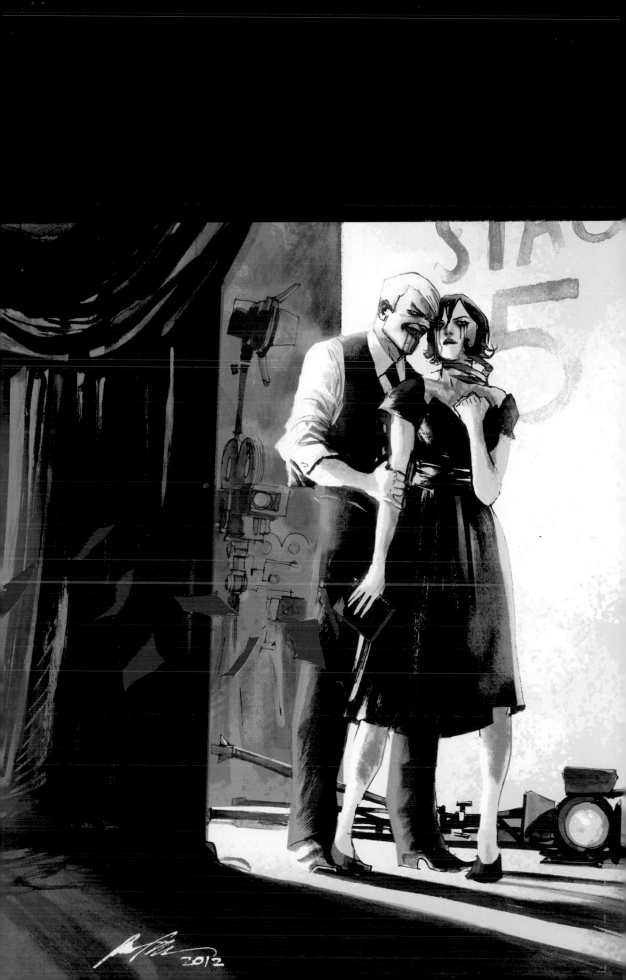

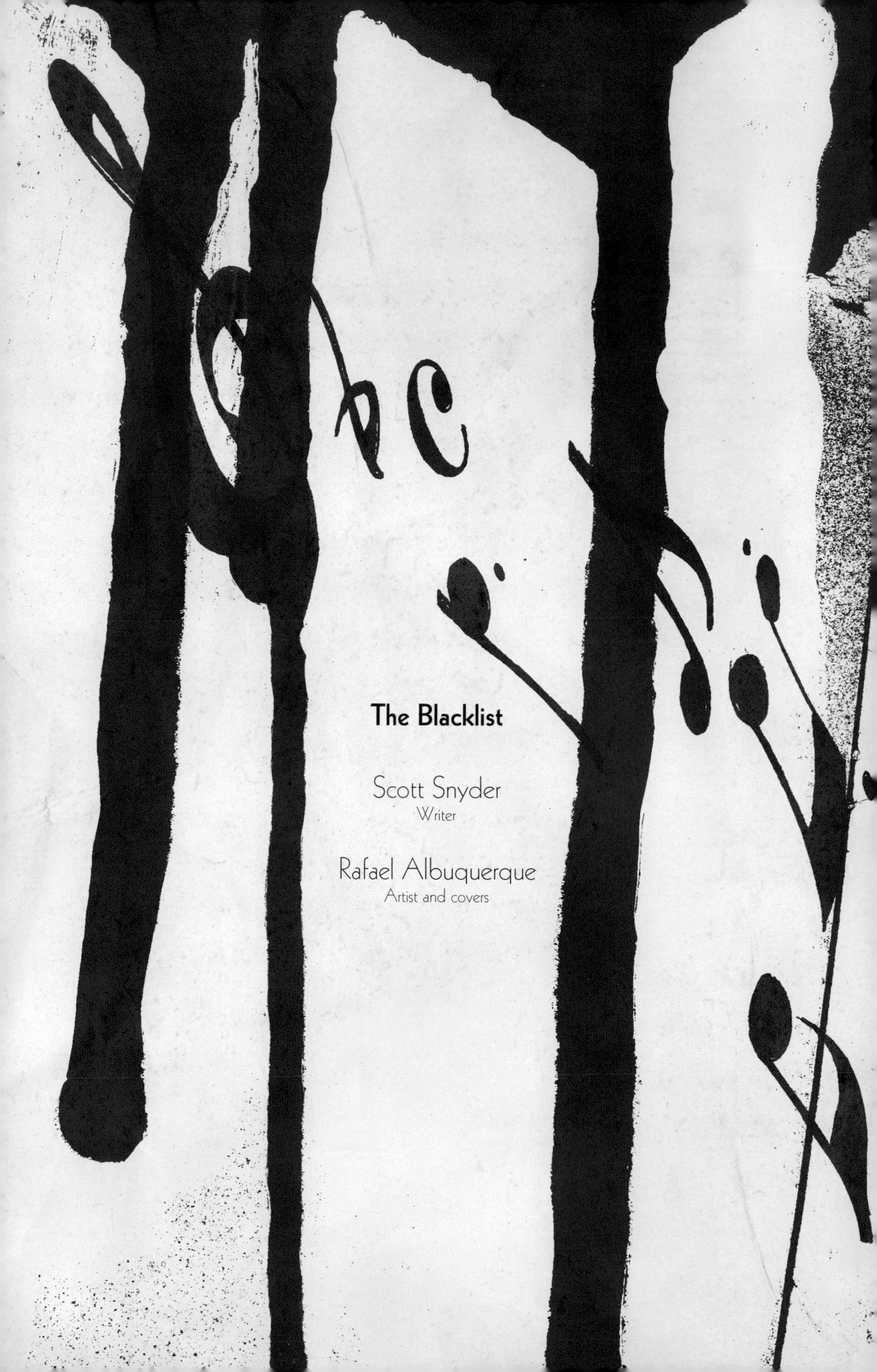

The Blacklist

Scott Snyder
Writer

Rafael Albuquerque
Artist and covers

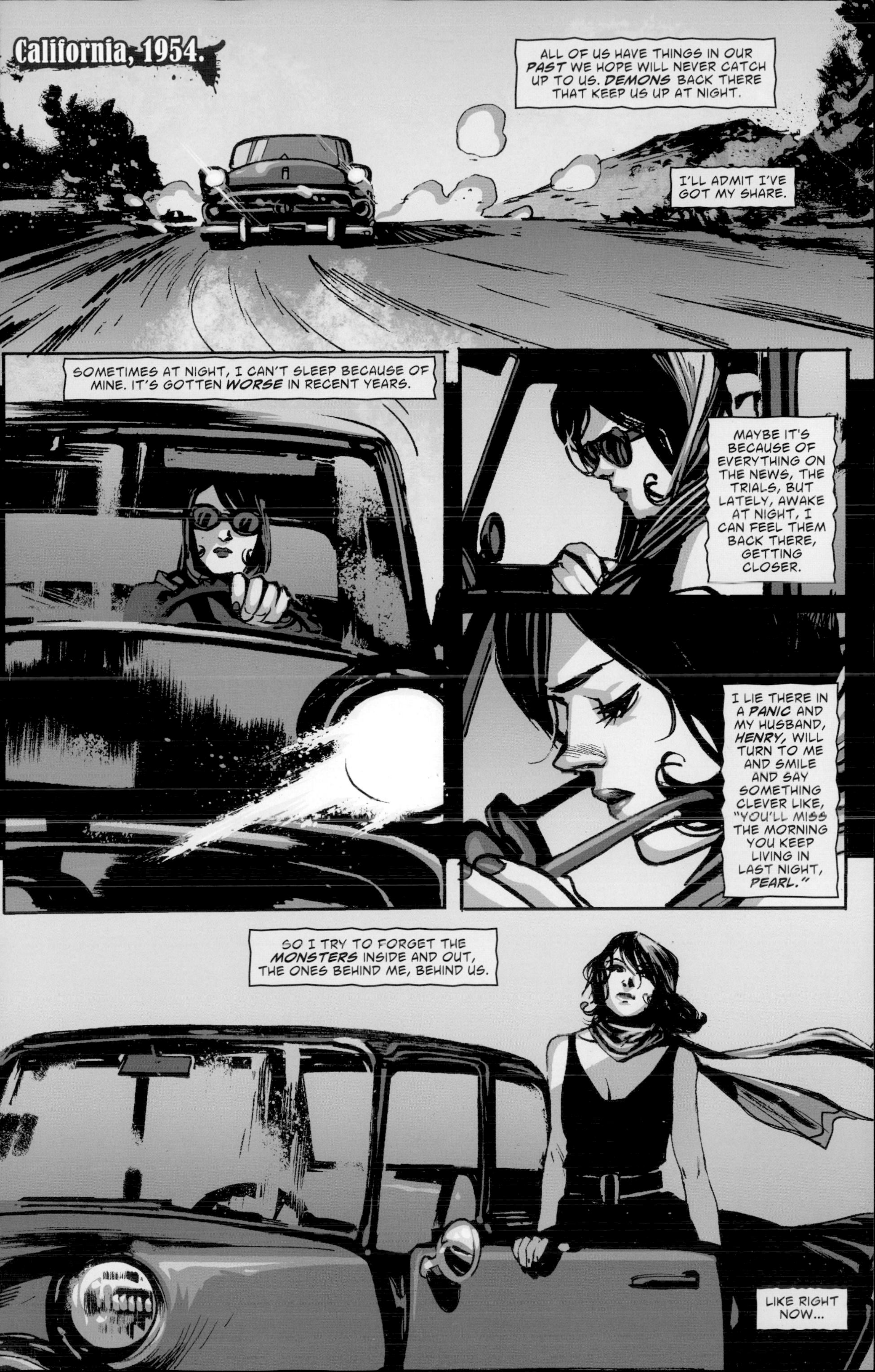
California, 1954.
ALL OF US HAVE THINGS IN OUR PAST WE HOPE WILL NEVER CATCH UP TO US. DEMONS BACK THERE THAT KEEP US UP AT NIGHT.
I'LL ADMIT I'VE GOT MY SHARE.
SOMETIMES AT NIGHT, I CAN'T SLEEP BECAUSE OF MINE. IT'S GOTTEN WORSE IN RECENT YEARS.
MAYBE IT'S BECAUSE OF EVERYTHING ON THE NEWS, THE TRIALS, BUT LATELY, AWAKE AT NIGHT, I CAN FEEL THEM BACK THERE, GETTING CLOSER.
I LIE THERE IN A PANIC AND MY HUSBAND, HENRY, WILL TURN TO ME AND SMILE AND SAY SOMETHING CLEVER LIKE, "YOU'LL MISS THE MORNING YOU KEEP LIVING IN LAST NIGHT, PEARL."
SO I TRY TO FORGET THE MONSTERS INSIDE AND OUT, THE ONES BEHIND ME, BEHIND US.
LIKE RIGHT NOW...

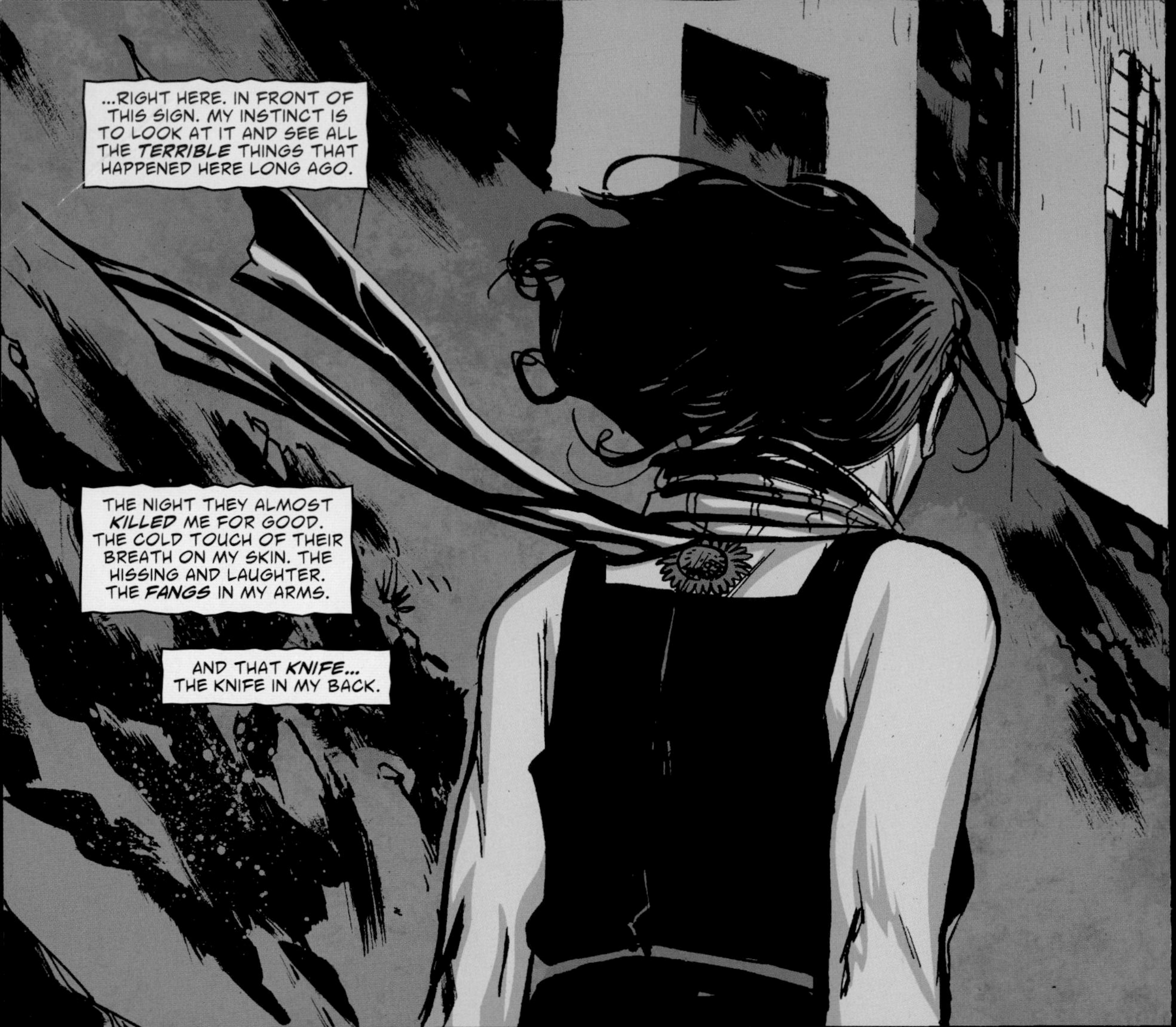
...RIGHT HERE. IN FRONT OF THIS SIGN. MY INSTINCT IS TO LOOK AT IT AND SEE ALL THE *TERRIBLE* THINGS THAT HAPPENED HERE LONG AGO.
THE NIGHT THEY ALMOST *KILLED* ME FOR GOOD. THE COLD TOUCH OF THEIR BREATH ON MY SKIN. THE HISSING AND LAUGHTER. THE *FANGS* IN MY ARMS.
AND THAT *KNIFE...* THE KNIFE IN MY BACK.

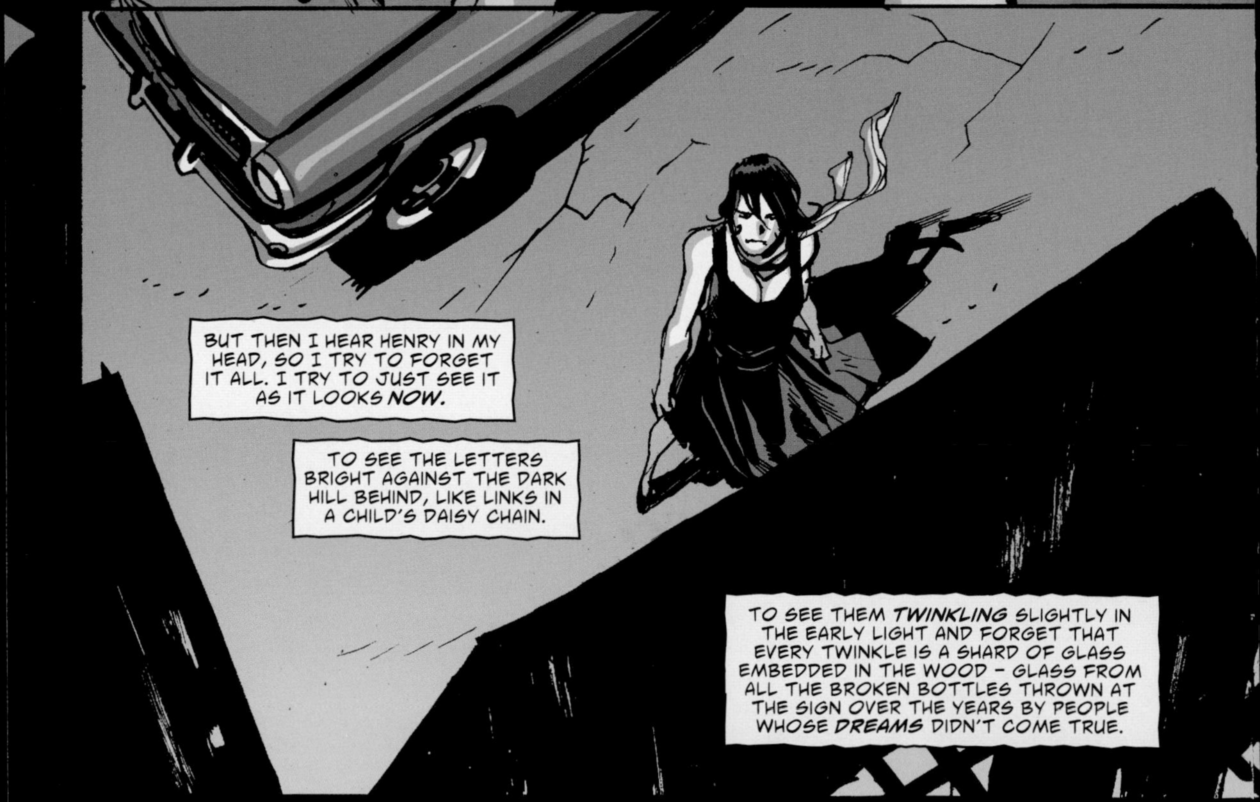
BUT THEN I HEAR HENRY IN MY HEAD, SO I TRY TO FORGET IT ALL. I TRY TO JUST SEE IT AS IT LOOKS *NOW.*
TO SEE THE LETTERS BRIGHT AGAINST THE DARK HILL BEHIND, LIKE LINKS IN A CHILD'S DAISY CHAIN.
TO SEE THEM *TWINKLING* SLIGHTLY IN THE EARLY LIGHT AND FORGET THAT EVERY TWINKLE IS A SHARD OF GLASS EMBEDDED IN THE WOOD – GLASS FROM ALL THE BROKEN BOTTLES THROWN AT THE SIGN OVER THE YEARS BY PEOPLE WHOSE *DREAMS* DIDN'T COME TRUE.

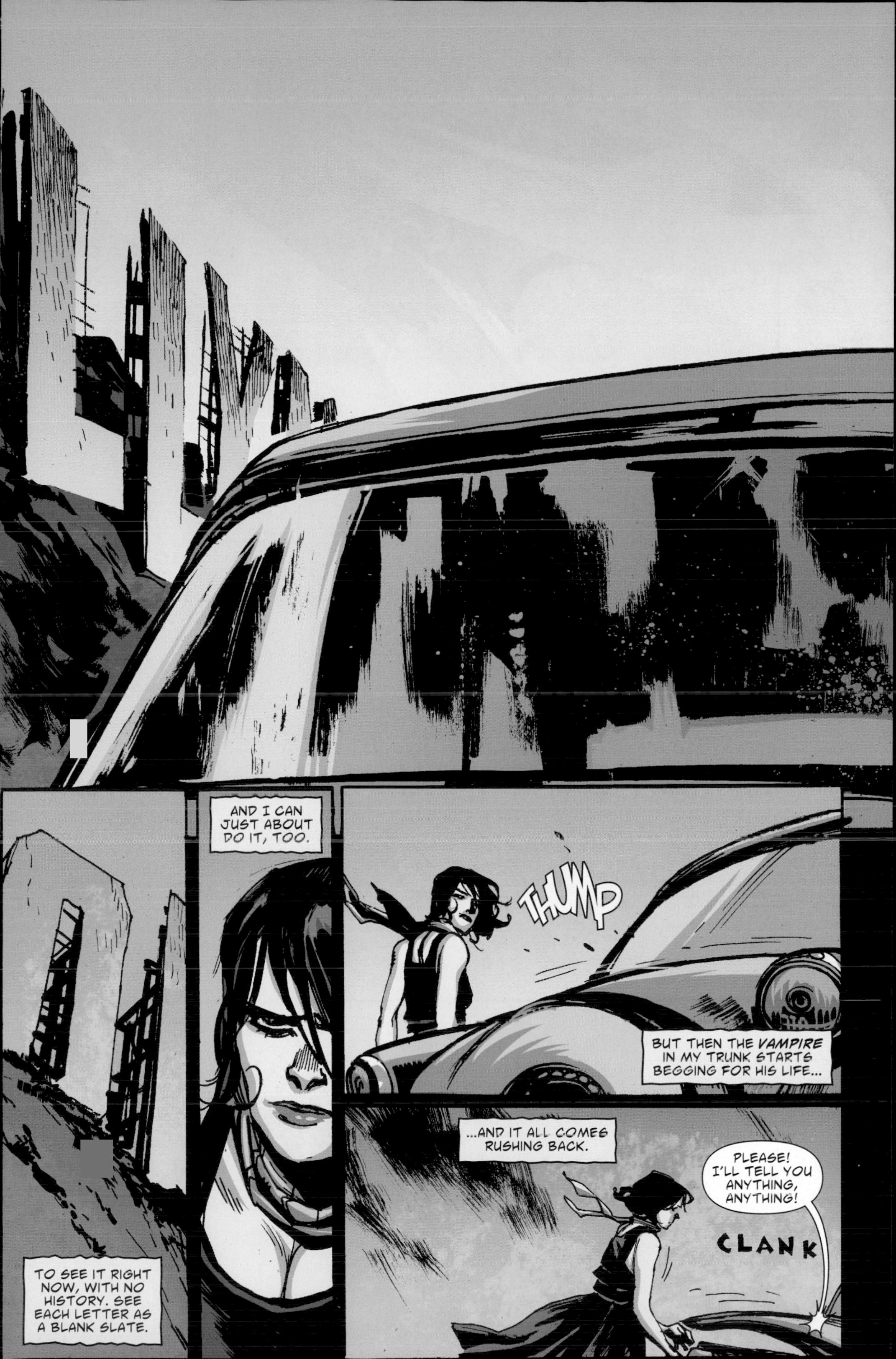
AND I CAN JUST ABOUT DO IT, TOO.
TO SEE IT RIGHT NOW, WITH NO HISTORY. SEE EACH LETTER AS A BLANK SLATE.
THUMP
BUT THEN THE *VAMPIRE* IN MY TRUNK STARTS BEGGING FOR HIS LIFE...
...AND IT ALL COMES RUSHING BACK.
PLEASE! I'LL TELL YOU ANYTHING, ANYTHING!
CLANK

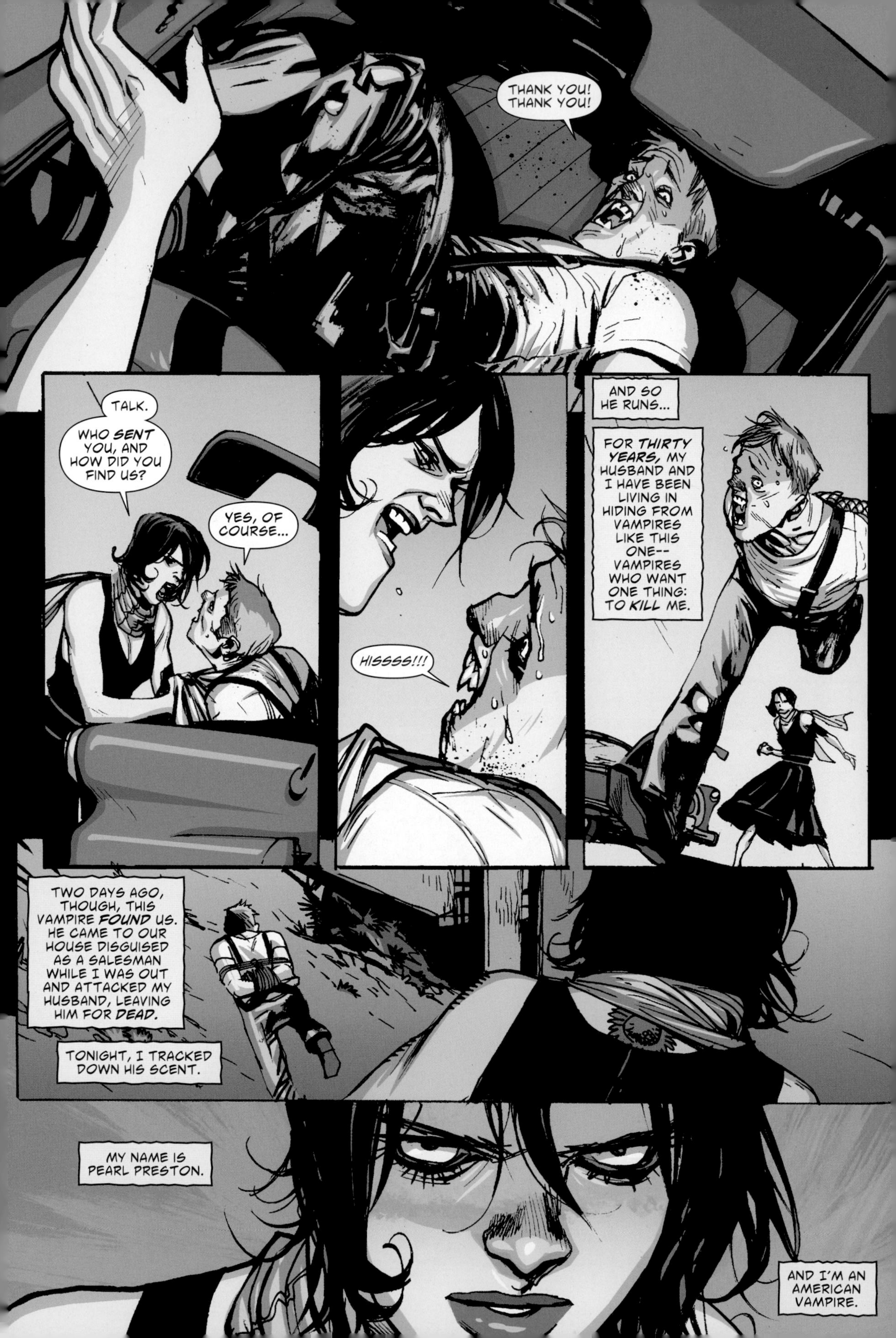

THANK YOU! THANK YOU!
TALK.
WHO SENT YOU, AND HOW DID YOU FIND US?
YES, OF COURSE...
HISSSS!!!
AND SO HE RUNS...
FOR THIRTY YEARS, MY HUSBAND AND I HAVE BEEN LIVING IN HIDING FROM VAMPIRES LIKE THIS ONE--VAMPIRES WHO WANT ONE THING: TO KILL ME.
TWO DAYS AGO, THOUGH, THIS VAMPIRE FOUND US. HE CAME TO OUR HOUSE DISGUISED AS A SALESMAN WHILE I WAS OUT AND ATTACKED MY HUSBAND, LEAVING HIM FOR DEAD.
TONIGHT, I TRACKED DOWN HIS SCENT.
MY NAME IS PEARL PRESTON.
AND I'M AN AMERICAN VAMPIRE.

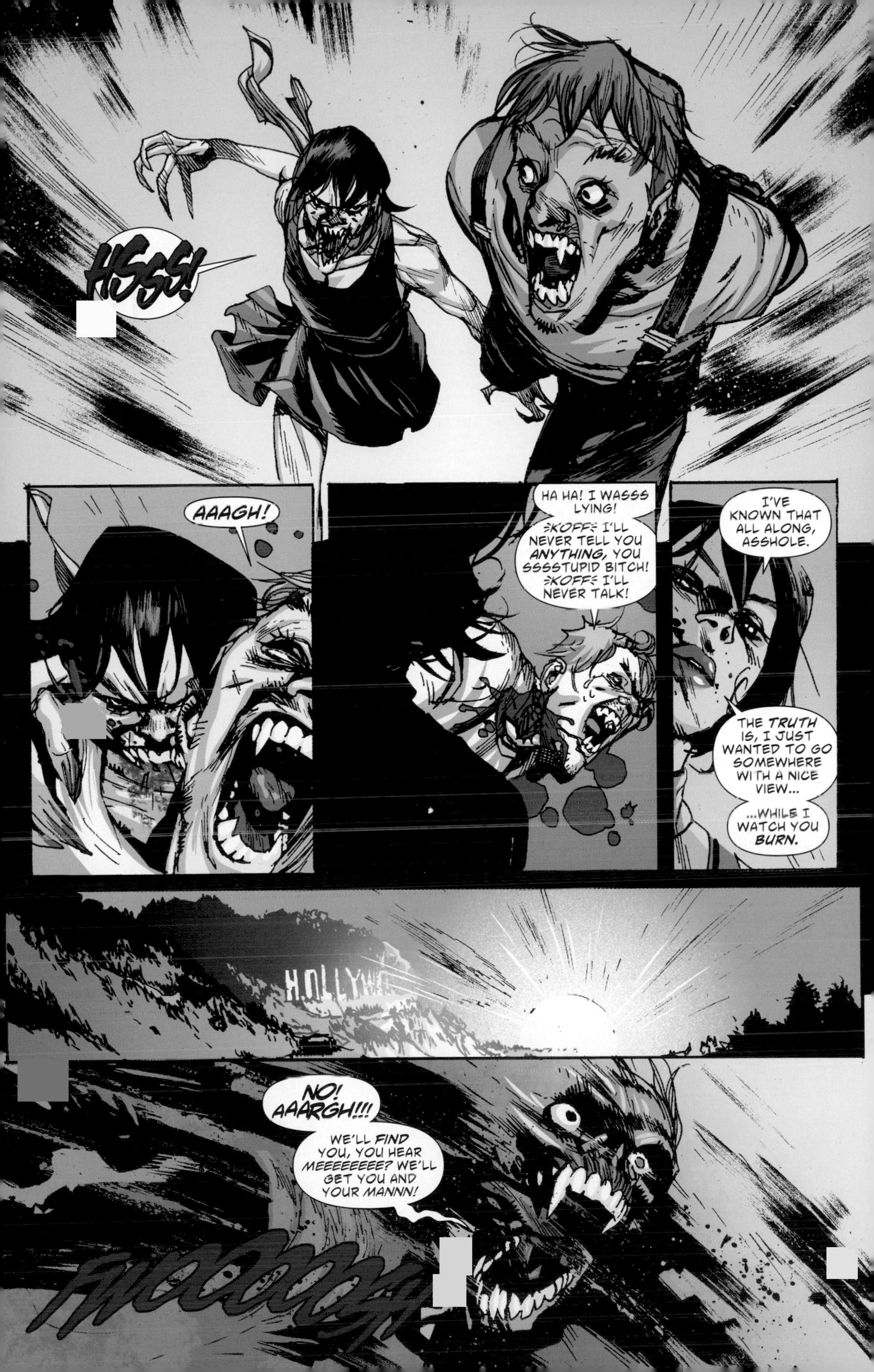
HSSS!
AAAGH!
HA HA! I WASSS LYING!
=KOFF= I'LL NEVER TELL YOU ANYTHING, YOU SSSSTUPID BITCH! =KOFF= I'LL NEVER TALK!
I'VE KNOWN THAT ALL ALONG, ASSHOLE.
THE TRUTH IS, I JUST WANTED TO GO SOMEWHERE WITH A NICE VIEW...
...WHILE I WATCH YOU BURN.
H.OLLYW
NO! AAARGH!!!
WE'LL FIND YOU, YOU HEAR MEEEEEEEE? WE'LL GET YOU AND YOUR MANNN!

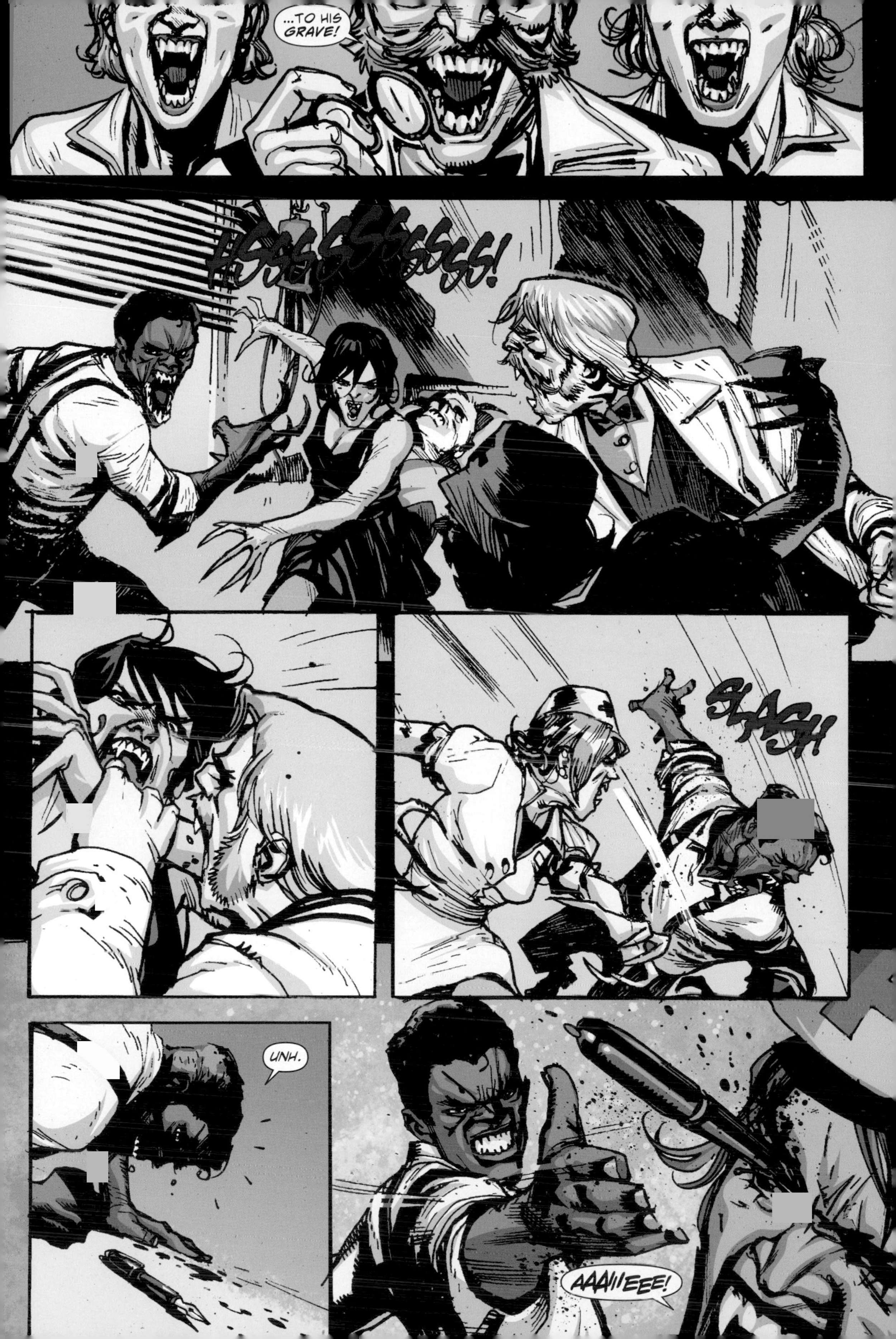

...TO HIS GRAVE!
HSSSSSSSSSSS!
SLASH!
UNH.
AAAIIIEEE!

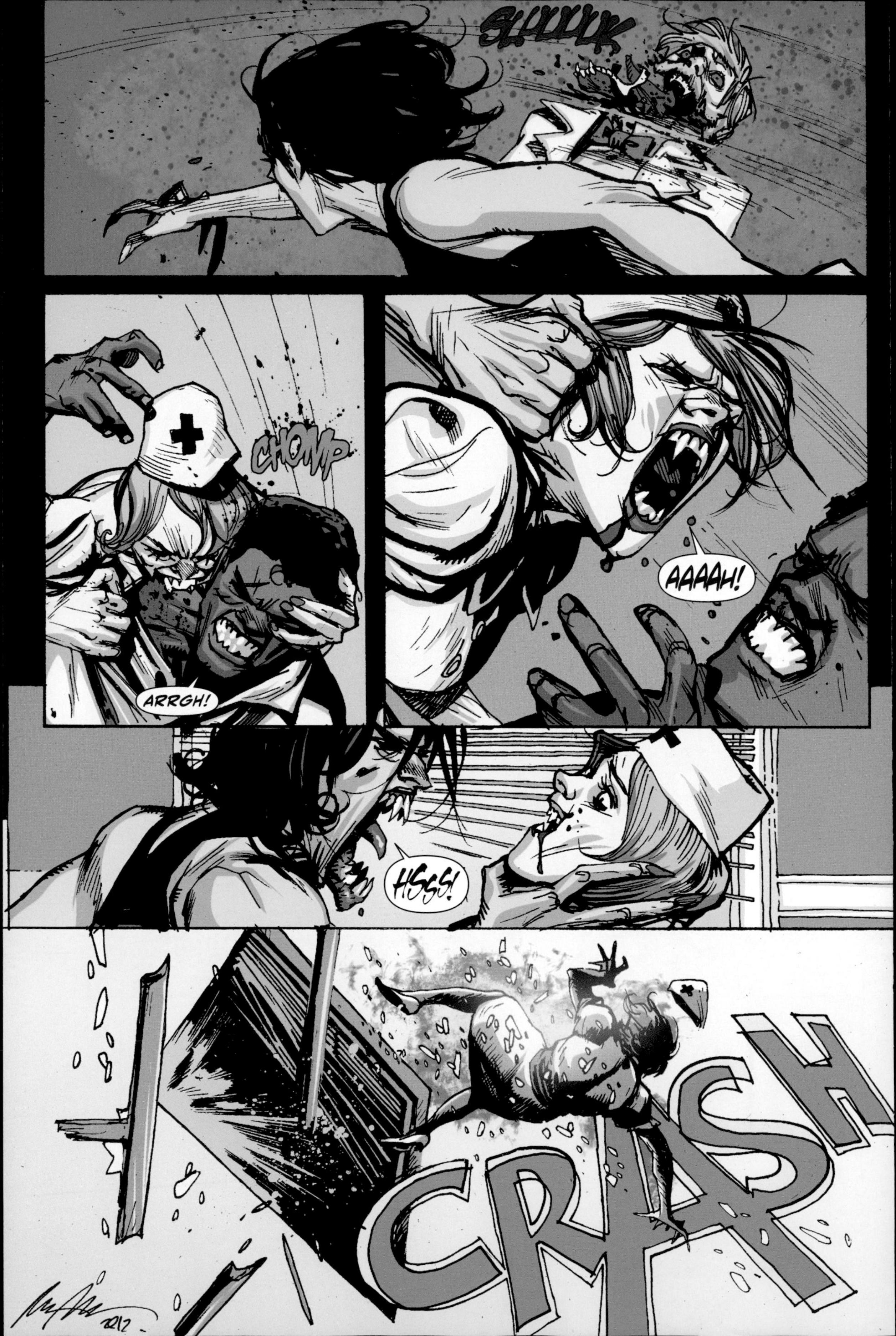
SHLUUK
CHOMP
ARRGH!
AAAAH!
HSSS!
CRASH

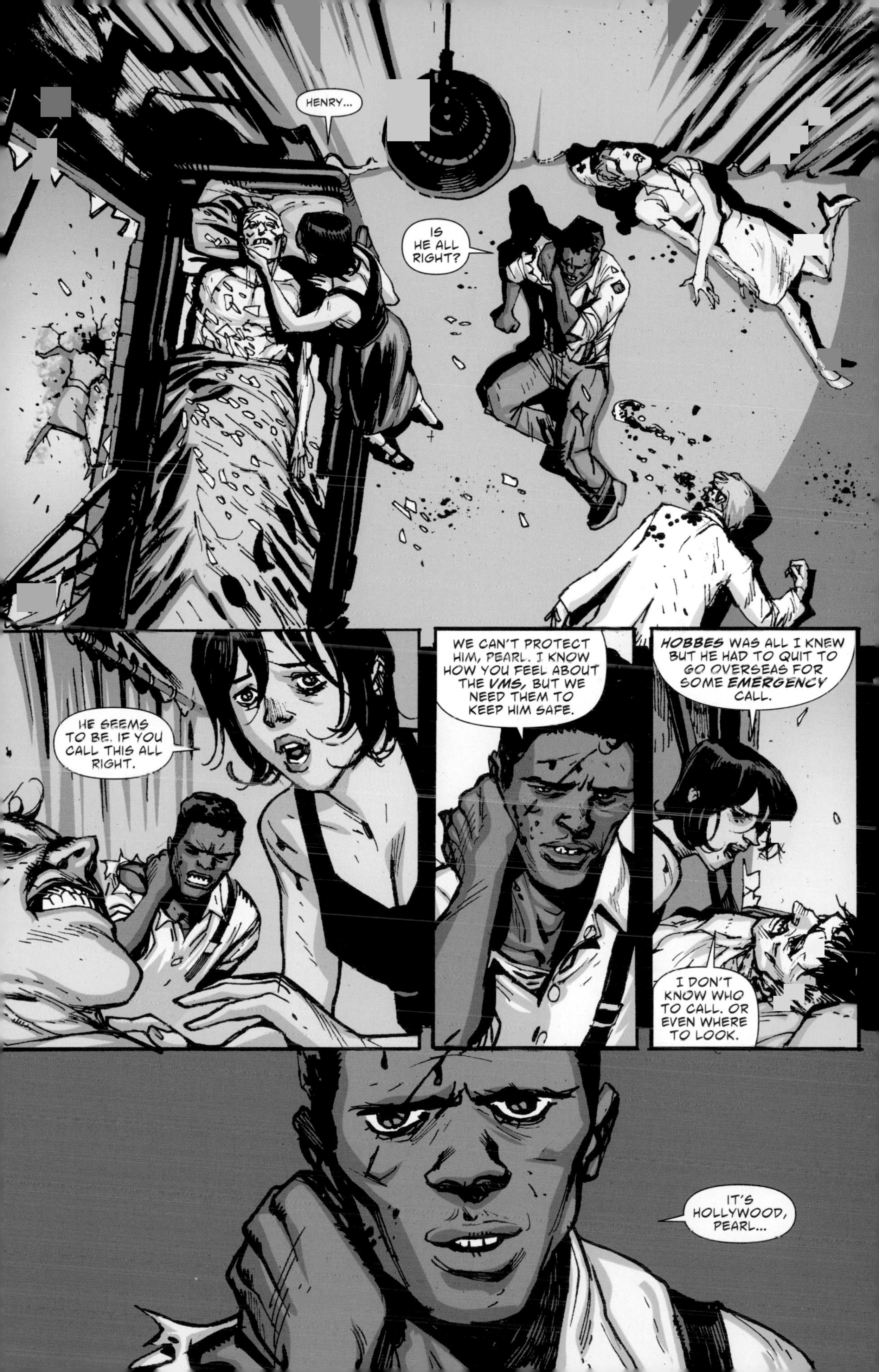
HENRY...
IS HE ALL RIGHT?
HE SEEMS TO BE. IF YOU CALL THIS ALL RIGHT.
WE CAN'T PROTECT HIM, PEARL. I KNOW HOW YOU FEEL ABOUT THE VMS, BUT WE NEED THEM TO KEEP HIM SAFE.
HOBBES WAS ALL I KNEW BUT HE HAD TO QUIT TO GO OVERSEAS FOR SOME EMERGENCY CALL.
I DON'T KNOW WHO TO CALL. OR EVEN WHERE TO LOOK.
IT'S HOLLYWOOD, PEARL...

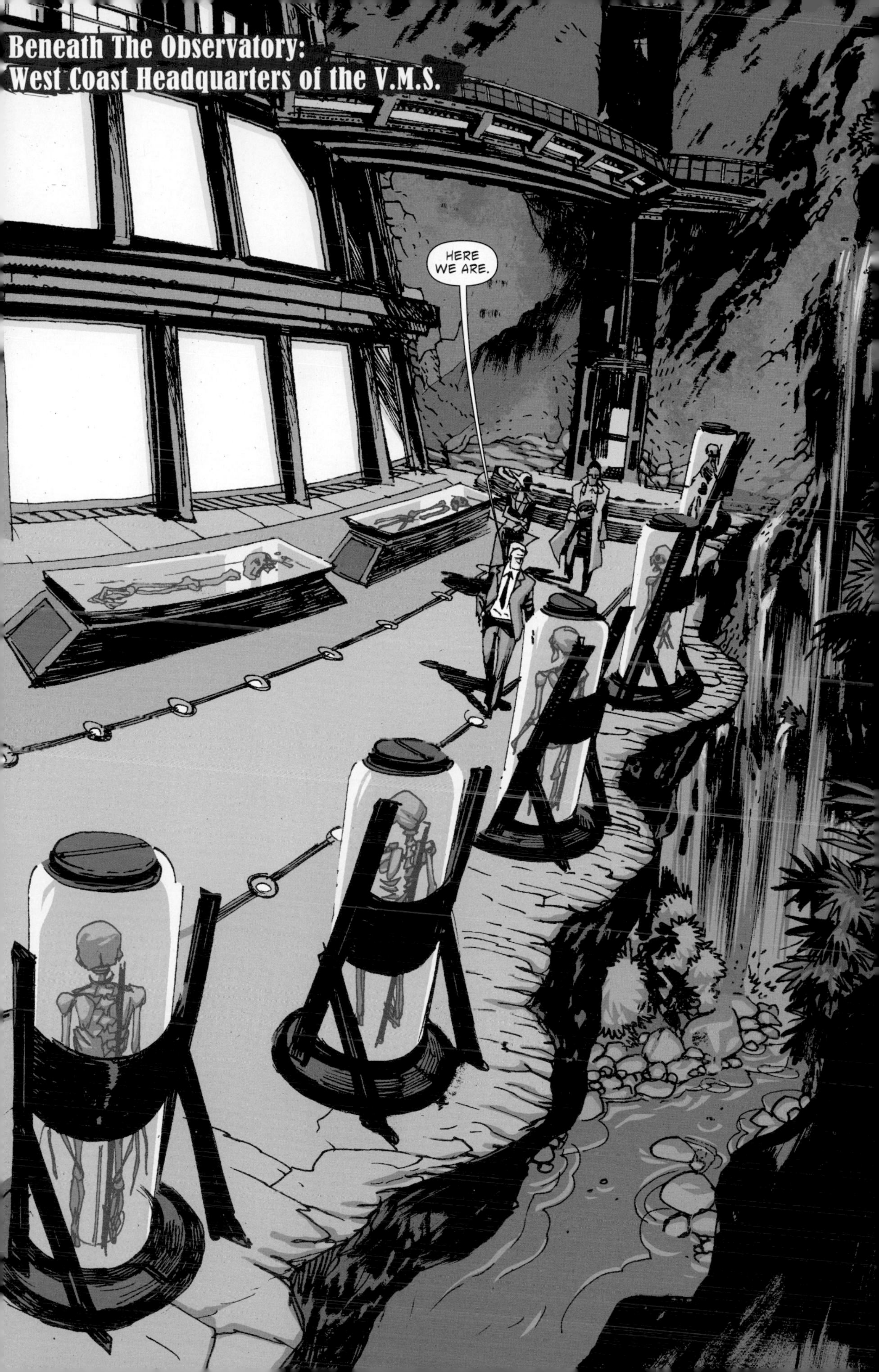
Beneath The Observatory:
West Coast Headquarters of the V.M.S.
HERE WE ARE.

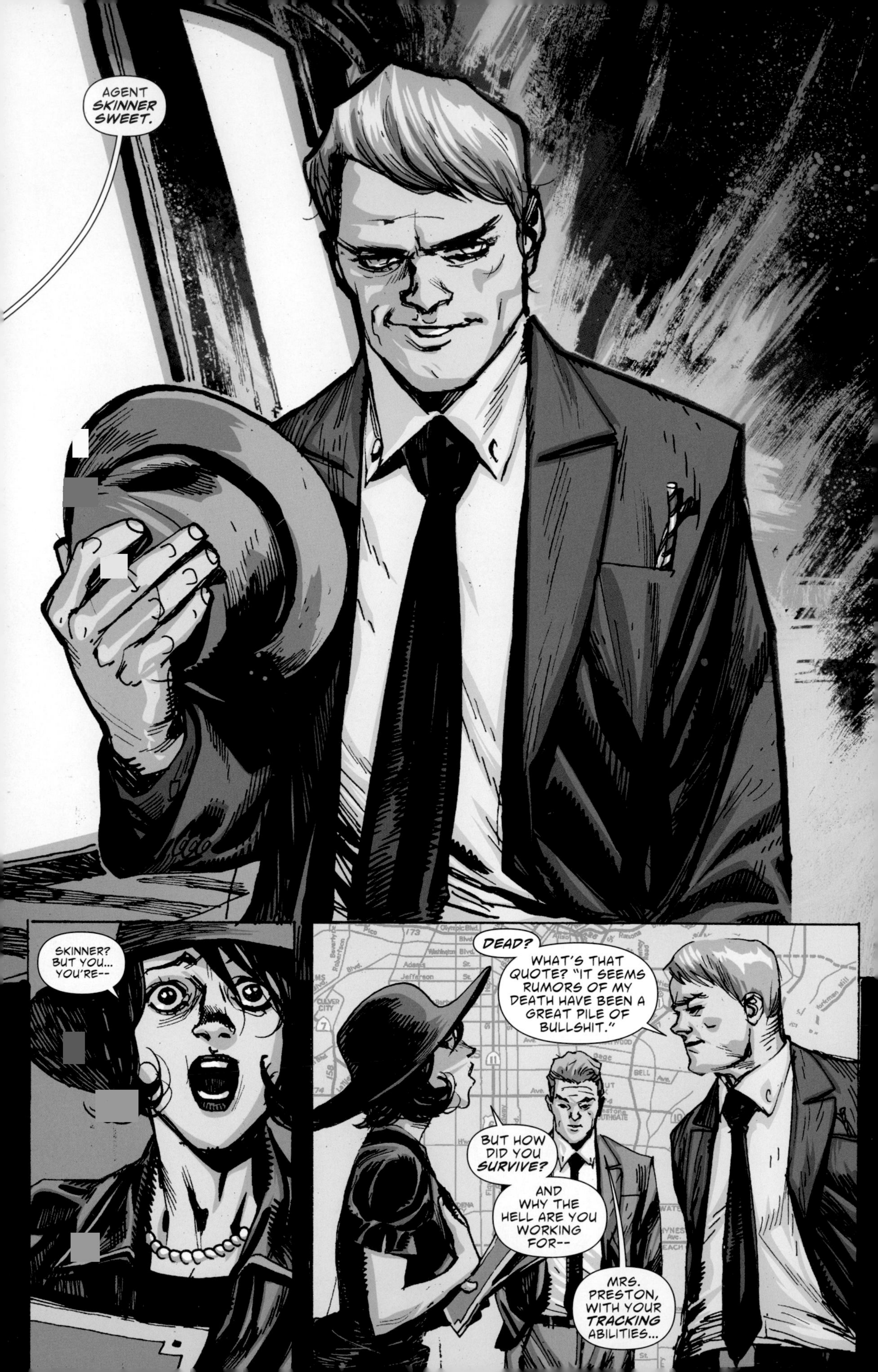
AGENT SKINNER SWEET.
SKINNER? BUT YOU... YOU'RE--
DEAD?
WHAT'S THAT QUOTE? "IT SEEMS RUMORS OF MY DEATH HAVE BEEN A GREAT PILE OF BULLSHIT."
BUT HOW DID YOU SURVIVE?
AND WHY THE HELL ARE YOU WORKING FOR--
MRS. PRESTON, WITH YOUR TRACKING ABILITIES...

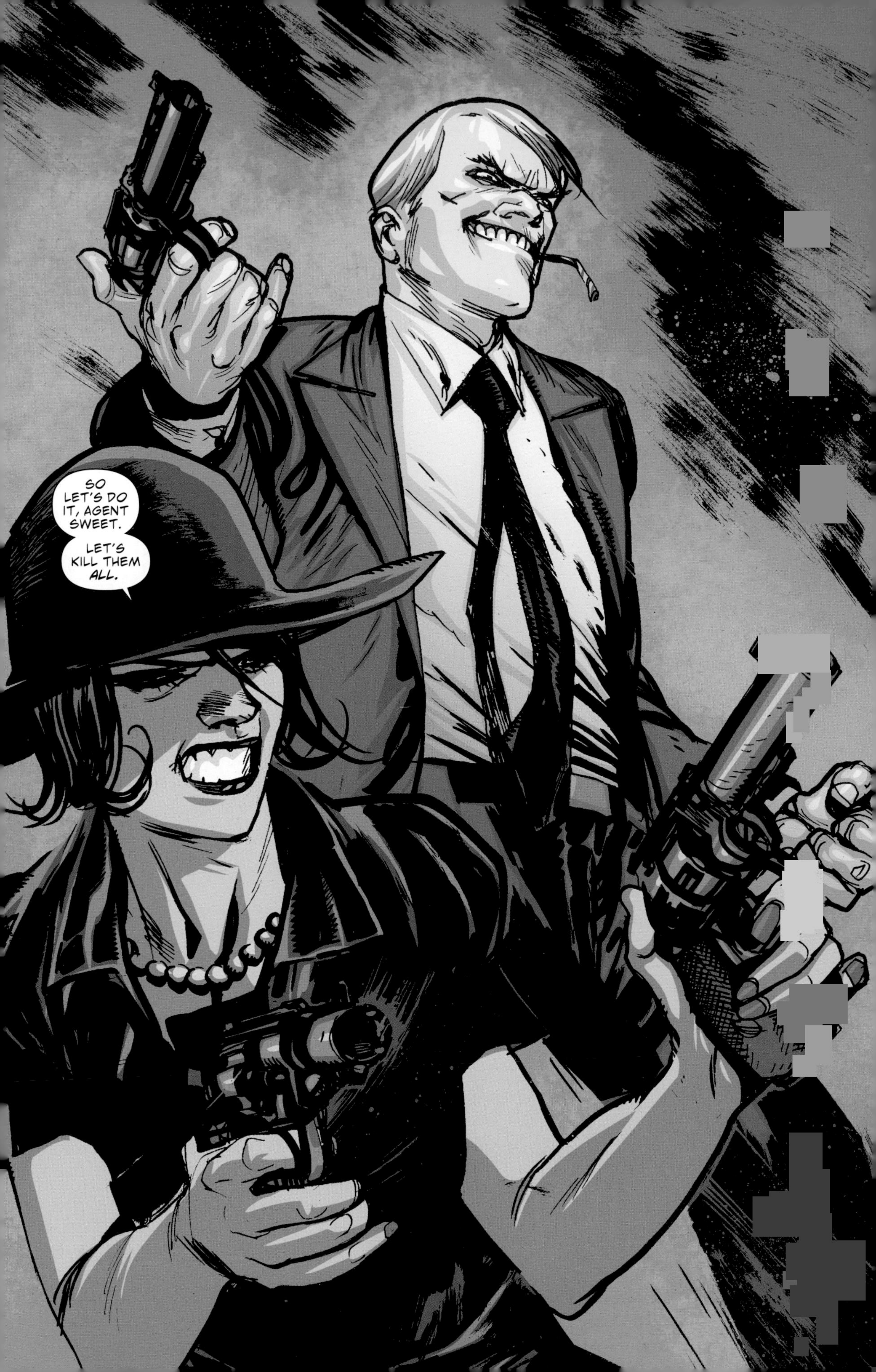
SO LET'S DO IT, AGENT SWEET.
LET'S KILL THEM *ALL*.

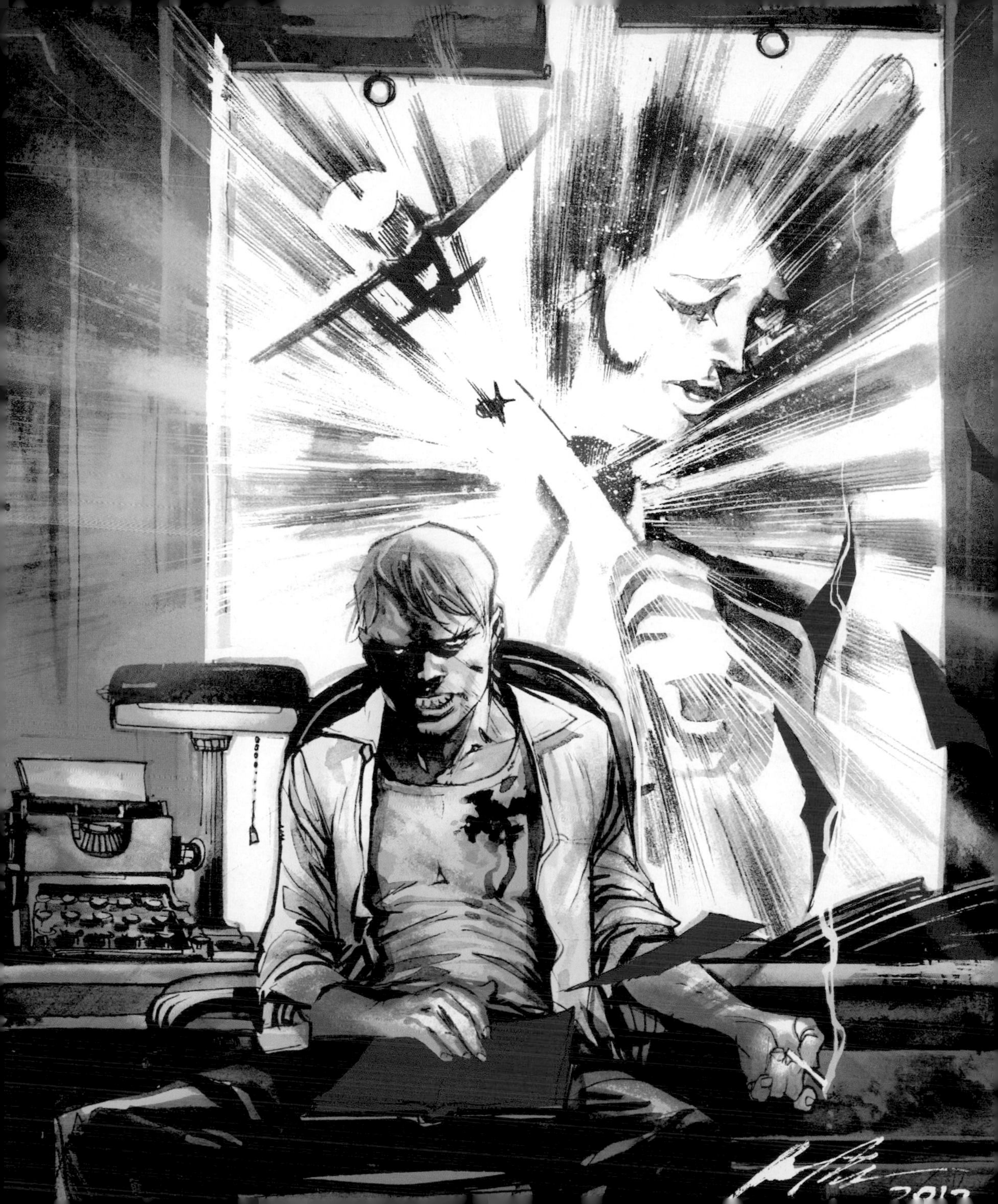

IT WAS THIRTY YEARS AGO THAT I FIRST SET FOOT IN LOS ANGELES.

I WAS TWENTY-FIVE YEARS OLD. I HAD SOME MONOLOGUES MEMORIZED, I HAD ENOUGH RENT FOR THREE MONTHS IN THE CHEAPEST BOARDING HOUSE ON SUNSET.

THE FIRST NIGHT I WAS THERE, THE OWNER, MS. DONNER, SAT US NEW GIRLS DOWN AND GAVE US A *SPEECH*.

"LOS ANGELES," SHE SAID, "IS ABOUT MEETING PEOPLE WHO'LL *CHANGE* YOUR LIFE, LADIES. THE TRICK, THOUGH, IS BEING ABLE TO KNOW WHO TO *TRUST*."

THEN OUT OF NOWHERE, SHE POINTED AT ME AND SHE SAID...

LADIE'S BOARDING HOUSE

"*YOU* FOR EXAMPLE, MS. JONES, YOU'RE GOING TO BE *VERY* BAD AT THIS. YOU'VE GOT A WIDE EYE. WATCH OUT FOR THAT. SQUINT, SQUINT, SQUINT."

I MOVED OUT THAT NIGHT.

I STAYED AT THE BUS STATION FOR A WEEK, UNTIL A ROOM OPENED UP AT MRS. PRUITT'S. I TOLD MYSELF MRS. DONNER DIDN'T KNOW WHAT THE HELL SHE WAS TALKING ABOUT. I WAS DETERMINED TO PROVE HER WRONG...

...BUT WITHIN A YEAR, I'D BE *DEAD*.

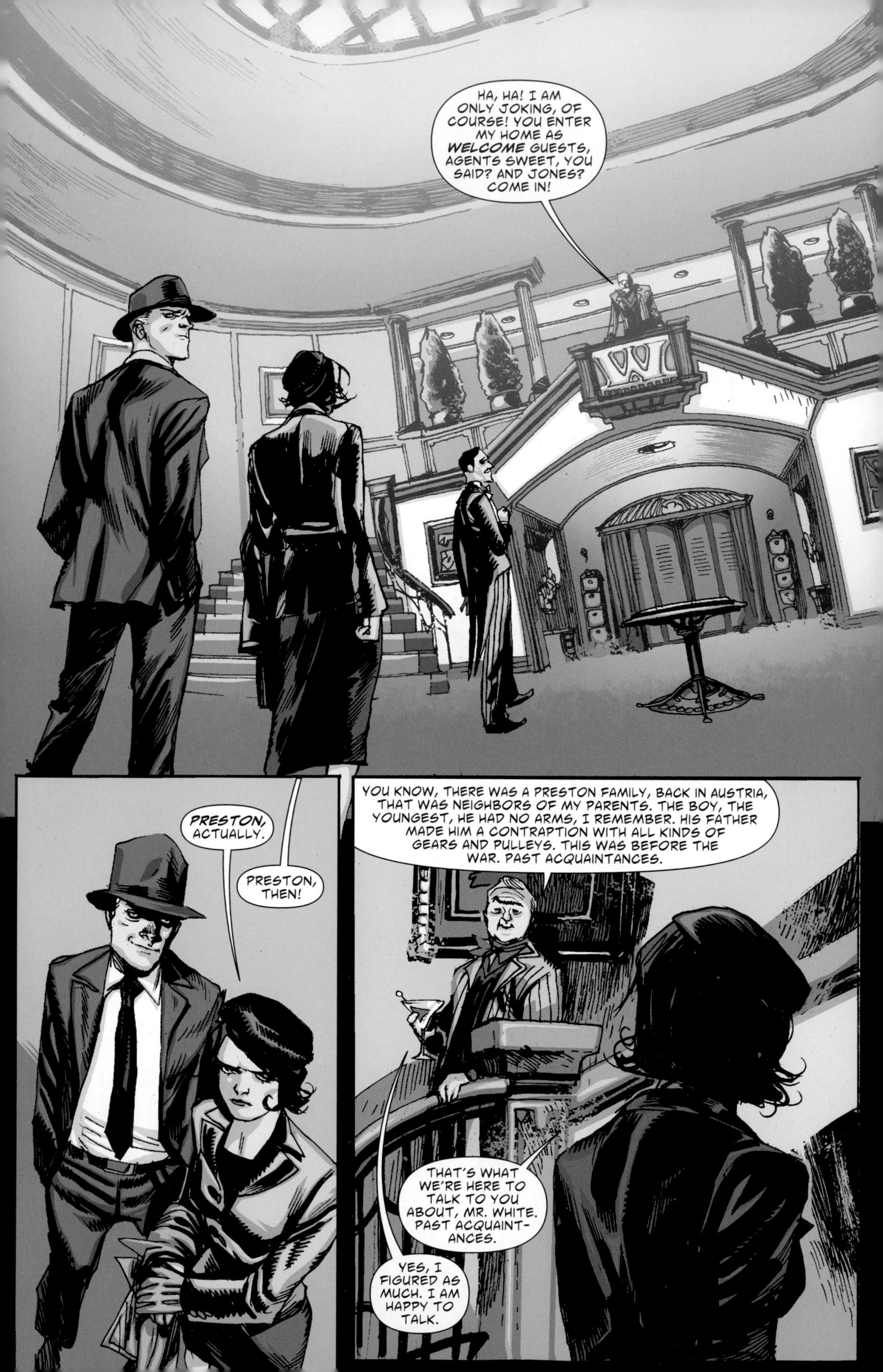
HA, HA! I AM ONLY JOKING, OF COURSE! YOU ENTER MY HOME AS *WELCOME* GUESTS, AGENTS SWEET, YOU SAID? AND JONES? COME IN!
PRESTON, ACTUALLY.
PRESTON, THEN!
YOU KNOW, THERE WAS A PRESTON FAMILY, BACK IN AUSTRIA, THAT WAS NEIGHBORS OF MY PARENTS. THE BOY, THE YOUNGEST, HE HAD NO ARMS, I REMEMBER. HIS FATHER MADE HIM A CONTRAPTION WITH ALL KINDS OF GEARS AND PULLEYS. THIS WAS BEFORE THE WAR. PAST ACQUAINTANCES.
THAT'S WHAT WE'RE HERE TO TALK TO YOU ABOUT, MR. WHITE. PAST ACQUAINT-ANCES.
YES, I FIGURED AS MUCH. I AM HAPPY TO TALK.

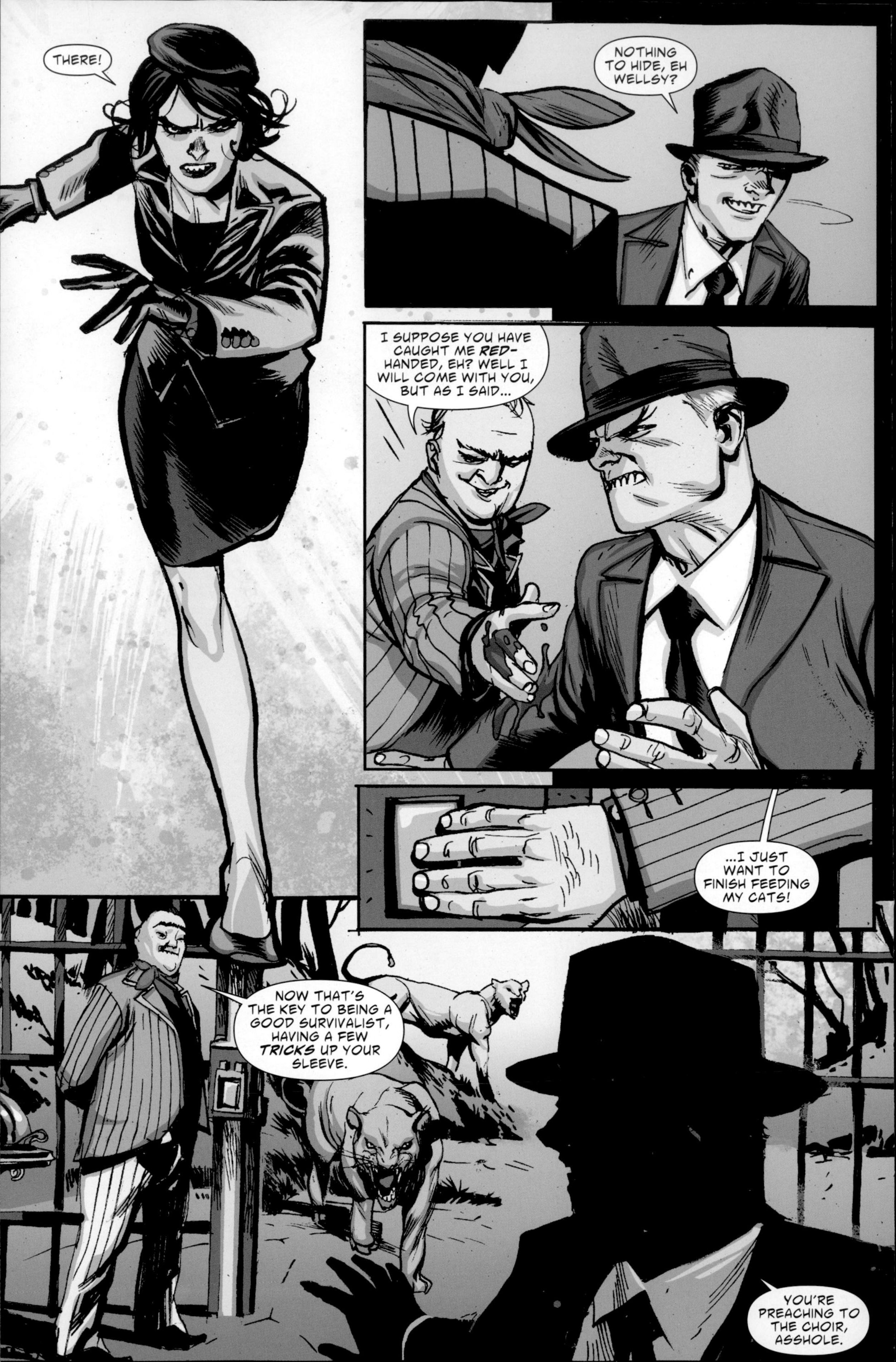
THERE!
NOTHING TO HIDE, EH WELLSY?
I SUPPOSE YOU HAVE CAUGHT ME RED-HANDED, EH? WELL I WILL COME WITH YOU, BUT AS I SAID...
...I JUST WANT TO FINISH FEEDING MY CATS!
NOW THAT'S THE KEY TO BEING A GOOD SURVIVALIST, HAVING A FEW TRICKS UP YOUR SLEEVE.
YOU'RE PREACHING TO THE CHOIR, ASSHOLE.

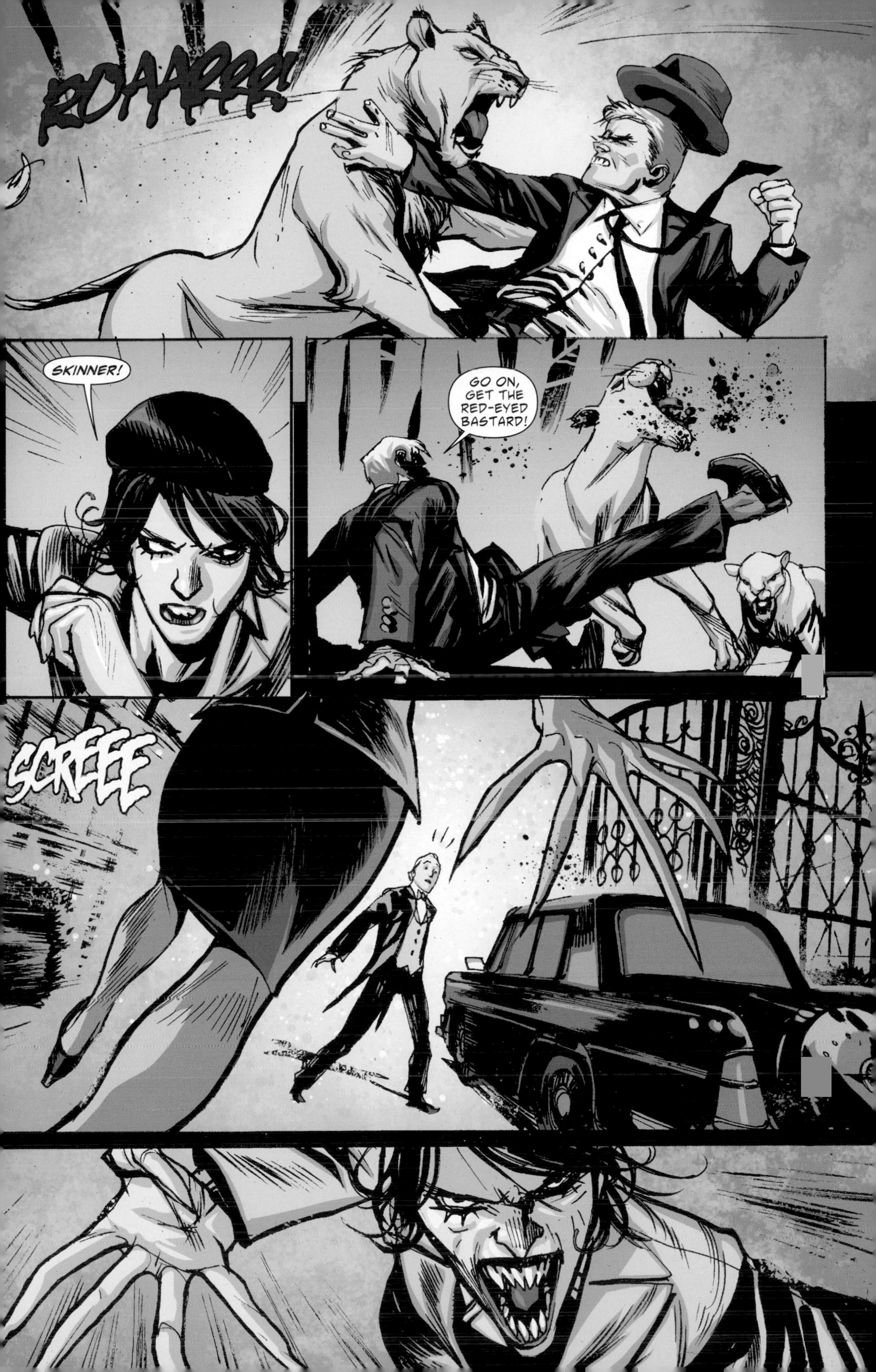
ROAARRR!
SKINNER!
GO ON, GET THE RED-EYED BASTARD!
SCREEE

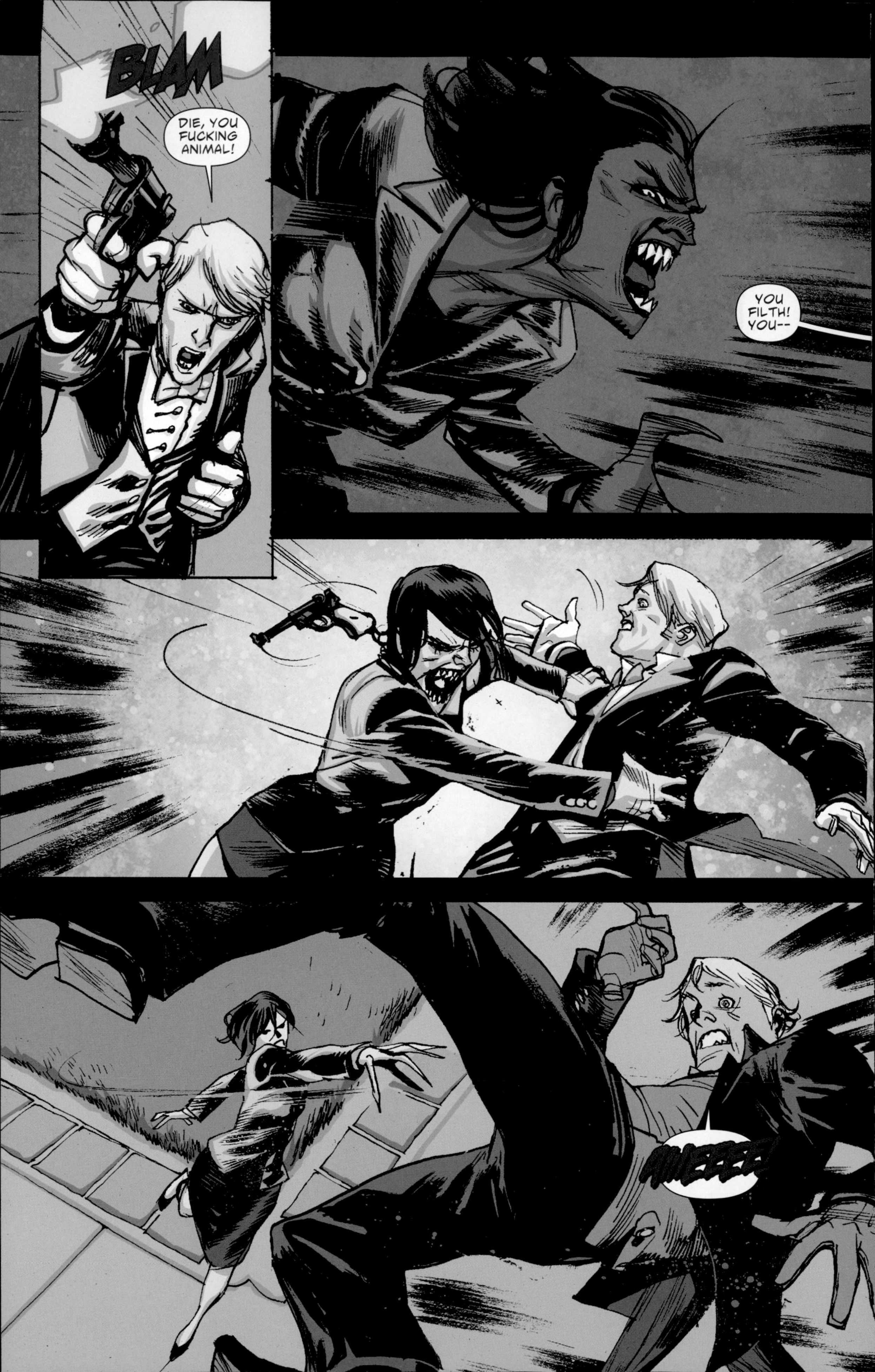
BLAM
DIE, YOU FUCKING ANIMAL!
YOU FILTH! YOU--
AIIEEEEE

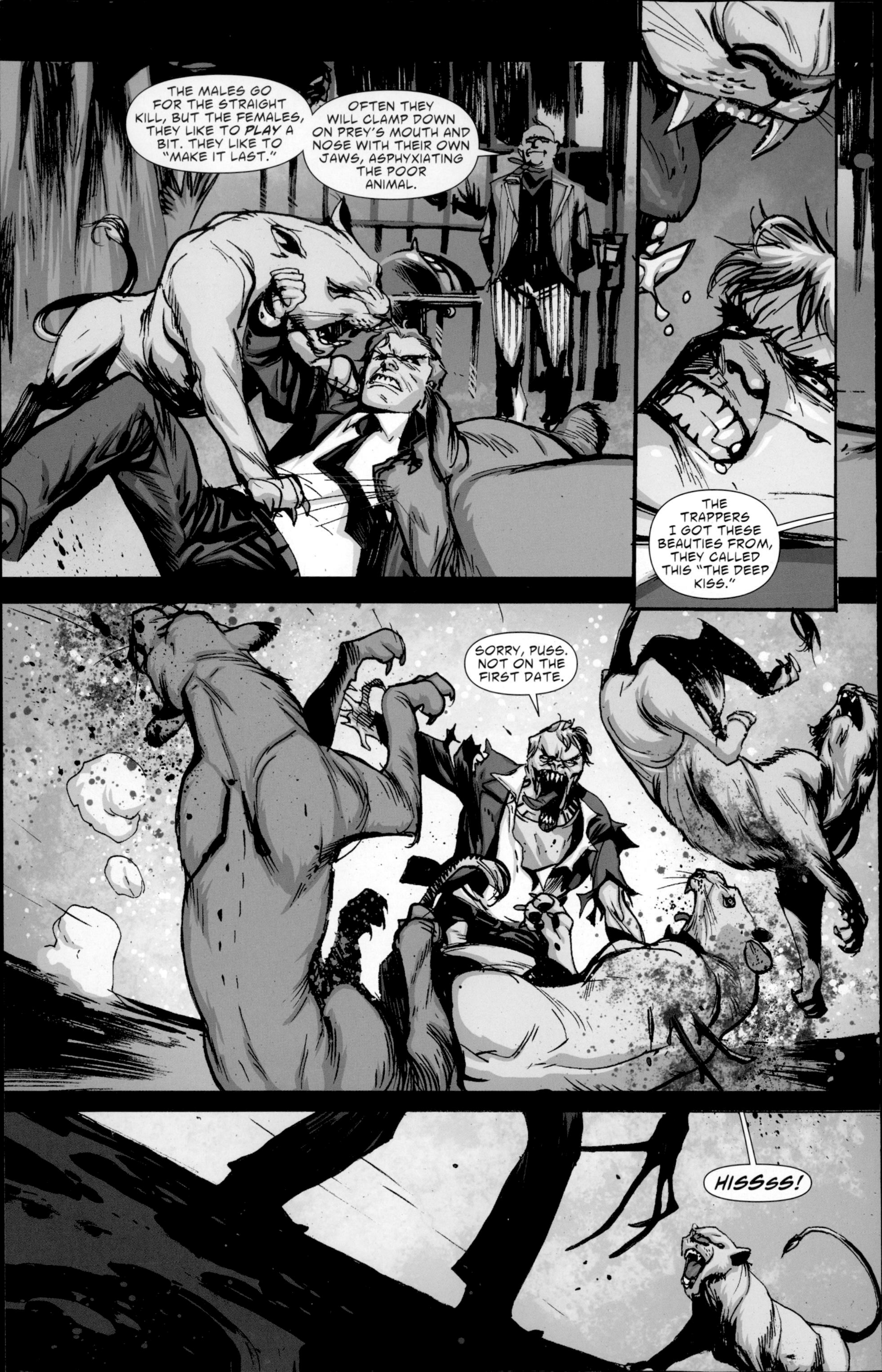
THE MALES GO FOR THE STRAIGHT KILL, BUT THE FEMALES, THEY LIKE TO PLAY A BIT. THEY LIKE TO "MAKE IT LAST."
OFTEN THEY WILL CLAMP DOWN ON PREY'S MOUTH AND NOSE WITH THEIR OWN JAWS, ASPHYXIATING THE POOR ANIMAL.
THE TRAPPERS I GOT THESE BEAUTIES FROM, THEY CALLED THIS "THE DEEP KISS."
SORRY, PUSS. NOT ON THE FIRST DATE.
HISSSS!

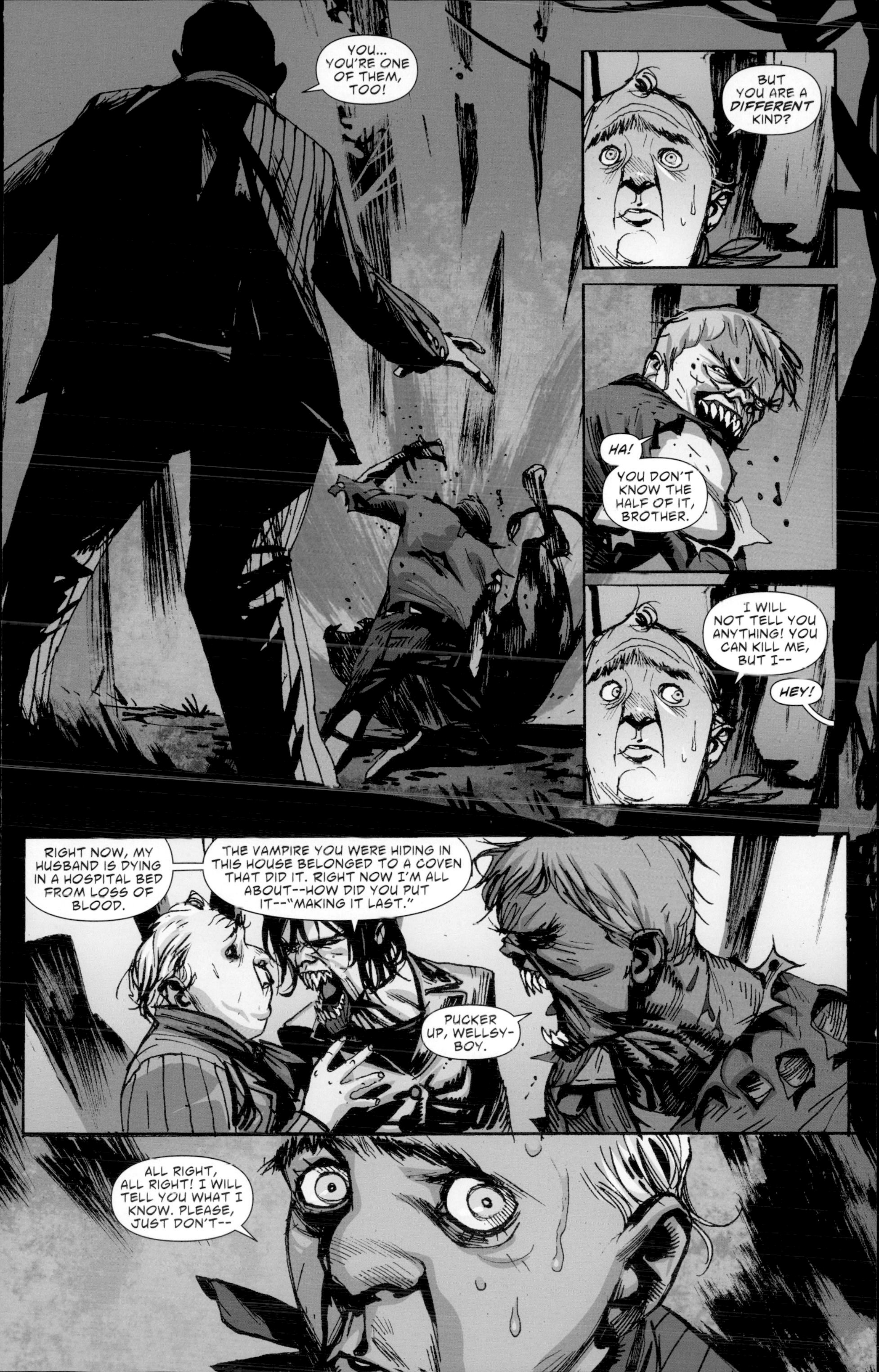
YOU... YOU'RE ONE OF THEM, TOO!
BUT YOU ARE A DIFFERENT KIND?
HA!
YOU DON'T KNOW THE HALF OF IT, BROTHER.
I WILL NOT TELL YOU ANYTHING! YOU CAN KILL ME, BUT I--
HEY!
RIGHT NOW, MY HUSBAND IS DYING IN A HOSPITAL BED FROM LOSS OF BLOOD.
THE VAMPIRE YOU WERE HIDING IN THIS HOUSE BELONGED TO A COVEN THAT DID IT. RIGHT NOW I'M ALL ABOUT--HOW DID YOU PUT IT--"MAKING IT LAST."
PUCKER UP, WELLSY-BOY.
ALL RIGHT, ALL RIGHT! I WILL TELL YOU WHAT I KNOW. PLEASE, JUST DON'T--

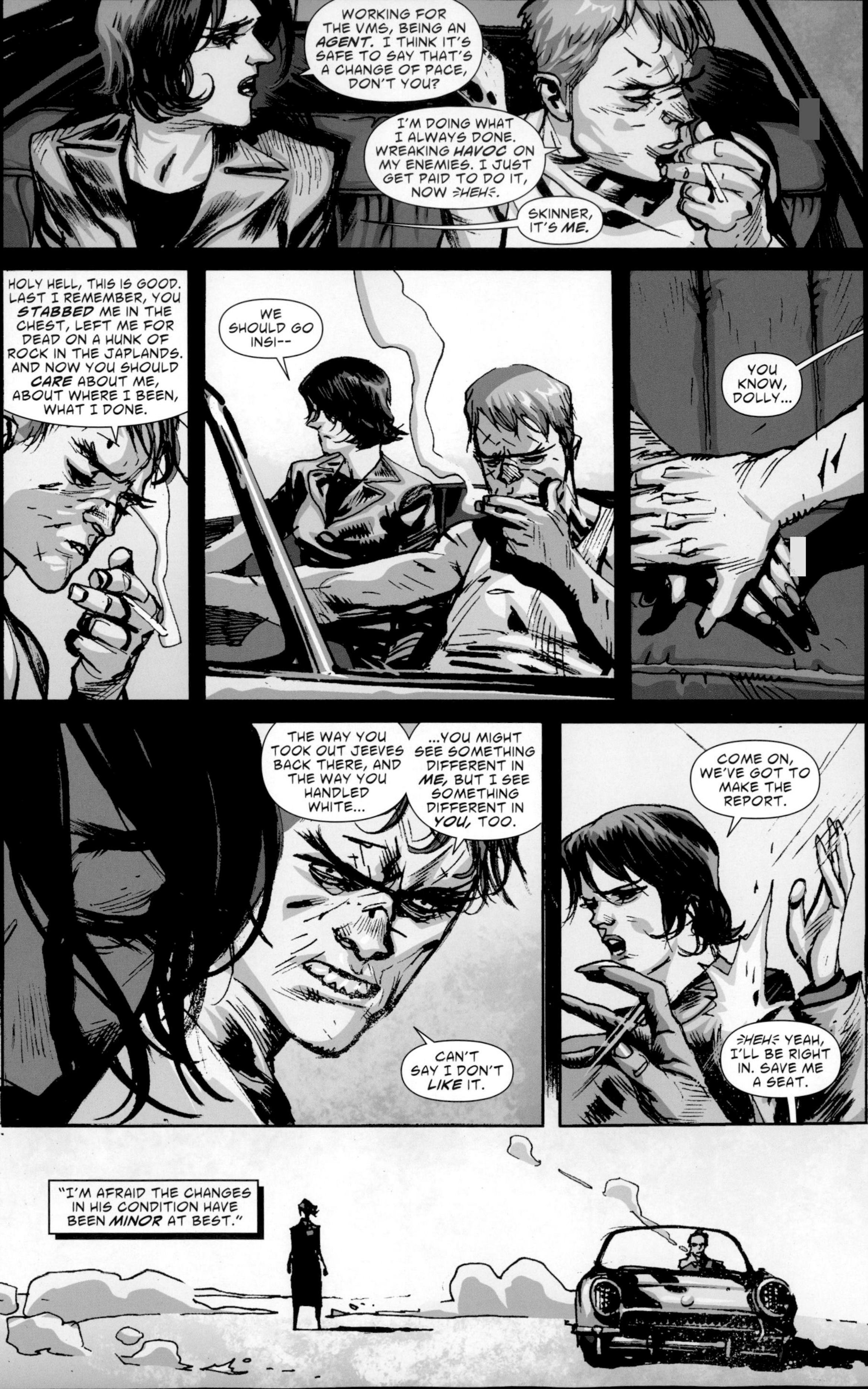

WORKING FOR THE VMS, BEING AN AGENT. I THINK IT'S SAFE TO SAY THAT'S A CHANGE OF PACE, DON'T YOU?
I'M DOING WHAT I ALWAYS DONE. WREAKING HAVOC ON MY ENEMIES. I JUST GET PAID TO DO IT, NOW =HEH=.
SKINNER, IT'S ME.
HOLY HELL, THIS IS GOOD. LAST I REMEMBER, YOU STABBED ME IN THE CHEST, LEFT ME FOR DEAD ON A HUNK OF ROCK IN THE JAPLANDS. AND NOW YOU SHOULD CARE ABOUT ME, ABOUT WHERE I BEEN, WHAT I DONE.
WE SHOULD GO INSI--
YOU KNOW, DOLLY...
THE WAY YOU TOOK OUT JEEVES BACK THERE, AND THE WAY YOU HANDLED WHITE...
...YOU MIGHT SEE SOMETHING DIFFERENT IN ME, BUT I SEE SOMETHING DIFFERENT IN YOU, TOO.
CAN'T SAY I DON'T LIKE IT.
COME ON, WE'VE GOT TO MAKE THE REPORT.
=HEH= YEAH, I'LL BE RIGHT IN. SAVE ME A SEAT.
"I'M AFRAID THE CHANGES IN HIS CONDITION HAVE BEEN MINOR AT BEST."

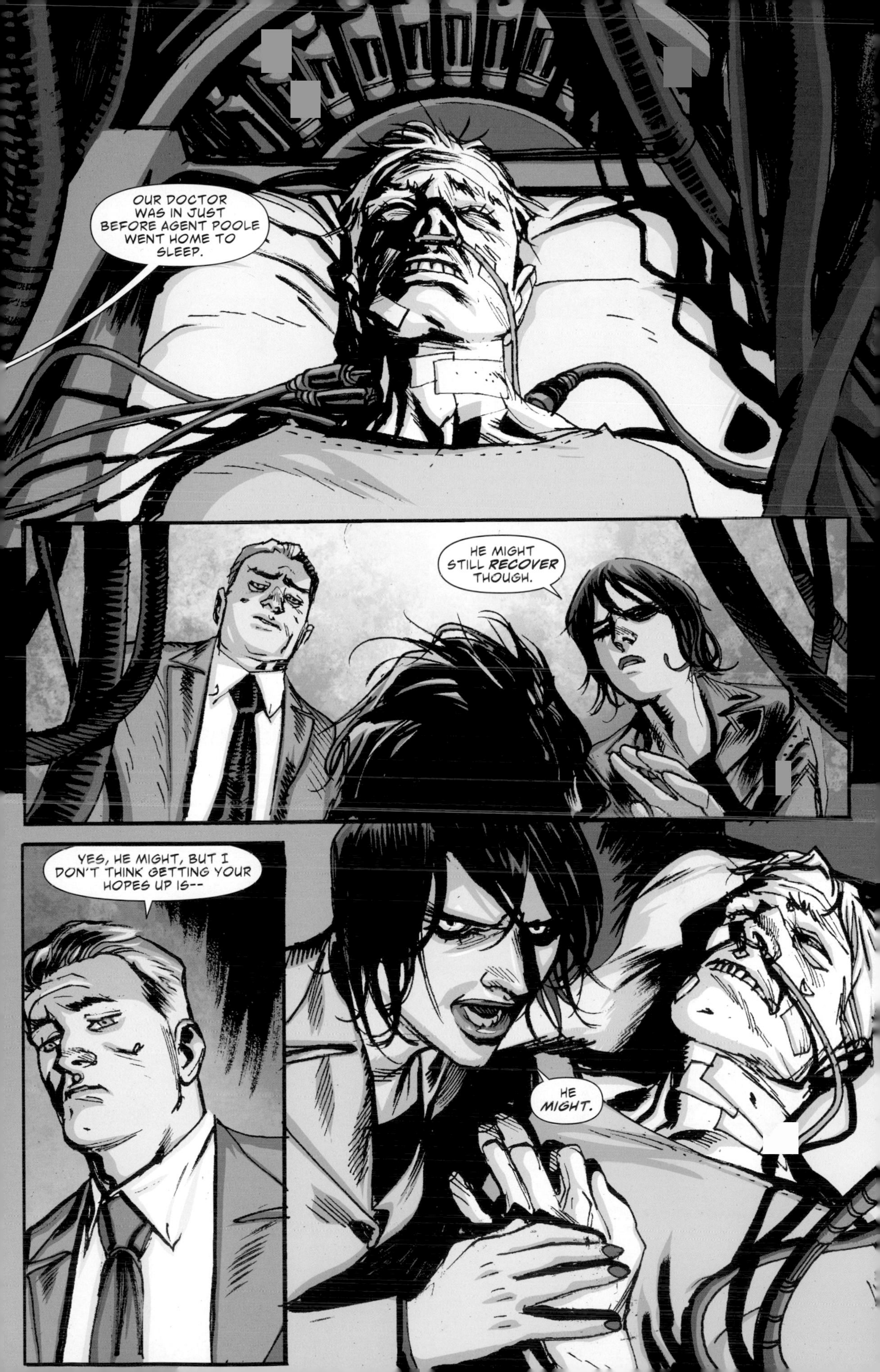
OUR DOCTOR WAS IN JUST BEFORE AGENT POOLE WENT HOME TO SLEEP.
HE MIGHT STILL *RECOVER* THOUGH.
YES, HE MIGHT, BUT I DON'T THINK GETTING YOUR HOPES UP IS--
HE *MIGHT.*

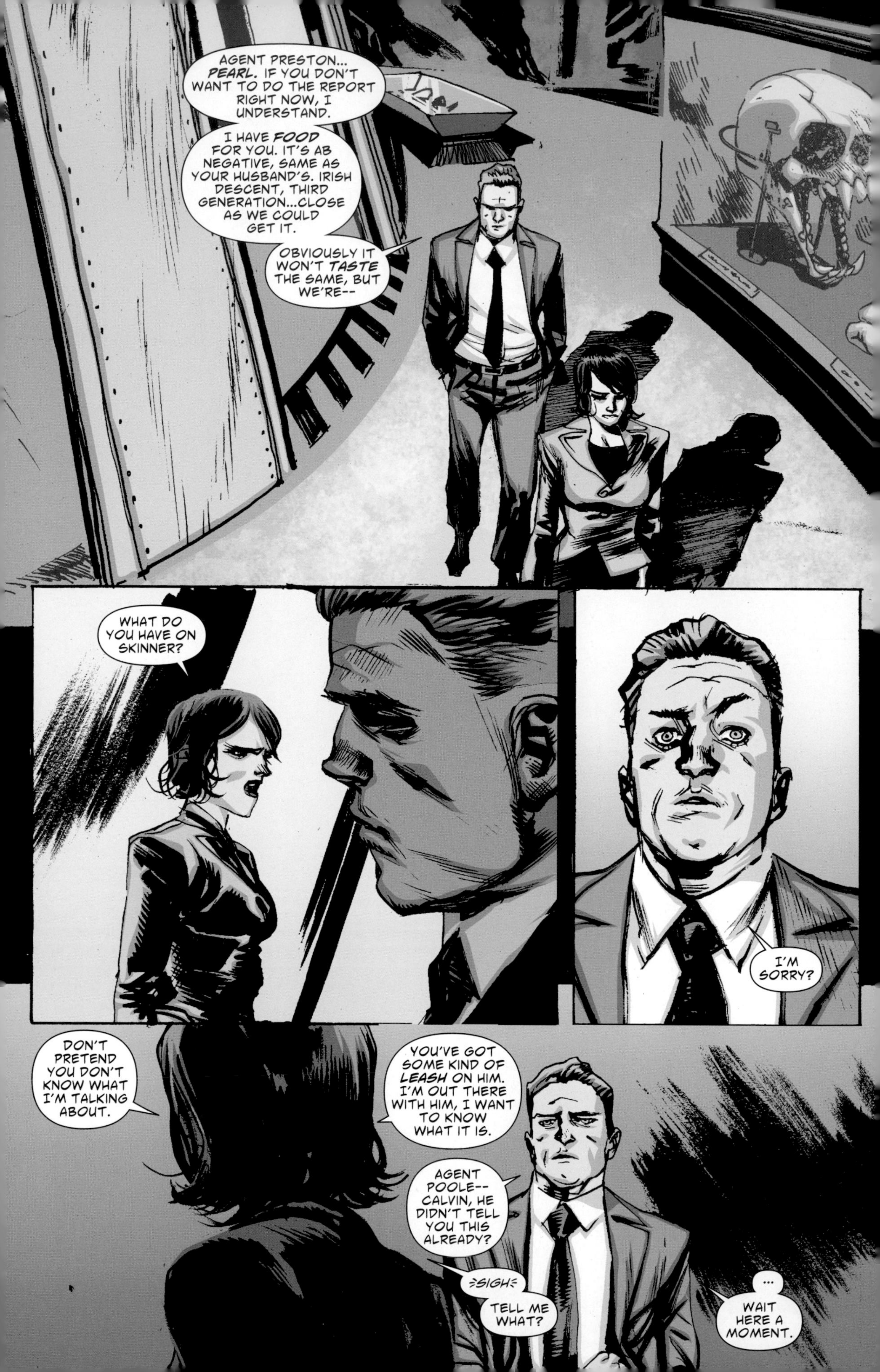
AGENT PRESTON... PEARL. IF YOU DON'T WANT TO DO THE REPORT RIGHT NOW, I UNDERSTAND.
I HAVE FOOD FOR YOU. IT'S AB NEGATIVE, SAME AS YOUR HUSBAND'S. IRISH DESCENT, THIRD GENERATION...CLOSE AS WE COULD GET IT.
OBVIOUSLY IT WON'T TASTE THE SAME, BUT WE'RE--
WHAT DO YOU HAVE ON SKINNER?
I'M SORRY?
DON'T PRETEND YOU DON'T KNOW WHAT I'M TALKING ABOUT.
YOU'VE GOT SOME KIND OF LEASH ON HIM. I'M OUT THERE WITH HIM, I WANT TO KNOW WHAT IT IS.
AGENT POOLE--CALVIN, HE DIDN'T TELL YOU THIS ALREADY?
<SIGH>
TELL ME WHAT?
...
WAIT HERE A MOMENT.

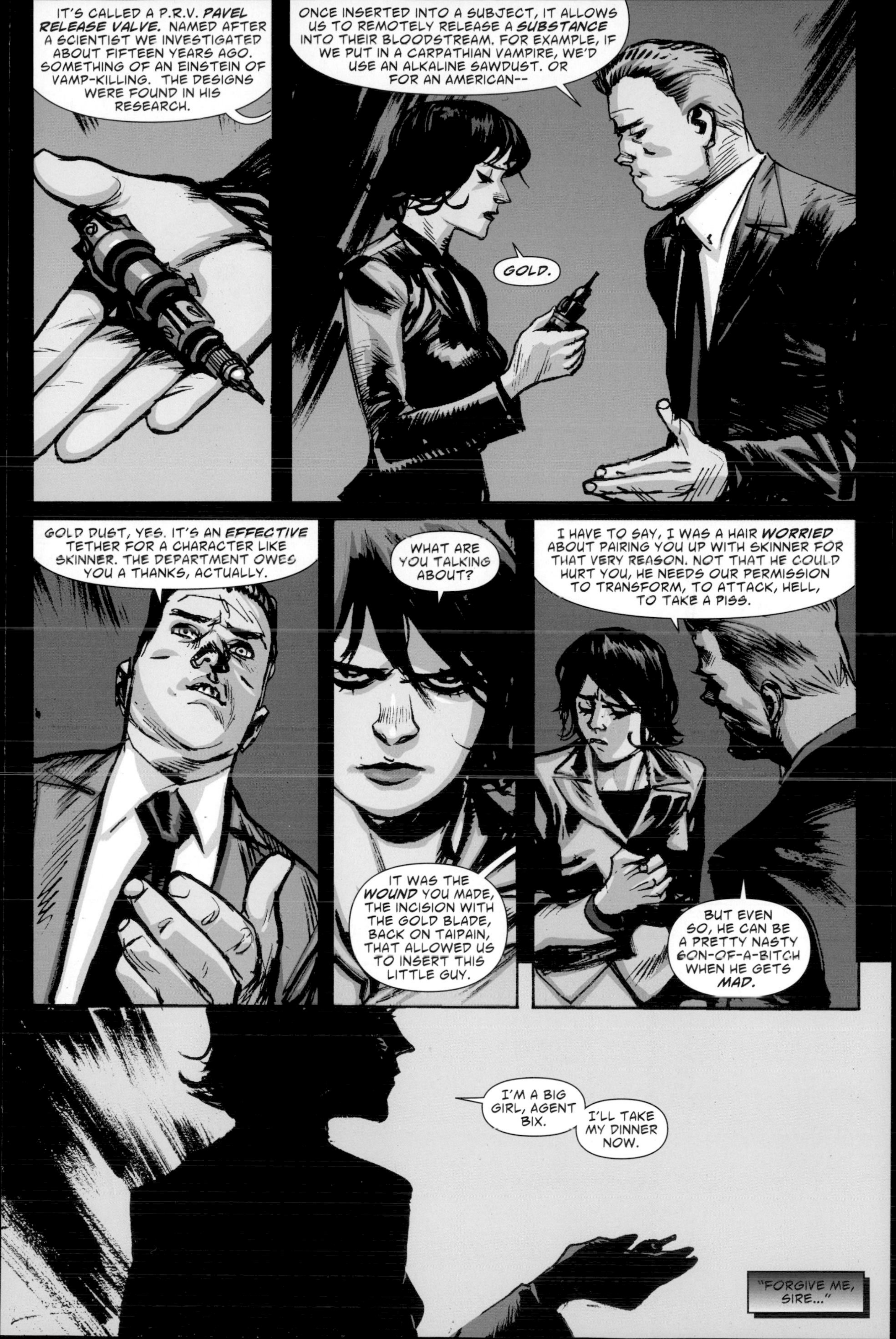
IT'S CALLED A P.R.V. PAVEL RELEASE VALVE. NAMED AFTER A SCIENTIST WE INVESTIGATED ABOUT FIFTEEN YEARS AGO. SOMETHING OF AN EINSTEIN OF VAMP-KILLING. THE DESIGNS WERE FOUND IN HIS RESEARCH.
ONCE INSERTED INTO A SUBJECT, IT ALLOWS US TO REMOTELY RELEASE A SUBSTANCE INTO THEIR BLOODSTREAM. FOR EXAMPLE, IF WE PUT IN A CARPATHIAN VAMPIRE, WE'D USE AN ALKALINE SAWDUST. OR FOR AN AMERICAN--
GOLD.
GOLD DUST, YES. IT'S AN EFFECTIVE TETHER FOR A CHARACTER LIKE SKINNER. THE DEPARTMENT OWES YOU A THANKS, ACTUALLY.
WHAT ARE YOU TALKING ABOUT?
IT WAS THE WOUND YOU MADE, THE INCISION WITH THE GOLD BLADE, BACK ON TAIPAIN, THAT ALLOWED US TO INSERT THIS LITTLE GUY.
I HAVE TO SAY, I WAS A HAIR WORRIED ABOUT PAIRING YOU UP WITH SKINNER FOR THAT VERY REASON. NOT THAT HE COULD HURT YOU, HE NEEDS OUR PERMISSION TO TRANSFORM, TO ATTACK, HELL, TO TAKE A PISS.
BUT EVEN SO, HE CAN BE A PRETTY NASTY SON-OF-A-BITCH WHEN HE GETS MAD.
I'M A BIG GIRL, AGENT BIX.
I'LL TAKE MY DINNER NOW.
"FORGIVE ME, SIRE..."

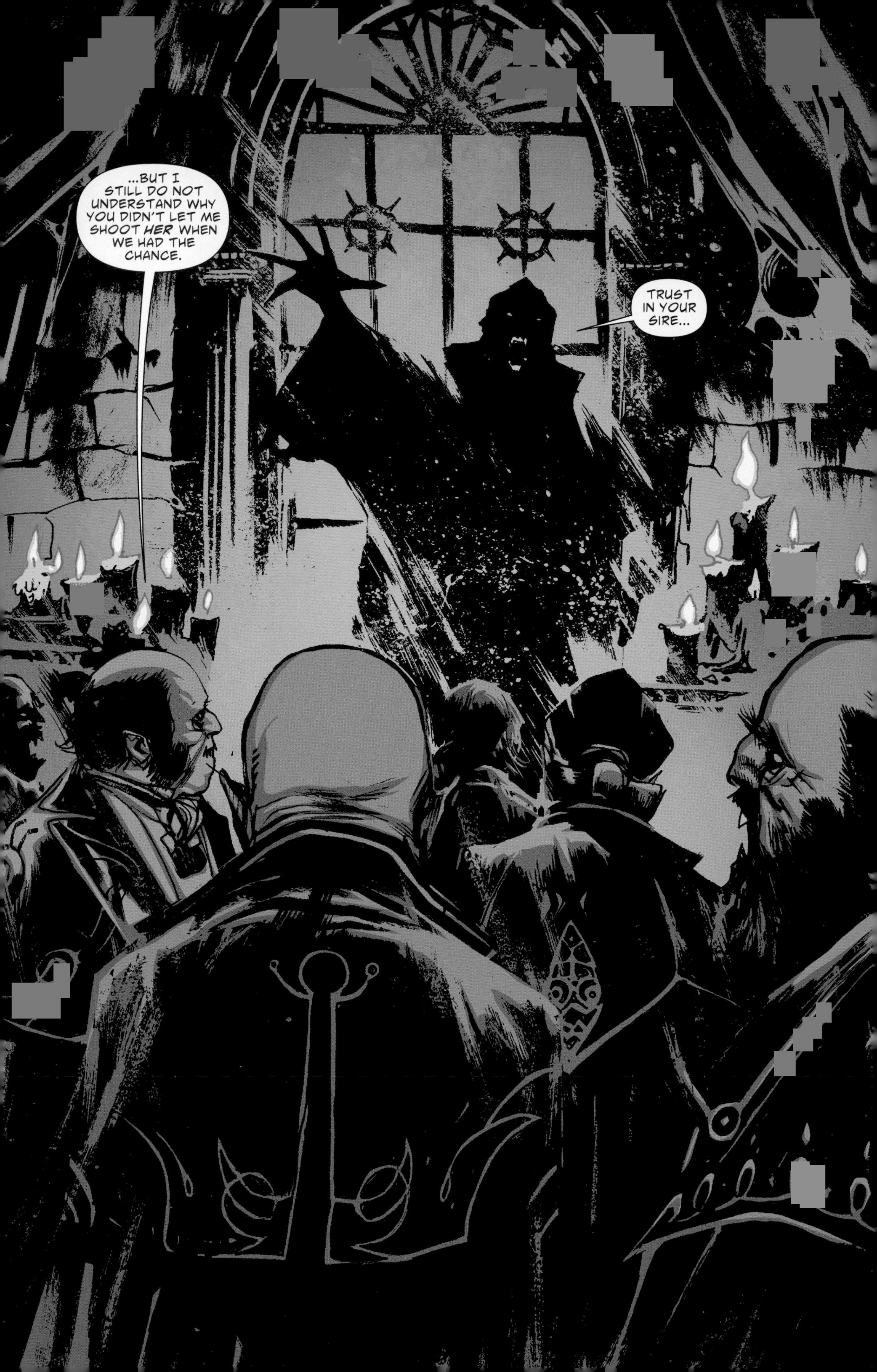
...BUT I STILL DO NOT UNDERSTAND WHY YOU DIDN'T LET ME SHOOT HER WHEN WE HAD THE CHANCE.
TRUST IN YOUR SIRE...

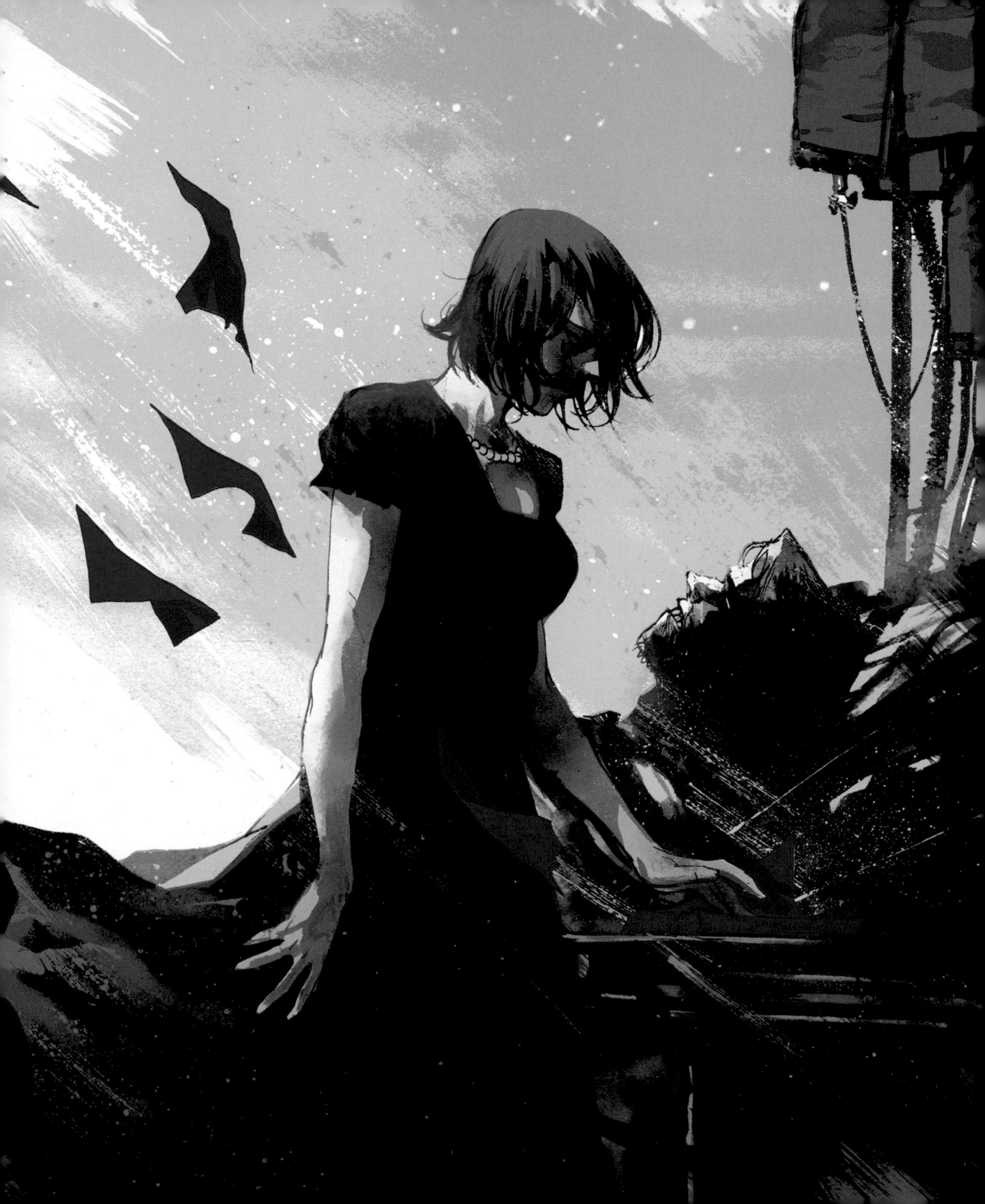

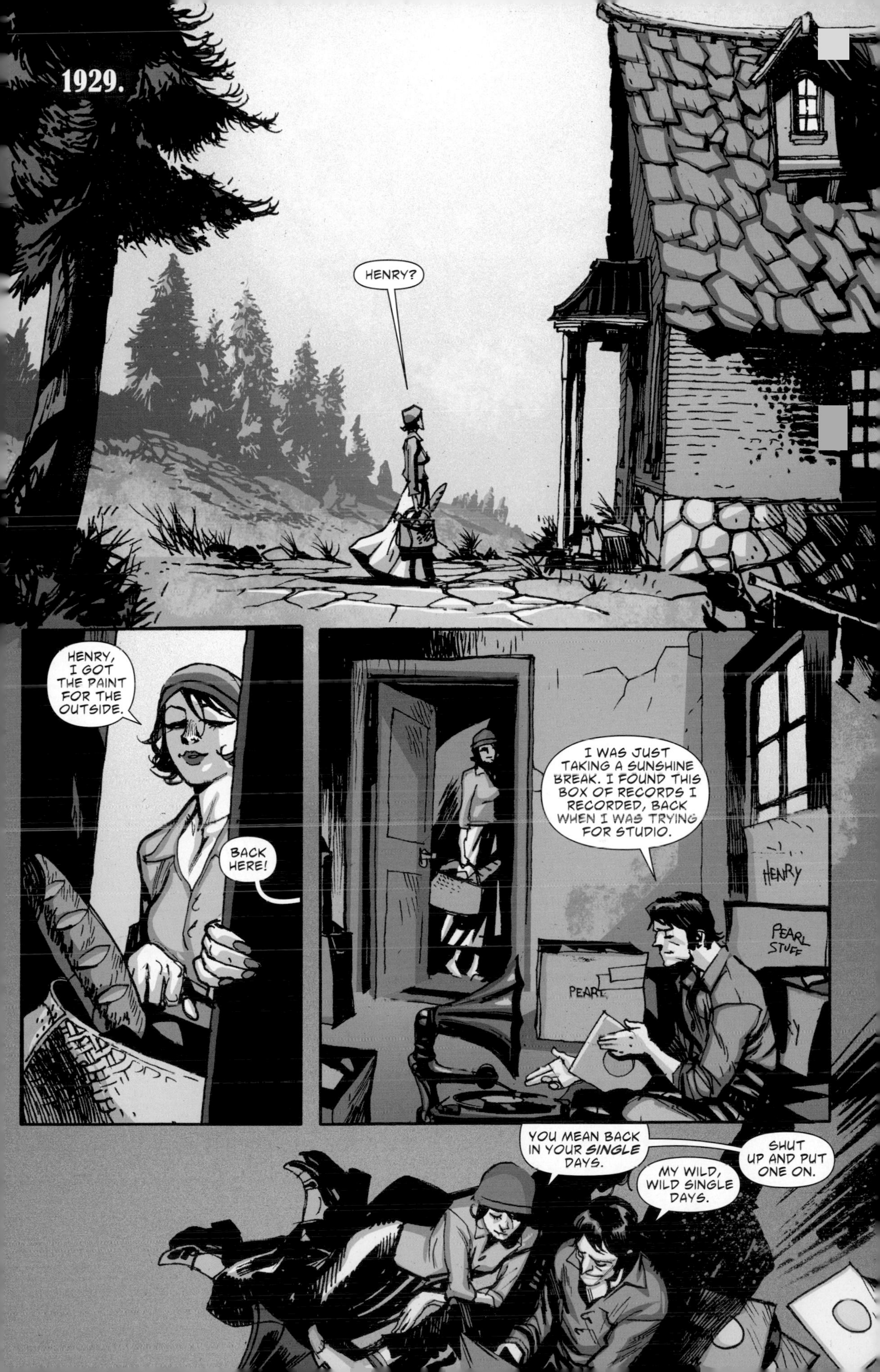

1929.
HENRY?
HENRY, I GOT THE PAINT FOR THE OUTSIDE.
BACK HERE!
I WAS JUST TAKING A SUNSHINE BREAK. I FOUND THIS BOX OF RECORDS I RECORDED, BACK WHEN I WAS TRYING FOR STUDIO.
HENRY
PEARL STUFF
PEARL
YOU MEAN BACK IN YOUR *SINGLE* DAYS.
MY WILD, WILD SINGLE DAYS.
SHUT UP AND PUT ONE ON.

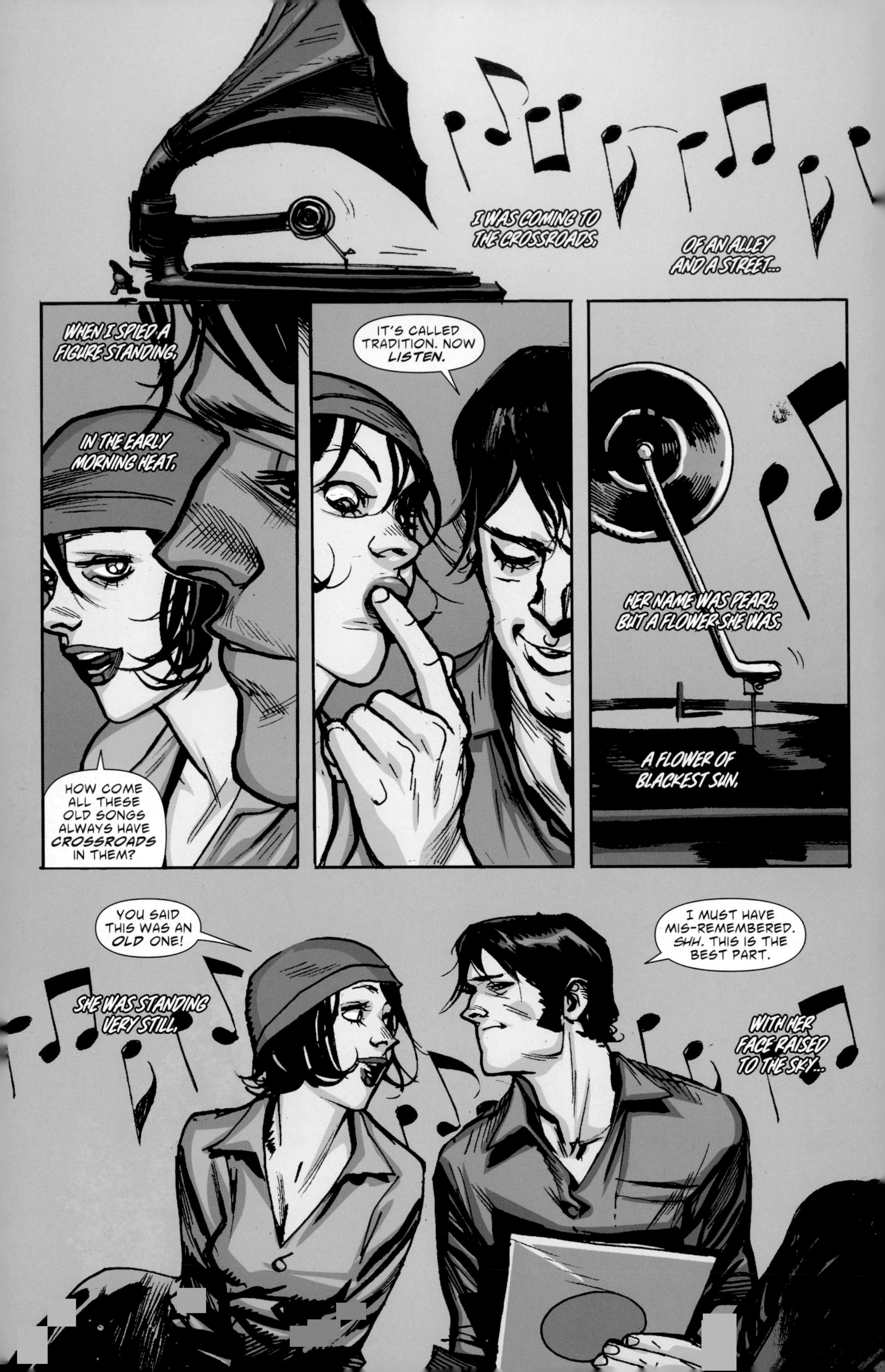
I WAS COMING TO THE CROSSROADS.
OF AN ALLEY AND A STREET...
WHEN I SPIED A FIGURE STANDING,
IN THE EARLY MORNING HEAT.
HOW COME ALL THESE OLD SONGS ALWAYS HAVE CROSSROADS IN THEM?
IT'S CALLED TRADITION. NOW LISTEN.
HER NAME WAS PEARL, BUT A FLOWER SHE WAS.
A FLOWER OF BLACKEST SUN.
YOU SAID THIS WAS AN OLD ONE!
I MUST HAVE MIS-REMEMBERED. SHH. THIS IS THE BEST PART.
SHE WAS STANDING VERY STILL.
WITH HER FACE RAISED TO THE SKY...

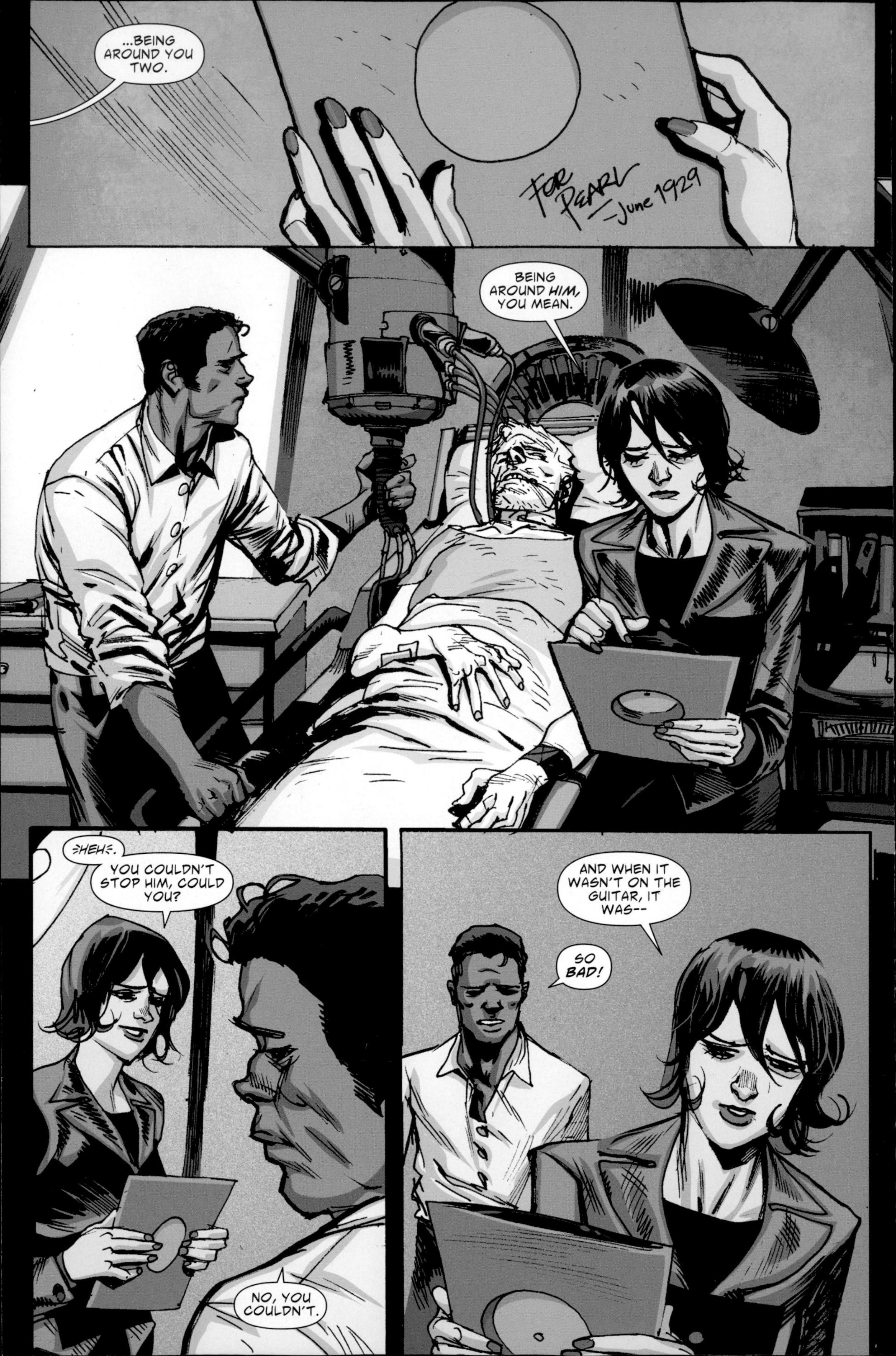
...BEING AROUND YOU TWO.
FOR PEARL —June 1929
BEING AROUND *HIM*, YOU MEAN.
HEH. YOU COULDN'T STOP HIM, COULD YOU?
NO, YOU COULDN'T.
AND WHEN IT WASN'T ON THE GUITAR, IT WAS--
SO BAD!

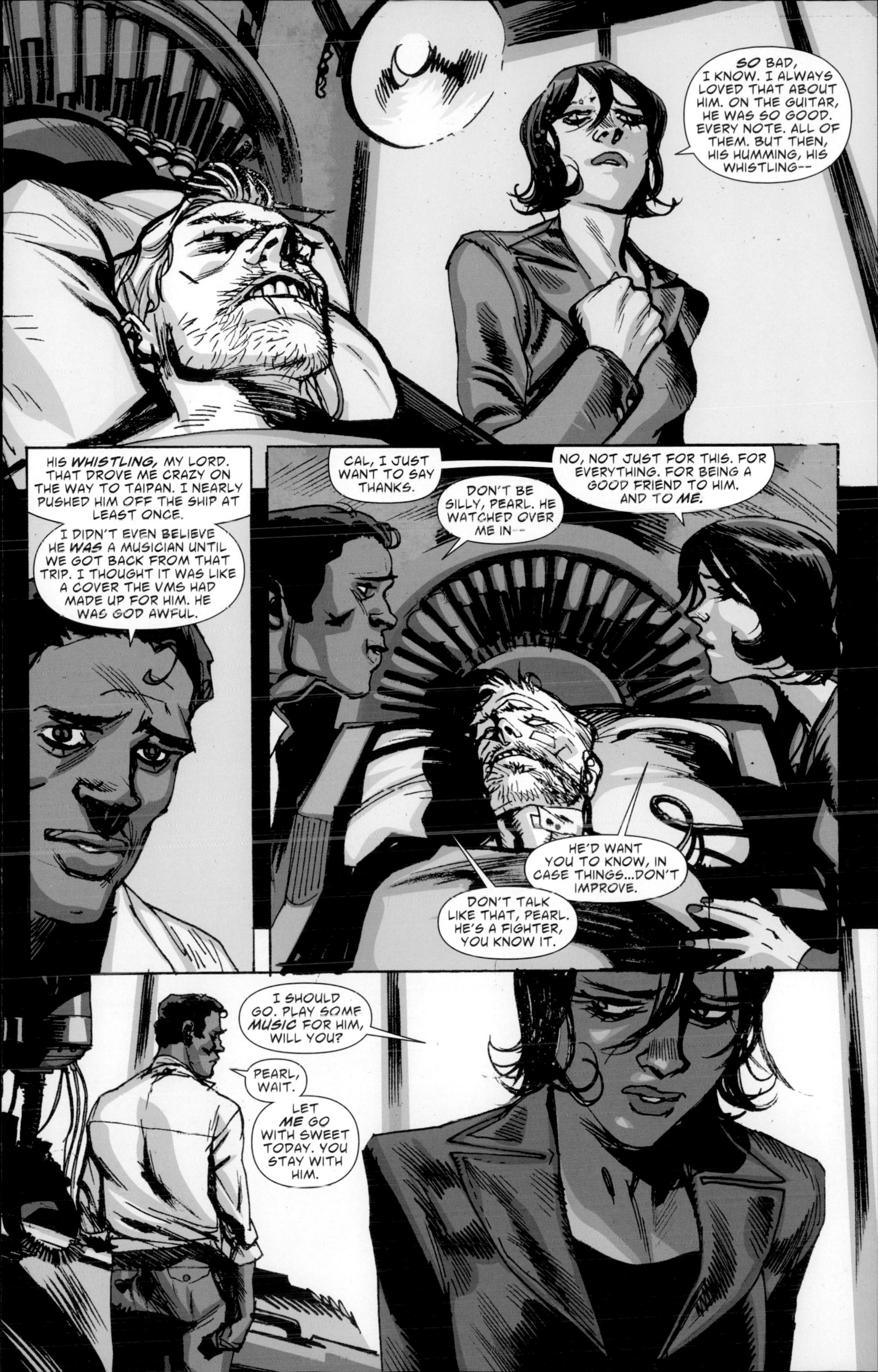
SO BAD, I KNOW. I ALWAYS LOVED THAT ABOUT HIM. ON THE GUITAR, HE WAS SO GOOD. EVERY NOTE. ALL OF THEM. BUT THEN, HIS HUMMING, HIS WHISTLING--
HIS WHISTLING, MY LORD. THAT DROVE ME CRAZY ON THE WAY TO TAIPAN. I NEARLY PUSHED HIM OFF THE SHIP AT LEAST ONCE.
I DIDN'T EVEN BELIEVE HE WAS A MUSICIAN UNTIL WE GOT BACK FROM THAT TRIP. I THOUGHT IT WAS LIKE A COVER THE VMS HAD MADE UP FOR HIM. HE WAS GOD AWFUL.
CAL, I JUST WANT TO SAY THANKS.
DON'T BE SILLY, PEARL. HE WATCHED OVER ME IN--
NO, NOT JUST FOR THIS. FOR EVERYTHING. FOR BEING A GOOD FRIEND TO HIM. AND TO ME.
HE'D WANT YOU TO KNOW, IN CASE THINGS...DON'T IMPROVE.
DON'T TALK LIKE THAT, PEARL. HE'S A FIGHTER, YOU KNOW IT.
I SHOULD GO. PLAY SOME MUSIC FOR HIM, WILL YOU?
PEARL, WAIT.
LET ME GO WITH SWEET TODAY. YOU STAY WITH HIM.

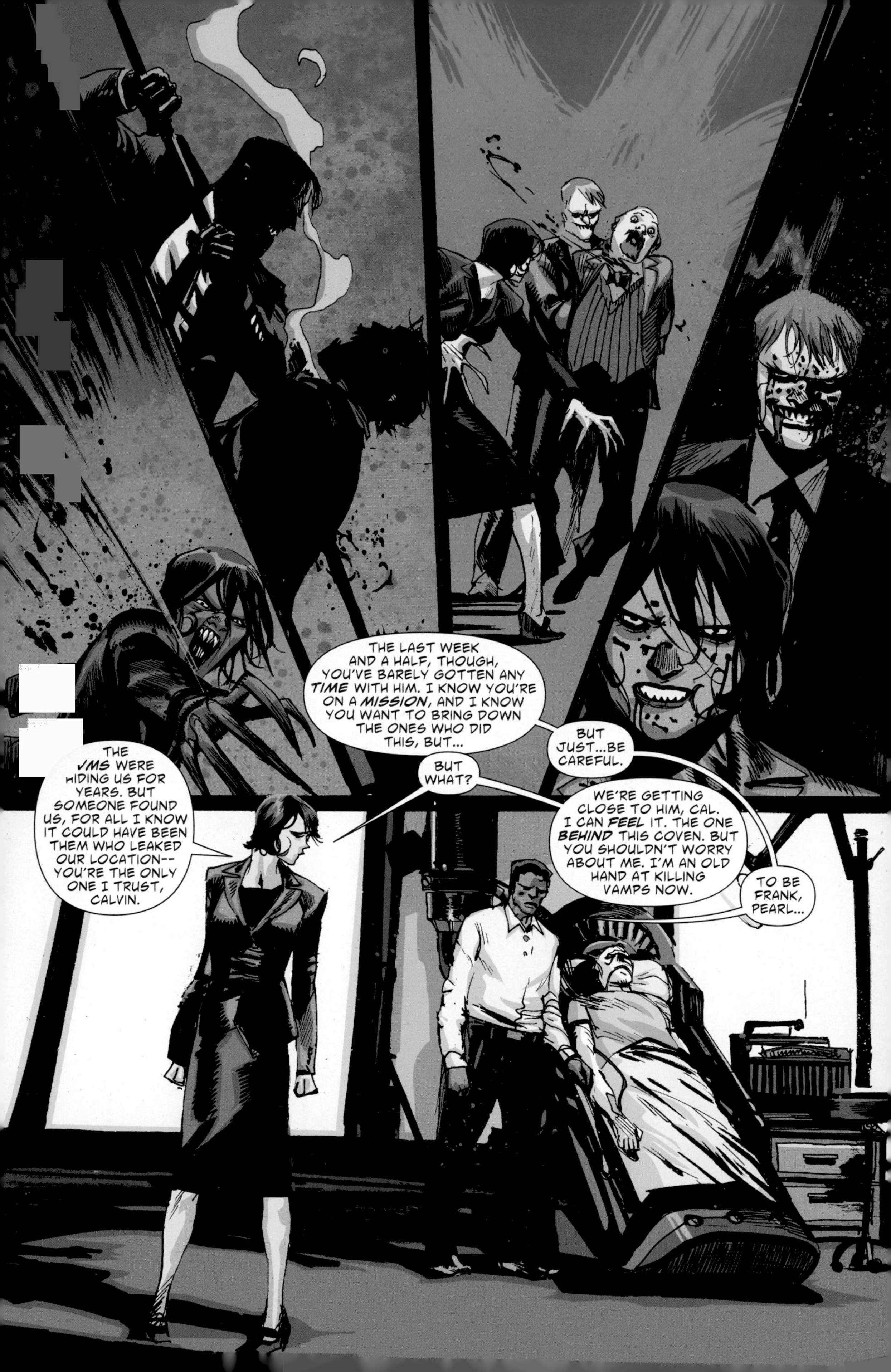
THE VMS WERE HIDING US FOR YEARS. BUT SOMEONE FOUND US, FOR ALL I KNOW IT COULD HAVE BEEN THEM WHO LEAKED OUR LOCATION--YOU'RE THE ONLY ONE I TRUST, CALVIN.
TO BE FRANK, PEARL...
THE LAST WEEK AND A HALF, THOUGH, YOU'VE BARELY GOTTEN ANY *TIME* WITH HIM. I KNOW YOU'RE ON A *MISSION*, AND I KNOW YOU WANT TO BRING DOWN THE ONES WHO DID THIS, BUT...
BUT WHAT?
BUT JUST...BE CAREFUL.
WE'RE GETTING CLOSE TO HIM, CAL. I CAN *FEEL* IT. THE ONE *BEHIND* THIS COVEN. BUT YOU SHOULDN'T WORRY ABOUT ME. I'M AN OLD HAND AT KILLING VAMPS NOW.

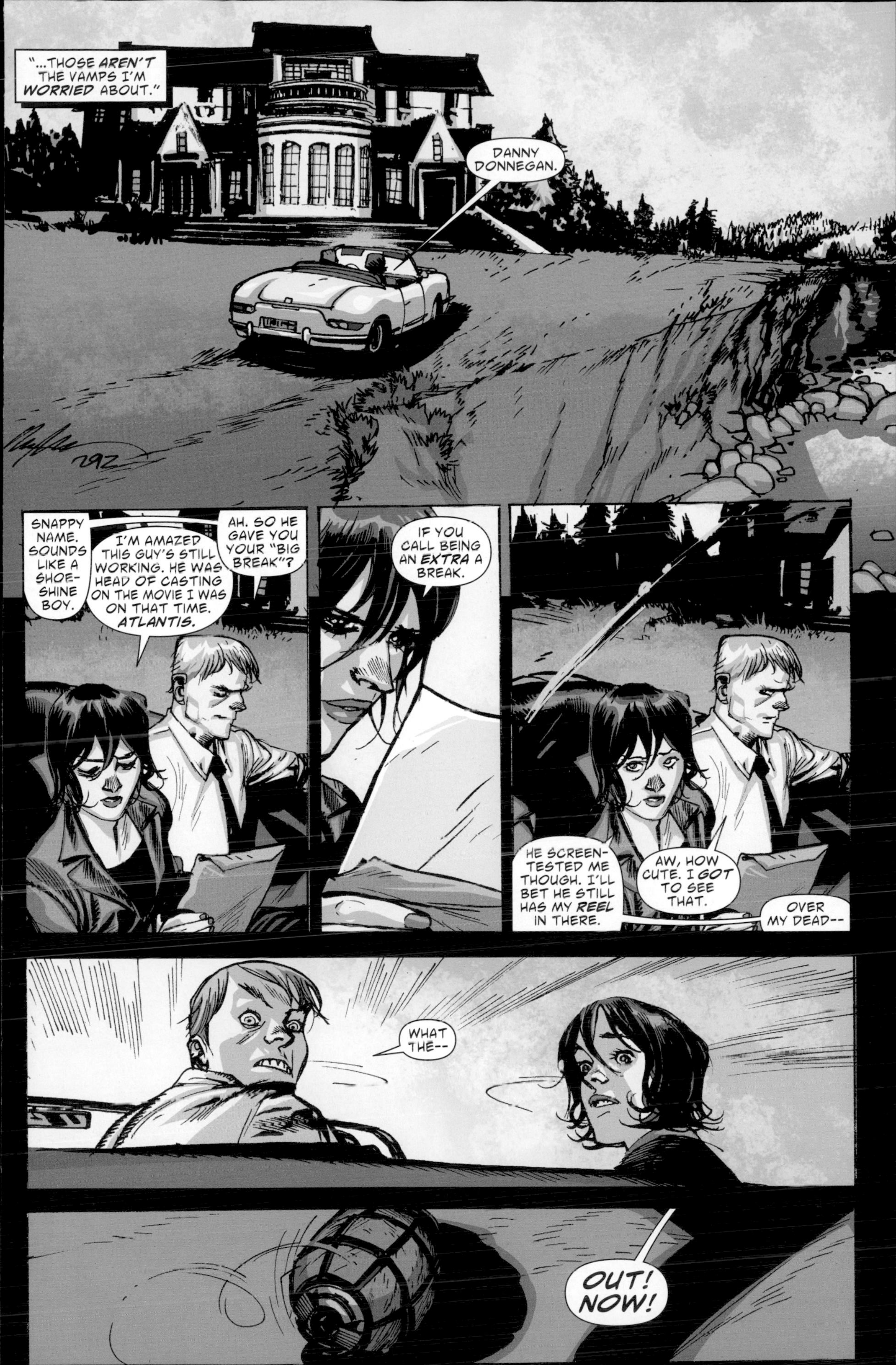

"...THOSE AREN'T THE VAMPS I'M WORRIED ABOUT."
DANNY DONNEGAN.
SNAPPY NAME. SOUNDS LIKE A SHOE-SHINE BOY.
I'M AMAZED THIS GUY'S STILL WORKING. HE WAS HEAD OF CASTING ON THE MOVIE I WAS ON THAT TIME. ATLANTIS.
AH. SO HE GAVE YOU YOUR "BIG BREAK"?
IF YOU CALL BEING AN EXTRA A BREAK.
HE SCREEN-TESTED ME THOUGH. I'LL BET HE STILL HAS MY REEL IN THERE.
AW, HOW CUTE. I GOT TO SEE THAT.
OVER MY DEAD--
WHAT THE--
OUT! NOW!

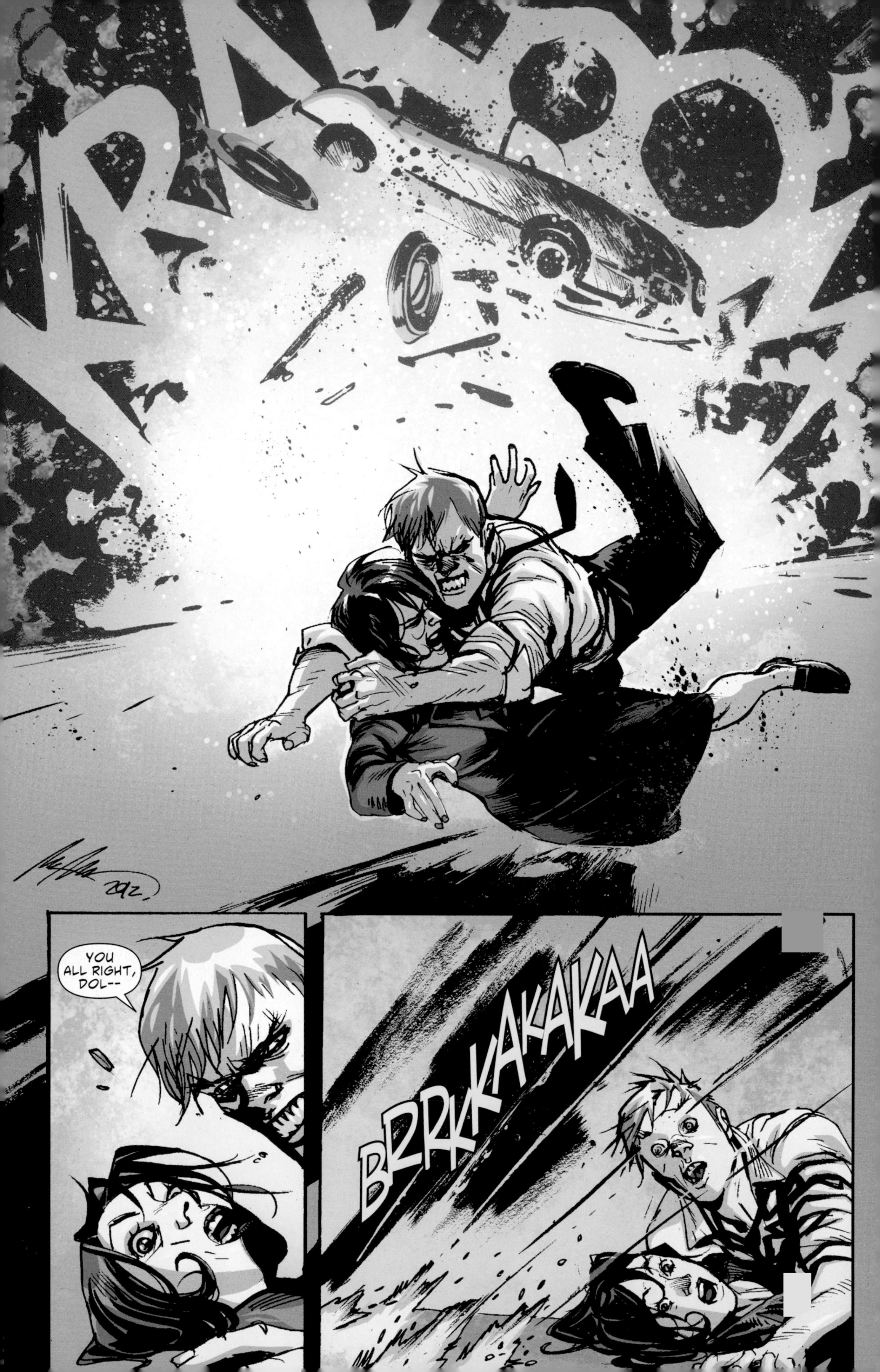
YOU ALL RIGHT, DOL--
BRRKKAKAKAA

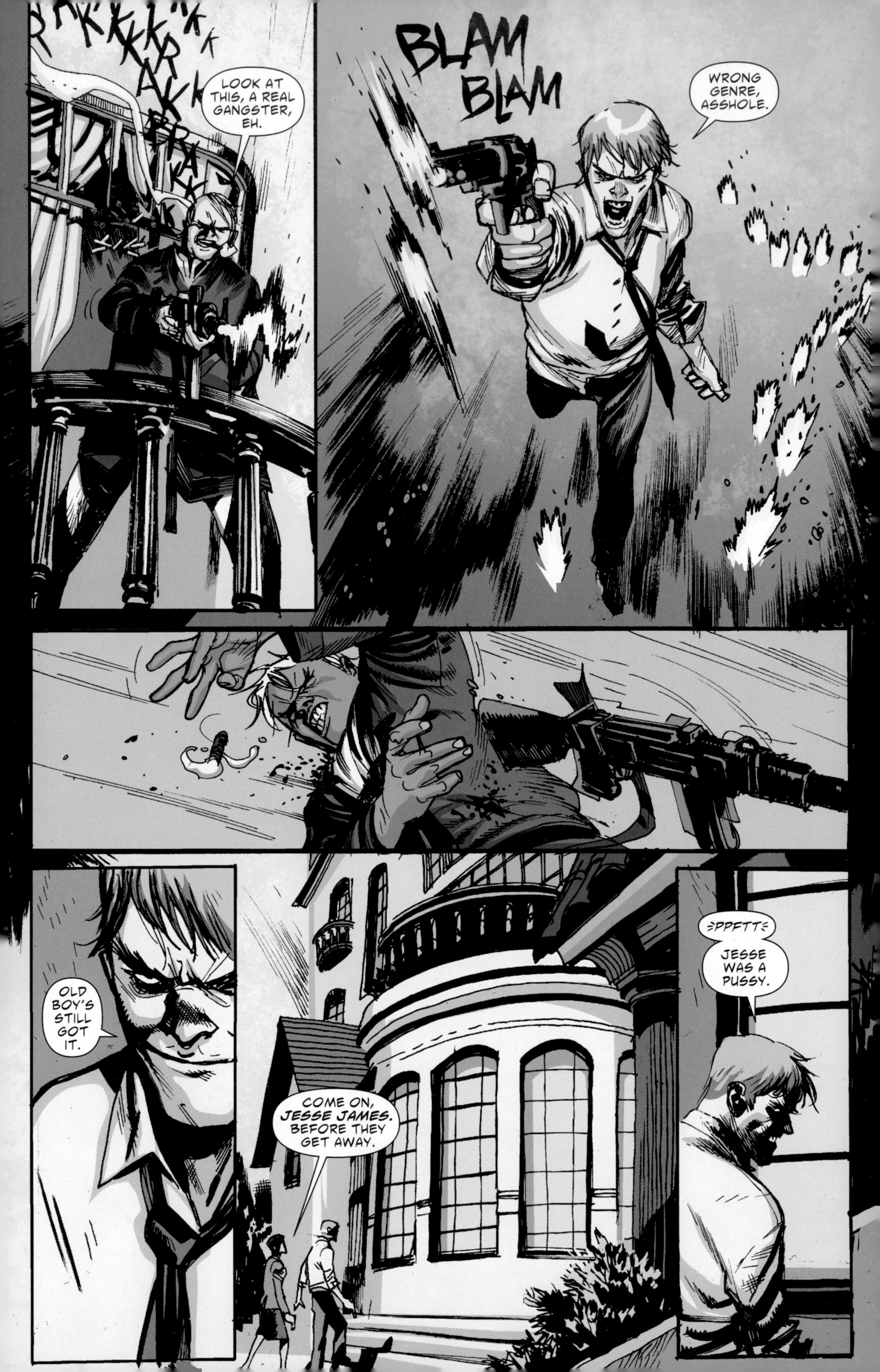

RAKKKKAKK KRAKKKRAKK
LOOK AT THIS, A REAL GANGSTER, EH.
BLAM BLAM
WRONG GENRE, ASSHOLE.
OLD BOY'S STILL GOT IT.
COME ON, JESSE JAMES. BEFORE THEY GET AWAY.
PPFTT
JESSE WAS A PUSSY.

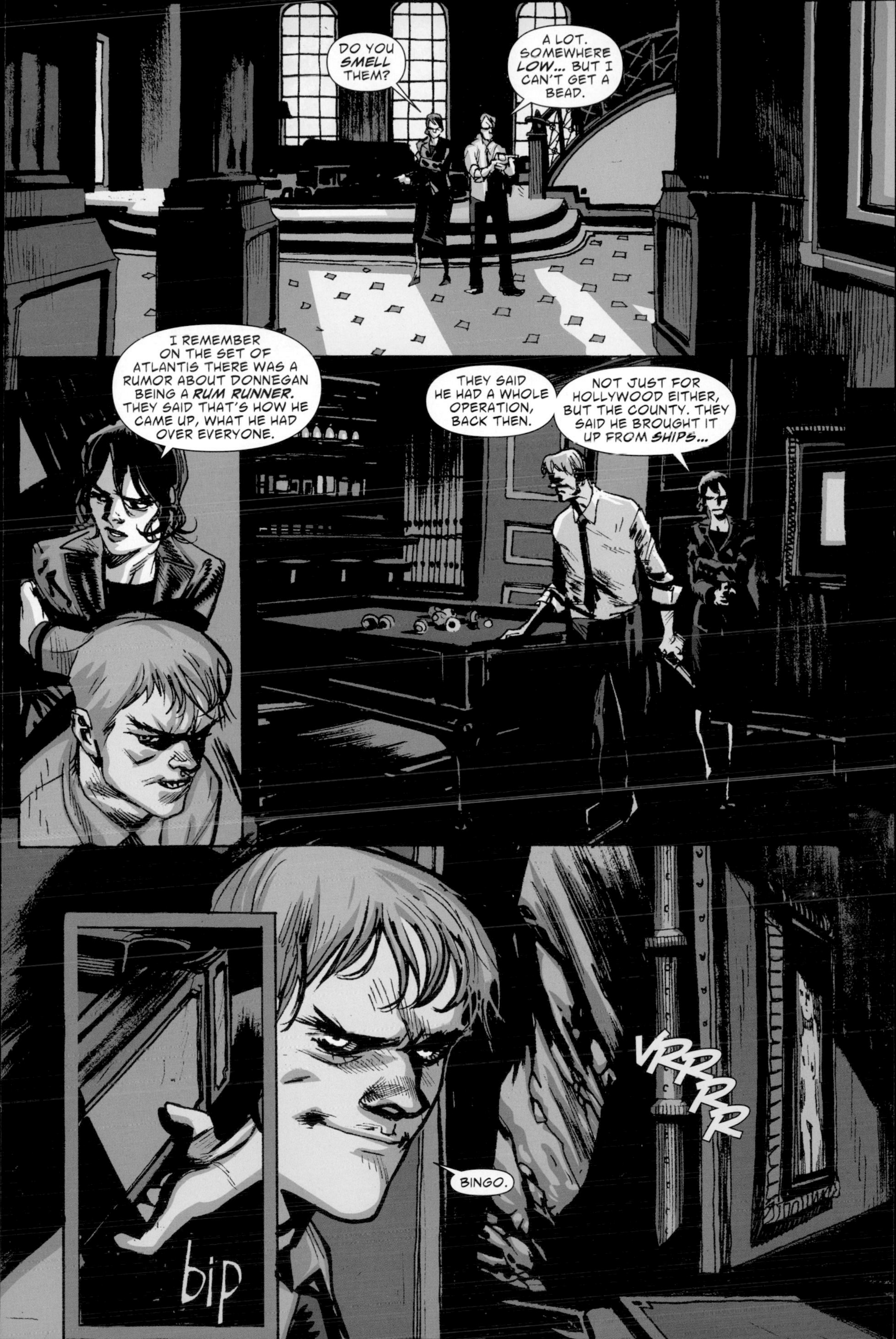
DO YOU SMELL THEM?
A LOT. SOMEWHERE LOW... BUT I CAN'T GET A BEAD.
I REMEMBER ON THE SET OF ATLANTIS THERE WAS A RUMOR ABOUT DONNEGAN BEING A RUM RUNNER. THEY SAID THAT'S HOW HE CAME UP, WHAT HE HAD OVER EVERYONE.
THEY SAID HE HAD A WHOLE OPERATION, BACK THEN.
NOT JUST FOR HOLLYWOOD EITHER, BUT THE COUNTY. THEY SAID HE BROUGHT IT UP FROM SHIPS...
VRRRR
BINGO.
bip

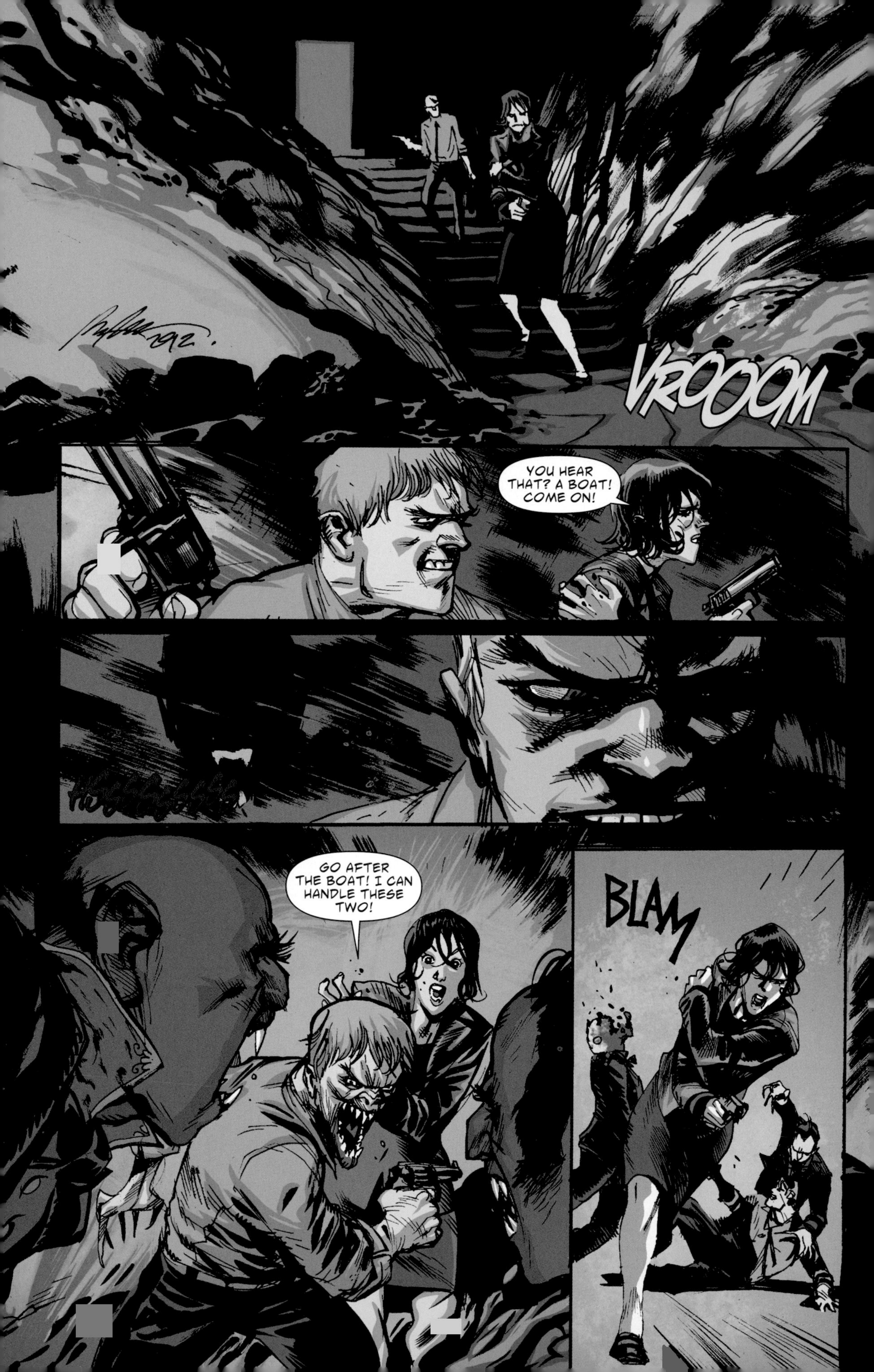
VROOOM
YOU HEAR THAT? A BOAT! COME ON!
GO AFTER THE BOAT! I CAN HANDLE THESE TWO!
BLAM

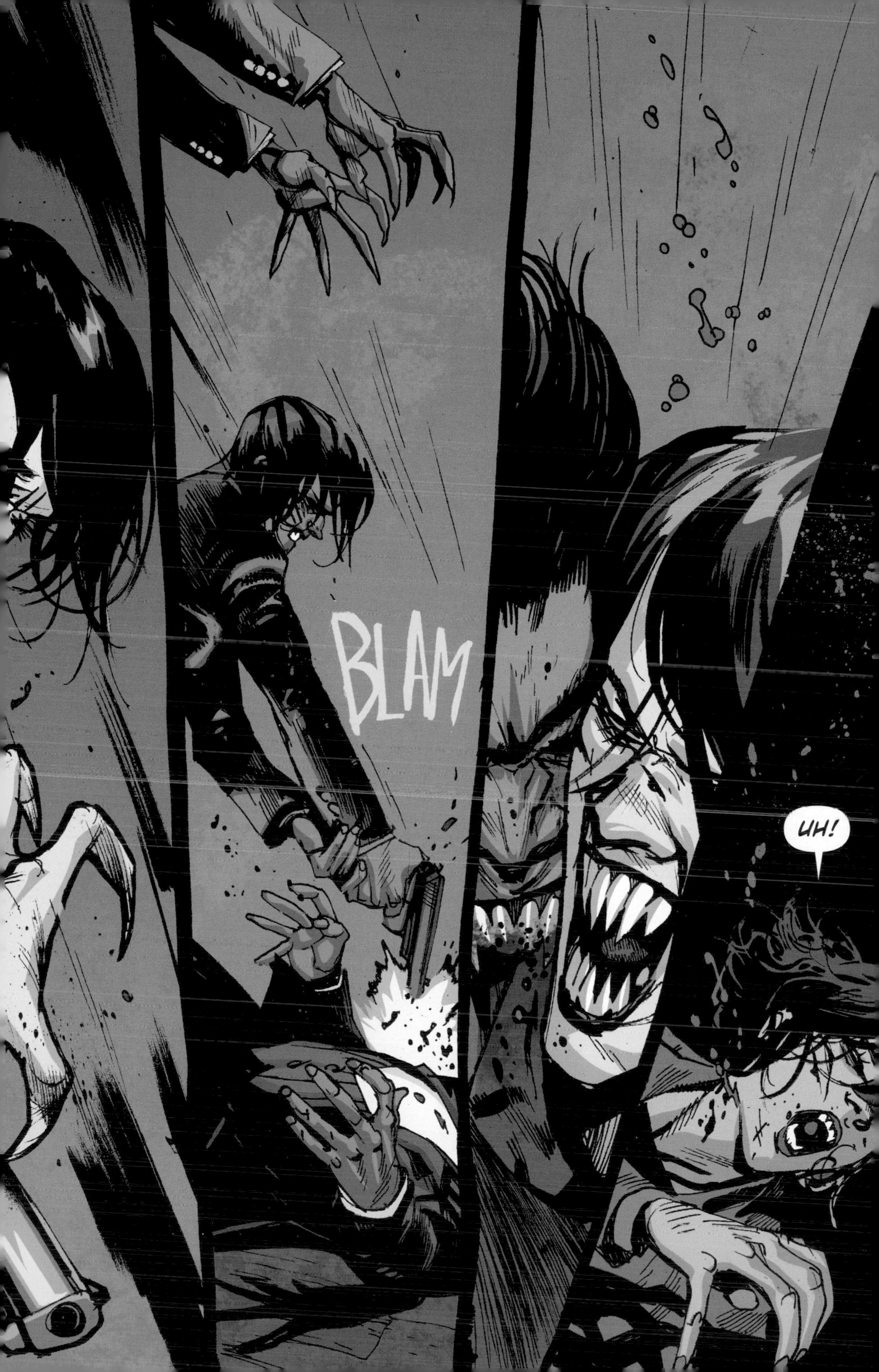
BLAM
UH!

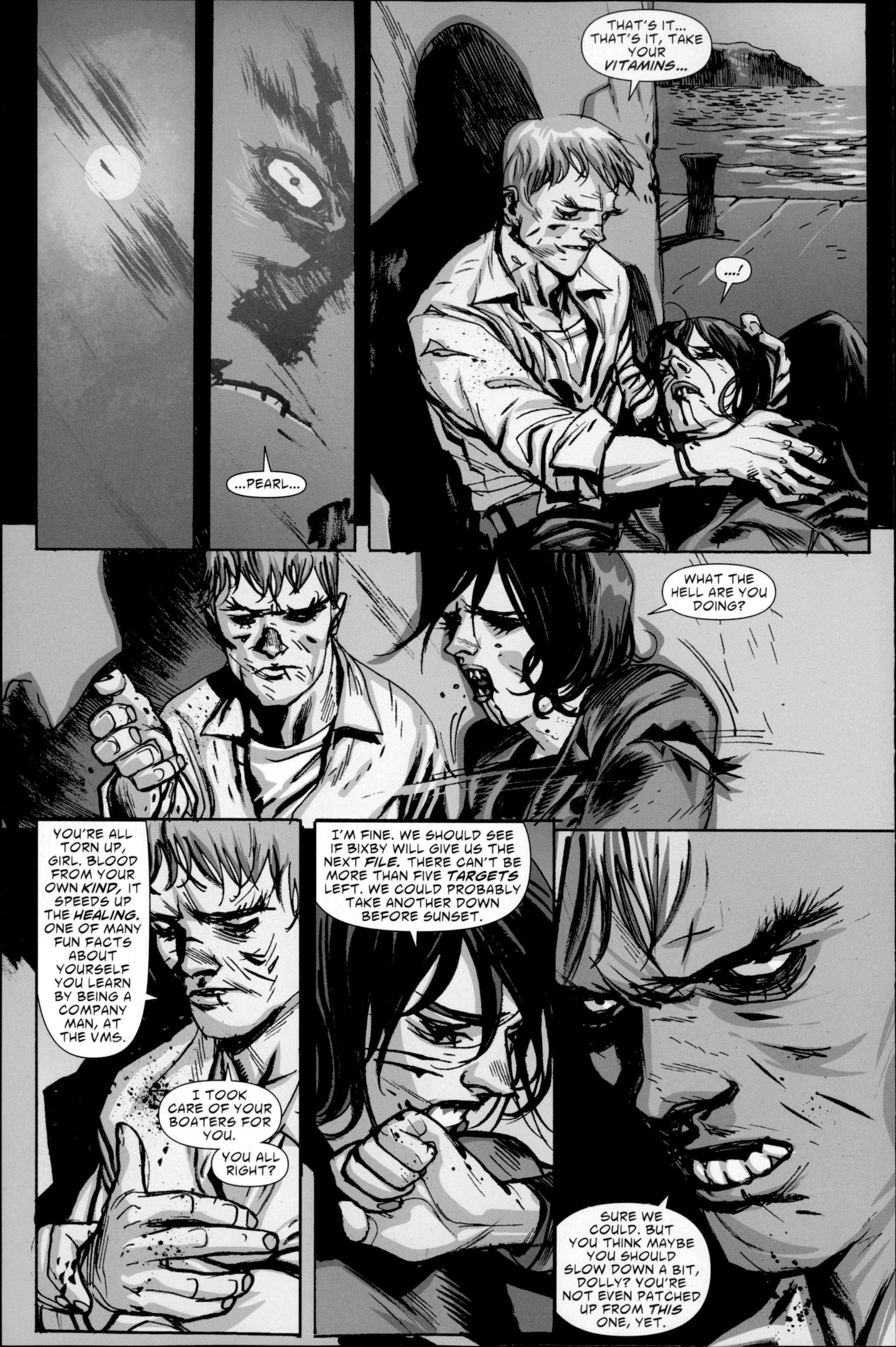
...PEARL...
THAT'S IT... THAT'S IT, TAKE YOUR *VITAMINS*...
...!
WHAT THE HELL ARE YOU DOING?
YOU'RE ALL TORN UP, GIRL. BLOOD FROM YOUR OWN *KIND*, IT SPEEDS UP THE *HEALING*. ONE OF MANY FUN FACTS ABOUT YOURSELF YOU LEARN BY BEING A COMPANY MAN, AT THE VMS.
I TOOK CARE OF YOUR BOATERS FOR YOU.
YOU ALL RIGHT?
I'M FINE. WE SHOULD SEE IF BIXBY WILL GIVE US THE NEXT *FILE*. THERE CAN'T BE MORE THAN FIVE *TARGETS* LEFT. WE COULD PROBABLY TAKE ANOTHER DOWN BEFORE SUNSET.
SURE WE COULD. BUT YOU THINK MAYBE YOU SHOULD SLOW DOWN A BIT, DOLLY? YOU'RE NOT EVEN PATCHED UP FROM *THIS* ONE, YET.

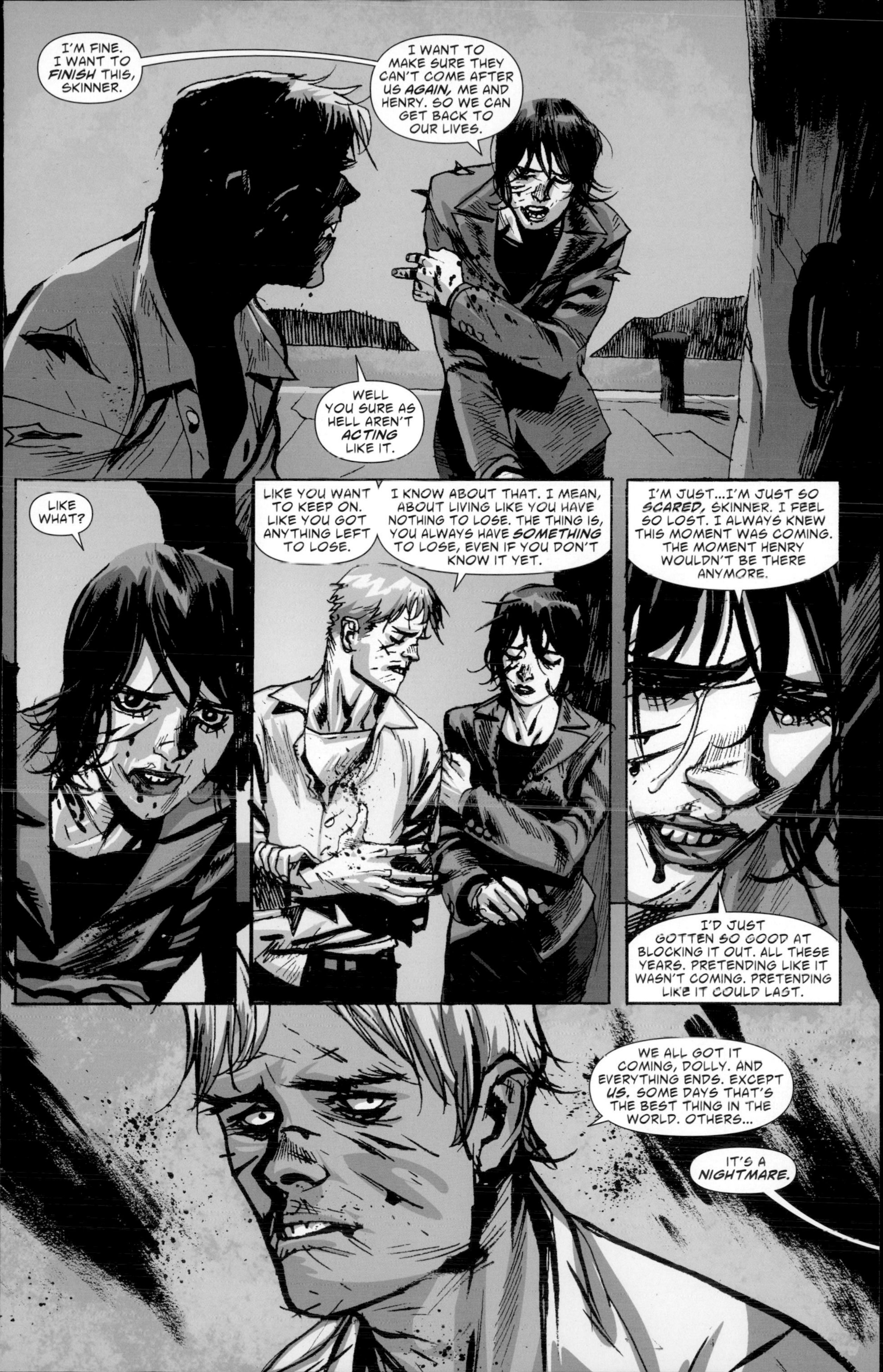
I'M FINE. I WANT TO FINISH THIS, SKINNER.
I WANT TO MAKE SURE THEY CAN'T COME AFTER US AGAIN, ME AND HENRY. SO WE CAN GET BACK TO OUR LIVES.
WELL YOU SURE AS HELL AREN'T ACTING LIKE IT.
LIKE WHAT?
LIKE YOU WANT TO KEEP ON. LIKE YOU GOT ANYTHING LEFT TO LOSE.
I KNOW ABOUT THAT. I MEAN, ABOUT LIVING LIKE YOU HAVE NOTHING TO LOSE. THE THING IS, YOU ALWAYS HAVE SOMETHING TO LOSE, EVEN IF YOU DON'T KNOW IT YET.
I'M JUST...I'M JUST SO SCARED, SKINNER. I FEEL SO LOST. I ALWAYS KNEW THIS MOMENT WAS COMING. THE MOMENT HENRY WOULDN'T BE THERE ANYMORE.
I'D JUST GOTTEN SO GOOD AT BLOCKING IT OUT. ALL THESE YEARS. PRETENDING LIKE IT WASN'T COMING. PRETENDING LIKE IT COULD LAST.
WE ALL GOT IT COMING, DOLLY. AND EVERYTHING ENDS. EXCEPT US. SOME DAYS THAT'S THE BEST THING IN THE WORLD. OTHERS...
IT'S A NIGHTMARE.

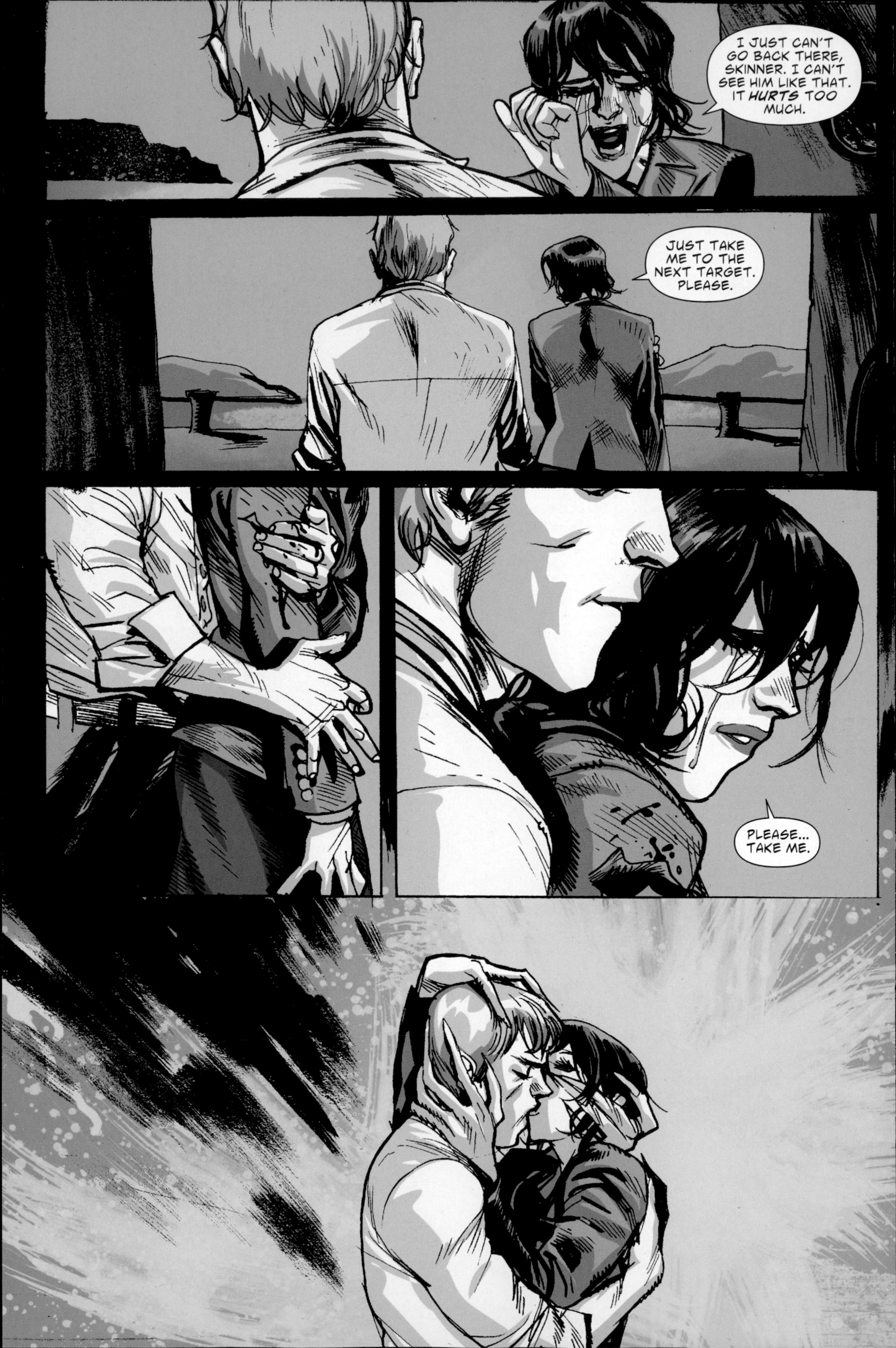
I JUST CAN'T GO BACK THERE, SKINNER. I CAN'T SEE HIM LIKE THAT. IT HURTS TOO MUCH.
JUST TAKE ME TO THE NEXT TARGET. PLEASE.
PLEASE... TAKE ME.

I WAS COMING TO THE CROSSROADS,

OF AN ALLEY AND THE STREET...

SHE WAS STANDING VERY STILL,

WITH HER FACE RAISED TO THE SKY...

AND I KNEW AT THAT VERY MOMENT,

I'D LOVE HER 'TIL I DIE.

CAL...?

"HER NAME WAS PEARL, BUT A FLOWER SHE WAS,

"WHEN I SPIED A FIGURE STANDING,

"IN THE EARLY MORNING HEAT,

"A FLOWER OF BLACKEST SUN.

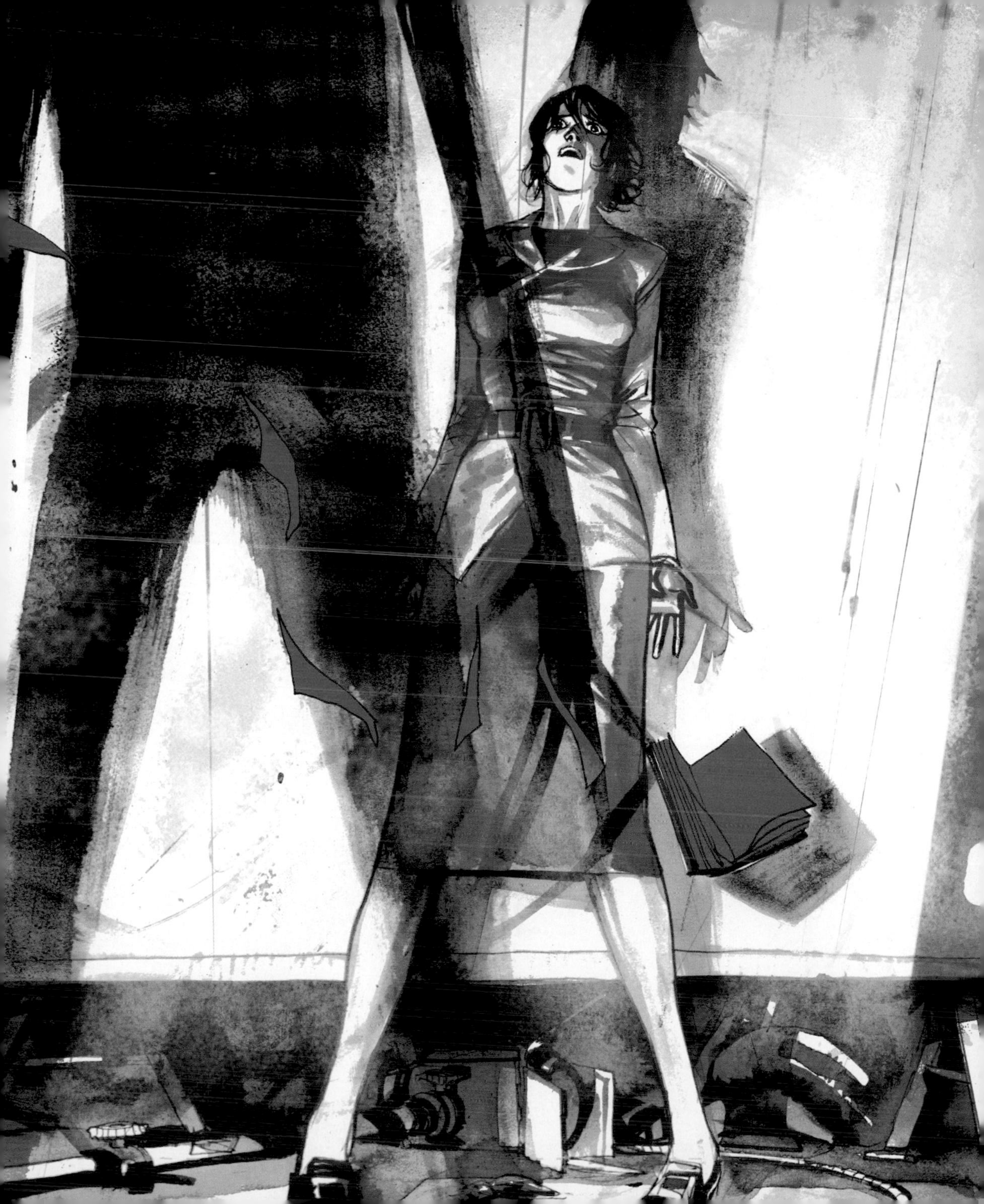

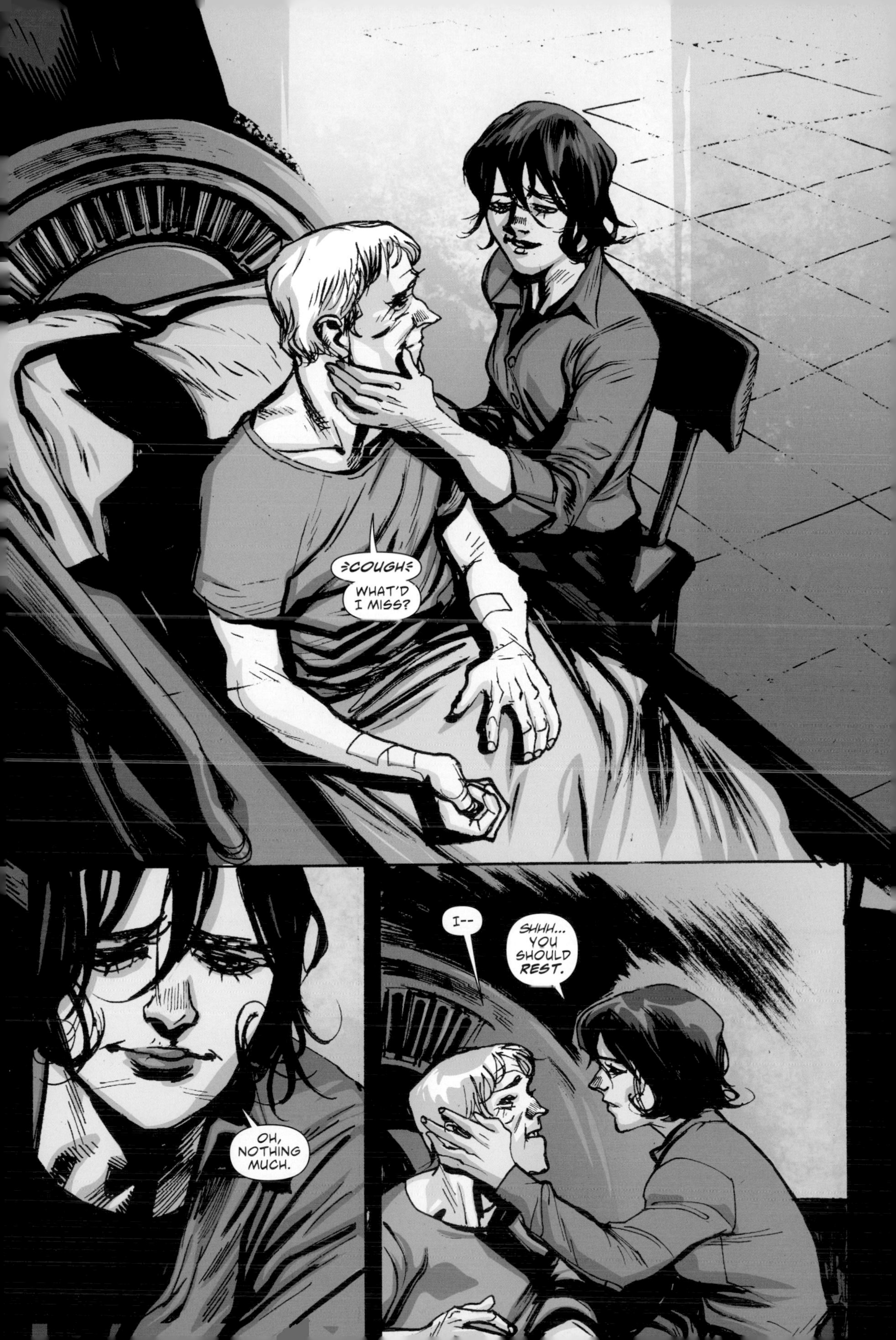

COUGH
WHAT'D I MISS?
OH, NOTHING MUCH.
I--
SHHH... YOU SHOULD REST.

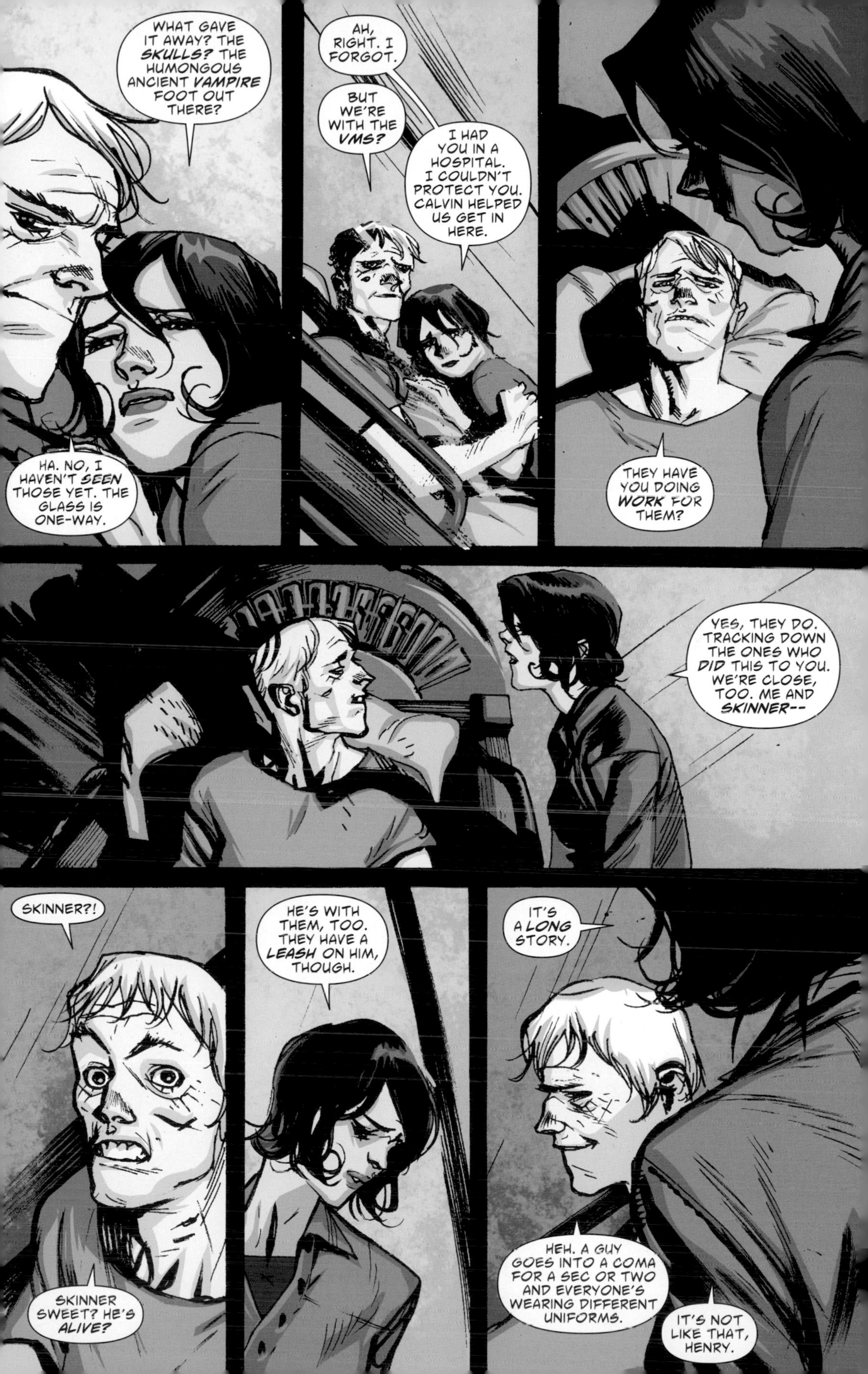
WHAT GAVE IT AWAY? THE SKULLS? THE HUMONGOUS ANCIENT VAMPIRE FOOT OUT THERE?
HA. NO, I HAVEN'T SEEN THOSE YET. THE GLASS IS ONE-WAY.
AH, RIGHT. I FORGOT.
BUT WE'RE WITH THE VMS?
I HAD YOU IN A HOSPITAL. I COULDN'T PROTECT YOU. CALVIN HELPED US GET IN HERE.
THEY HAVE YOU DOING WORK FOR THEM?
YES, THEY DO. TRACKING DOWN THE ONES WHO DID THIS TO YOU. WE'RE CLOSE, TOO. ME AND SKINNER--
SKINNER?!
SKINNER SWEET? HE'S ALIVE?
HE'S WITH THEM, TOO. THEY HAVE A LEASH ON HIM, THOUGH.
IT'S A LONG STORY.
HEH. A GUY GOES INTO A COMA FOR A SEC OR TWO AND EVERYONE'S WEARING DIFFERENT UNIFORMS.
IT'S NOT LIKE THAT, HENRY.

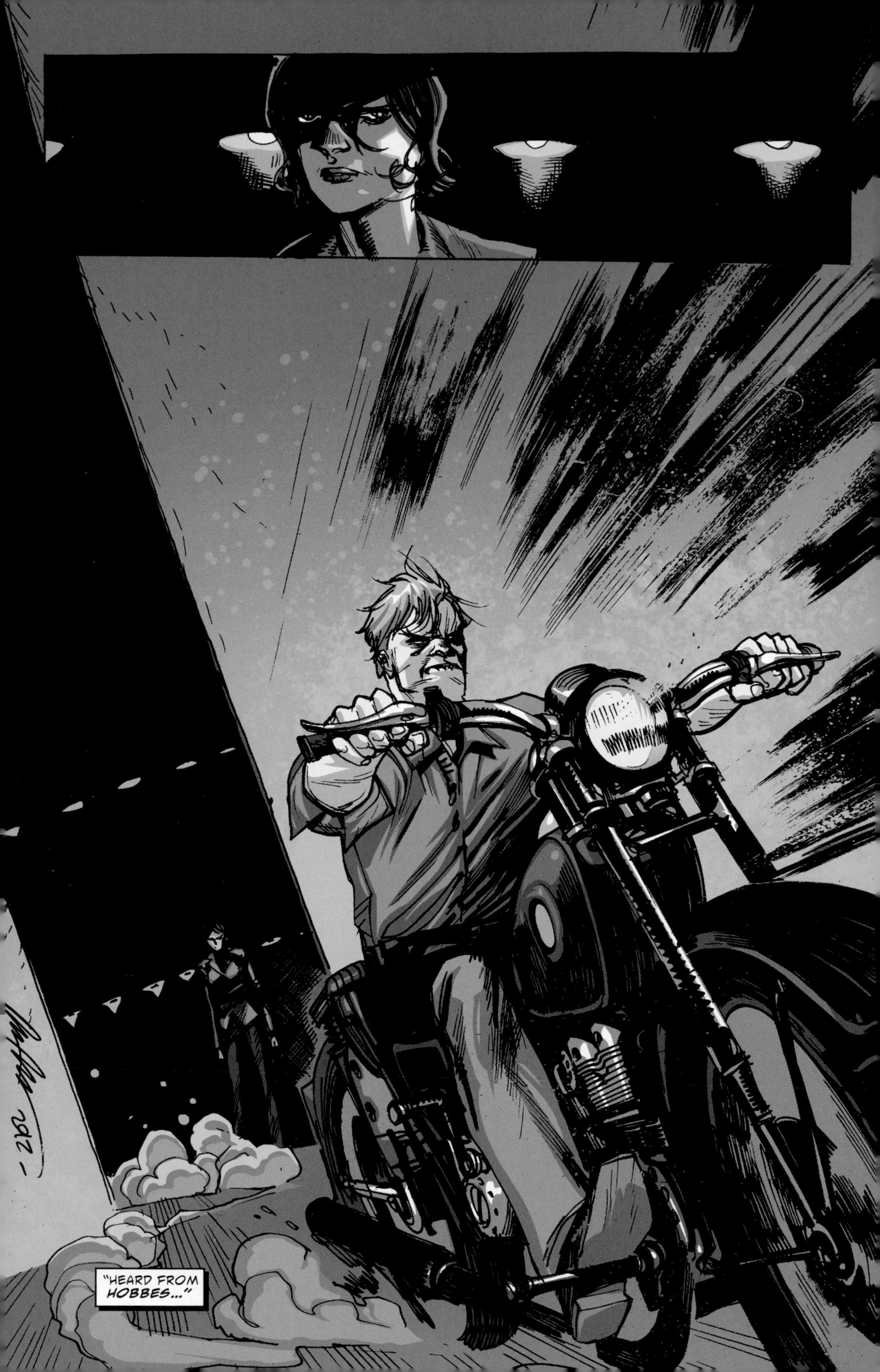
"HEARD FROM HOBBES..."

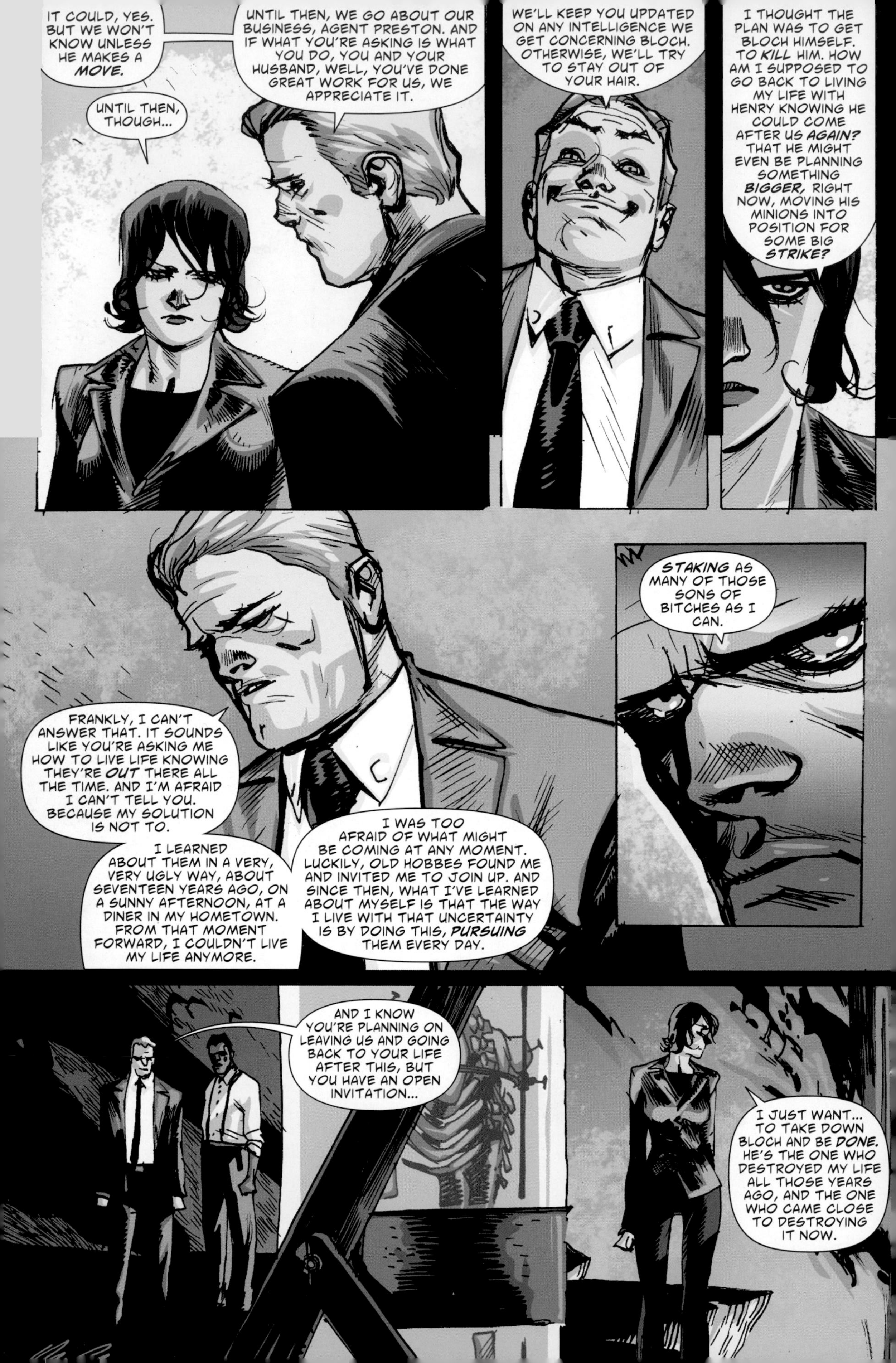
IT COULD, YES. BUT WE WON'T KNOW UNLESS HE MAKES A MOVE.
UNTIL THEN, THOUGH...
UNTIL THEN, WE GO ABOUT OUR BUSINESS, AGENT PRESTON. AND IF WHAT YOU'RE ASKING IS WHAT YOU DO, YOU AND YOUR HUSBAND, WELL, YOU'VE DONE GREAT WORK FOR US, WE APPRECIATE IT.
WE'LL KEEP YOU UPDATED ON ANY INTELLIGENCE WE GET CONCERNING BLOCH. OTHERWISE, WE'LL TRY TO STAY OUT OF YOUR HAIR.
I THOUGHT THE PLAN WAS TO GET BLOCH HIMSELF. TO KILL HIM. HOW AM I SUPPOSED TO GO BACK TO LIVING MY LIFE WITH HENRY KNOWING HE COULD COME AFTER US AGAIN? THAT HE MIGHT EVEN BE PLANNING SOMETHING BIGGER, RIGHT NOW, MOVING HIS MINIONS INTO POSITION FOR SOME BIG STRIKE?
FRANKLY, I CAN'T ANSWER THAT. IT SOUNDS LIKE YOU'RE ASKING ME HOW TO LIVE LIFE KNOWING THEY'RE OUT THERE ALL THE TIME. AND I'M AFRAID I CAN'T TELL YOU. BECAUSE MY SOLUTION IS NOT TO.
I LEARNED ABOUT THEM IN A VERY, VERY UGLY WAY, ABOUT SEVENTEEN YEARS AGO, ON A SUNNY AFTERNOON, AT A DINER IN MY HOMETOWN. FROM THAT MOMENT FORWARD, I COULDN'T LIVE MY LIFE ANYMORE.
I WAS TOO AFRAID OF WHAT MIGHT BE COMING AT ANY MOMENT. LUCKILY, OLD HOBBES FOUND ME AND INVITED ME TO JOIN UP. AND SINCE THEN, WHAT I'VE LEARNED ABOUT MYSELF IS THAT THE WAY I LIVE WITH THAT UNCERTAINTY IS BY DOING THIS, PURSUING THEM EVERY DAY.
STAKING AS MANY OF THOSE SONS OF BITCHES AS I CAN.
AND I KNOW YOU'RE PLANNING ON LEAVING US AND GOING BACK TO YOUR LIFE AFTER THIS, BUT YOU HAVE AN OPEN INVITATION...
I JUST WANT... TO TAKE DOWN BLOCH AND BE DONE. HE'S THE ONE WHO DESTROYED MY LIFE ALL THOSE YEARS AGO, AND THE ONE WHO CAME CLOSE TO DESTROYING IT NOW.

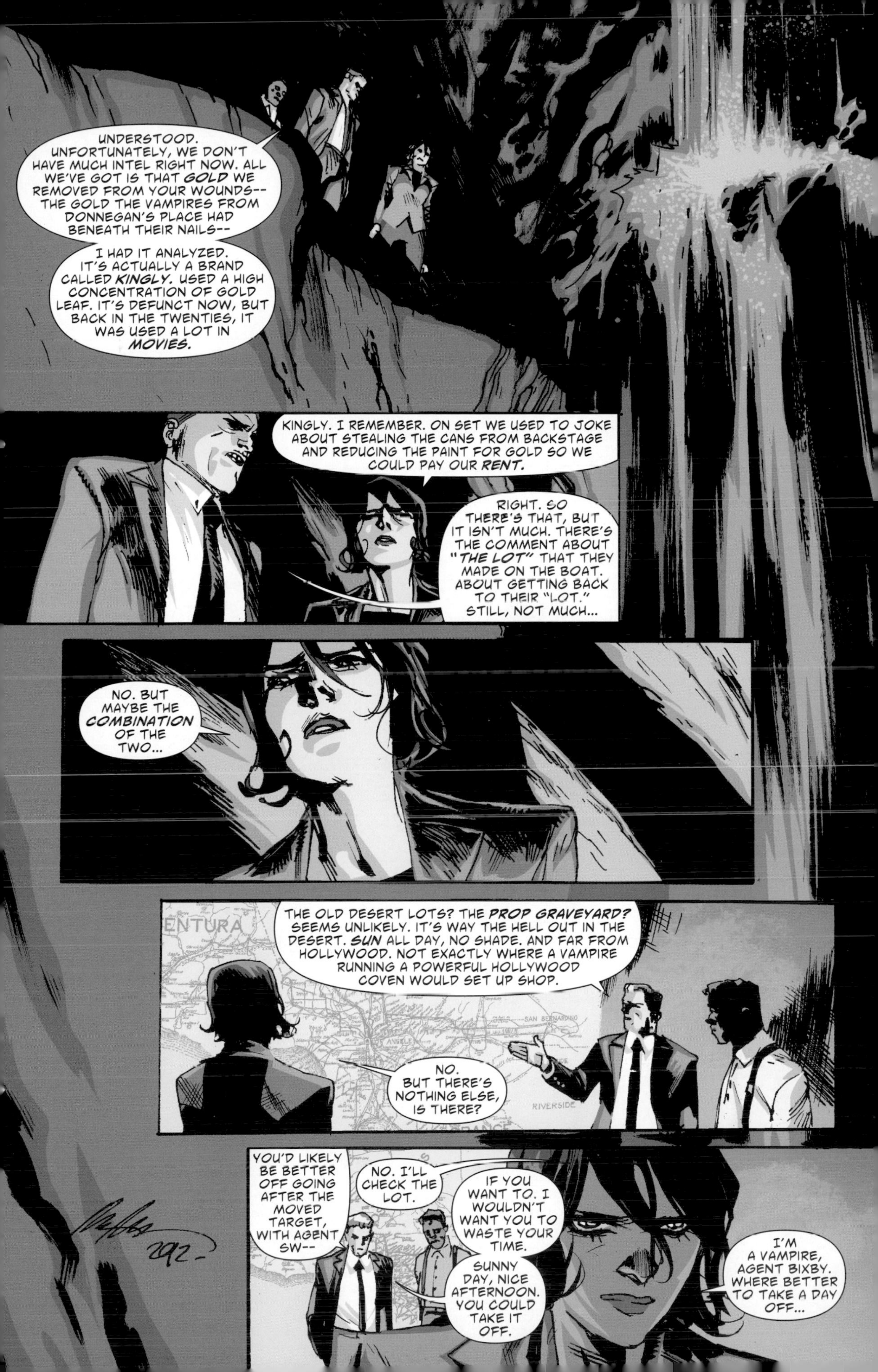
UNDERSTOOD. UNFORTUNATELY, WE DON'T HAVE MUCH INTEL RIGHT NOW. ALL WE'VE GOT IS THAT GOLD WE REMOVED FROM YOUR WOUNDS-- THE GOLD THE VAMPIRES FROM DONNEGAN'S PLACE HAD BENEATH THEIR NAILS--
I HAD IT ANALYZED. IT'S ACTUALLY A BRAND CALLED KINGLY. USED A HIGH CONCENTRATION OF GOLD LEAF. IT'S DEFUNCT NOW, BUT BACK IN THE TWENTIES, IT WAS USED A LOT IN MOVIES.
KINGLY. I REMEMBER. ON SET WE USED TO JOKE ABOUT STEALING THE CANS FROM BACKSTAGE AND REDUCING THE PAINT FOR GOLD SO WE COULD PAY OUR RENT.
RIGHT. SO THERE'S THAT, BUT IT ISN'T MUCH. THERE'S THE COMMENT ABOUT "THE LOT" THAT THEY MADE ON THE BOAT. ABOUT GETTING BACK TO THEIR "LOT." STILL, NOT MUCH...
NO. BUT MAYBE THE COMBINATION OF THE TWO...
THE OLD DESERT LOTS? THE PROP GRAVEYARD? SEEMS UNLIKELY. IT'S WAY THE HELL OUT IN THE DESERT. SUN ALL DAY, NO SHADE. AND FAR FROM HOLLYWOOD. NOT EXACTLY WHERE A VAMPIRE RUNNING A POWERFUL HOLLYWOOD COVEN WOULD SET UP SHOP.
NO. BUT THERE'S NOTHING ELSE, IS THERE?
ENTURA
SAN BERNARDINO
RIVERSIDE
YOU'D LIKELY BE BETTER OFF GOING AFTER THE MOVED TARGET, WITH AGENT SW--
NO. I'LL CHECK THE LOT.
IF YOU WANT TO. I WOULDN'T WANT YOU TO WASTE YOUR TIME.
SUNNY DAY, NICE AFTERNOON. YOU COULD TAKE IT OFF.
I'M A VAMPIRE, AGENT BIXBY. WHERE BETTER TO TAKE A DAY OFF...

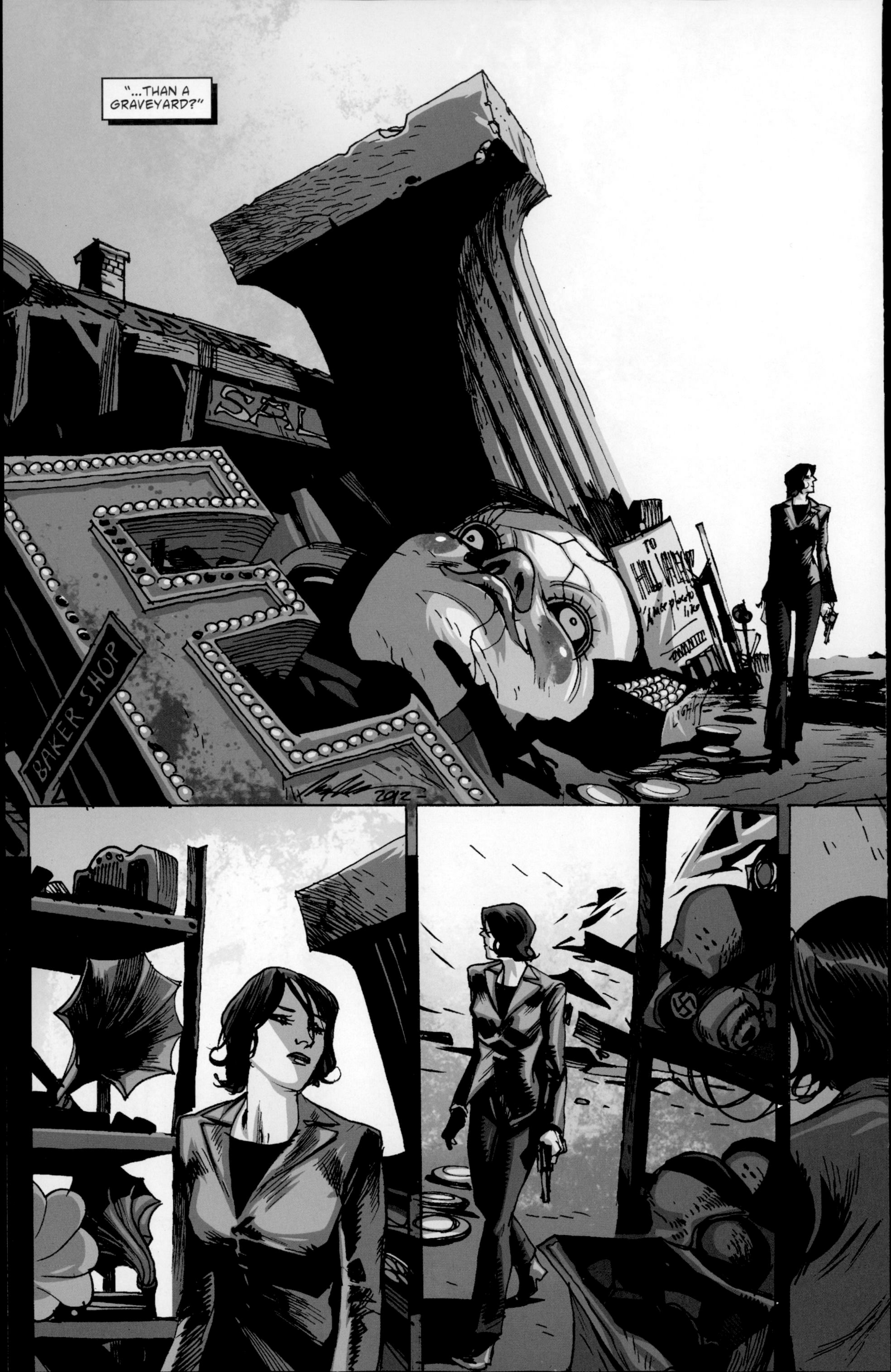
"...THAN A GRAVEYARD?"
BAKER SHOP

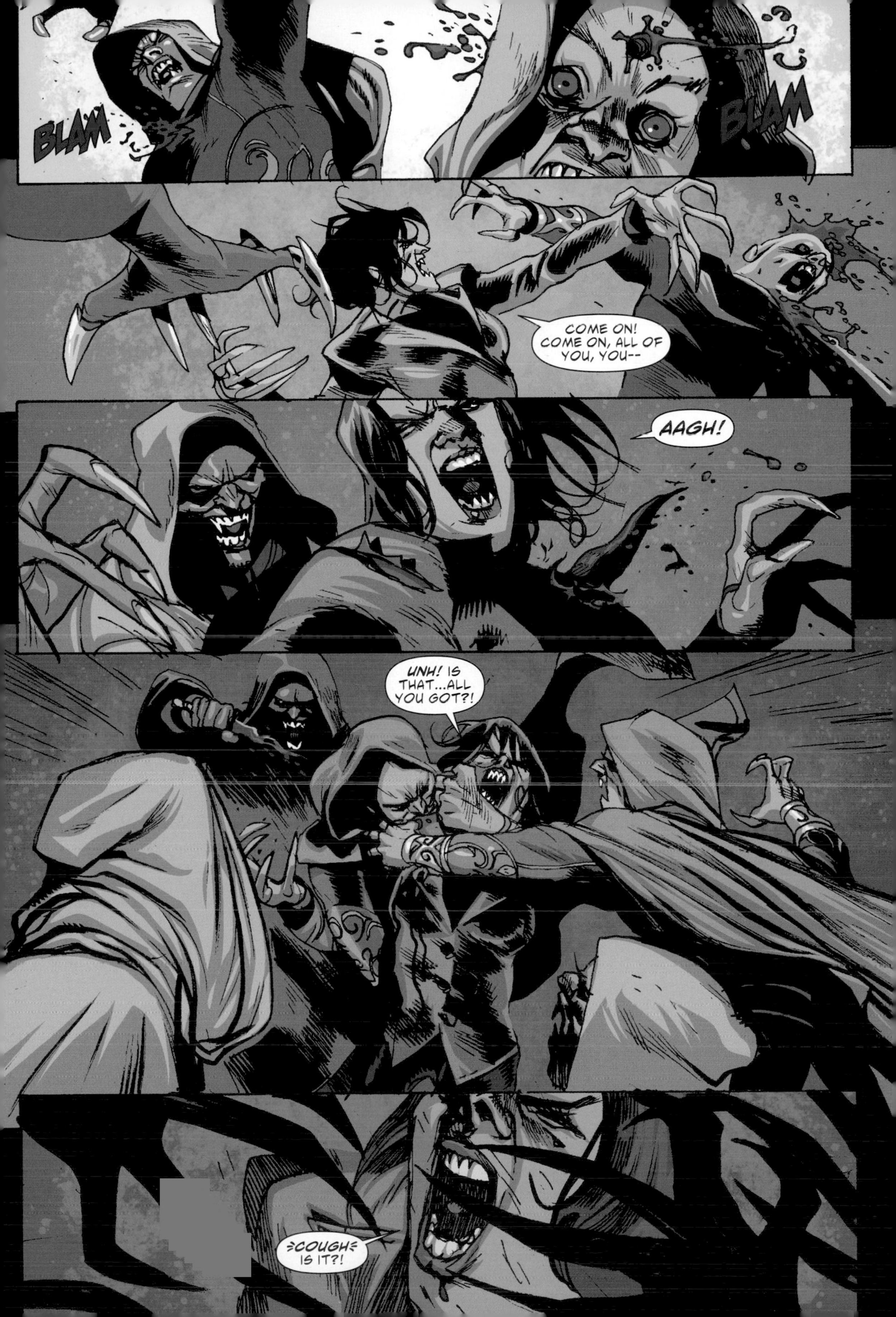
BLAM
BLAM
COME ON! COME ON, ALL OF YOU, YOU--
AAGH!
UNH! IS THAT...ALL YOU GOT?!
COUGH IS IT?!

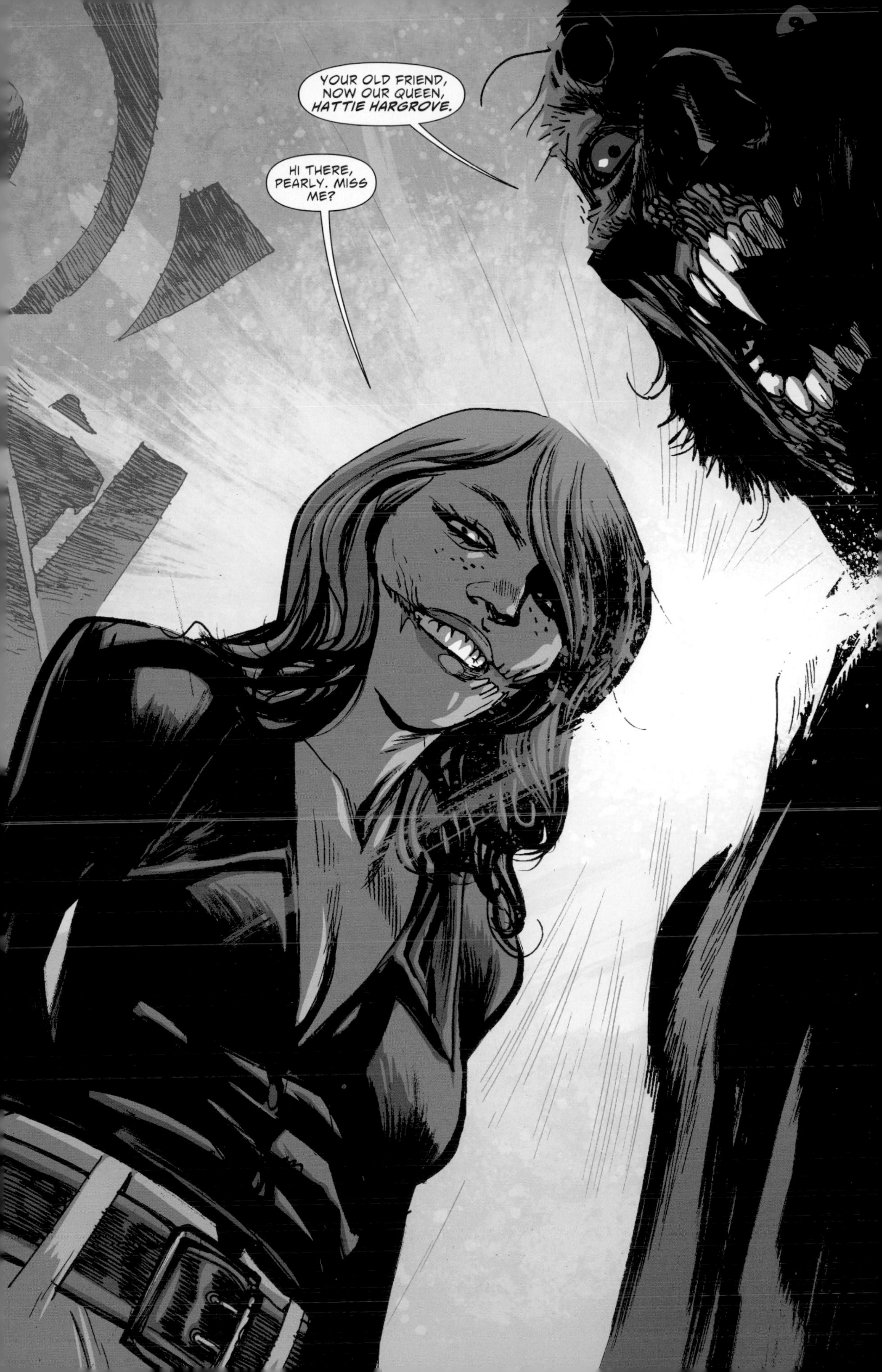
YOUR OLD FRIEND, NOW OUR QUEEN, HATTIE HARGROVE.
HI THERE, PEARLY. MISS ME?

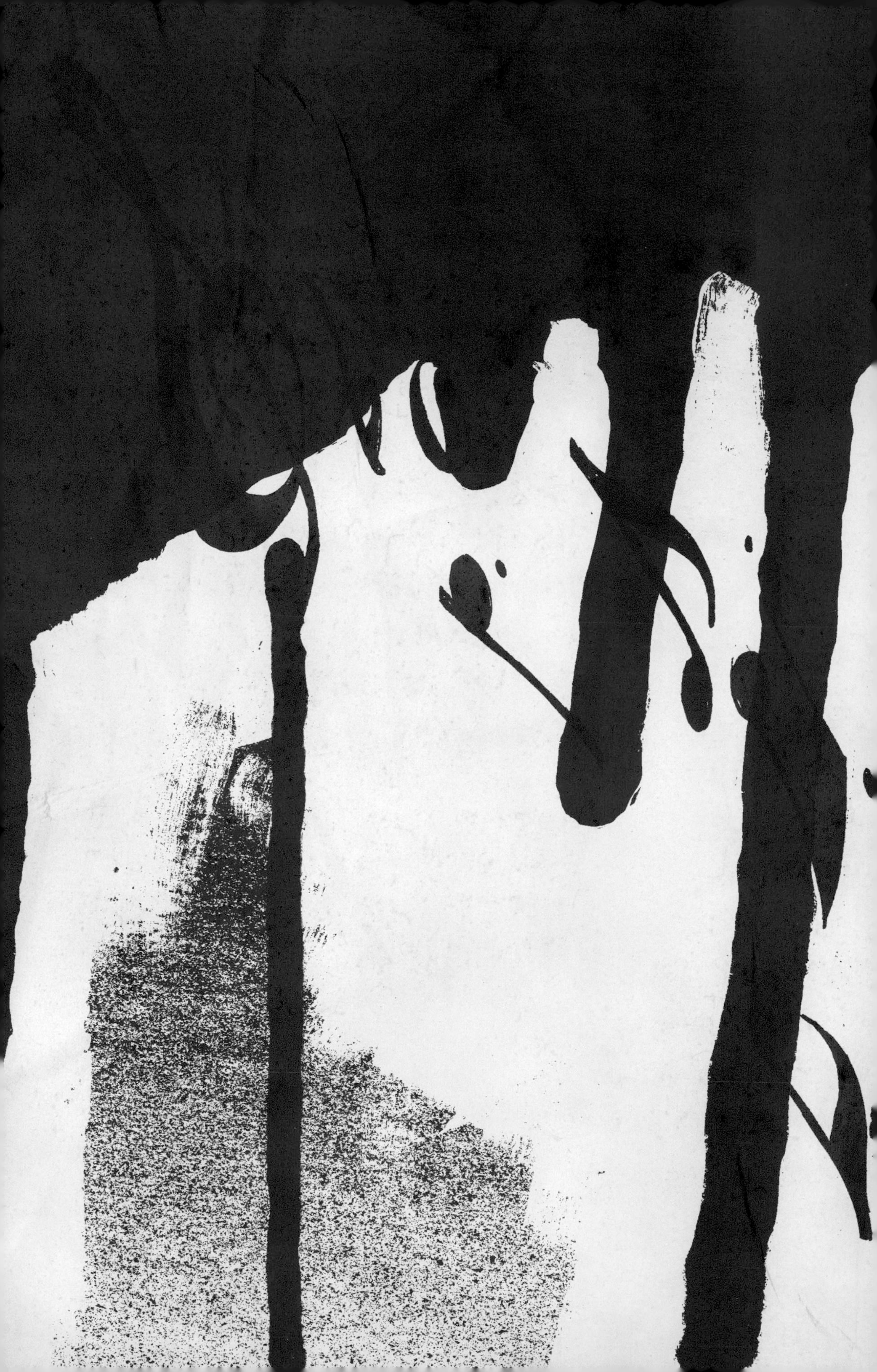

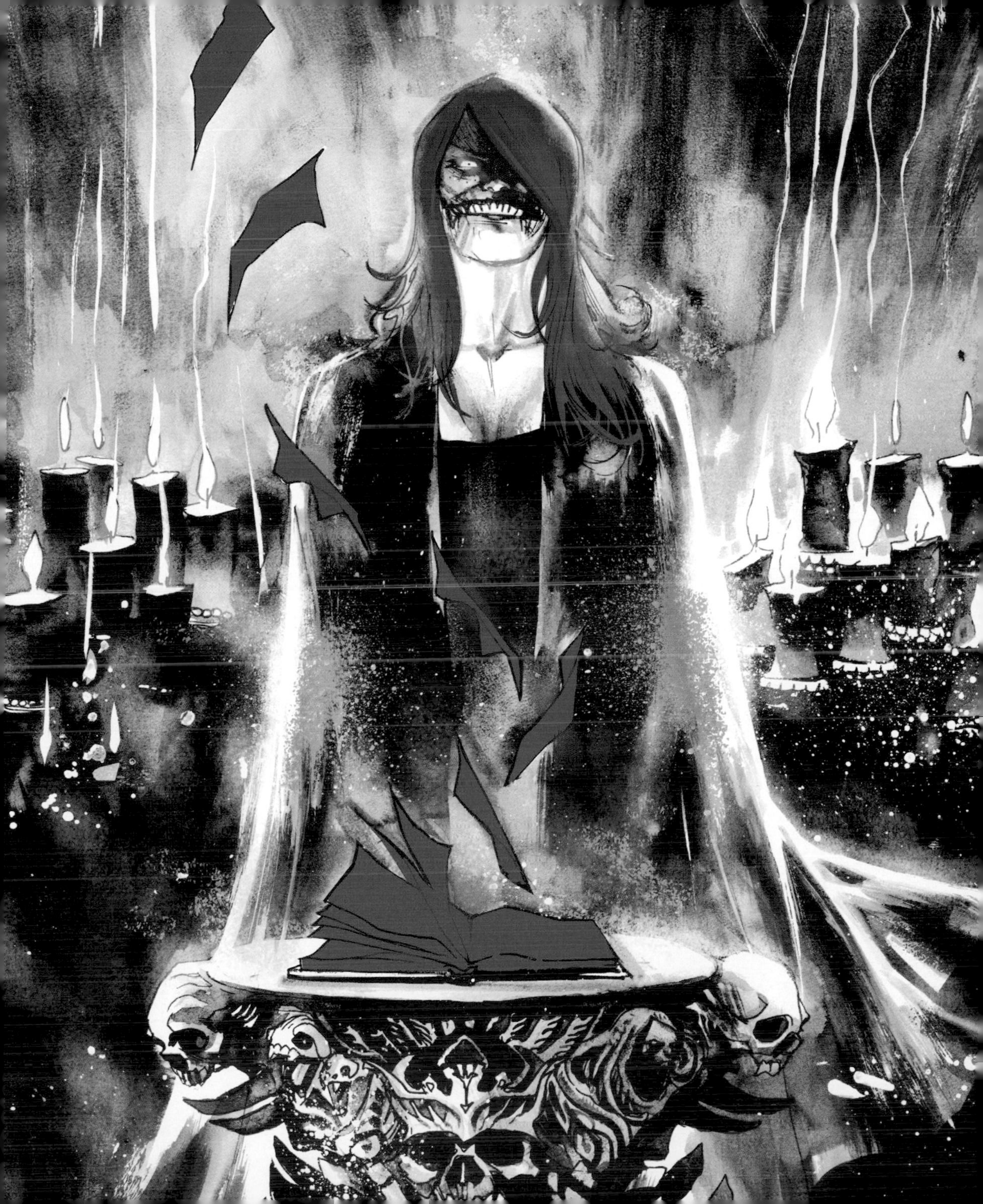

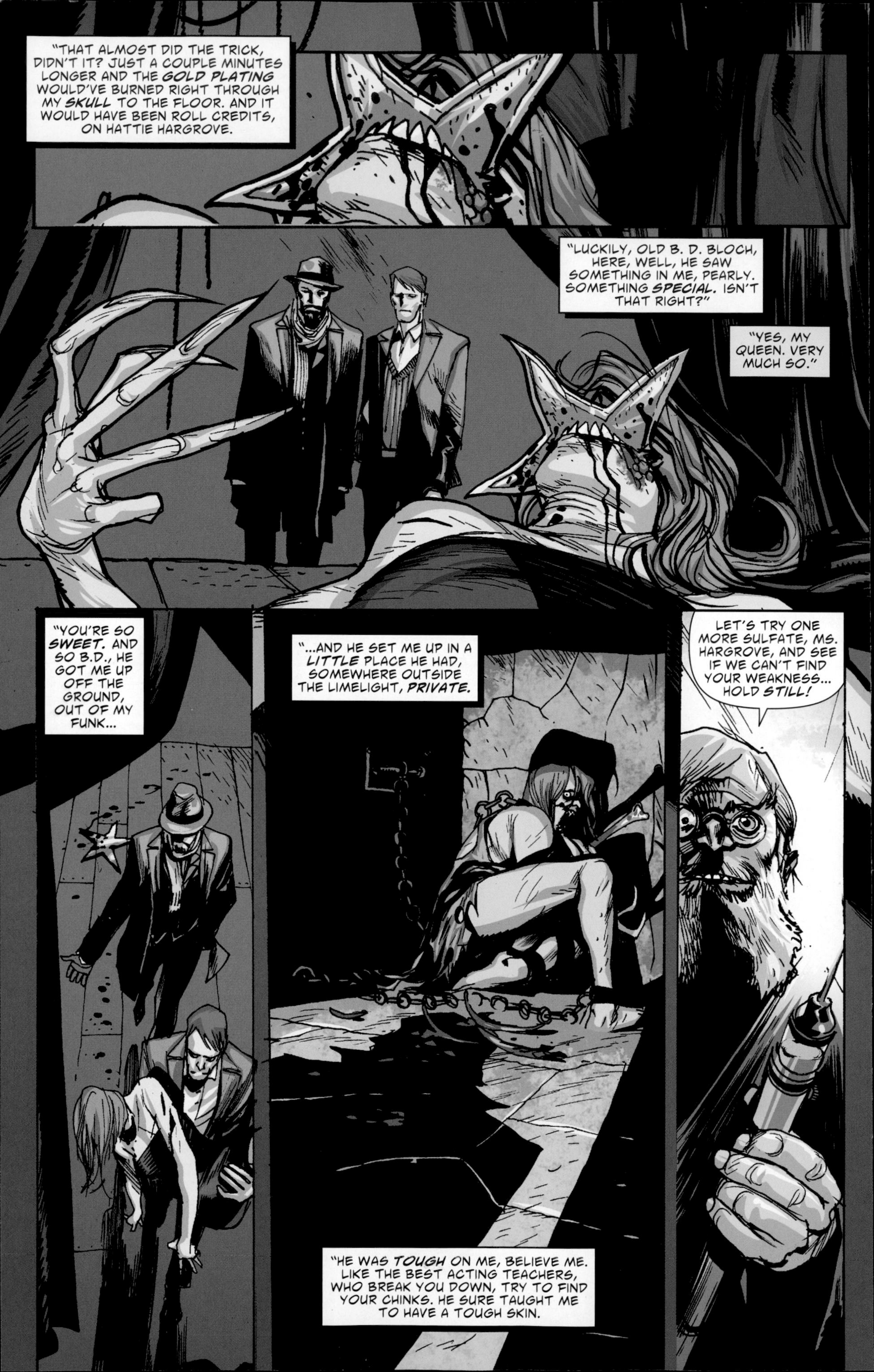
"THAT ALMOST DID THE TRICK, DIDN'T IT? JUST A COUPLE MINUTES LONGER AND THE GOLD PLATING WOULD'VE BURNED RIGHT THROUGH MY SKULL TO THE FLOOR. AND IT WOULD HAVE BEEN ROLL CREDITS, ON HATTIE HARGROVE.
"LUCKILY, OLD B. D. BLOCH, HERE, WELL, HE SAW SOMETHING IN ME, PEARLY. SOMETHING SPECIAL. ISN'T THAT RIGHT?"
"YES, MY QUEEN. VERY MUCH SO."
"YOU'RE SO SWEET. AND SO B.D., HE GOT ME UP OFF THE GROUND, OUT OF MY FUNK...
"...AND HE SET ME UP IN A LITTLE PLACE HE HAD, SOMEWHERE OUTSIDE THE LIMELIGHT, PRIVATE.
LET'S TRY ONE MORE SULFATE, MS. HARGROVE, AND SEE IF WE CAN'T FIND YOUR WEAKNESS... HOLD STILL!
"HE WAS TOUGH ON ME, BELIEVE ME. LIKE THE BEST ACTING TEACHERS, WHO BREAK YOU DOWN, TRY TO FIND YOUR CHINKS. HE SURE TAUGHT ME TO HAVE A TOUGH SKIN.

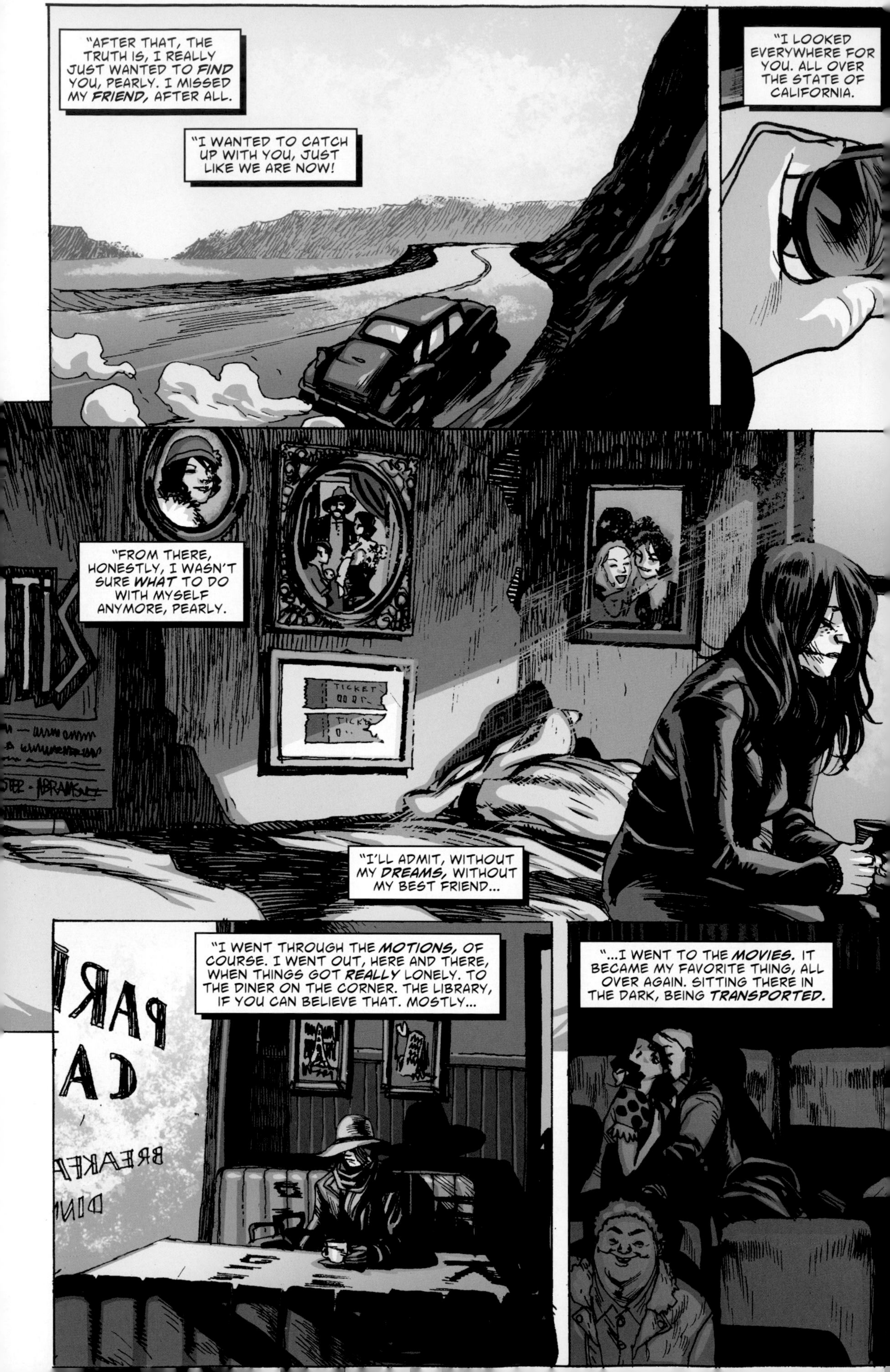
"AFTER THAT, THE TRUTH IS, I REALLY JUST WANTED TO *FIND* YOU, PEARLY. I MISSED MY *FRIEND,* AFTER ALL.
"I WANTED TO CATCH UP WITH YOU, JUST LIKE WE ARE NOW!
"I LOOKED EVERYWHERE FOR YOU. ALL OVER THE STATE OF CALIFORNIA.
"FROM THERE, HONESTLY, I WASN'T SURE *WHAT* TO DO WITH MYSELF ANYMORE, PEARLY.
TICKET
"I'LL ADMIT, WITHOUT MY *DREAMS,* WITHOUT MY BEST FRIEND...
"I WENT THROUGH THE *MOTIONS,* OF COURSE. I WENT OUT, HERE AND THERE, WHEN THINGS GOT *REALLY* LONELY. TO THE DINER ON THE CORNER. THE LIBRARY, IF YOU CAN BELIEVE THAT. MOSTLY...
"...I WENT TO THE *MOVIES.* IT BECAME MY FAVORITE THING, ALL OVER AGAIN. SITTING THERE IN THE DARK, BEING *TRANSPORTED.*

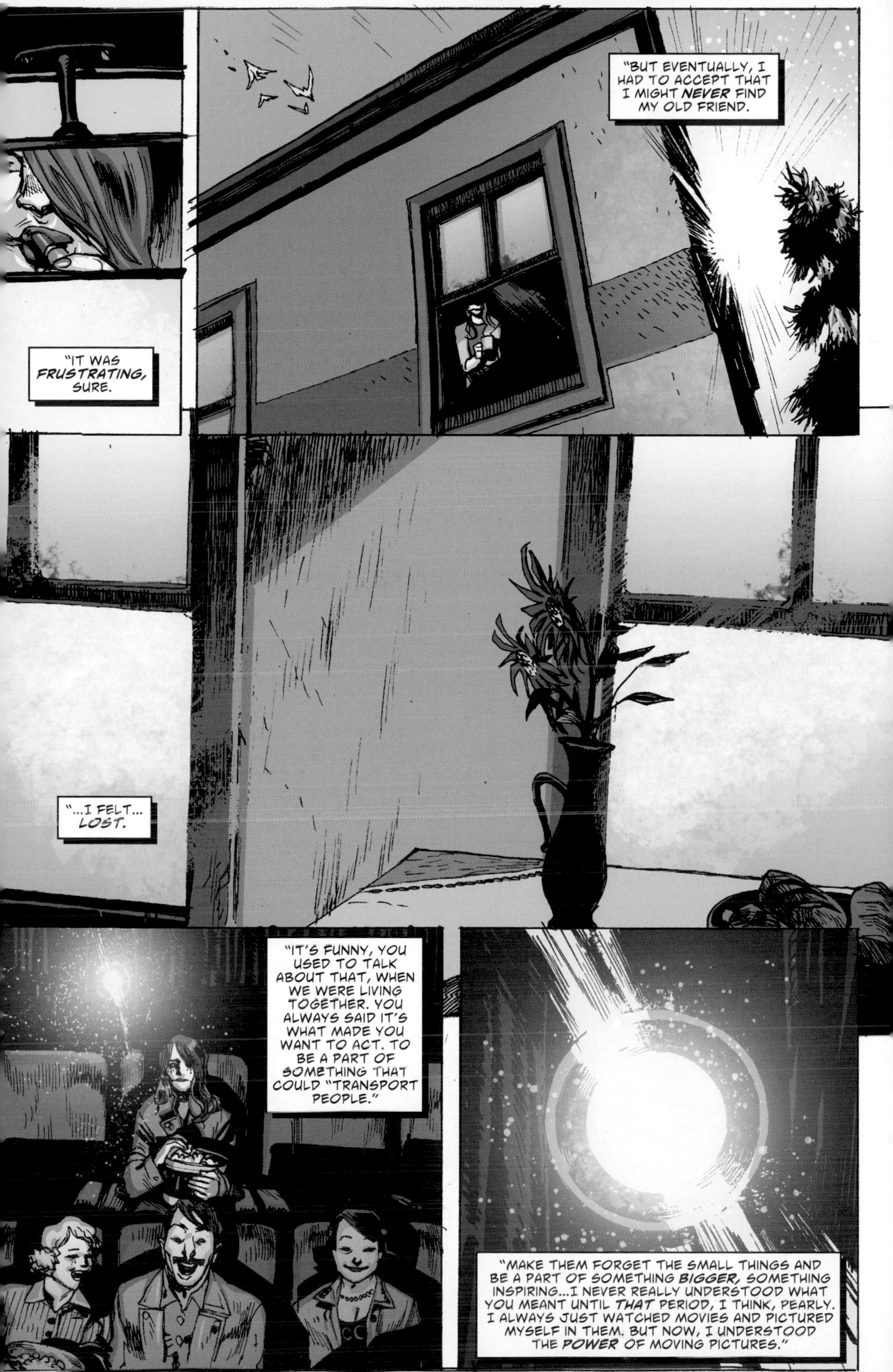
"IT WAS FRUSTRATING, SURE.
"BUT EVENTUALLY, I HAD TO ACCEPT THAT I MIGHT NEVER FIND MY OLD FRIEND.
"...I FELT... LOST.
"IT'S FUNNY, YOU USED TO TALK ABOUT THAT, WHEN WE WERE LIVING TOGETHER. YOU ALWAYS SAID IT'S WHAT MADE YOU WANT TO ACT. TO BE A PART OF SOMETHING THAT COULD "TRANSPORT PEOPLE."
"MAKE THEM FORGET THE SMALL THINGS AND BE A PART OF SOMETHING BIGGER, SOMETHING INSPIRING...I NEVER REALLY UNDERSTOOD WHAT YOU MEANT UNTIL THAT PERIOD, I THINK, PEARLY. I ALWAYS JUST WATCHED MOVIES AND PICTURED MYSELF IN THEM. BUT NOW, I UNDERSTOOD THE POWER OF MOVING PICTURES."

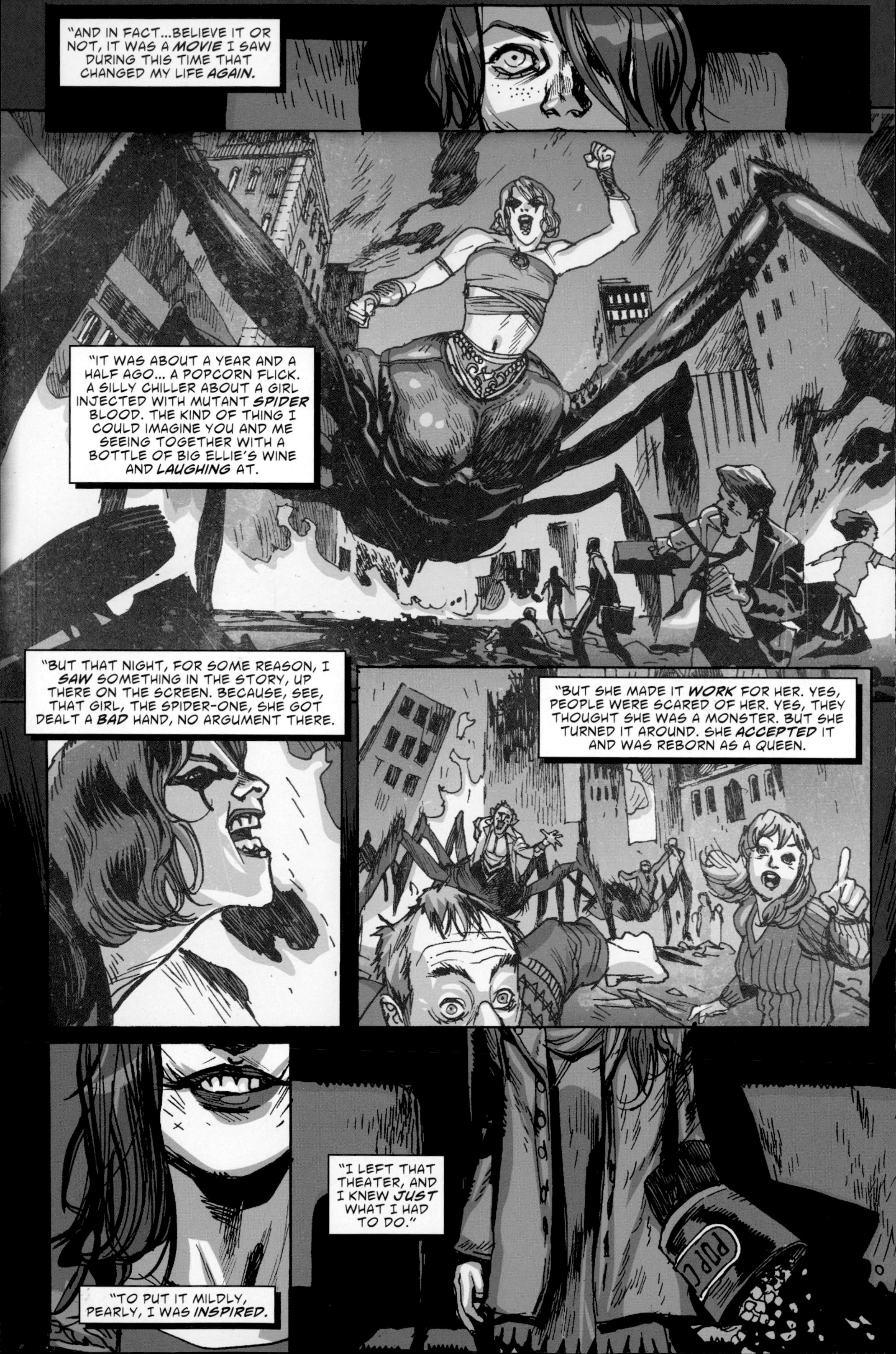
"AND IN FACT...BELIEVE IT OR NOT, IT WAS A *MOVIE* I SAW DURING THIS TIME THAT CHANGED MY LIFE *AGAIN*.
"IT WAS ABOUT A YEAR AND A HALF AGO... A POPCORN FLICK. A SILLY CHILLER ABOUT A GIRL INJECTED WITH MUTANT *SPIDER* BLOOD. THE KIND OF THING I COULD IMAGINE YOU AND ME SEEING TOGETHER WITH A BOTTLE OF BIG ELLIE'S WINE AND *LAUGHING* AT.
"BUT THAT NIGHT, FOR SOME REASON, I *SAW* SOMETHING IN THE STORY, UP THERE ON THE SCREEN. BECAUSE, SEE, THAT GIRL, THE SPIDER-ONE, SHE GOT DEALT A *BAD* HAND, NO ARGUMENT THERE.
"BUT SHE MADE IT *WORK* FOR HER. YES, PEOPLE WERE SCARED OF HER. YES, THEY THOUGHT SHE WAS A MONSTER. BUT SHE TURNED IT AROUND. SHE *ACCEPTED* IT AND WAS REBORN AS A QUEEN.
"TO PUT IT MILDLY, PEARLY, I WAS *INSPIRED*.
"I LEFT THAT THEATER, AND I KNEW *JUST* WHAT I HAD TO DO."

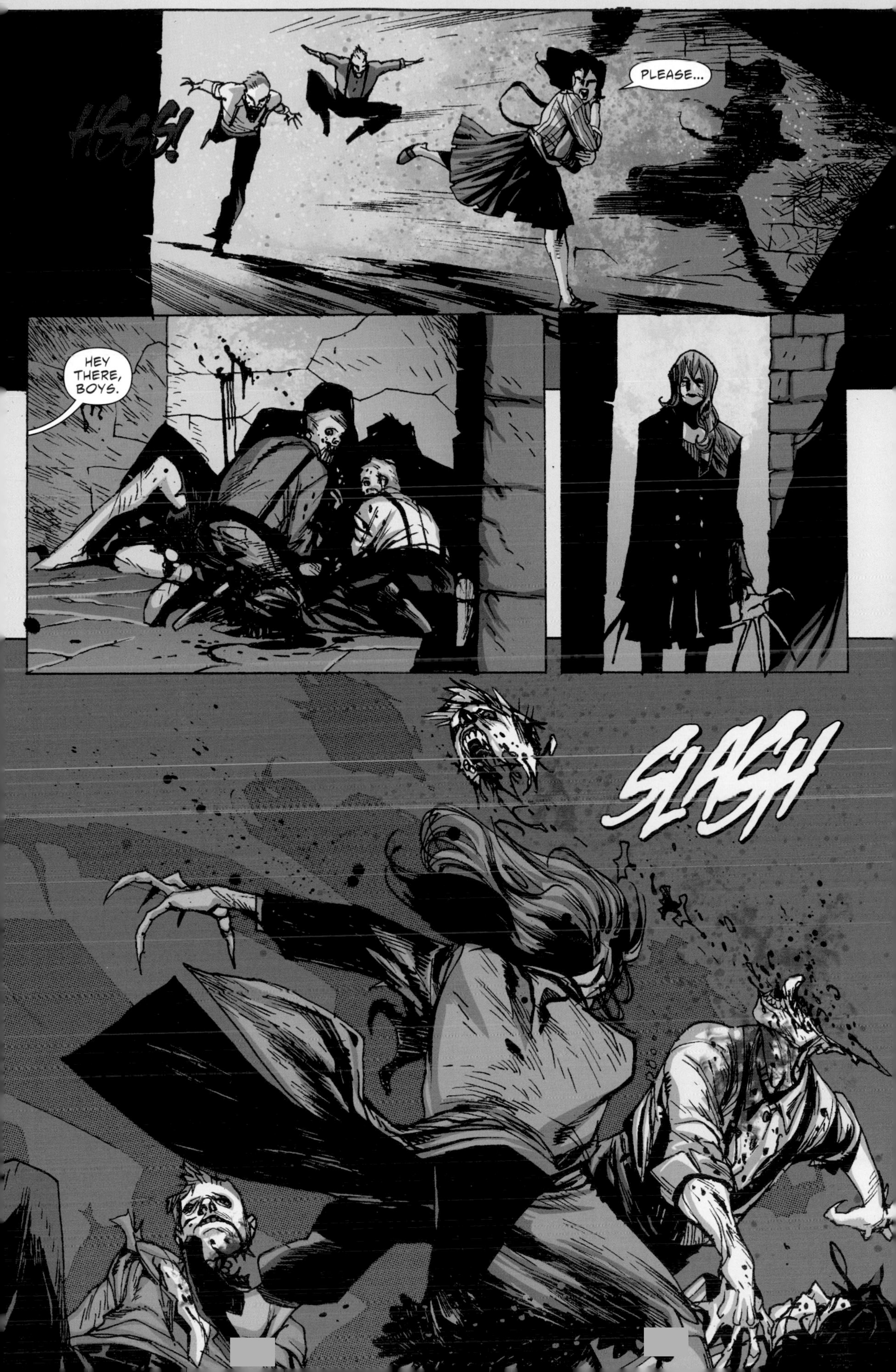
HSSS!
PLEASE...
HEY THERE, BOYS.
SLASH

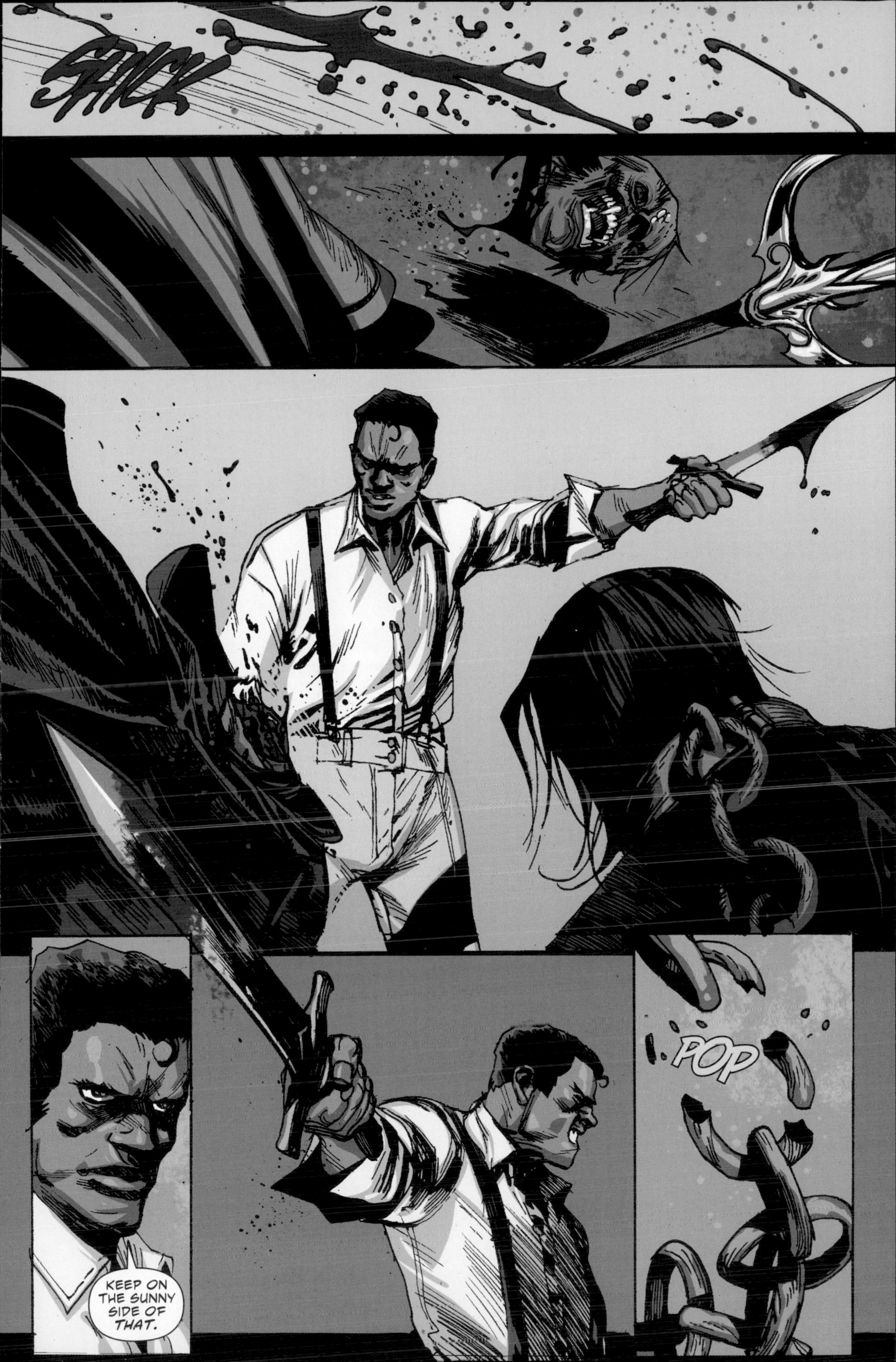
SHICK
KEEP ON THE SUNNY SIDE OF THAT.
POP

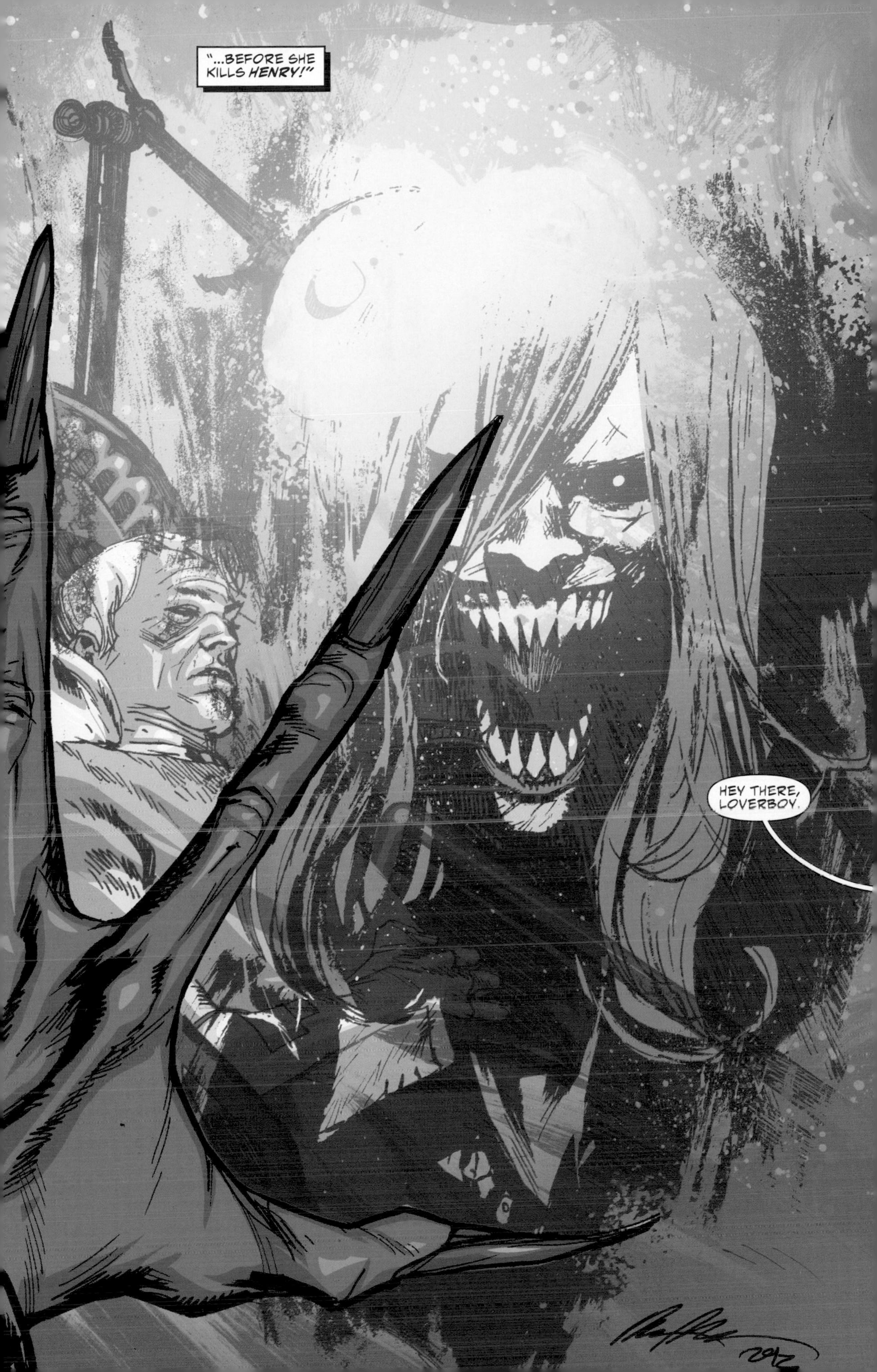
"...BEFORE SHE KILLS HENRY!"
HEY THERE, LOVERBOY.

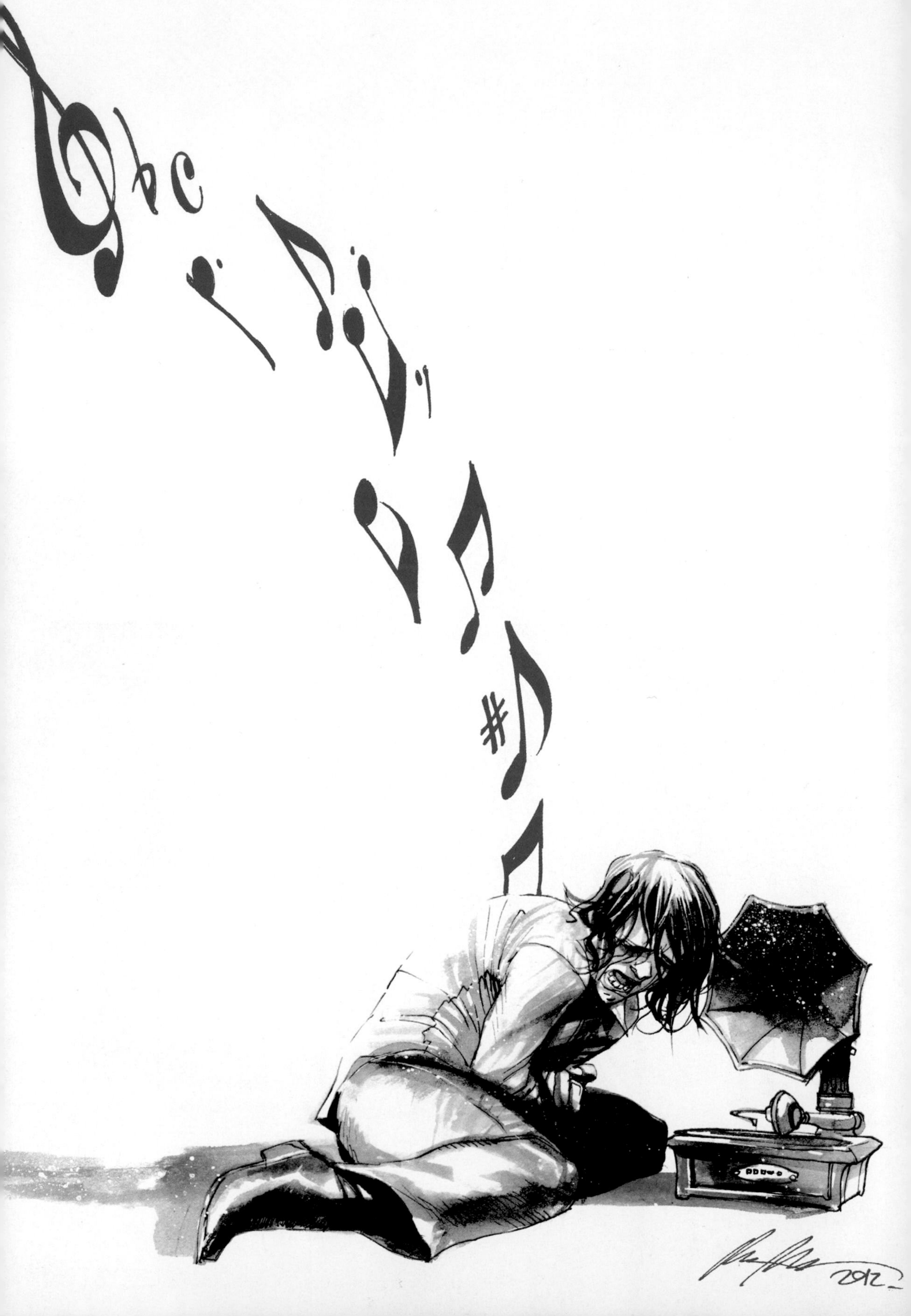

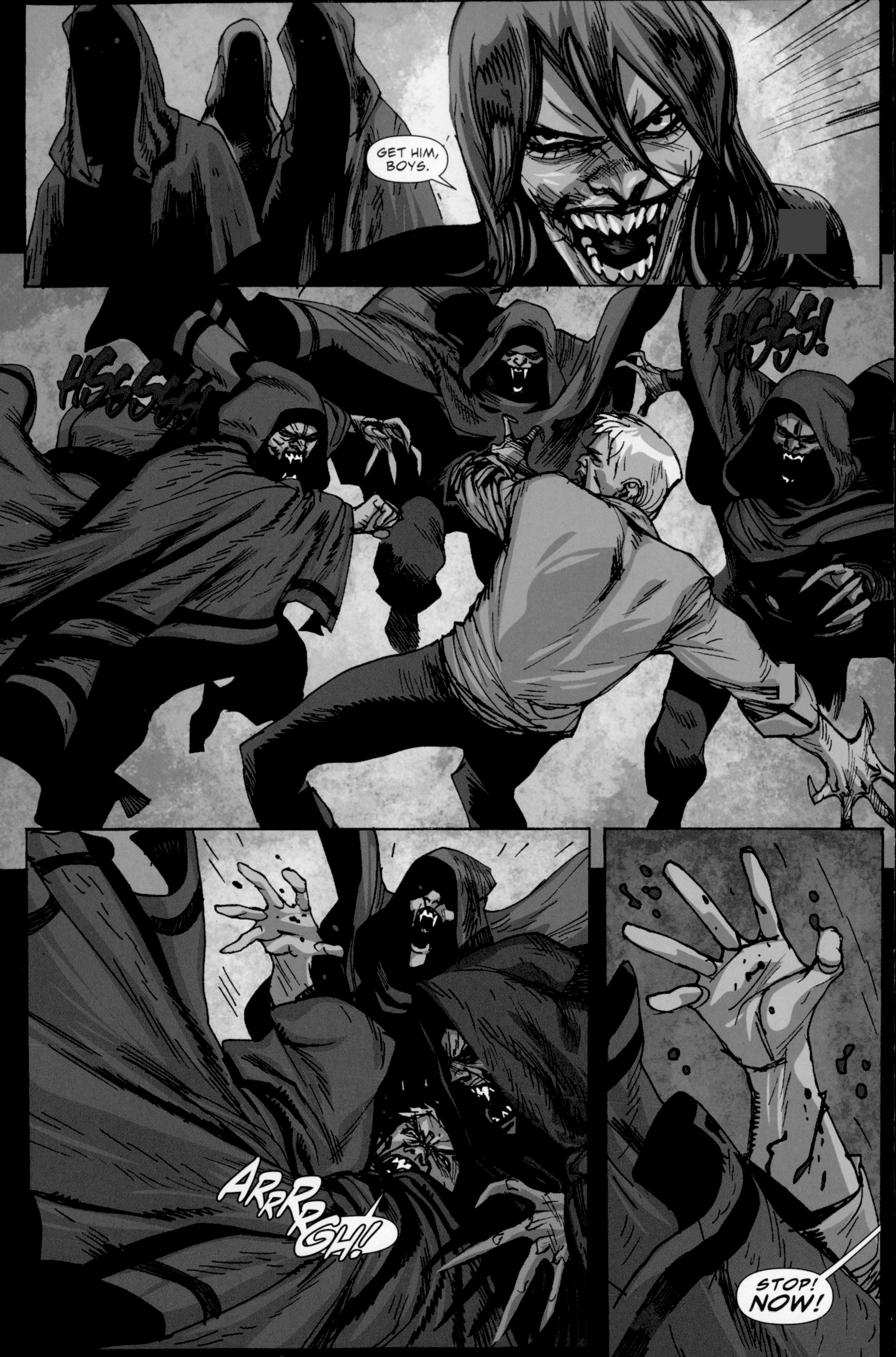
GET HIM, BOYS.
HSSSSS!
HSSS!
ARRRRGH!
STOP! NOW!

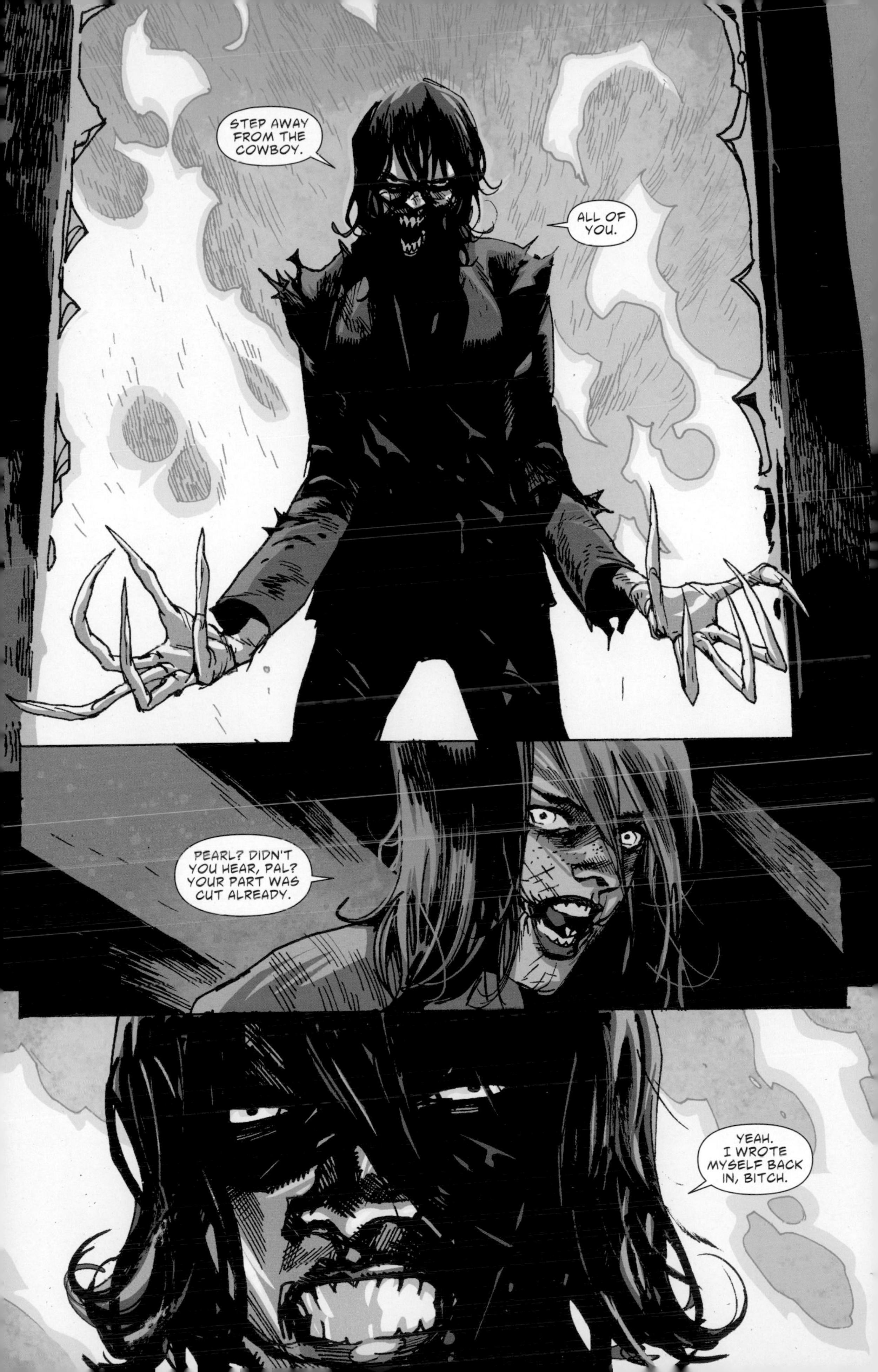
STEP AWAY FROM THE COWBOY.
ALL OF YOU.
PEARL? DIDN'T YOU HEAR, PAL? YOUR PART WAS CUT ALREADY.
YEAH. I WROTE MYSELF BACK IN, BITCH.

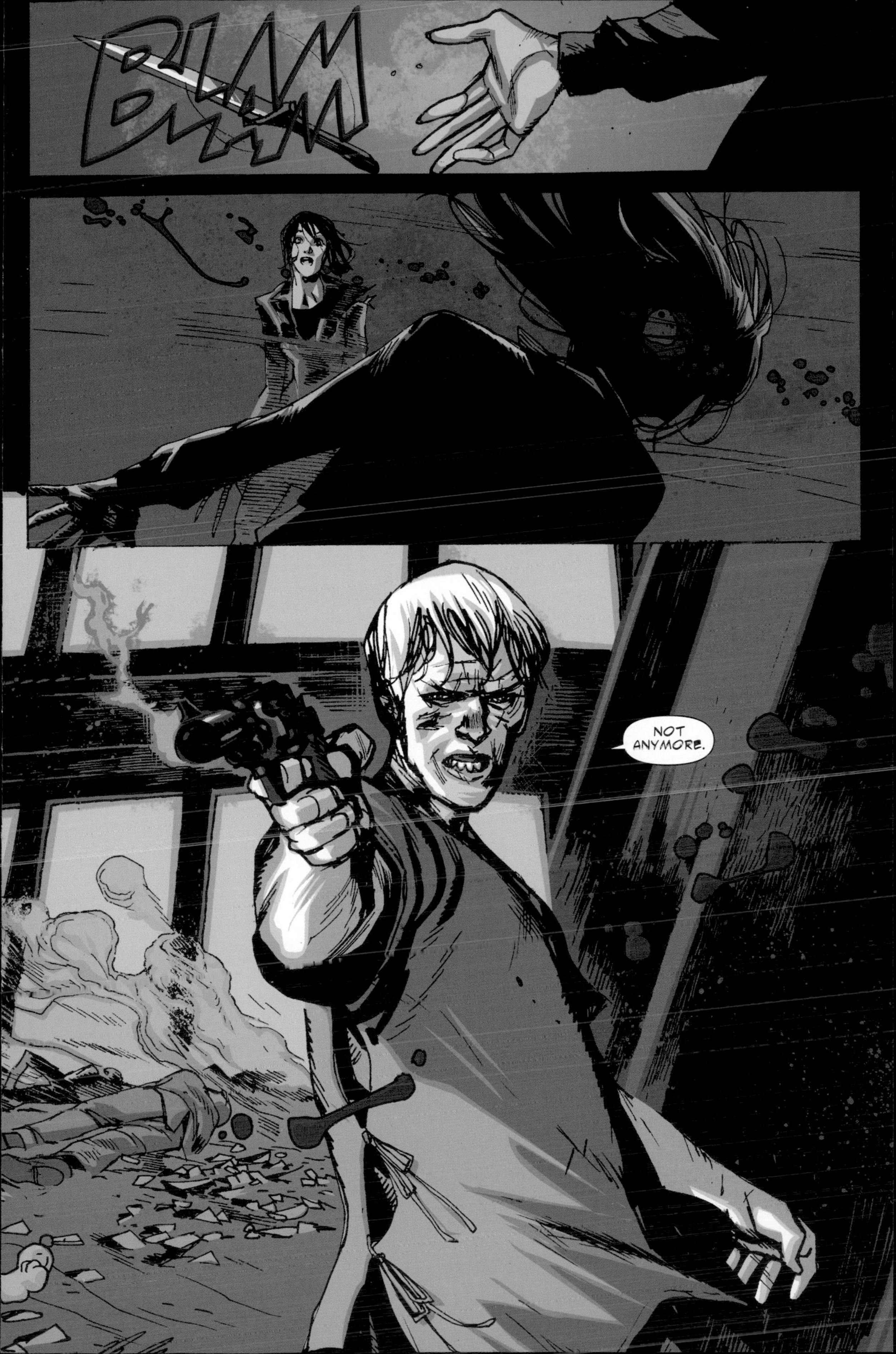
BLAM
BLAM
NOT ANYMORE.

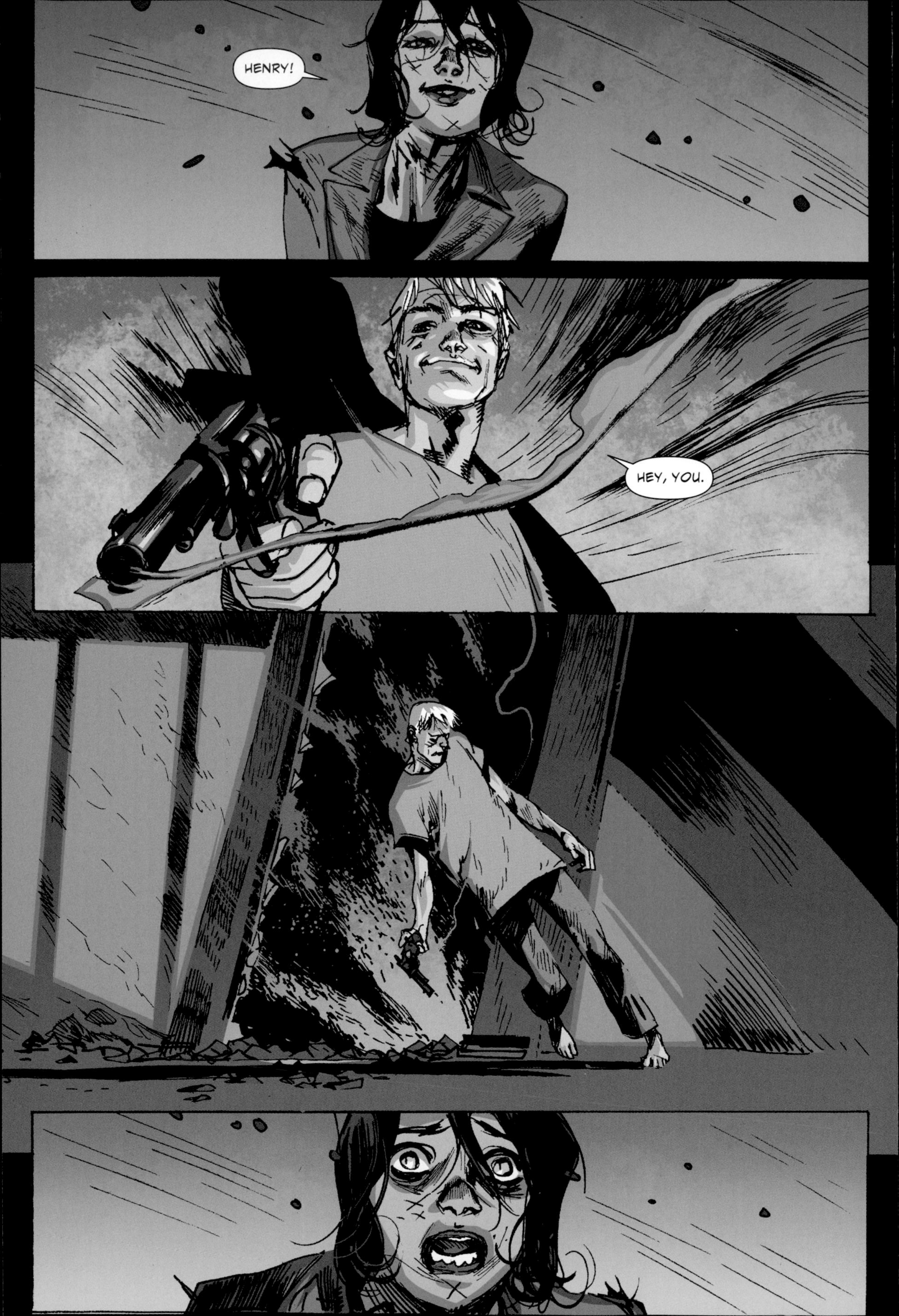
HENRY!
HEY, YOU.

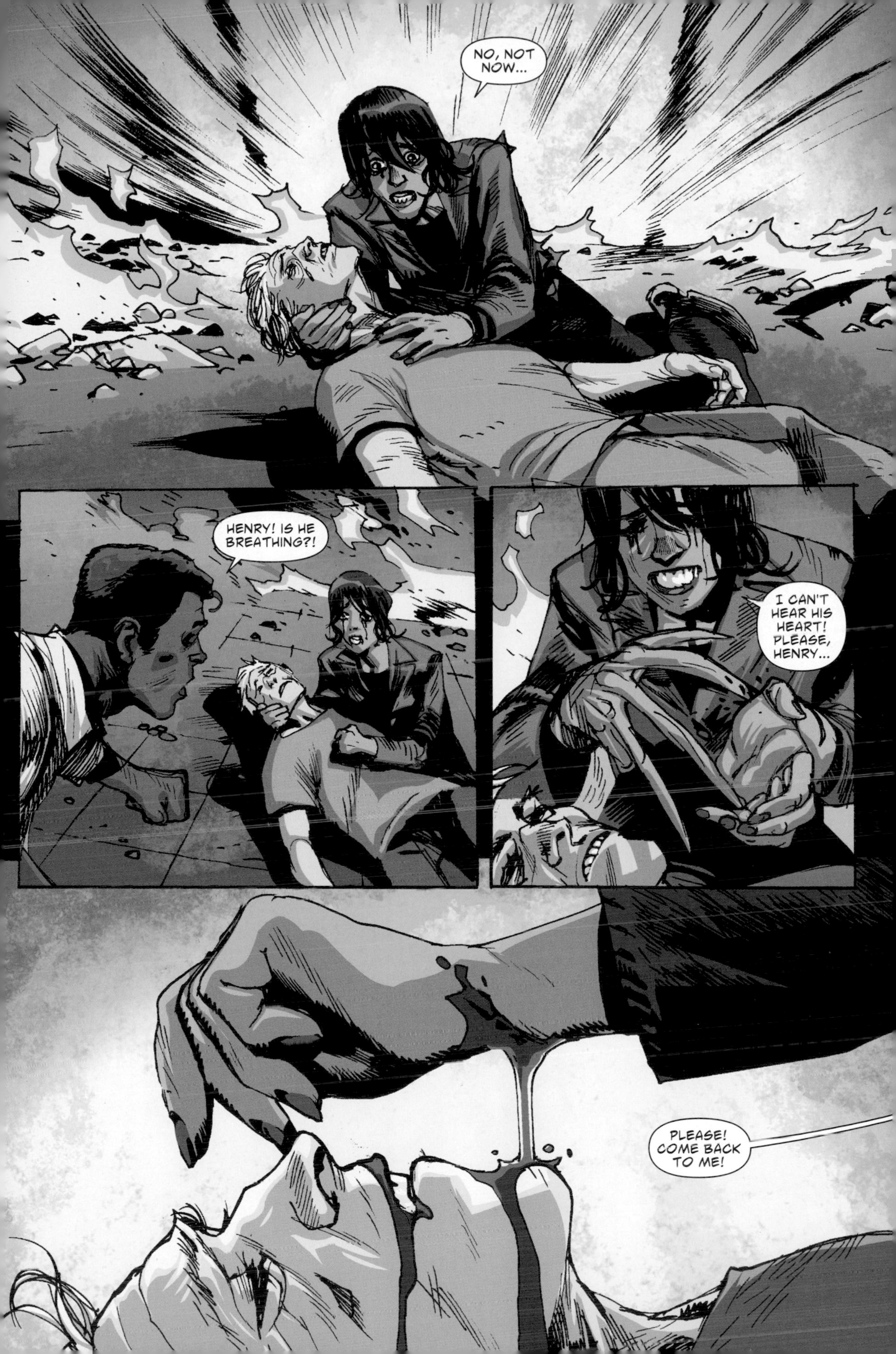
NO, NOT NOW...
HENRY! IS HE BREATHING?!
I CAN'T HEAR HIS HEART! PLEASE, HENRY...
PLEASE! COME BACK TO ME!

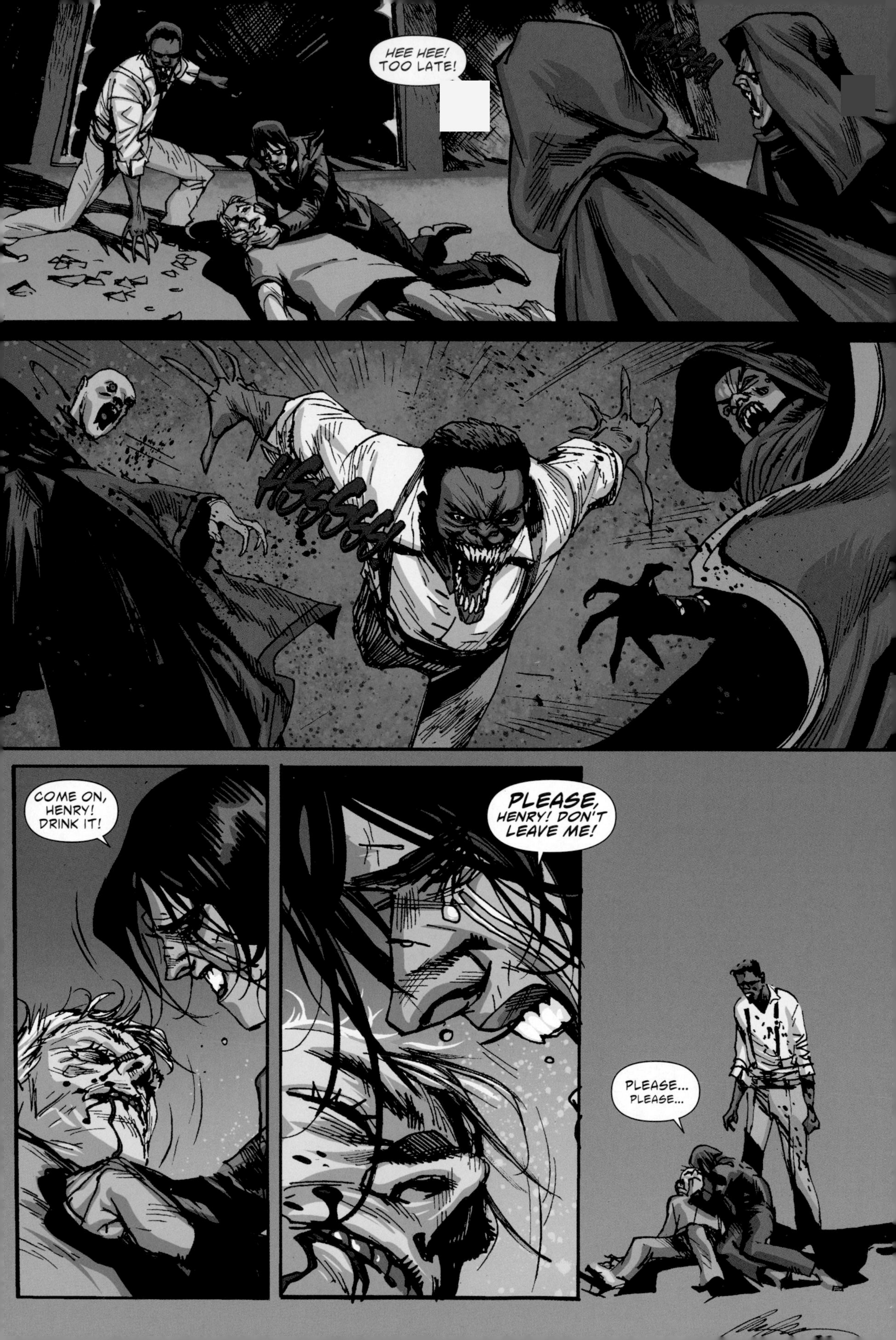
HEE HEE! TOO LATE!
COME ON, HENRY! DRINK IT!
PLEASE, HENRY! DON'T LEAVE ME!
PLEASE... PLEASE...

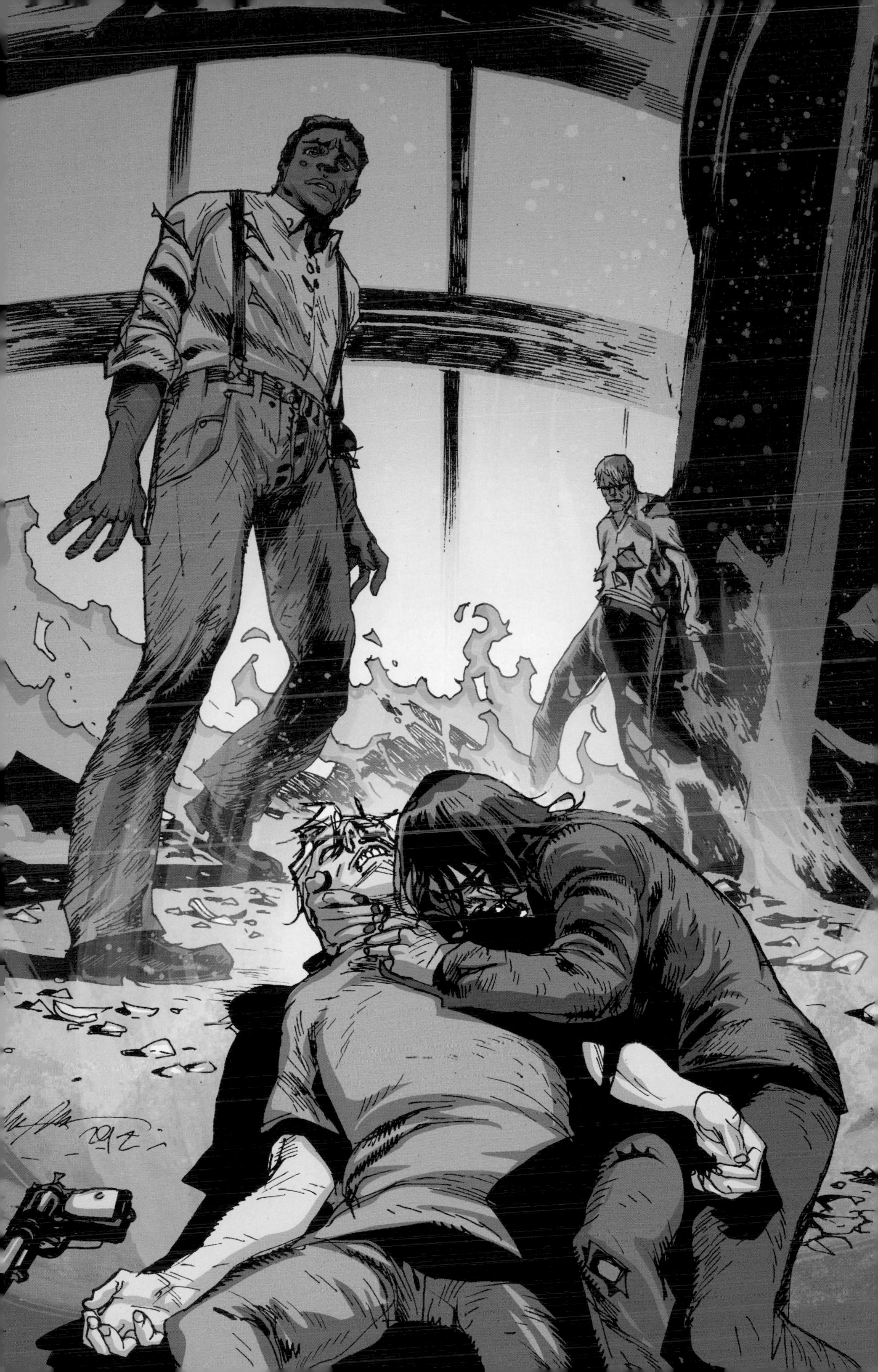

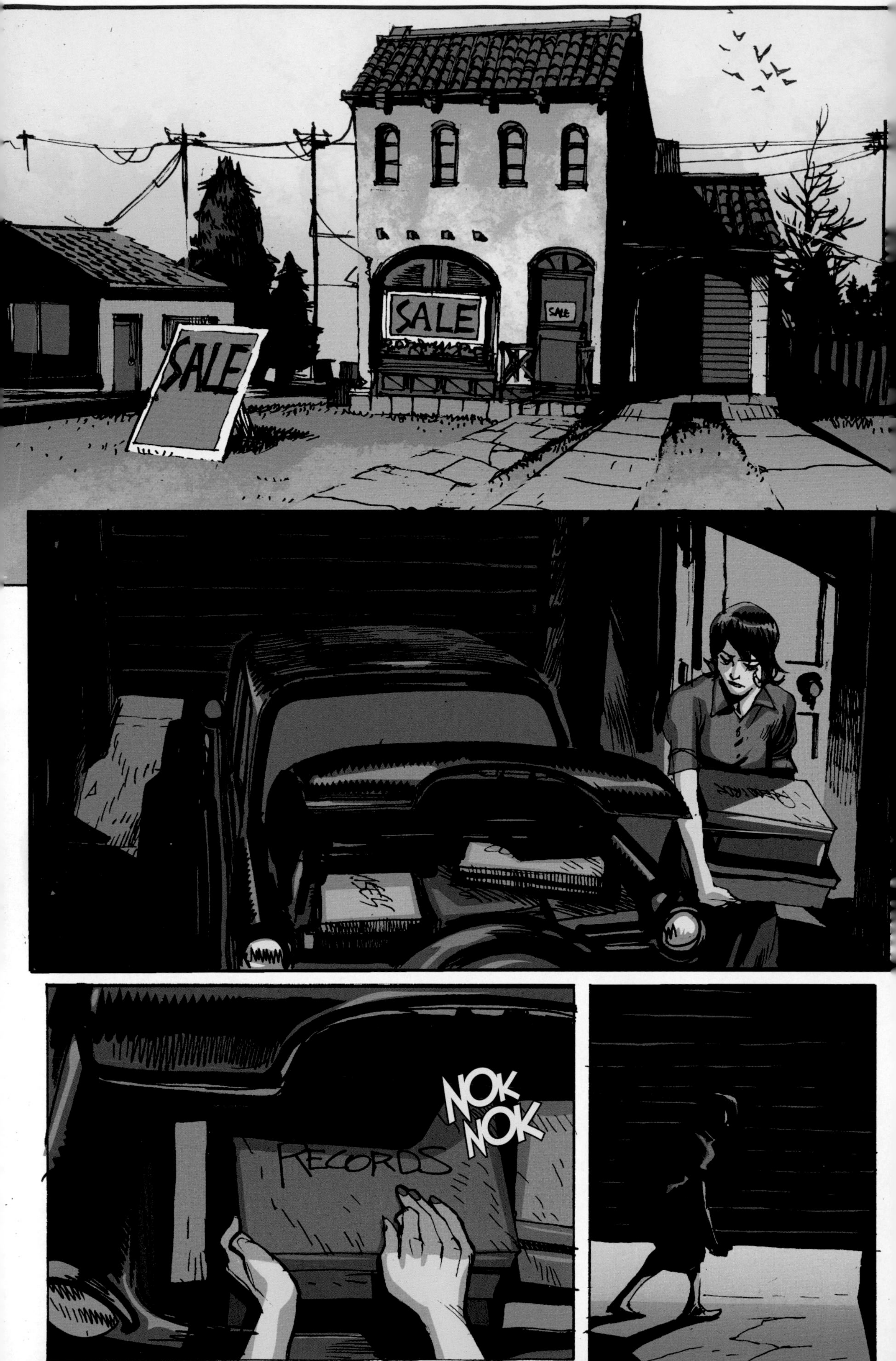
SALE
SALE
SALE
RECORDS
NOK
NOK

"PEARL, IF YOU'RE READING THIS, IT MEANS...WELL, I GUESS IT MEANS MY PART OF OUR SONG ENDED A LITTLE EARLIER THAN I'D HAVE LIKED.

"AND FOR THAT, HON, FOR BOWING OUT EARLY, I'M SO, SO SORRY.

"BUT WHAT I WANT YOU TO KNOW, PEARL, HERE AND NOW, IS WHAT I'M *NOT* SORRY FOR. I'M NOT SORRY FOR MAKING THE CHOICE, TOGETHER, NOT TO TURN ME.

"SEE, THE THING IS, I'VE ALWAYS KNOWN YOU WERE PART OF SOMETHING *BIGGER* THAN ME, THAN US. I KNEW IT BEFORE YOU BECAME A VAMPIRE, AND I KNEW IT AFTER. YOU GOT MORE LIFE, MORE FIRE IN YOU THAN A NORMAL BODY'LL HOLD, GIRL.

"ME, THOUGH, I'M DIFFERENT. I HAD A ROUGH TIME OF IT, AS A YOUNG MAN, AND IN MUSIC, IN LIFE, ALL I EVER WANTED WAS SOME KIND OF HOME, OF *PEACE*.

"AND FOR A LONG TIME, I FOUND THAT WITH YOU. IT'S WHERE I WANT TO STAY NOW, PEARL, HOME, EVEN THOUGH I CAN SEE YOU'RE READY FOR SOMETHING NEW.

"I KNOW YOU WANT THE SOMETHING NEW TO BE WITH ME, BUT I'M NOW SO TIRED, PEARL, TIRED AND GRATEFUL FOR ALL THE TIMES WE'VE HAD TOGETHER. FROM HERE TO THE OTHER SIDE OF THE WORLD AND BACK. I'M GRATEFUL FOR IT ALL.

"BEST THING I EVER DID WITH MY LIFE HAPPENED ON A MORNING IN 1925, WHEN I ASKED A GIRL TO JOIN ME FOR A CUP OF COFFEE.

"I LOVE YOU, PEARL, NOW AND ALWAYS.

"NOW GO ON. NO MORE LOOKING BACK, ONLY FORWARD. MY PART MIGHT BE OVER, BUT YOUR SONG IS ONLY JUST BEGINNING."

SNYDER/ALBUQUERQUE

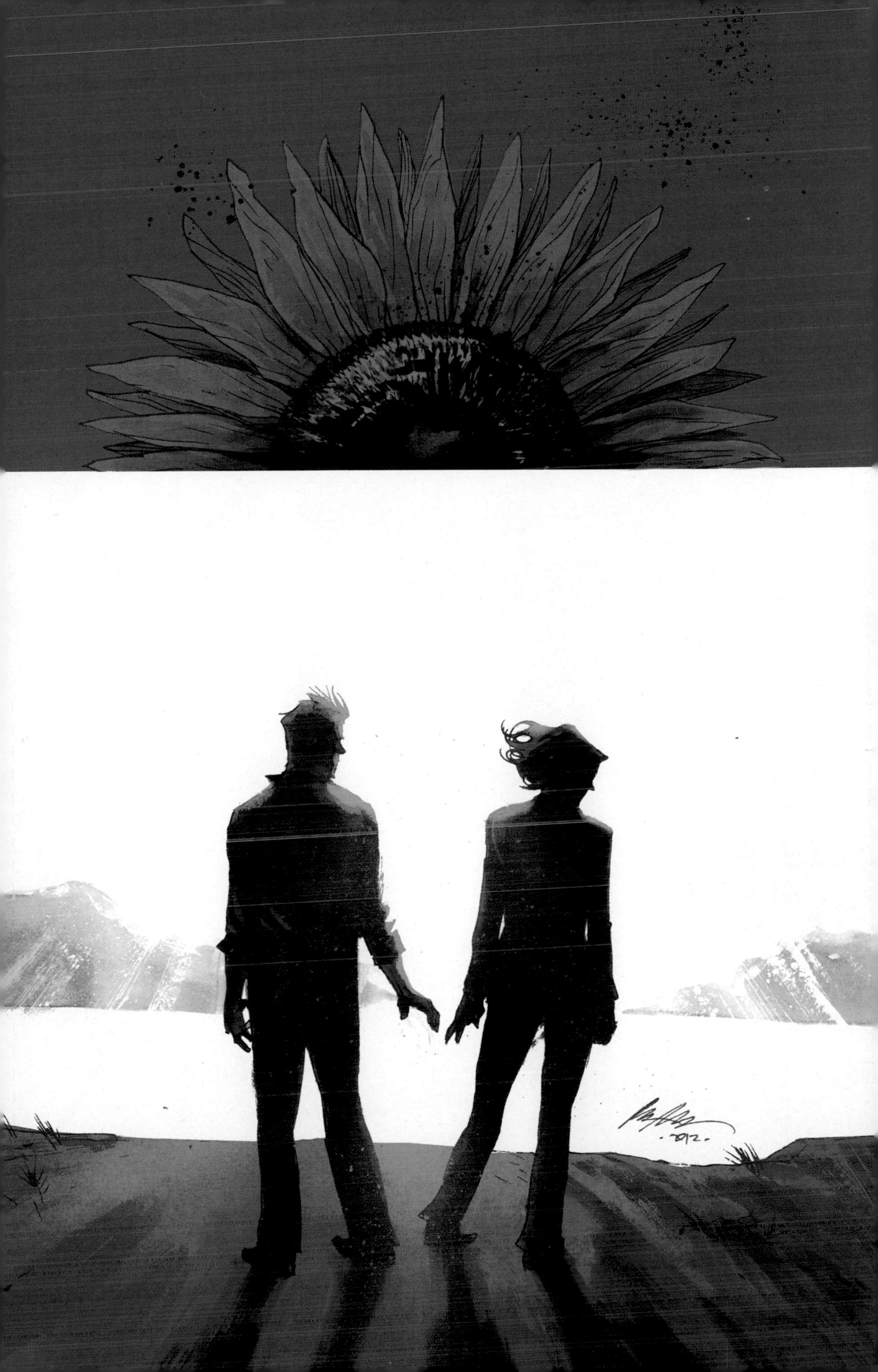

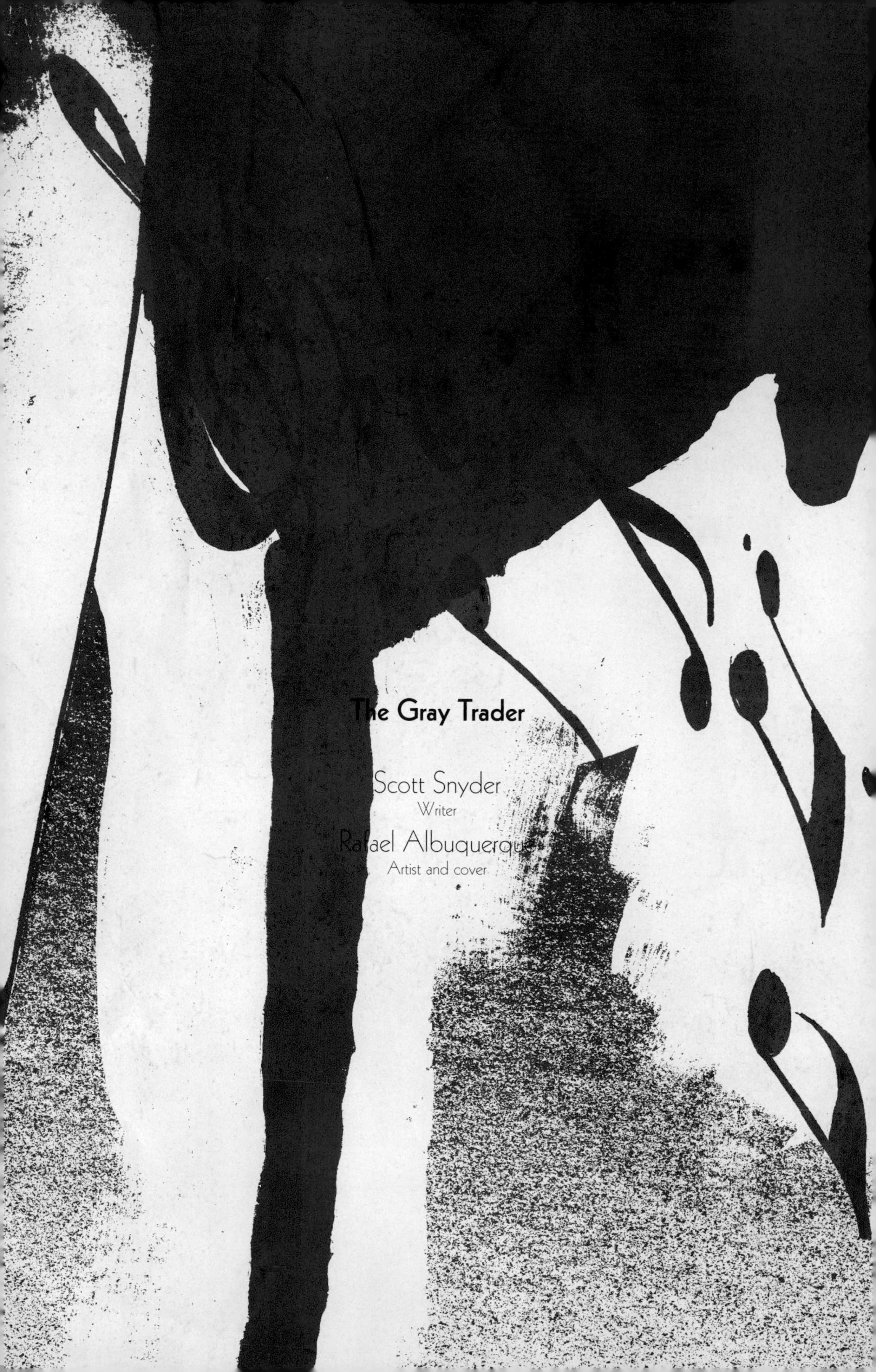

The Gray Trader

Scott Snyder
Writer

Rafael Albuquerque
Artist and cover

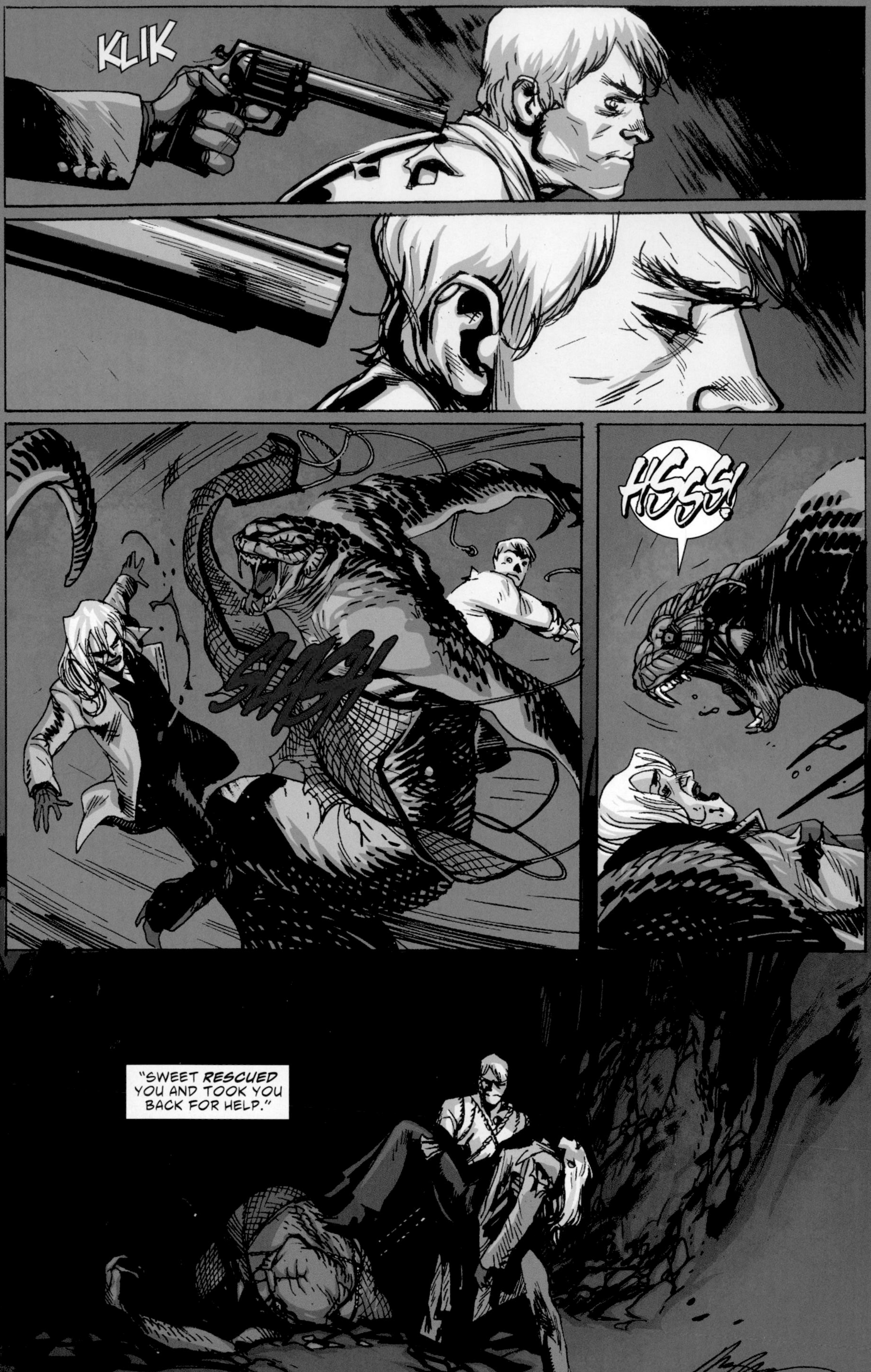
KLIK
SLASH
HSSS!
"SWEET RESCUED YOU AND TOOK YOU BACK FOR HELP."

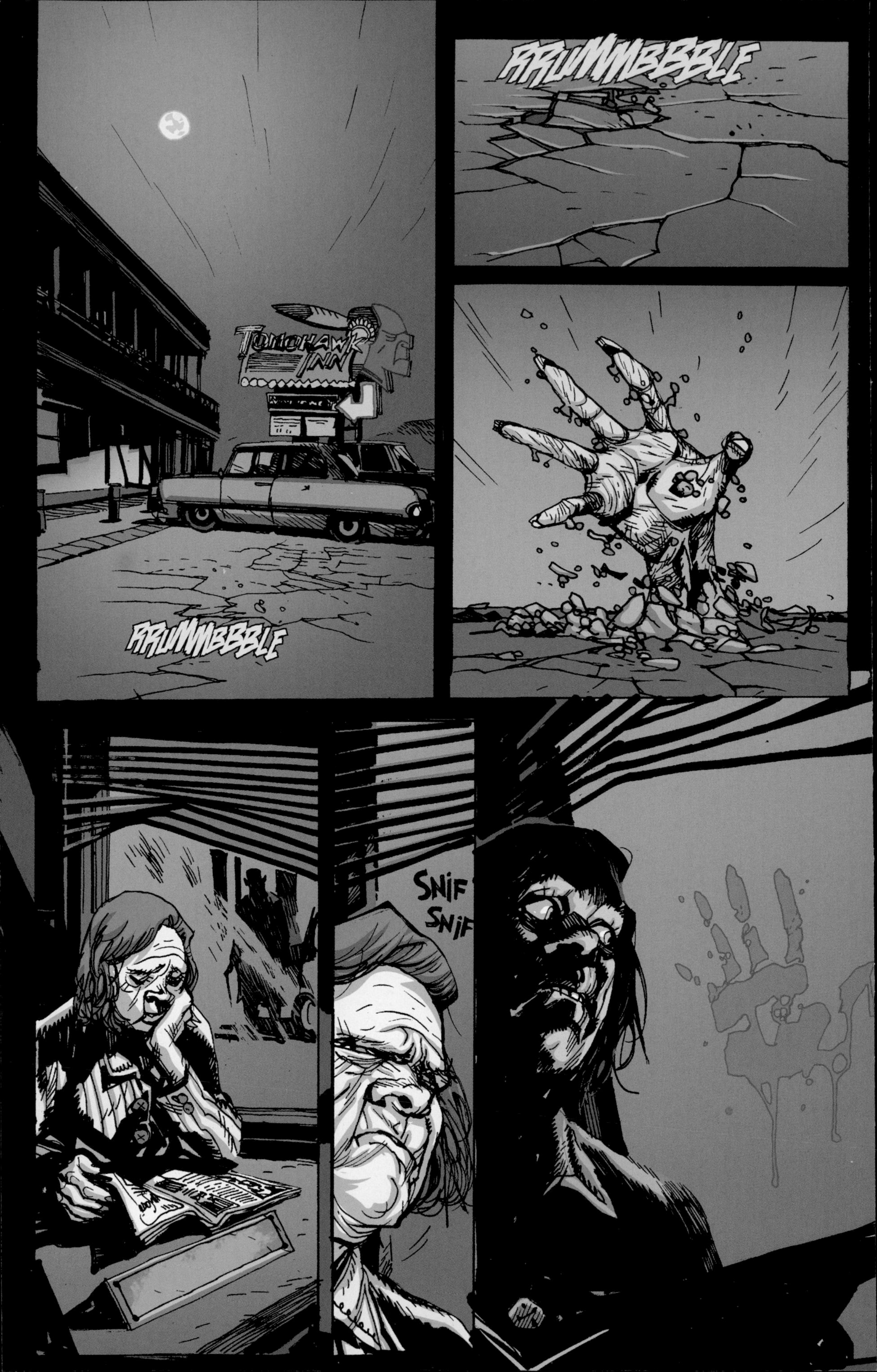
RRUMMBBBLE
RRUMMBBBLE
SNIF
SNIF

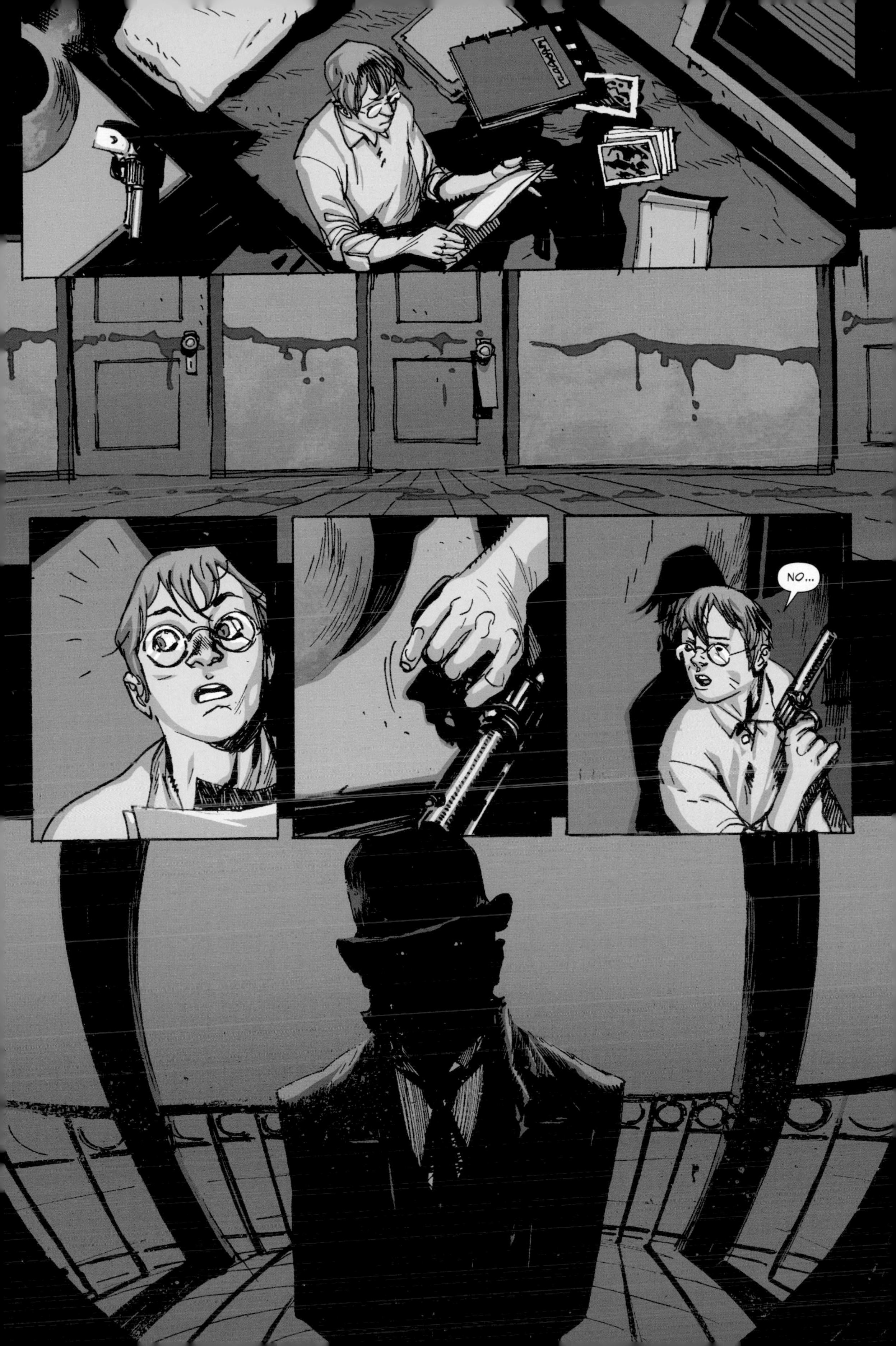
NO...

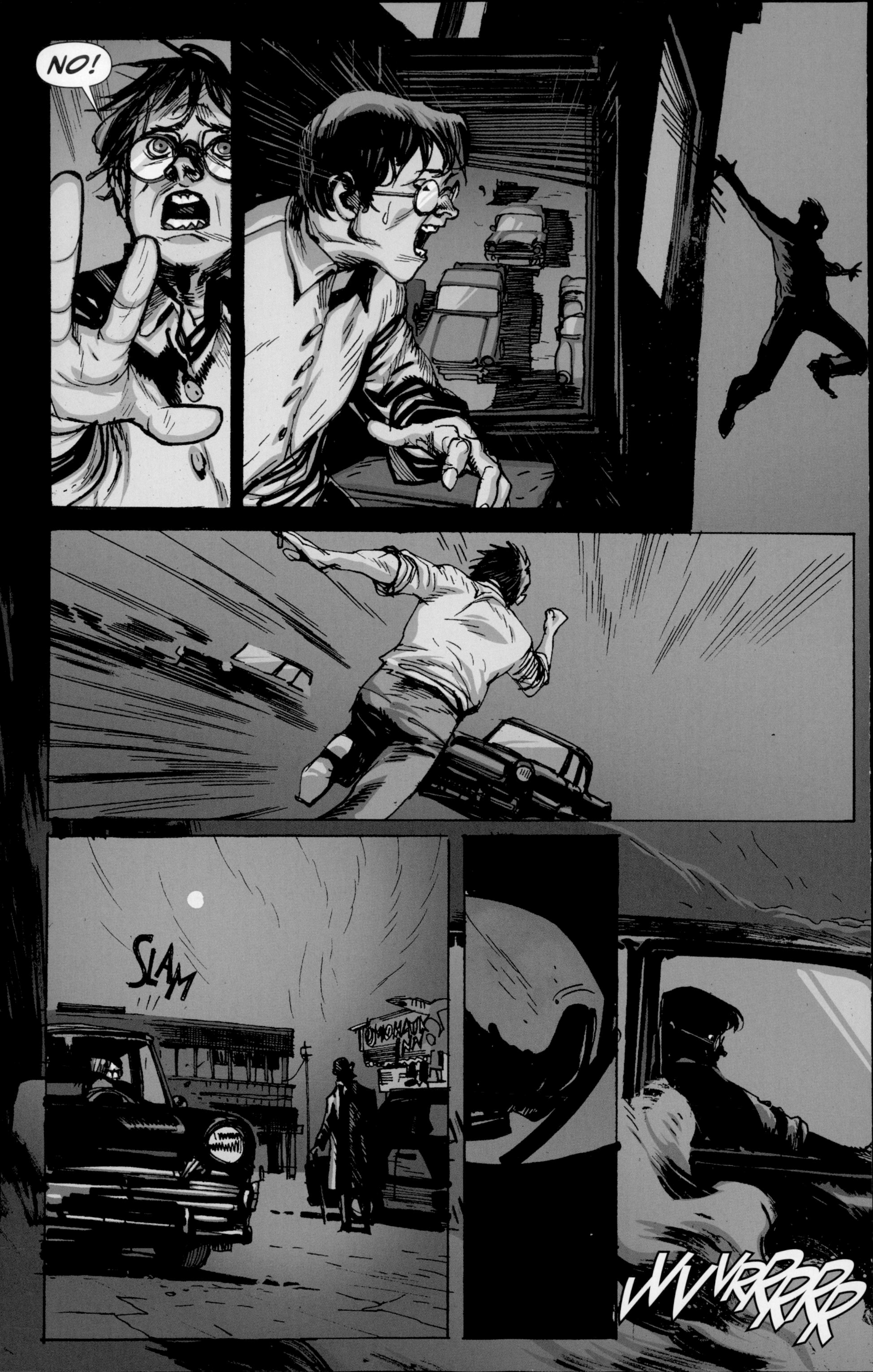
NO!
SLAM
TOMOHAWK INN
WVRRRRRR

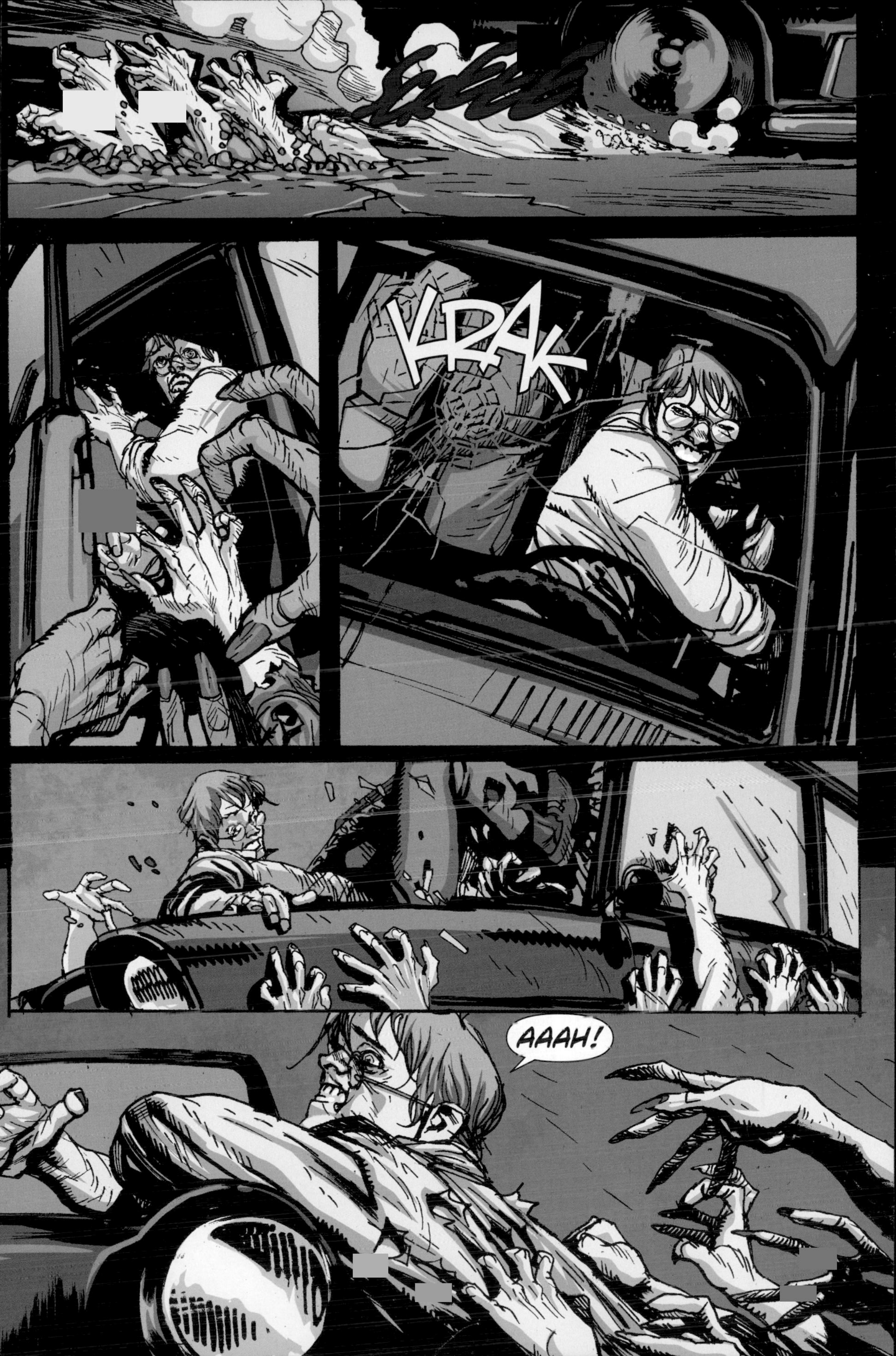
KRAK
AAAH!

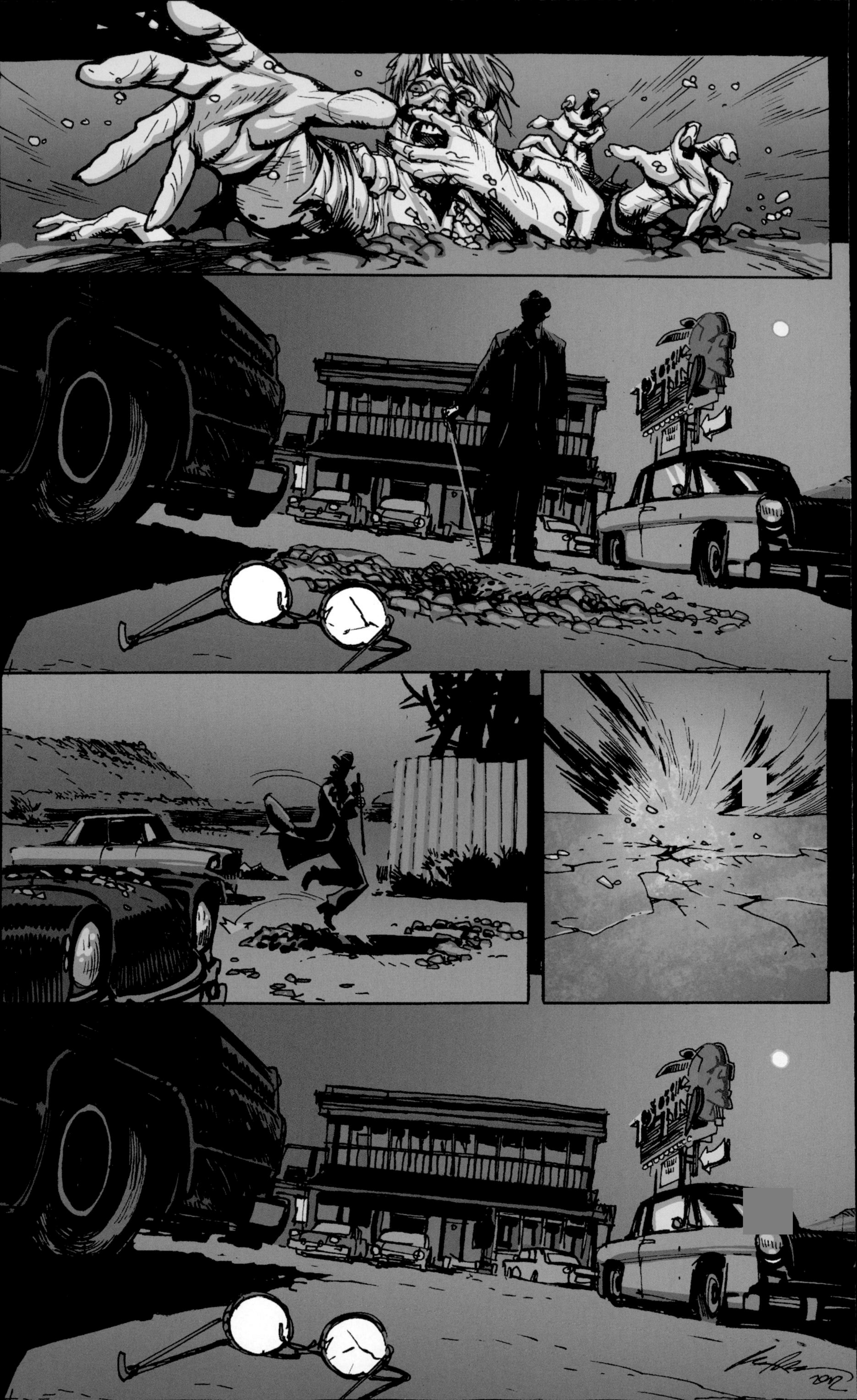

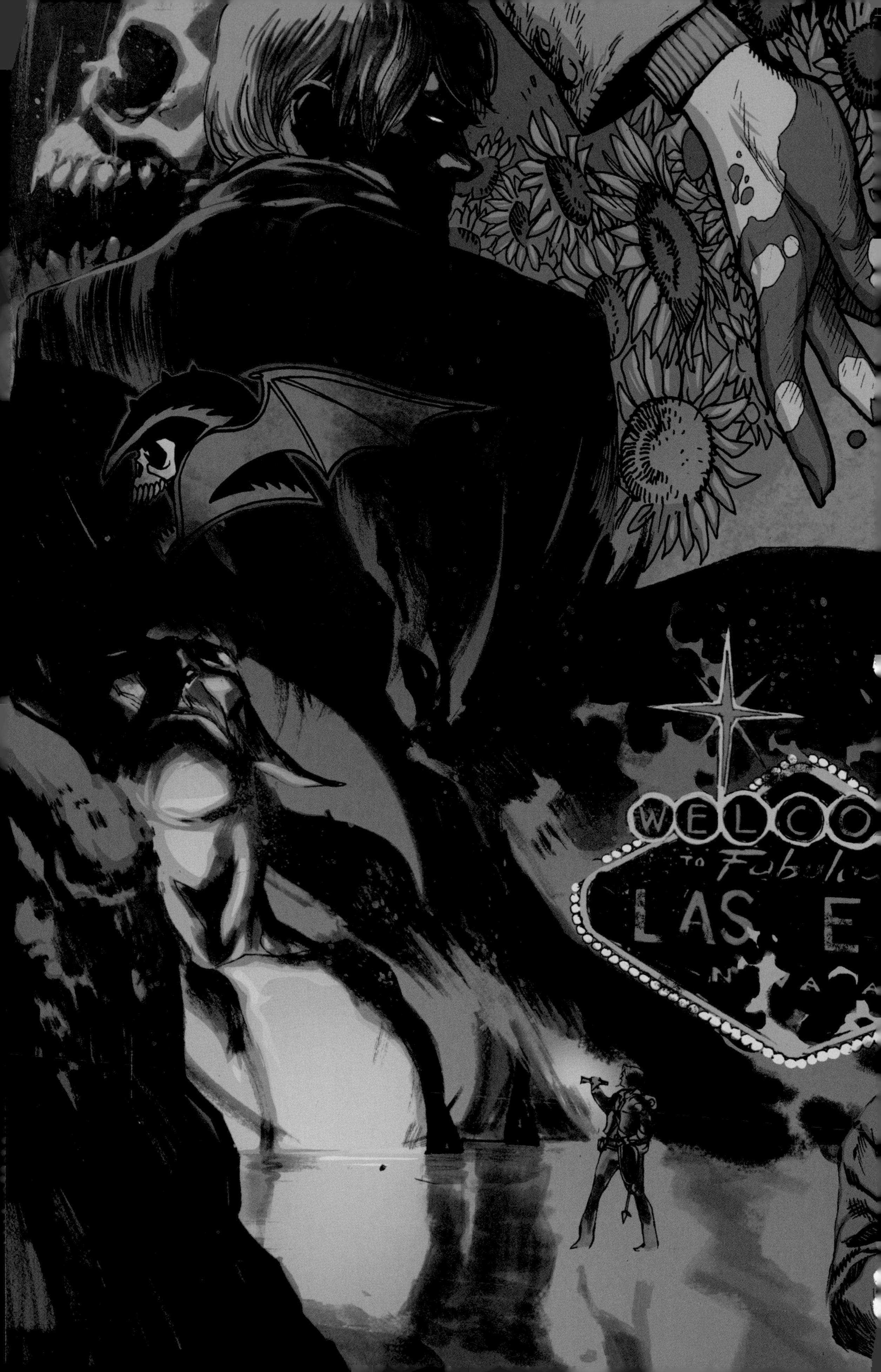
WELCO
LAS

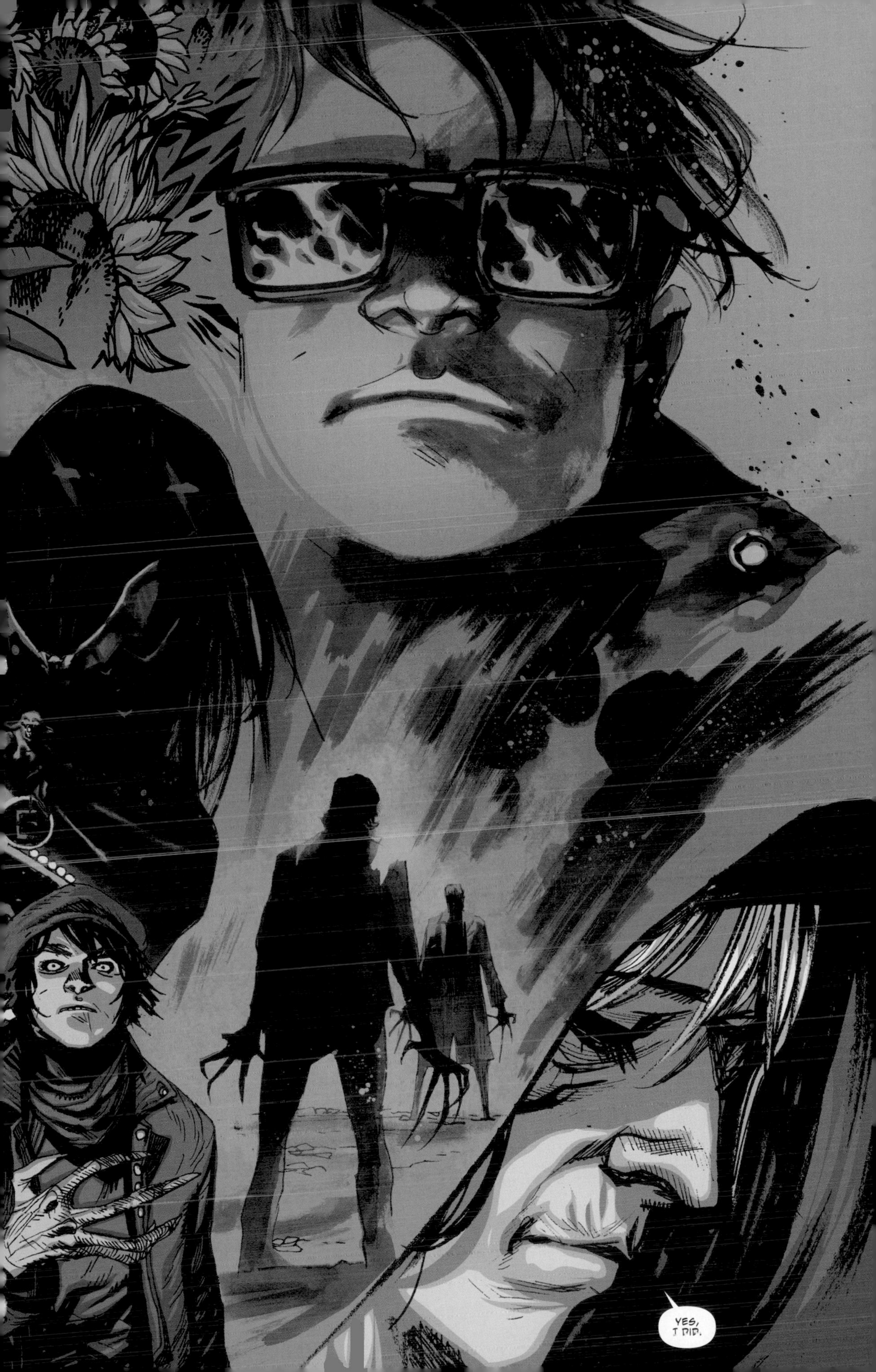
YES, I DID.

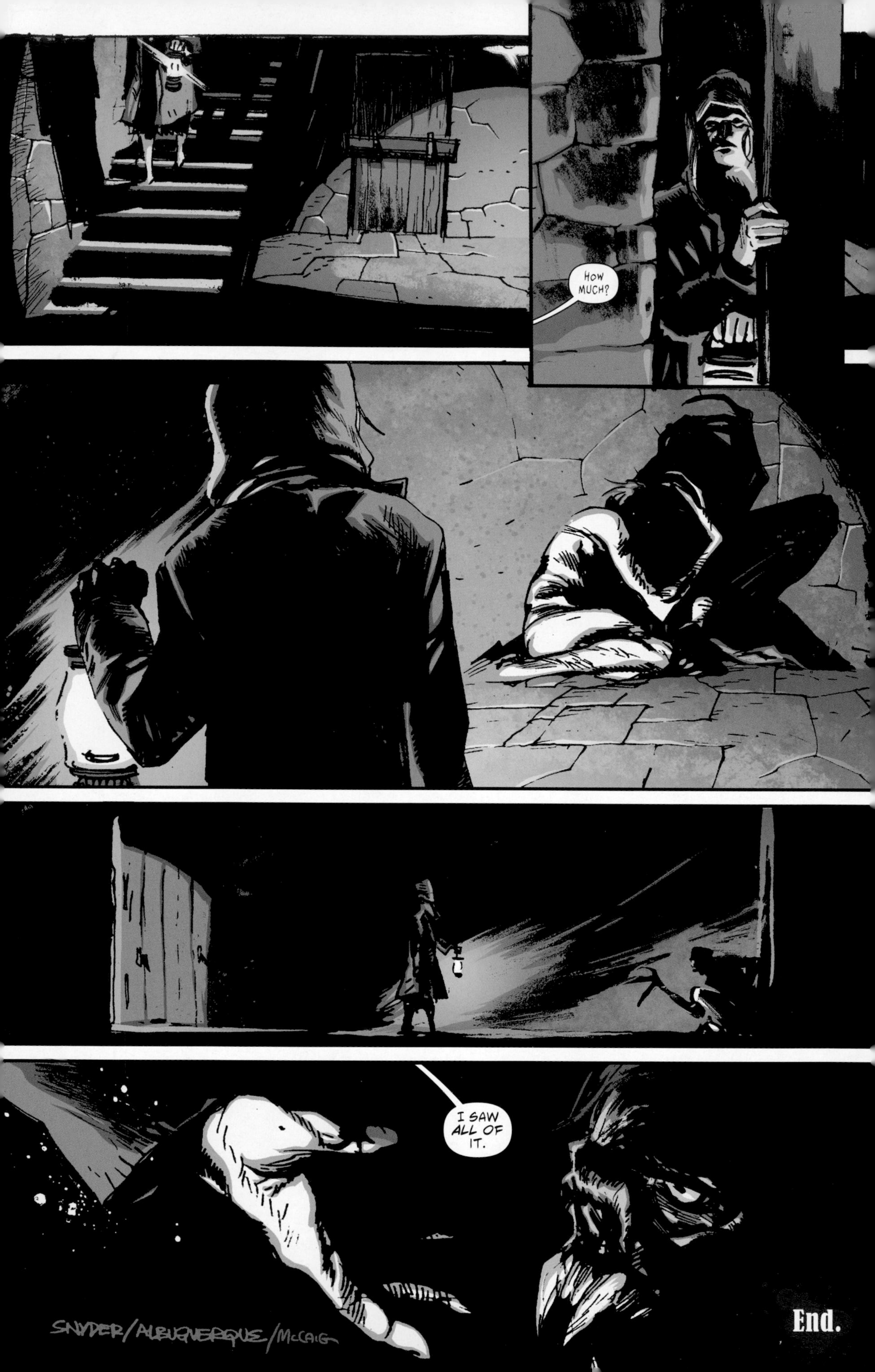
HOW MUCH?
I SAW ALL OF IT.
SNYDER/ALBUQUERQUE/McCAIG
End.

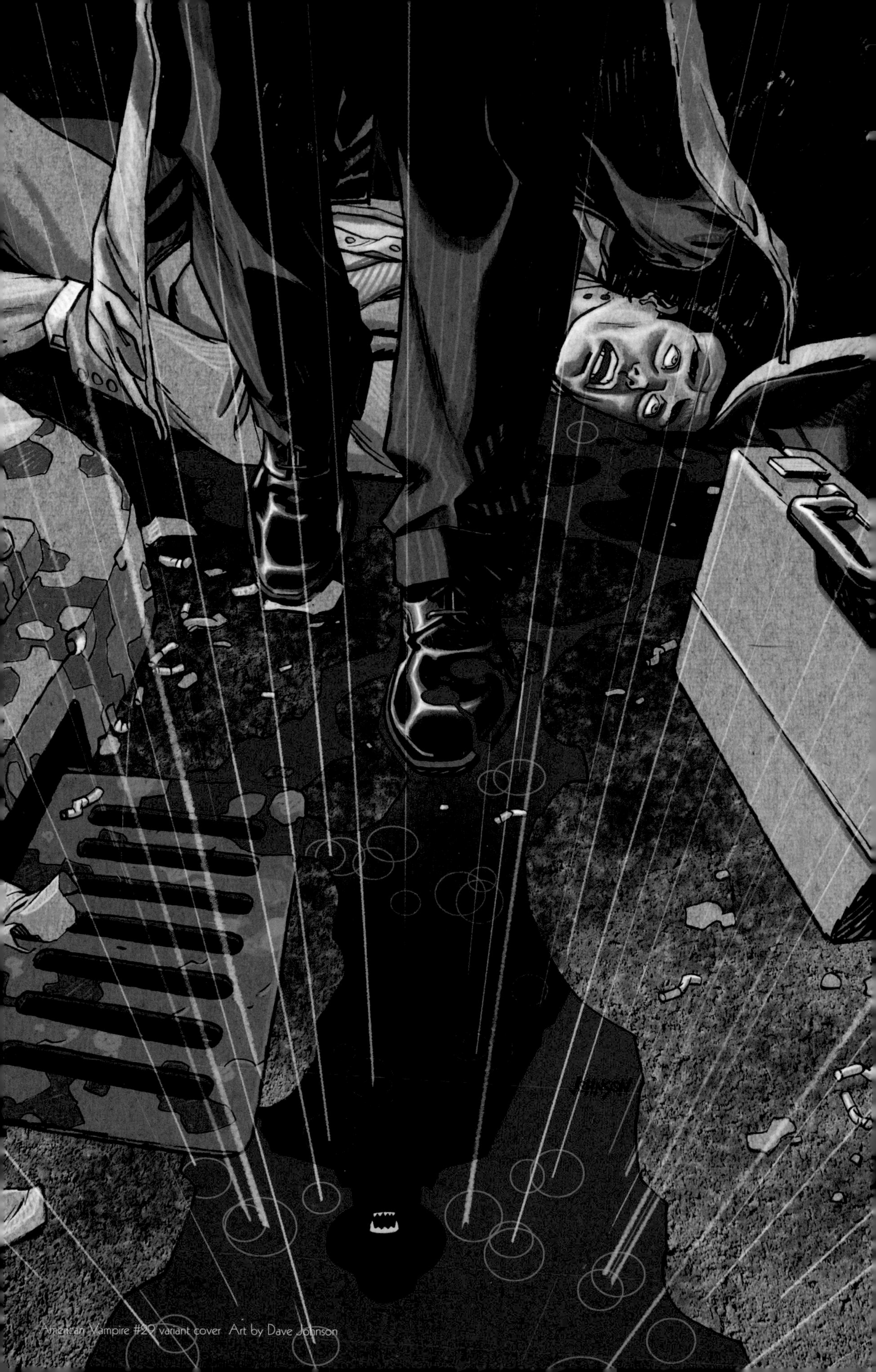

American Vampire #29 variant cover Art by Dave Johnson

American Vampire #30 variant cover Art by Francesco Francavilla

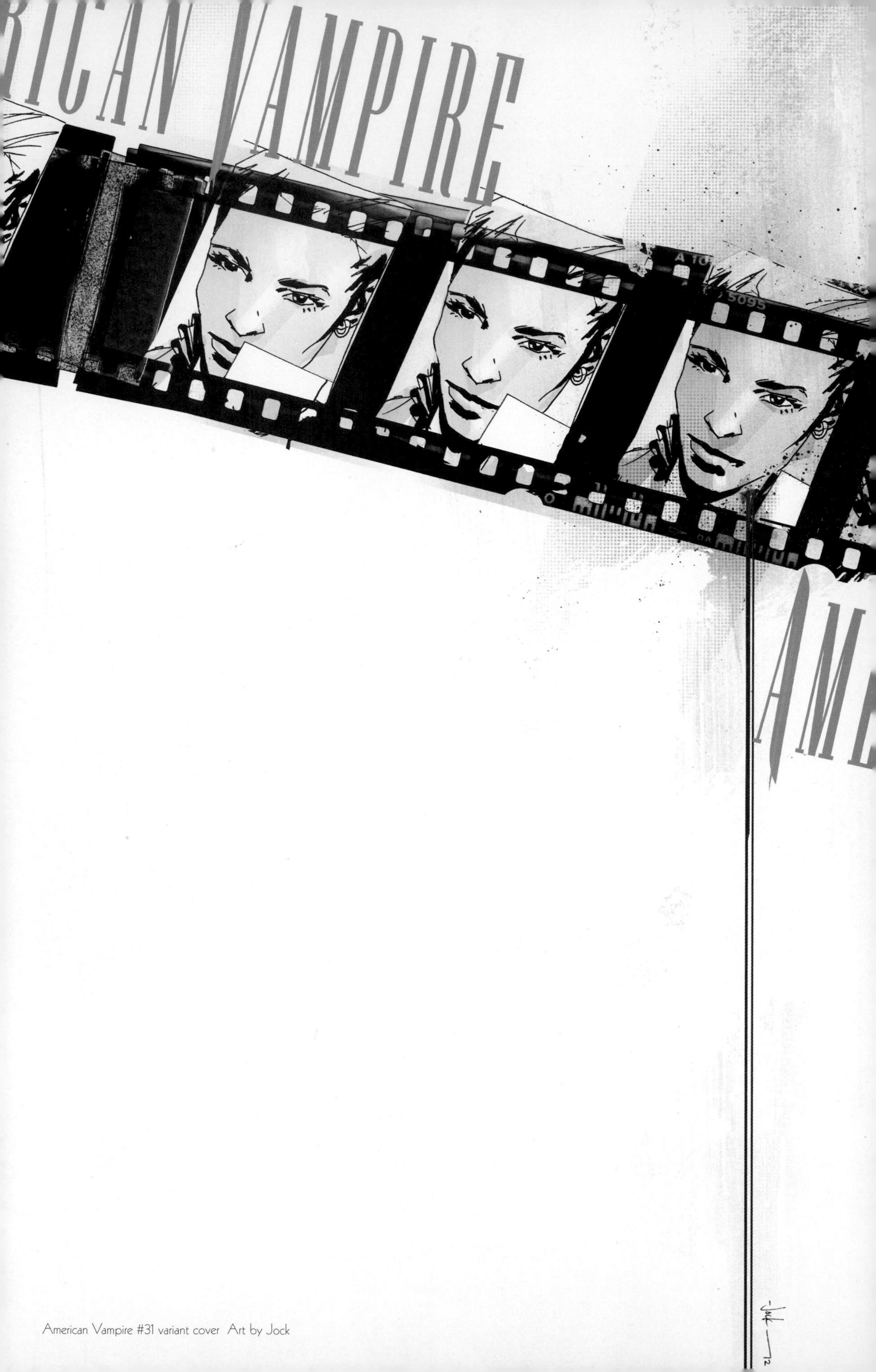
RICAN VAMPIRE
AME

American Vampire #31 variant cover Art by Jock

American Vampire #32 variant cover Art by Dustin Nguyen

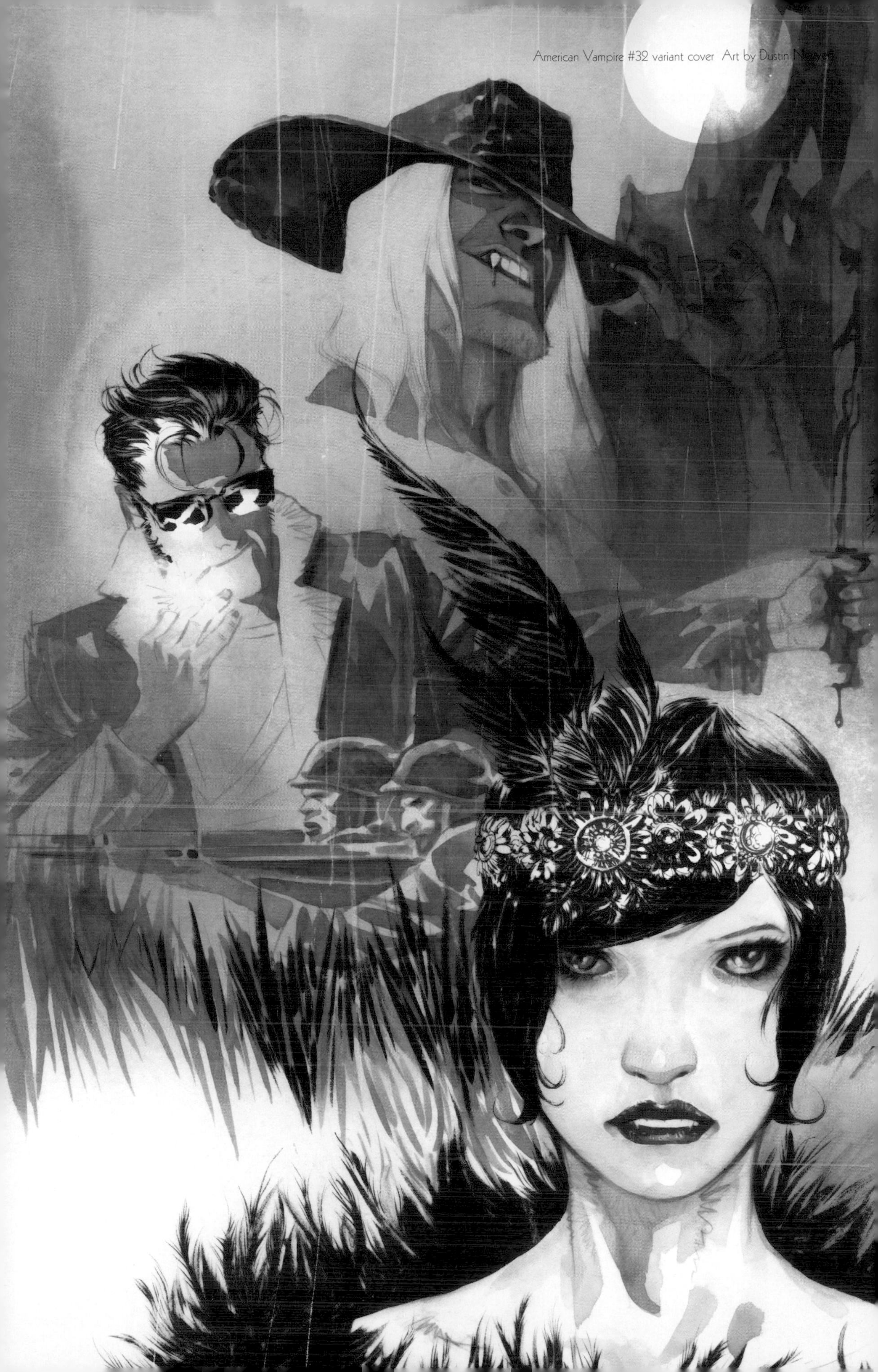

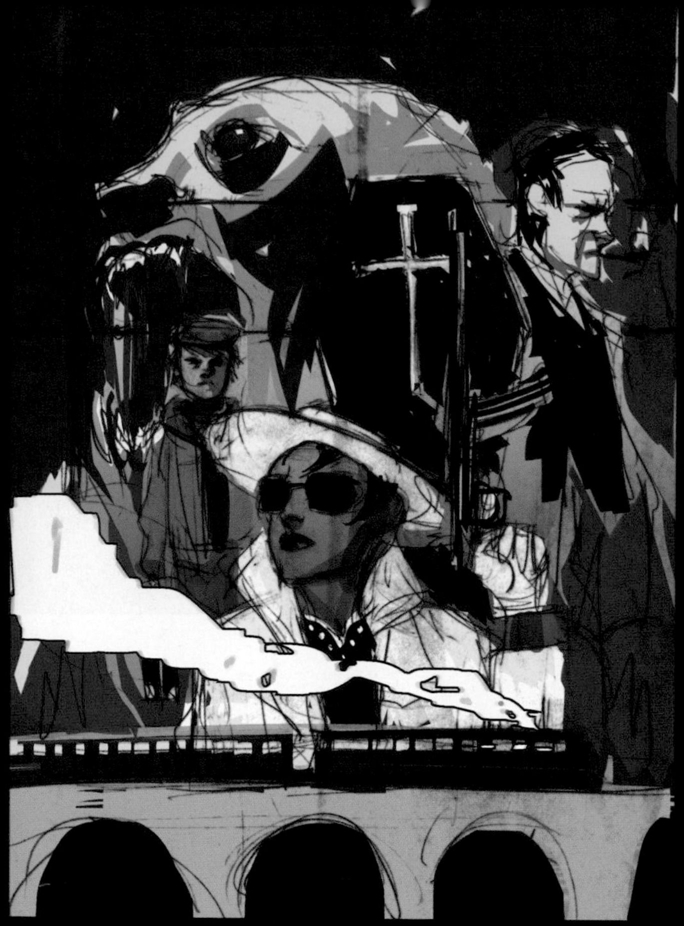

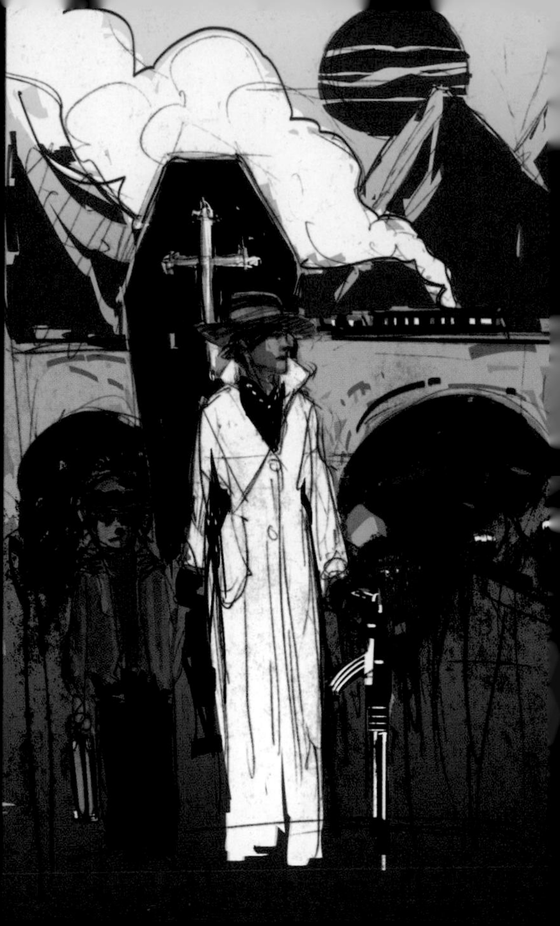

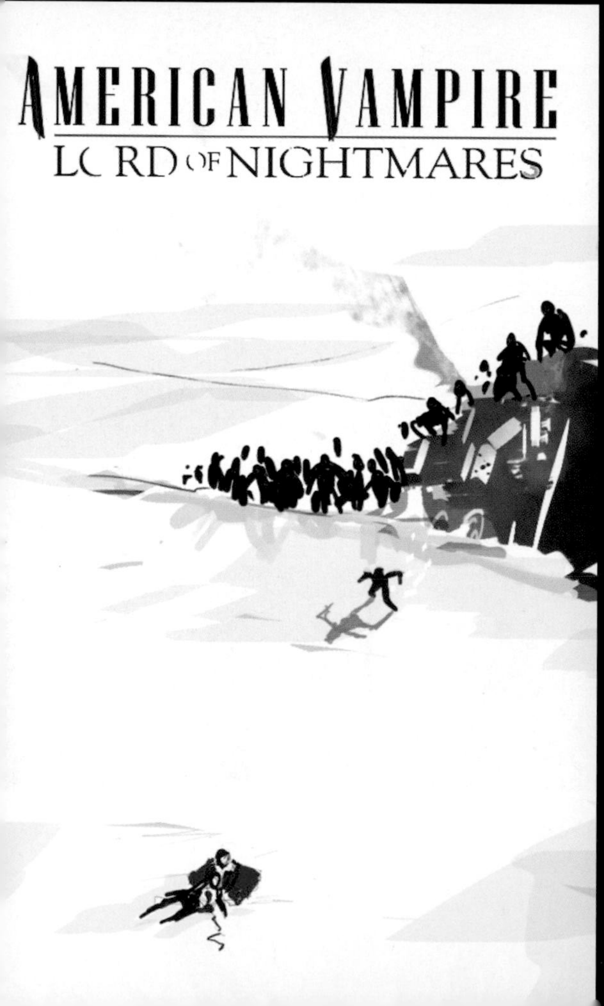
AMERICAN VAMPIRE
LORD OF NIGHTMARES

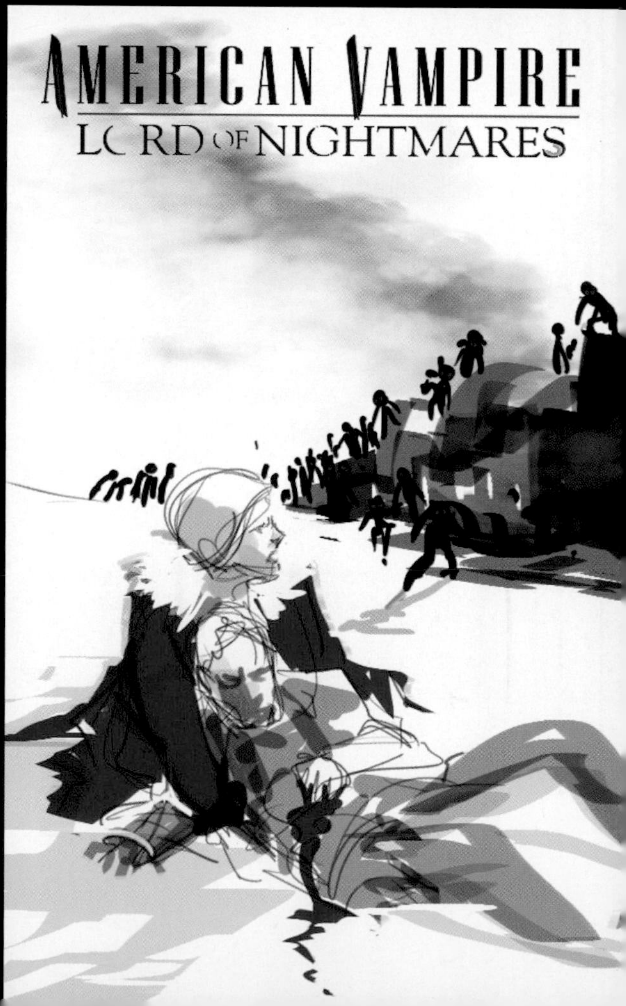
AMERICAN VAMPIRE
LORD OF NIGHTMARES

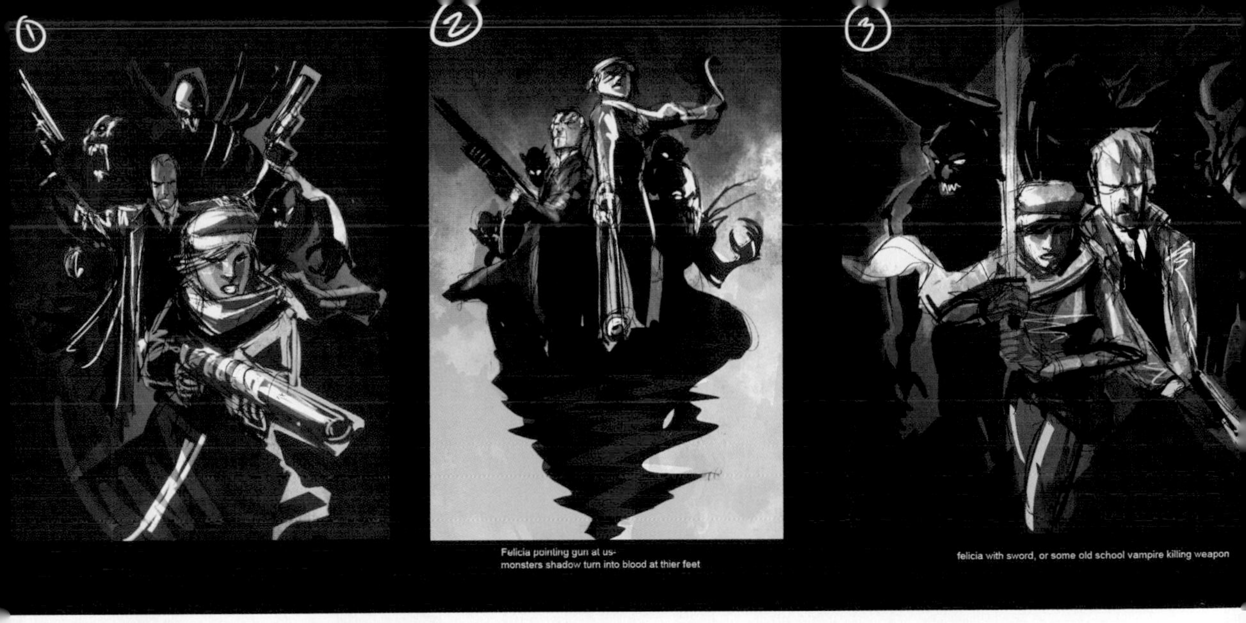
1
2
3
Felicia pointing gun at us-
monsters shadow turn into blood at thier feet
felicia with sword, or some old school vampire killing weapon

COVER SKETCHES AND CHARACTER DESIGNS BY DUSTIN NGUYEN FOR " LORD OF NIGHTMARES."

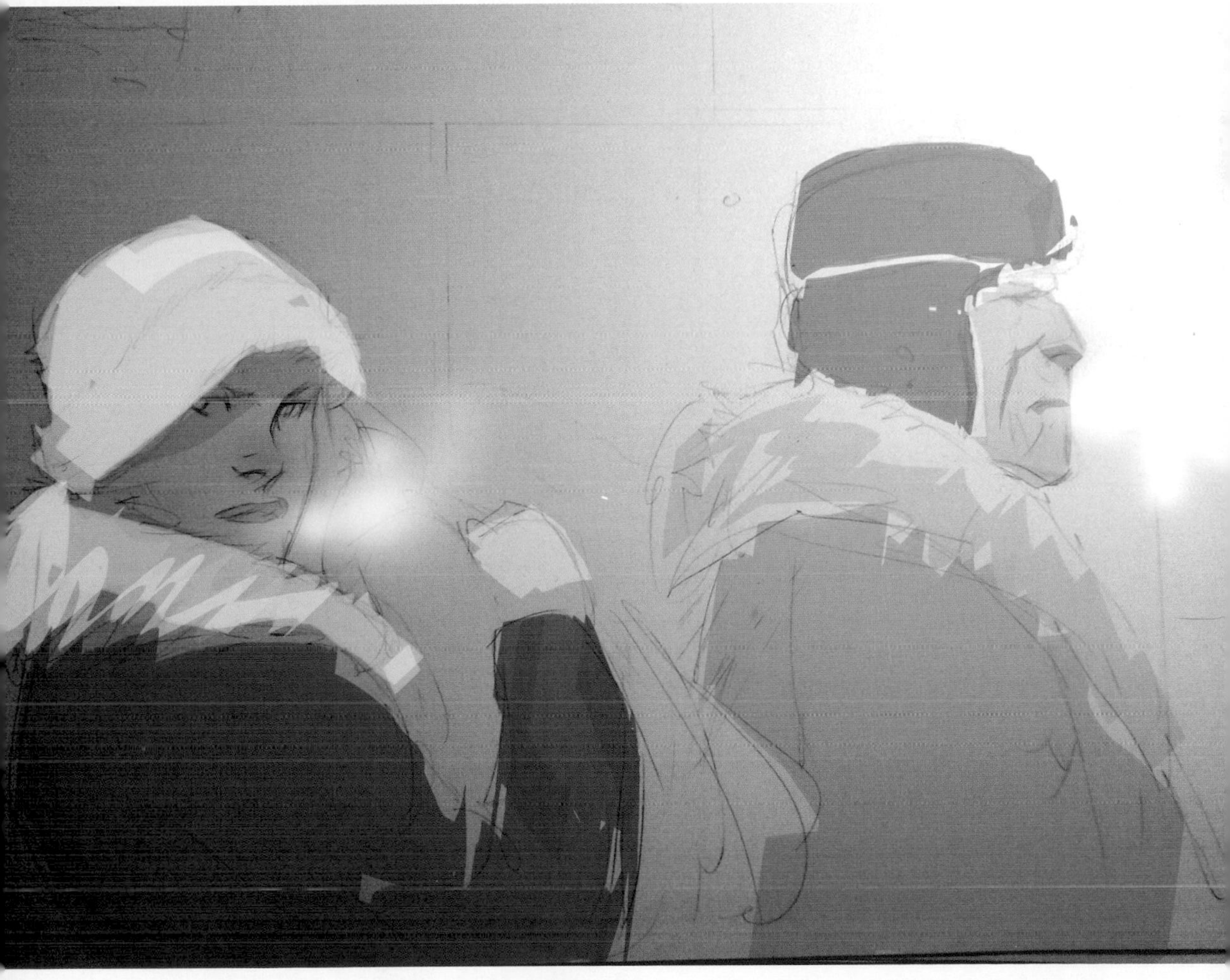

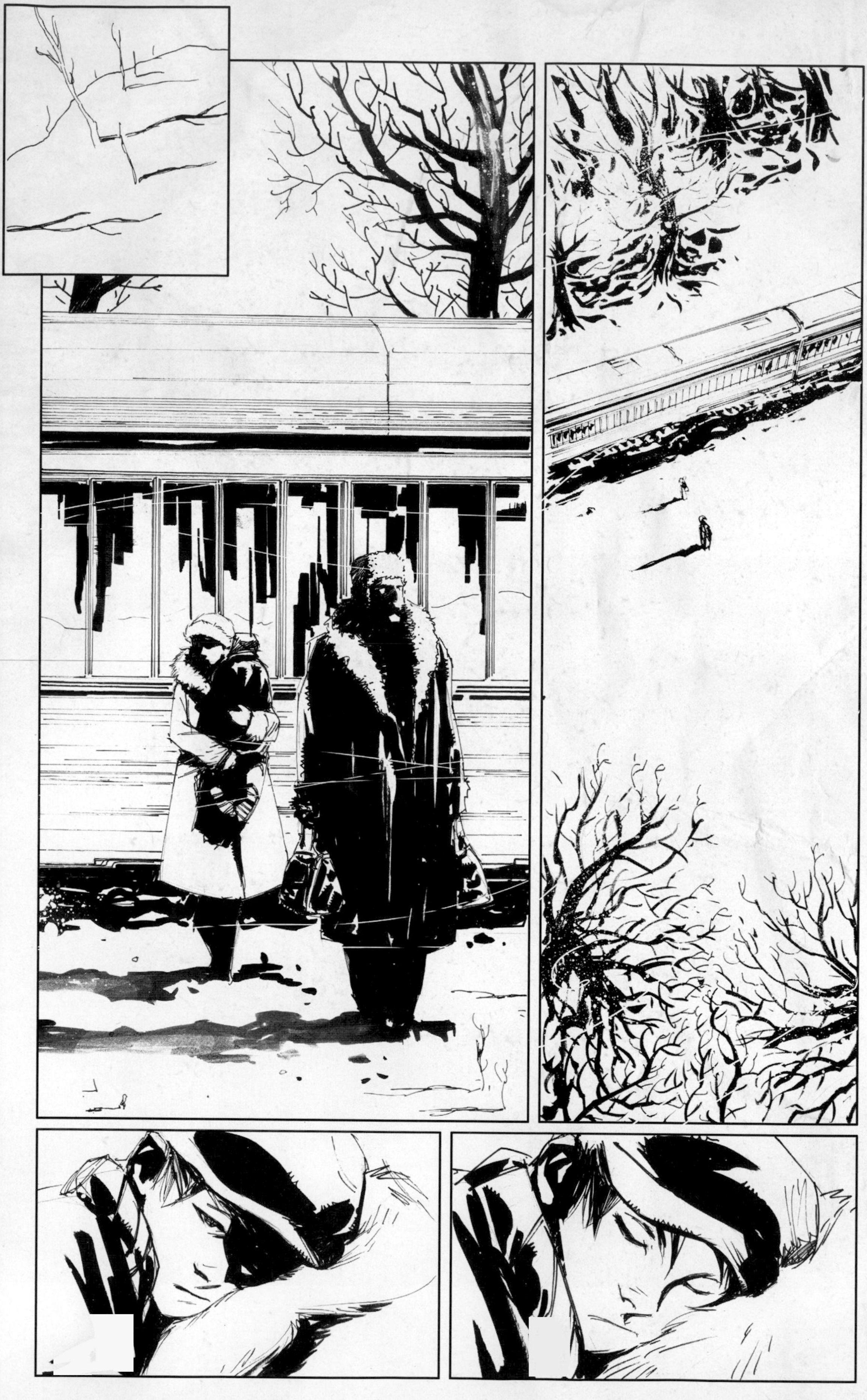

Bix

-AGENT BIX.

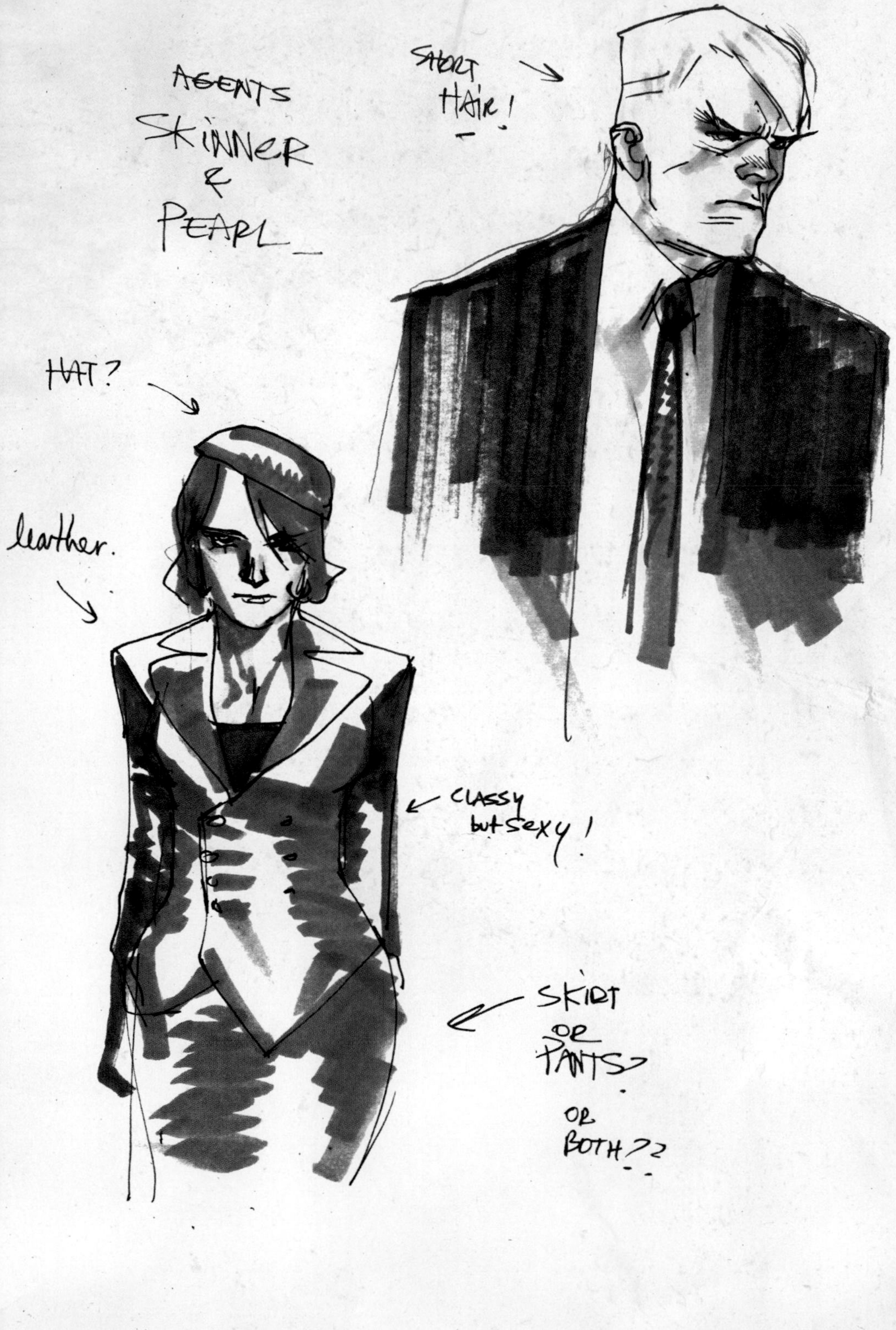
AGENTS
SKINNER
&
PEARL_
SHORT
HAIR!
HAT?
leather.
CLASSY
but sexy!
SKIRT
OR
PANTS?
OR
BOTH??

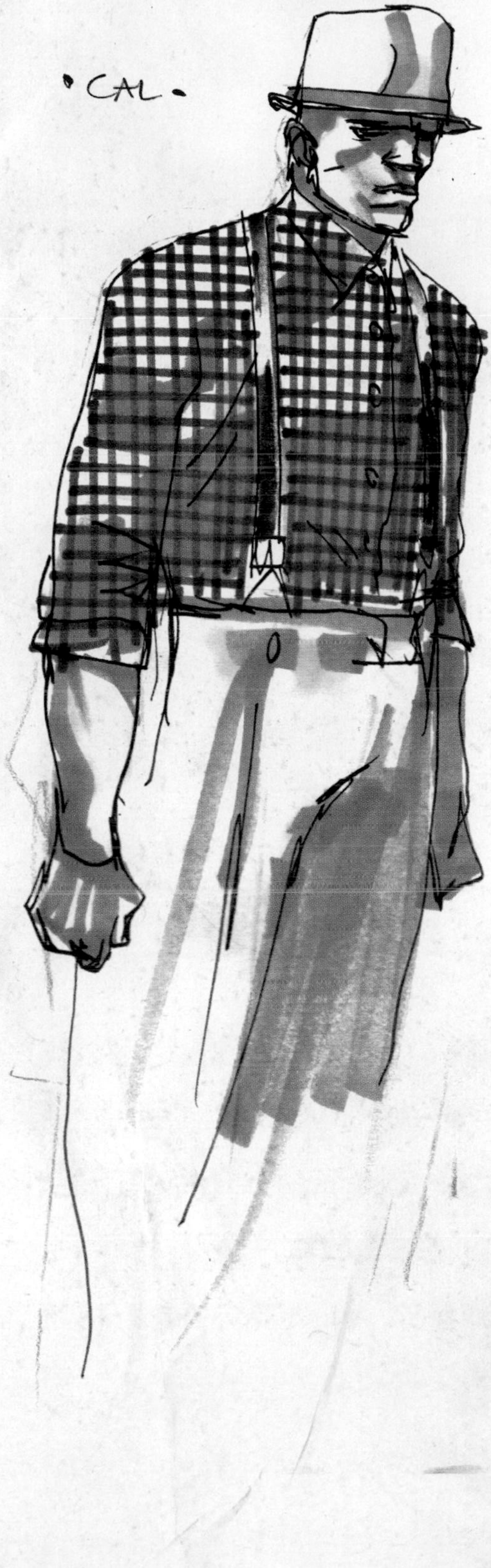
CAL

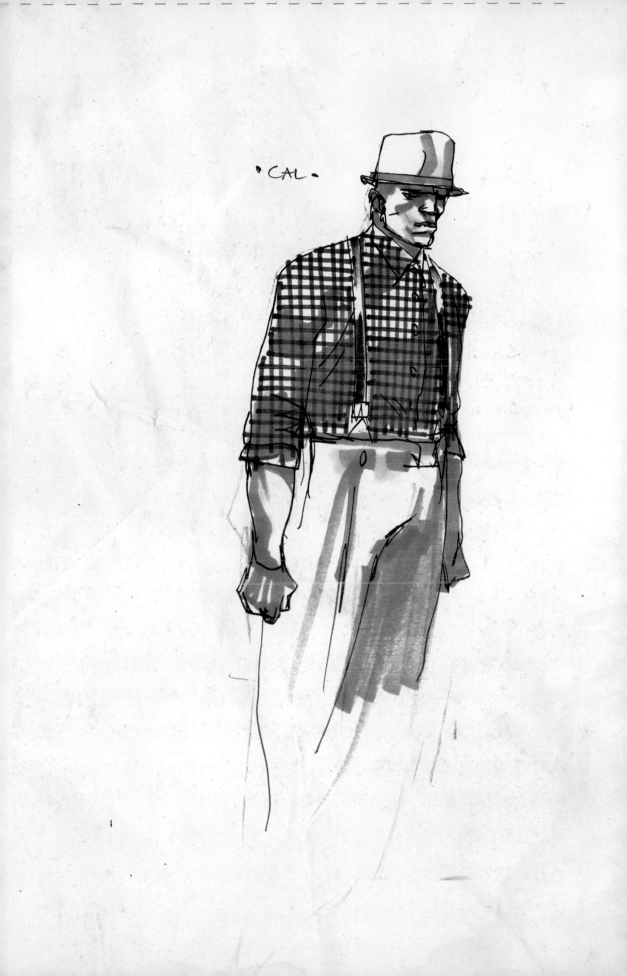

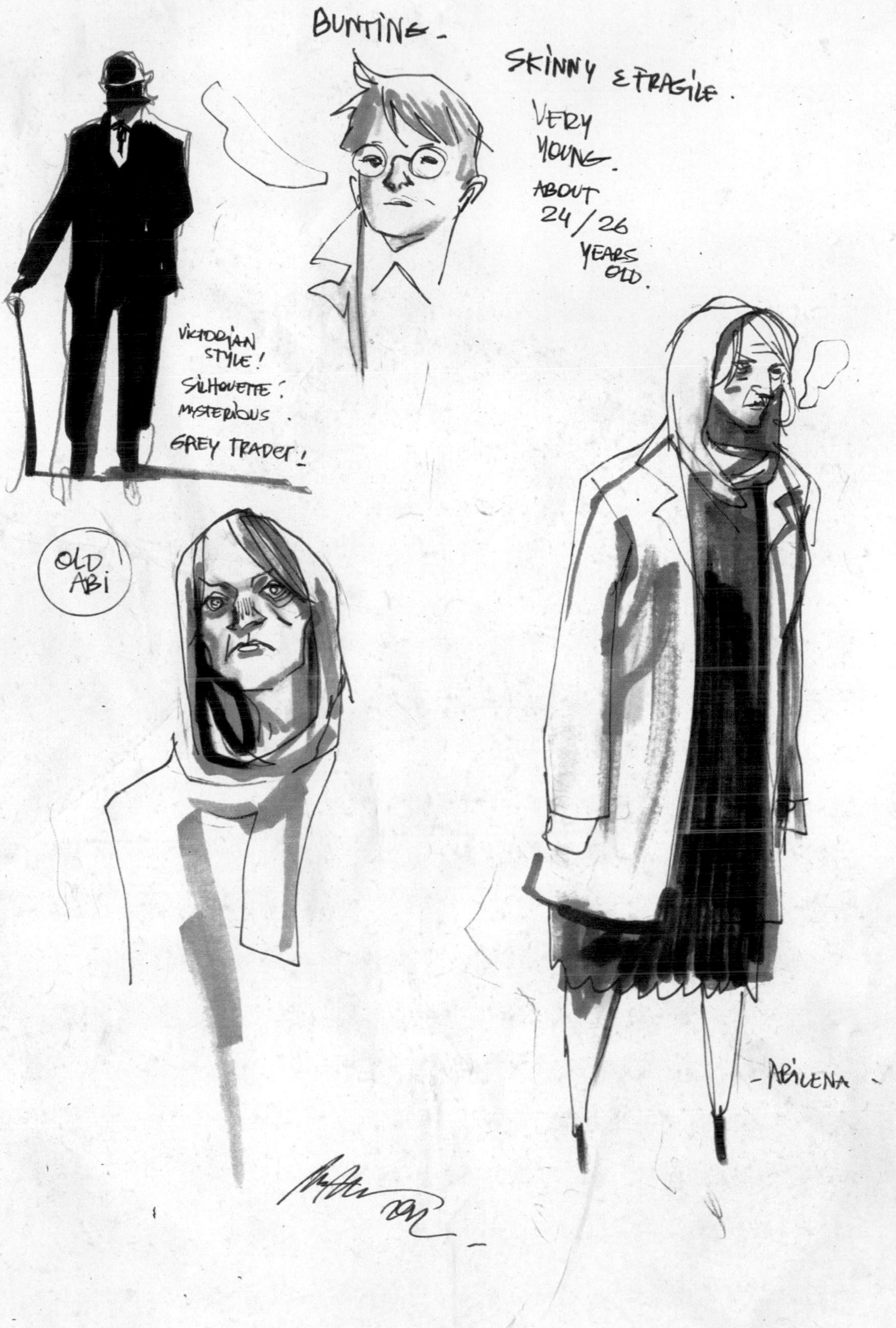
BUNTING -
SKINNY & FRAGILE.
VERY YOUNG.
ABOUT 24/26 YEARS OLD.
VICTORIAN STYLE!
SILHOUETTE!
MYSTERIOUS.
GREY TRADER!
OLD ABI
- ABILENA -

Scott Snyder is the best-selling and award-winning writer of BATMAN and SWAMP THING as well as the short story collection Voodoo Heart (The Dial Press). He teaches writing at Sarah Lawrence College, New York University and Columbia University. He lives on Long Island with his wife, Jeanie, and his sons Jack and Emmett. He is a dedicated and un-ironic fan of Elvis Presley.

Rafael Albuquerque was born in Porto Alegre, Brazil, and has been working in the American comic book industry since 2005. Best known from his work on the *Savage Brothers*, BLUE BEETLE and SUPERMAN/BATMAN, he has also published the creator-owned graphic novels *Crimeland* (2007) and *Mondo Urbano*, published in 2010.

Dustin Nguyen is an American comic artist whose body of work includes mainly titles throughout the DC Comics universe. His past projects include WILDCATS V3.0, BATMAN, BATGIRL, SUPERMAN/BATMAN, DETECTIVE COMICS, MANIFEST ETERNITY, BATGIRL, BATMAN: STREETS OF GOTHAM, and many others. Currently, he co-writes and illustrates DC's BATMAN: LI'L GOTHAM. He stays up late at night and resides somewhere in California with his lovely wife Nicole and their kids Bradley and Kaeli.

"Looking for a vampire story with some real bite? Then, boys and girls, Scott Snyder has a comic book for you."
—USA WEEKEND

FROM THE NEW YORK TIMES #1 BESTSELLING AUTHOR OF *BATMAN: THE BLACK MIRROR*

SCOTT SNYDER
with RAFAEL ALBUQUERQUE and STEPHEN KING

AMERICAN VAMPIRE
VOL. 2

with RAFAEL
ALBUQUERQUE and
MATEUS SANTOLOUCO

AMERICAN VAMPIRE
VOL. 3

with RAFAEL
ALBUQUERQUE and
SEAN MURPHY

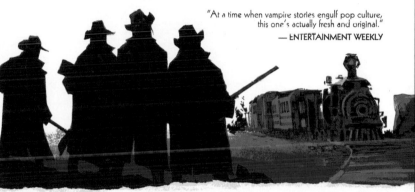

"At a time when vampire stories engulf pop culture, this one's actually fresh and original."
— ENTERTAINMENT WEEKLY

AMERICAN VAMPIRE

SCOTT SNYDER   RAFAEL ALBUQUERQUE
and
STEPHEN KING

VERTIGO